# A RADICAL POLITICAL THEOLOGY
# FOR THE ANTHROPOCENE AGE

# A Radical Political Theology for the Anthropocene Age

## —Thinking and Being Otherwise—

RYAN LAMOTHE

CASCADE *Books* · Eugene, Oregon

A RADICAL POLITICAL THEOLOGY FOR THE ANTHROPOCENE AGE
Thinking and Being Otherwise

Cascade Books
An Imprint of Wipf and Stock Publishers
199 W. 8th Ave., Suite 3
Eugene, OR 97401

www.wipfandstock.com

PAPERBACK ISBN: 978-1-7252-5354-4
HARDCOVER ISBN: 978-1-7252-5355-1
EBOOK ISBN: 978-1-7252-5356-8

*Cataloguing-in-Publication data:*

Names: LaMothe, Ryan, author.

Title: A radical political theology for the Anthropocene Age : thinking and being otherwise / Ryan LaMothe.

Description: Eugene, OR: Cascade Books, 2021. | Includes bibliographical references and index.

Identifiers: ISBN 978-1-7252-5354-4 (paperback). | ISBN 978-1-7252-5355-1 (hardcover). | ISBN 978-1-7252-5356-8 (ebook).

Subjects: LSCH: Theology. | Public theology. | Global warming—political aspects. | Environmental ethics.

Classification: BT695.5 L35 2021 (print). | BT695.5 (ebook).

*For Cyn*

And for all those who labor to care for
all residents of our one home

# Contents

# *Acknowledgments*

---

And then the pandemic hit. Most people around the world could begin their narratives with this phrase. Life before the pandemic was not idyllic. We had our personal, family, and national crises, but 2020 brought global disruptions, numerous unexpected and untimely deaths, rises in mental illness, domestic violence, suicides, and lost jobs. Is shared global suffering in the past year or so, enough to bring human beings together, cooperating to make sure that every human being has access to resources and vaccines? As of this writing, richer countries are way ahead in vaccinating their populations and U.S. pharmaceutical companies are more interested in profits and patents than in sharing their research with other companies and nations. All of this took place along with the rise of white supremacists and the insurrection of the cultish, conspiracy laden followers under the sway of a delusional, narcissistic, and profoundly incompetent leader. It is not simply that we live in interesting times, we seem to be living in an age of all manner of crises, including ongoing political polarization and disorder. Is the past year or so a harbinger for the decades to come as human beings face growing problems with global warming and political discord within and between nations?

My own response to "And then the pandemic hit" begins in the spring of 2019, when I was invited to deliver Princeton Seminary's Frederick Neumann Memorial Lecture in March of 2020. Few could have imagined that a year later the world would shut down for a time, because of a global pandemic. In the spring of 2019, I was honored to accept the invitation and, anticipating that I would give the lecture, I set about outlining my ideas about a political theology that considers the existential realities of the Anthropocene Age. For a number of years, I have been exploring issues associated with climate change, political theology, and psychoanalysis, and the invitation provided an opportunity to develop further thoughts. In short order, I realized that the topic far exceeded one lecture, which led me to consider writing a book that would encompass questions and problems of political theology given the nature of the crises we face today and will face in the years ahead. Later that summer, before the pandemic hit, I sent my proposal to Dr. K. C. Hanson, editor in chief of Cascade Books. I am grateful that the editorial team accepted the proposal and for K. C.'s generous comments about this and an earlier work.

And then the pandemic hit. In early February of 2020, there was a growing awareness that a dangerous virus was making its way around the world. By the third week of March lectures were cancelled, students were sent home, classes went online, businesses shuttered their doors, people lost jobs, and thousands of people began to die. The tragedy of the pandemic, coupled with the bumbling incompetence of the Trump Administration, demonstrated again that political leadership fell horribly short in addressing this crisis, as well as the climate crisis all humanity and other species face. By March of 2020 I was writing a chapter on the problem of sovereignty against the then-current spectacle of political leadership's state of exception, which provided a sobering and disturbing backdrop and illustration. Yet, in the midst of this and the self-induced isolation of writing came friends and colleagues who brought a balm to the worries of the day—a balm that provided the energy to continue writing, to continue giving voice to the unsaid.

Giorgio Agamben notes that "wanting to write is the desire to experience potentiality."[1] While I am not quite sure what he means, this resonated with me. There is in writing, for me, a reaching out toward making actual something potential, yet even actuality leaves something unsaid. To return to Agamben, "the properly philosophical element in any work, be it a work of scholarship, of literature, or of art, is that which goes unsaid therein, and thereby possesses a possibility for development."[2] In terms of this book, I see it as taking the said and unsaid from a variety of works and developing them into a radical political theology, recognizing that this work leaves things unsaid that hopefully will be developed by others. Let me add that the said and unsaid, in my view, emerge from relationships and conversations, even given the solitary nature of writing. I have benefited over the years from many conversations with colleagues such as Drs. Lewis Rambo, Carrie Doehring, Liston Mills, Robert Dykstra, Nancy Ramsay, Jaco Hamman, Bruce Rogers-Vaughn, Marcos McPeek Villatoro, Kirk Bingaman, and Lisa Cataldo. Indeed, Drs. Kirk Bingaman, Lisa Cataldo, and Mary Beth

1. In De La Durantaye, *Giorgio Agamben: A Critical Introduction*, 3.
2. De La Durantaye, *Giorgio Agamben: A Critical Introduction*, 9.

Werdel were respondents to the three lectures I gave at Fordham University (just a day before Fordham closed because of the pandemic) and gained from their insights and questions regarding a radical political theology for the Anthropocene Age. For these and many more conversations I am deeply grateful.

I would also like to acknowledge the said and unsaid that comes with attending conferences and participating in one's guild. Drs. Donald Capps and Robert Dykstra started Group for New Directions of Pastoral Theology more than a decade ago. These yearly conferences, interrupted by the pandemic, have provided opportunities to learn from others and to play with ideas. Another group I have benefited from is the Society for Pastoral Theology and, in particular, the Postcolonial Study Group. These presentations and conversations have enriched me and my work. It is important to thank Saint Meinrad Seminary and School of Theology for providing sabbaticals and grant money for research. The School's generosity is central to having time and support for research and writing. Special thanks to Mary Jeanne Schumacher and Rev. Cindy Geisen for their editorial acumen. They read various drafts of all the chapters with graceful criticism and affirmation. Of course, any errors in this work are mine alone. I offer my deepest gratitude for Cyn—friend, partner, lover, community activist, life-long learner, and good soul. If we have to endure a pandemic or the looming realities of the Anthropocene Age, it is best to be surrounded by thoughtful, mostly sane, caring friends and family.

# Introduction

I think it is only through metaphysical, religious,
and theological paradigms that one can truly approach
the contemporary—the political—situation.[1]

Philosophy as such is nothing but genuine awareness of the problems,
i.e., of the fundamental and comprehensive problems. It is impossible
to think about these problems without becoming inclined toward a
solution, toward one or the other of the very few typical solutions.
Yet as long as there is no wisdom but only quest for wisdom, the
evidence of all solutions is necessarily smaller than the evidence of the
problems. Therefore, the philosopher ceases to be a philosopher at the
moment at which the "subjective certainty" [quoting M. Alexandre
Kojève] of a solution becomes stronger than his awareness of the
problematic character of that solution. At that moment the sectarian
is born.[2]

(T)he prophecy of doom is to be given greater heed than the prophecy
of bliss.[3]

We cannot construct an eco-theology without offering a radical political theology. An eco-theology/philosophy depends on thinking and
being otherwise politically.

---

1. Giorgio Agamben in De La Durantaye, *Giorgio Agamben*, 369.
2. Strauss, "What Is Political Philosophy?"
3. Hans Jonas quoted in Bromwich, "Natural Piety and Human Responsibility," 274.

1

The news is bleak—increasing temperatures, melting glaciers, rising and more acidic seas, catastrophic storms, desertification of vast tracts of land, decimated rain forests, frequent massive forest fires, extinctions of millions of species,[4] failed and failing states, increases in political violence, and mass migrations of peoples within and between borders.[5] Bleaker still is the news that a number of climate scientists believe that we have already passed the threshold of making significant changes to avert global warming.[6] Even if we were to magically reduce carbon emissions to near zero, it would take centuries for the $CO_2$ already present to diminish to earlier pre-Anthropocene Age levels. One climate scientist, responding to a reporter's question about what he really thought about the consequences of climate change, said, "We're fucked."[7] We are, as Elizabeth Kolbert[8] and Naomi Klein[9] note, in the midst of a sixth extinction event,[10] which they and others call the Anthropocene Era[11]—an era of mass extinctions caused by human beings.[12] This extinction event reveals, as historian Dipesh Chakrabarty rightly claims, that human beings are a force of nature, which means that natural and human history can no longer be considered separate.[13] Put differently, we have long recognized that human beings have political agency, but we are now realizing in this era that human beings also have eco-agency, though for decades human beings were blissfully, perhaps willfully, ignorant of our role in climate change.

4. Famed biologist Edward Wilson predicts that half of the known species will be extinct by the end of this century; Wilson, *The Future of Life*.

5. Climate Science Special Report, 2017; see also Northcott, *A Political Theology of Climate Change*, 1–9; Parenti, *Tropic of Chaos*; Sassen, *Expulsions*.

6. Nield, "Scientists Say It Could Be 'Game Over' for Climate Change."

7. Quoted in Dufresne, *The Democracy of Suffering*, 93.

8. Kolbert, *The Sixth Extinction*.

9. Klein, *This Changes Everything*.

10. There is considerable debate about the use of the term Anthropocene and, if used, what date is to be used to the beginning of this age. See Northcott, "On Going Gently into the Anthropocene"; and Nichols and Gogineni, "The Anthropocene Dating Problem."

11. Scientist Paul Crutzen, decades ago, coined the term Anthropocene Age to indicate we are now out of the Holocene Age. There is much debate about when this new age began, but there is little doubt we are in the midst of a sixth extinction event brough on by human activities. See Bilgrami, *Nature and Value*.

12. Jason Moore prefers the term Capitalocene Era because, he argues, capitalism is the primary culprit in global warming. While there is much to be said for this term, I will use the more common Anthropocene Era, in part because it is more inclusive of the many human factors causing climate change and species extinctions. Moore, "Name the System! Anthropocene & the Capitalocene Alternative."

13. Chakrabarty, *The Climate of History*.

Of course, it was not as if we were not aware that human beings could destroy the earth and most, if not all, of its residents. Growing up in the turbulence of the 1960s, I remember grade-school drills where we hid under our desks, not because of an active shooter, but in case of a nuclear attack. Nuclear war and nuclear winter captured our imaginations and heightened our sense of vulnerability and helplessness. During this time, though, almost no one had any idea that we were well on the way toward damaging our habitat, not by nuclear weapons, but by the very way we lived our lives in the profligacy of market societies. The great leap forward in science, technology, and industry in the late eighteenth century accompanied costs we have only begun to calculate during the last forty years. While we have found ways to constrain the proliferation of nuclear weapons, we (the United States in particular) have not and may not find the political-economic will to engage in real and comprehensive international cooperation to restrain, let alone stop, the trajectory of climate change and its dire consequences. Despite incredible human creativity and ingenuity in the face of these threats, I am neither optimistic nor hopeful, primarily because of human/collective anthropocentrism, narcissism (tribalism, classism, racism, sexism), and myopia evident in the ongoing prevalence of militarism, global capitalism, nationalism, and imperialism, all of which are seemingly insurmountable obstacles to global political cooperation toward making significant advances in reducing human degradation of the planet—our one and only home.

Yet, this is neither a counsel for despair nor nihilism, though these are understandable responses, even if they are unhelpful. And while I am aware of the prevalence of narcissism and parochialism, I also recognize that human beings are capable of extraordinary acts of love, self-sacrifice, and courageous generosity.[14] Between the poles of optimism/hope and pessimism/despair are routine acts of care, acceptance, humility, patience, kindness, and hospitality. Care,[15] not hope motivates me to write this book, to write

14. See Ricard, *Altruism*.

15. Let me offer a brief definition of care: Care is everything we do to help individuals, families, communities, and societies to 1) meet vital biological, psychosocial, and existential or spiritual needs of individuals, families, and communities, 2) develop or maintain basic capabilities with the aim of human flourishing, 3) facilitate participation in the polis's space of appearances, and 4) maintain a habitable environment for all. I add to this definition that care as a political concept involves shared critical and constructive reflection on how the structures (and their accompanying narratives and practices) of the state, governing authorities, and non-state organizations (e.g., businesses, labor unions, religious and secular communities, etc.) and actors meet or fail to meet the four features of this definition of care. See LaMothe, *Care of Souls, Care of Polis*; and LaMothe, *Pastoral Reflections on Global Citizenship*.

in the face of present and coming disasters. It is care for the residents of the earth, care for other creatures who similarly depend on a good-enough habitat, care for the earth itself as an extraordinary, complex living system. This is echoed in Pope Francis' encyclical, *Laudato Si*, wherein he uses the example of St. Francis to exhort human beings to care for all that exists, because every creature is a sister or brother.[16] Whether care is sufficient to turn the tide is not the question. It may very well be that care is not enough, but care is not necessarily contingent on or determined by the realization of a particular vision or outcome, which I will say more about in the last chapter. Care is sufficient in itself, in the present, in the moment. As Martin Luther is credited with saying, "If the world was going to end tomorrow, I would plant a tree today."

Care, then, is what goads me to write a book proposing a radical political theology for the Anthropocene Era. This radical political theology rests on five premises. First, human beings possess both political agency, which we have known and commented on for millennia, and ecological agency. The former undergirds a particular political ethos and mythos, wherein citizens, living a life in common, possess sufficient mutual fidelity, trust, and care to cooperate toward the well-being of society and its members. The latter founds the belief that human beings, as a force of nature, are responsible for caring for their habitats,[17] which includes the vast diversity of creatures who, likewise, are dependent on a viable habitat for their existence and well-being.[18] And we are now more aware than ever that our particular habitats are part of one larger, single, deeply complex living habitat—the earth. It is also increasingly apparent that political and ecological agencies

16. Francis, *Laudato Si*, para. 11.

17. Culpability for climate change does not rest equally on all human beings. People in so-called first world countries contribute much more to greenhouse gases than those countries with fewer resources. Within the U.S., responsibility varies as well, depending on income, wealth, and status.

18. Readers may wonder whether this means all creatures. Why not get rid of pesky mosquitoes that carry diseases (e.g., malaria, dengue fever)? A British biotech company, Oxitec, is already doing this. Decades ago, Gregory Bateson coined the term "schismogenesis" to refer to the human tendency to introduce technological changes vis-à-vis the environment without being able to comprehend the effects, precisely because there are too many variables and nature is an incredibly complex system. We cannot know, in other words, what all the consequences will be. If we were to eliminate dengue fever and malaria by killing off mosquitoes, we would also remove a food source for other creatures. That is what we know, but there are other consequences we cannot know. My point here is not that we ought not be concerned with human suffering by letting the mosquitoes carry on as they will, but to point out that human attempts to control nature for the benefit of humankind often results in harm to other creatures and eventually ourselves. Bateson, *Steps to an Ecology of Mind*, 68–73.

are intertwined, for without care of the habitat, there will be no political ethos or mythos. Moreover, political and ecological agencies combine the universal and the particular. We all dwell and are dependent on one spaceship, despite all the rich varieties of cultures that inhabit the earth. The idea of the universal does not necessarily imply homogeneity vis-à-vis political and ecological agency. Just as one earth has diverse habitats, so, too, human beings, as universally dependent on the earth, have a diversity of cultures and political responses regarding how human beings are to dwell together.

In Western philosophy there is a long history of contested discourse regarding being and becoming, potentiality and actuality, essence and existence. If I may be overly reductionistic, from being to becoming, from potential to actual, from essence to existence occurs, for human beings, only if there is care. The second premise of a radical political theology, then, is that care founds subjectivity, intersubjectivity, and agency (political and ecological). At the same time, the fact of ecological agency also means that care necessarily extends to the earth—the very possibility of a viable habitat. In other words, subjectivity (becoming, actuality, and existence) is contingent on caring for the habitat, and not simply the care provided by human beings. We know, for instance, that for ages competent farmers, while dependent on the weather (which they could not influence), knew that they must care for the land for their very existence. Their agency as farmers was contingent on adapting to and nurturing the earth. If the land is ill, then human beings will also suffer.[19] Today, more and more people are realizing that if we do not care for the earth, care for each other will be negatively impacted. Care of and for human beings, then, means caring for the earth, which now includes acknowledging that our embodied subjectivity is dependent on the viability of our habitat. The third and related premise is that God's infinite and indeterminate care, evident in the act of creation and the incarnation, is partially manifested in human acts of care for Others, other-than-human beings, and the earth. Being created in the image and likeness of God, in other words, includes eco-agency and political agency of caring for others and care for the earth as a foundation of human life.

The fourth premise is that all human beings are residents of the earth. This is obvious, but it has implications with regard to the political. I avoid using the term "citizen" to refer to human beings as citizens of the earth. The notion "citizen" is a political and juridical concept, demarcating itself from those who are not citizens. In the case of a particular polis, citizens are deemed to have rights, responsibilities, protections, and privileges that

19. For clear examples of this see Hedges and Sacco, *Days of Destruction, Days of Revolt*.

are denied those who reside in society but deemed to be non-citizens.[20] Residents who are not citizens are both included and excluded, at best, and completely excluded, at worse. Today, there are persons, residing in the U.S. who are constructed as "illegal," because they have not followed the guidelines for entry into the country. They are residents, but not citizens, which means they have fewer rights and are vulnerable to exploitation.[21] If we shift to the Anthropocene Age and the reality that the earth is one habitat, we might entertain the idea that all human beings are citizens. Unfortunately, the legacy of exclusion (including identity) would continue in the sense that animals could not be considered citizens.[22] Of course, it would be a category mistake to apply the concept of citizenry to animals, since they lack political agency. Therefore, I prefer the term "resident" in referring to all living creatures of the earth. This is not necessarily a juridical or political term, but rather an existential fact that eschews any attempt at exclusion. Human beings and other-than-human beings, then, are residents first and foremost. Human beings are secondarily citizens of their specific societies.

There is another reason for avoiding the term "global citizenship." "Citizenship" implies that a particular state or governing body provides the juridical and political basis for who is and who is not a citizen. The idea of global citizenship would suggest some kind of world government, which is difficult to imagine as being currently possible or feasible given the plethora of nation states and the challenges of arriving at consensus about human rights and addressing issues of identity. Global citizenship is not impossible, however numerous obstacles limit it to the realm of metaphor or idea. I add here that global citizenship would continue to be exclusive with regard to nature and those residents of the earth that are more-than-human. Since they share the same habitat and are residents, are they to be excluded from protections and resources?

James Hunter argues that an essential task of political theology is to reflect critically on the world, as well as theological perspectives aimed at engaging the public-political realm.[23] A critical stance is the final premise,

---

20. Dimitry Kochenov vigorously details the problems of citizenship and its relation to stateless persons. Kochenov, *Citizenship*.

21. The notion of "residents" is also juridical and political, but for me it also has a broader non-juridical meaning, which is a reason for including it. It can refer to human beings and other creatures residing in and on this one habitat.

22. Giorgio Agamben points out that for millennia in the West, the political has been separated from nature. Nature exists outside the political. His point is to mend this gap. See Whyte, *Catastrophe and Redemption*, 78. See also Bechtel, Eaton, Harvie, *Encountering Earth*.

23. Hunter, *To Change the World*, 185.

but a radical political theology extends this by critiquing "the tradition from within so to suspend its authority and free it for a new use."[24] Decades ago Alan Watts made a similar comment, stating that "To be free from convention is not to spurn it but not to be deceived by it. It is to be able to use it as an instrument instead of being used by it."[25] Scripture and theology, then, need to be problematized, because they can be used to promote and sustain ideologies that undermine political theologies that are more fitting to the demands of the Anthropocene Age. So, for instance, in chapter 1 I critique theologies of subjugation and subordination evident in scripture and many Judeo-Christian theologies with the aim of highlighting a theology of vulnerability and dependency that is latently evident in scripture. This will serve as the basis of a radical political theology that addresses the Anthropocene Age.

These premises undergird this work, which leads me to offer a comment about the method used in this book. The title, *A Radical Political Theology for the Anthropocene*, would seem to suggest, for some readers, the systematic construction of a political theology. This is not the approach taken here, in part, because any systematic creation of a political theology, as I hope to make clear, is already a problem.[26] It is a problem for two reasons. First, it would be a vision of what would be definitive for human beings. Instead, I would rather begin moving toward notion of a specific political theology (e.g., radical democracy) by identifying problems and principles so that we could discuss how we will dwell together.[27] Second, it is

24. Kotsko, "Agamben's Messianic Nihilism," 123.

25. Watts, *The Way of Zen*, 11.

26. Giorgio Agamben discusses the early twentieth-century work of Erik Peterson on political theology, wherein Peterson raises the notion of the impossibility of a Christian political theology. Agamben does not believe Peterson pulled this off, though he did contribute to the discussion regarding the separation of kingdom and government. My point here is that political theology suggests some form of government and rule that are often legitimated by framing the political in terms of God. As I will address in other chapters, any systematic construction of a political theology is fundamentally flawed because it seeks to legitimate a particular form of sovereignty, which usually means it is imposed on others through coercion, the threat of violence, or violence. While the political is a theological concern, it is not an attribute of God, but one that is projected onto God. More on this later. Agamben, *The Kingdom and Glory*, 73.

27. There are a number of political theologians writing about radical democracy, which I will address briefly in chapter 3. For now, it is important to acknowledge my sympathies for this approach, but point out that the issue of God and God's sovereignty remain. If anything, I lean more toward a polis that is anarchic and that does not depend on the mythos of a sovereign God. See Hauerwas and Coles, *Christianity, Democracy, and the Radical Ordinary*; Schüssler Fiorenza, *Discipleship of Equals*; West, *Democracy Matters*.

also a problem because it would likely support a particular type of political sovereignty, which, as I note in chapter 3, is inimical to the theological idea of a non-sovereign God. Instead of constructing or defending a systematic edifice, my approach is to identify and respond to various problems associated with any political theology and philosophy so that we might begin to see more clearly how we might work together to develop a "provisional politics" that is a means without a particular defined end.[28] The main reason for this approach is that political theology, at its best, is critical[29] and responsive to the questions, issues, and sufferings of the time (and geography) without imposing a particular vision of sovereignty, government, etc.[30] Or to turn to Paul Kahn's view, political theology "offers not theory of justice against which to reform our political life. It asks only to think carefully (and critically) about our own belief that we are and must be free."[31] Therefore, a radical political theology is not, in my view, utopian in terms of seeking a particular vision of an unrealizable polis, in part, because to do so would suggest a universality that does not exist or, if it were to exist, would involve coercion, violence, and oppression toward those who have a different vision. This, however, does not mean there is an absence of a vision or mythos. Instead, it is a vision informed by, but not determined by, Christian mythoi that contain principles for dwelling together, principles of working toward a shared idea of the common well-being of others and the habitat. The approach here is realistic and respectful in that it recognizes the incredible diversity of human beings and their manifold ways of living a life in common, though my approach is also critically grounded in the theological mythos of the infinite, indeterminate care of God for all of creation and the incarnation of Jesus Christ. In terms of using this mythos, I follow, in part,

28. See Smith, *Against Ecological Sovereignty*, 215. See also Agamben, *Means Without Ends*.

29. I will say more about this below, but for now let me mention that this perspective is connected to Max Horkheimer's view that "The future of humanity depends on the existence today of the critical attitude." In Wolin, *Politics and Vision*, 231. Karl Popper also indicated that a critical stance is necessary for an open society. Even democracies, which usually have a greater chance of openness, can foreclose critique, which is evident in the U.S.'s long history of slavery and Jim Crow. Popper, *The Open Society and Its Enemies*.

30. Leo Strauss' comment about political theology and problems is relevant here. Political theologians, like political philosophers, are adept at identifying and discussing myriad of problems. The temptation is to offer solutions and when we do, we become sectarian. I am also concerned with recognizing that identifying problems can lead to responses that are not solutions, but rather ways of thinking about how we might converse together to consider varied solutions to the problems we face.

31. Kahn, *Political Theology*, 152.

Giorgio Agamben's approach in deactivating a tradition in order to put it to new use.[32]

My approach, while not aimed at constructing a particular polity, is also aimed at thinking and being otherwise given the particular polis in which we reside, as well as our use of theology. By this I mean, both possessing a critical stance and inoperativity (more about this later) vis-à-vis the governing structures and apparatuses[33] of our particular society (and theological apparatuses).[34] This critical stance and inoperativity emerge from a notion of care, and it is care in the Anthropocene Age that avoids both hope and despair. In other words, hope is contingent on some realization of a particular vision, and one is vulnerable to despair when this vision is not realized. A radical political theology rests on the idea of care, which is connected to a mythos and vision, but is not contingent on realizing the vision in the present moment of care. I intend to explicate this further in the last chapter.

Let me add a few related thoughts regarding political theologizing. French philosophers Gilles Deleuze and Félix Guattari write that "philosophy is the art of forming, inventing, and fabricating concepts."[35] The history of philosophy, then, is not about the history of moving toward greater articulation of Truth(s). Instead, it is a history wherein persons create concepts that have meaning and significance given the questions, concerns, and issues of their time and location. I think theology and, in particular, political theology can be understood in this way as well, though with a qualification.

Any theology is, in my view, a creation that emerges from the issues of the day. I say a creation for two reasons. First, as Paul noted, we see through

32. See Kotsko and Salzani, *Agamben's Philosophical Lineage*, 4.

33. For Agamben the term apparatus refers to "a set of practices, bodies of knowledge, measures and institutions that aim to manage, govern, control, and orient—in a way that purports to be useful—the behaviors, gestures, and thoughts of human beings." Referencing Foucault, Agamben writes that "in a disciplinary society, apparatuses aim to create—through a series of practices, discourses, and bodies of knowledge—docile, yet free, bodies that assume their identity and their 'freedom' as subjects." Agamben, *What Is an Apparatus?*, 13, 19.

34. Leland De La Durantaye discusses Agamben's notion of profanation as a radical existential step to avoid the destructive distinctions between the sacred and profane, which are ensconced in notions of sovereignty and the state of exception. To profane religion is to free it for another use that does not lead to destructive relations. While I do not frame a radical political theology in terms of profanation, I do use term of inoperativity in subsequent chapters in the sense of freeing us to think and be otherwise in the Anthropocene Age. De La Durantaye, *Giorgio Agamben*, 351–58.

35. Deleuze and Guattari, *What Is Philosophy?* 2. Philosopher Richard Rorty has a similar view about the role of philosophy, though he clearly leans toward the pragmatic side of the philosophical endeavor. Rorty, *Truth and Progress*.

the glass darkly, which I take to mean that in grasping reality or truth, we distort it.[36] No human being has a privileged access to the Truth—a Truth that is universal and timeless. Second, our theological constructions of reality are creations that are inextricably linked to our projections. From Xenophanes[37] to Spinoza, from Voltaire to Feuerbach and Freud people have noted the projective element in human constructions and discussions about God. How could it be otherwise? Does this, then, mean that political theology lacks any foundational truth? Is it merely a construction, like philosophy? Are we doomed to relativity of perspectives, since there is no Truth? I have two responses. First, while I believe that political theology is a creative, critical enterprise that involves some projection, I do not think or believe it is merely this. This is where I part company with Deleuze's and Guattari's perspective. To say that we see through the glass darkly presupposes some Truth, though we inevitably distort it because of human finitude, which, I believe, is a fact or truth that might give rise to some degree of humility and even hospitality for diverse views among theologians who create political theologies. This said, the theological premise above is the Truth that I derive out of my seeing through the dark glass. The truth is the non-sovereign God's infinite and indeterminate care, evident in creation, *imago dei*, and the incarnation. Daniel Black's novel provides a brief illustration. On the slave ship the narrator looks across the ship and sees a fellow African, noting there was "Something deep in the soul that could not be spoken. Something the oppressors could not disturb or destroy. Something unnamable, immeasurable, indestructible."[38] This man loved a woman, who was also brutally enslaved on the ship. That which could not be spoken, but was also immeasurable and unnamable, was also ungovernable, beyond the sovereignty of the oppressors and their terroristic machinations. Theologically, the man's and woman's love, in my view, can be understood as an incarnation of the non-sovereign care of God, though like Jesus' forgiveness of his tormentors, had no apparent effect. That said, their love exceeded their chains. The belief in and truth of God's infinite and determinate care, then, is the theological premise/truth that undergirds the political theological discussion in this book.

A second and related response concerns the silence of God. Frequently, theologies operate as apparatuses or disciplinary regimes, presuming to inform people about what God said, believes, or God's attributes. Indeed,

36. Farley, *Good and Evil*, 10.

37. Xenophanes wrote that "if oxen and horses or lion had hands, and could paint with their hands, and produce works of art as men do, horses would paint the forms of gods like horses, and oxen like oxen." In Grayling, *The History of Philosophy*, 26.

38. Black, *The Coming*, 37.

as will be discussed in the next chapter, theologies of subjugation/subordination serve as anthropological machines, differentiating between human beings and other-than-human beings in terms of the illusions of superiority and inferiority, which necessarily are linked to the notion of dominion that, more often than not, leads to exclusion and exploitation.[39] These theologies, in other words, are used to justify and legitimate forms of exploitation and political exclusion (e.g., sexism, racism, etc.). Colby Dickinson and Adam Kotsko note that Agamben did not articulate a theology, though "we might suggest that if he did venture into this territory, it would be one wherein God is silent, behind the wall of 'absolute immanence' that at once undoes centuries of theological speculation and yet might preserve the nature of whatever 'mystery' such a divinity might actually be."[40] I appreciate this view, but out of this silence I will posit one attribute of this "absolute immanent" God and that is the infinite mystery of the indeterminate care of God.

Given these general comments, it is necessary in this introductory chapter to explain, albeit briefly, what is meant by polis, politics, political, and political theology, including a brief explication of how climate change shapes them. I hasten to add that these concepts, by themselves, are complex and contested, making it impossible to do justice to them in such a short space. Nevertheless, it is important to provide some foundation for the chapters that follow, and I do so by adding my own views regarding these concepts. Once this is accomplished, I conclude with a brief depiction of subsequent chapters.

## Clarifying Terms:
## The Polis, Political, Politics, and the Anthropocene Age

I recall a Jewish colleague remarking humorously that if there are three Jews conversing, there will be four, perhaps five opinions. One could see this as the perennial problem of arriving at consensus, but I think it is what provides richness to conversations, especially discussions addressing topics of importance. The same can be said of academics who write about politics and political theology. As a group many theologians are deeply concerned about politics, which in the Anthropocene Age takes on even greater weight.

---

39. Mick Smith writes that "the modern anthropological machine makes humanity recursively, in its own image, as an act of sovereign power, an act declaring human dominion over the world." This "modern" anthropological machine has roots in scripture where scriptural writers claim the sovereign God's proclamation that human being have dominion. Smith, *Against Ecological Sovereignty*, 9.

40. Kotsko and Dickinson, *Agamben's Coming Philosophy*, 252.

While we may not arrive at consensus, the discussion itself may clarify our thoughts and methods. With this in mind, let me plunge ahead in depicting these terms, recognizing that these ideas will be explored further in subsequent chapters.

It is readily observed that the notions "political" and "politics" are derived from the Greek term "polis," which is often translated as city-state.[41] Political philosophers Leo Strauss and Joseph Cropsey argue that the term "city-state" is not an accurate translation.[42] They write, "When people speak today of 'the state,' they ordinarily understand the 'state' in contradistinction to 'society.' This distinction is alien to classical political philosophy."[43] Classical political philosophers, they argue, emphasized society vis-à-vis the city-state and they lacked the concept of the state, though this did not mean that they lacked a notion of governance or sovereignty.[44] Instead, as Melissa Lane points out, the polis, in Greek thought, was understood primarily to be "a community in which citizens share; it is a community of common activities"[45] for the "sake of life."[46] In Aristotle's view, for instance, the polis is a "sphere of conscious creation," which is allied with humankind's nature to associate and dwell together—life lived in common.[47] The polis, in other words, reflects the intersection of the given and the made, necessity and freedom. Human beings create the polis and its institutions, yet human beings by nature are finite social/political animals.

In terms of the "made," philosopher Hannah Arendt, relying on her reading of Plato and Aristotle, views the polis as a space wherein people *speak and act together* toward living a life in common and sharing in common a vision of the good life.[48] She argues further that "the polis properly speaking is not a city-state in its physical location, it is an organization of

41. Lane, *The Birth of Politics*.

42. Strauss and Cropsey, "Introduction," 5–6.

43. Strauss and Cropsey, "Introduction," 6.

44. See Barker, *The Politics of Aristotle*.

45. Lane, *The Birth of Politics*, 206–7.

46. Lane, *The Birth of Politics*, 197.

47. Barker, *The Politics of Aristotle*, xlix. See also Scottish philosopher John Macmurray who argued that governments are human creations and, as such, can be altered or overthrown. Macmurray, *Persons in Relation*, 137.

48. Arendt, *The Human Condition*. It is important to mention that Arendt believed Socrates epitomized philosophy acting in the public square, while Plato, shocked at the political killing of his teacher, retreated from engaging in the political domain. Plato set the West, she argues, on a trajectory of philosophers not actively engaging in the political sphere. I add here that Arendt differentiates between labor (our work to survive, e.g., our job), culture (the work of creating meaning, e.g., the arts, ritual), and action (speaking and acting together in the public political realm).

the people as it arises out of speaking and acting together."[49] Arendt, following though amending Aristotle's view, believed the polis was necessary for human beings to "attain their full humanity, not only because they are (as in the privacy of the household) but also because they appear."[50] In other words, "Politics arises in what lies between [persons] and is established as relationships."[51] Her views are echoed later in Agamben's work, wherein he argues that politics is humankind's "most proper dimension."[52] Similarly, contemporary political philosophers Axel Honneth[53] and Nancy Fraser[54] contend that the political—this space of speaking and acting together—depends on interpersonal recognition, which could be said to mean that individuals are constructed as persons and they appear in their singularity or suchness. To "appear" in the polis means that there must be recognition and treatment of human beings as persons—unique, valued, inviolable, responsive subjects.[55] To experience oneself as a person, to appear as a unique human being, is both a social and political achievement, and one that necessarily implies plurality, which is, for Arendt, necessary for a viable polis.[56] Politics, then, is constitutive of being human in all its diversity—a Western notion that has deep roots in both Plato and Aristotle.[57]

To return to Arendt, she rightly stresses communication and community, rather than locating geography (or identity) as the principal factor in understanding the notion "city-state," though this will need to be further qualified below. Analogously, philosopher Giorgio Agamben argues that it is in speaking and acting together that one becomes a political being, which suggests that geography or specific location and particular governing structures are secondary to speaking and acting together.[58] For moderns, when it comes to the "polis," we often focus on the "state" and geography instead of the community of citizens/residents speaking and acting together toward the common good. For instance, I might say I am a North American, which locates me not only within a specific geographical setting, but it also implies

49. Arendt, *The Human Condition*, 198.

50. Arendt, *The Promise of Politics*, 21.

51. Arendt, *The Promise of Politics*, 95.

52. Agamben, *The Kingdom and the Glory*, xiii.

53. Honneth, *The Struggle for Recognition*. See also, Macmurray, *Persons in Relation*.

54. Fraser and Honneth, *Redistribution or Recognition?*

55. See Macmurray, *Persons in Relation*.

56. Arendt, *The Human Condition*.

57. Any political theology is limited by the traditions upon which it relies. In my case, I rely primarily on Western political philosophers and theologians.

58. Colebrook and Maxwell, *Agamben*, 150.

an identity that is exclusionary and linked to the state. For Arendt, who had the experience of being a stateless person fleeing the Nazis, the emphasis is on speaking and acting together, which paves the way for the possibility of political identity wherein geography and the state are secondary or in Agamben's term, inoperative. Briefly, inoperative means deactivating the apparatus or disciplinary regime that establishes the political in terms of geography and identity.[59]

Before identifying other features of a "polis," let me linger for the moment to note a connection between polis and *ekklesia*. For Richard Horsley, the community of faith or *ekklesia* has a political character. He notes that the term *ekklesia* "referred to the assembly of citizens in a self-governing city-state."[60] To be sure, modern understandings of the community of faith might eschew the notion of it being a polis or city-state. Naturally, there are distinctions to be made, but for my purposes the *ekklesia* falls within the notion of the polis, given that it involves an assembly of people engaged in mutual-personal recognition while speaking and acting together toward the common good. This will be important in later discussions regarding a radical political theology. For now, the political character of the *ekklesia* links it to the larger political reality of society, but, at the same time, paradoxically (ideally) incarnates the non-sovereign God, making inoperative—in the case of the early communities of faith—Roman political governance.

Several features of the polis are worth briefly identifying, because they will be important for subsequent chapters. When we say the polis is an assembly of people living and speaking together (Arendt's space of appearances[61]), we immediately notice that this means its members or citizens have, in varying degrees, a shared language, narratives, and practices, which accompany a shared identity and vision(s) of the good. Implicit here for

59. Agamben, *Kingdom and the Glory*, 251. Sergei Prozorov that inoperativity "is the process of becoming or rendering something inoperative, deactivating its functioning in the apparatus and making it available for free use." He stress that to "affirm inoperativity is not to affirm inertia, inactivity, or apraxia." Inoperativity, which will be used throughout this book, is an action. Prozorov, *Agamben and Politics*, 31, 33.

60. Horsely, *Covenant Economics*, 14. It should also be noted that Giorgio Agamben, in reading Paul, argues that "*ekklesia* is 'economic' not political." This said, I am inclined to agree with Horsely, because in Acts we clearly see a group of individuals speaking and acting together toward the well-being of all—a polis. Agamben, *The Kingdom and the Glory*, 24.

61. Philosopher Hannah Arendt used this term to refer to the public-political space of speaking and acting together vis-à-vis the polis. Steeped in the works of classical philosophers, Arendt sought to correct Western philosophies trajectory of considering contemplation as the highest form of life, which she attributes to Plato's turn away from Socratic political engagement (action) in the polis. This term will be used frequently and expanded in the subsequent chapters. Arendt, *The Human Condition*.

a polis or *ekklesia* to be viable, to flourish, shared personal recognition as fellow citizens is foundational for "appearing" as a political subject. This recognition, which I will discuss in more detail in the next chapter, necessarily accompanies and is supported by shared public-political narratives, communicative practices, and social rituals. These narratives, practices, and rituals not only contain representations for political recognition, they also contain the values that comprise a common, though often contested, vision of the common good. Even during instances of contestation regarding the common vision, people will be arguing from a set of shared narratives, while at the same time ideally sharing common representations for mutual-personal recognition.

Of course, the very same narratives and practices that make possible mutual personal recognition and that are necessary for speaking and acting together, are also involved in excluding persons from participating. As Claire Colebrook and Jason Maxwell note about Agamben's political philosophy, "Being recognized before the law, having the political identity of a citizen, is an event of inclusion that necessarily entails exclusion."[62] If we turn to the Greeks, Aristotle's polis excluded women, children, and slaves from the public-political process of speaking and acting together as citizens, though women, children, and slaves were included in the polis—residents, but not citizens. Others who were not politically recognized and who were excluded were men (foreigners, barbarians) from other city-states. They may have been residents, but they were excluded from full participation in the polis. In the history of the United States, slaves, African Americans, Native peoples, and women have, at times, not been recognized as political agents, though they resided within the U.S. They were, in other words, excluded from the political space of appearances, to use Arendt's term, yet included in the polis-excluded-included Others.[63] The shared narratives and practices legitimated the attenuation of the space of appearances and accompanying mis or non-recognitions.

The struggle between exclusion and inclusion vis-à-vis human beings may have sparked Emmanuel Kant's interest in cosmopolitanism.[64] How do we live in a polis that is pluralistic and diverse was an issue for Kant's times, and our own as well, though there is a key difference. The realization that we are in the Anthropocene Age, wherein all human beings are residents,

62. Colebrook and Maxwell, *Agamben*, 56.

63. As will be noted in subsequent chapters, in much of Western philosophy and theology nature is included-excluded Other. To care for nature and other species means to open a space for them to appear as they are and not simply or solely as we wish them to be.

64. Kant, *Idea for a Universal History from a Cosmopolitan Point of View*.

might offer opportunities to move beyond inclusion-exclusion dynamics within and between diverse political communities. Agamben envisions the possibility of a political community—coming community—that does not have the problem of inclusion-exclusion. Can we dwell in the polis such that we "co-belong without any representable condition of belonging," "without affirming identity"?[65] He believes so, though not without recognizing the countervailing headwinds confronting any approximation of this type of polis. To embody and appear as singular and to belong without making either singularity or belonging contingent on the representations of a particular identity are intolerable to the state apparatus, according to Agamben. "What the State cannot tolerate in any way," he writes, "is that the singularities form a community without affirming an identity, that human beings co-belong without any representable condition of belonging."[66] We might hear counter-echoes of this in Galatians (3:28): "There is no longer Jew or Greek, there is no longer slave or free, there is no longer male and female; for all of you are one in Christ." The point here is not simply to live in a polis without the necessity of relying on identity, but how we are to live and cooperate together toward the well-being of all residents of the earth and the earth itself, while affirming the incredible diversity and plurality of cultures/identities. Can the space of appearances be extended to include all human beings (and other-than-human beings) without resorting to one state or universal government (Leviathan)? Or can we speak and act together without making identity the criterion for participation? I will return to this below.

Giorgio Agamben further broadens the vision of exclusion and inclusion vis-à-vis the polis. In Western philosophy, starting with the Greeks, Agamben notes, there has been a split between the political and natural world,[67] which means that more-than-human beings are not considered to be residents—existentially or juridically. Of course, there is no hint here of making animals legal residents or citizens, for that, as noted above, would be a category mistake. The point, rather, with regard to living in the Anthropocene, is to acknowledge that other-than-human beings and the earth are part of the polis and the political.[68] Nature, in other words, is the very

---

65. Agamben, *The Coming Community*, 5. I am assuming that Agamben was referring to political identity.

66. Agamben, *The Coming Community*, 5.

67. Colebrook and Maxwell, *Agamben*, 6–17. See also Prozorov, *Agamben and Politics*, 103–7.

68. Mick Smith notes that Hannah Arendt states that "*politics will, from now on, be inherently, not just accidently, a politics of nature.*" For Arendt, Agamben, and others the exclusion of nature from politics is a devastatingly destructive illusion, which we are reaping the benefits of in the Anthropocene Age. Smith, *Against Ecological Sovereignty*, 141.

foundation for the possibility of a polis. While we may agree with Arendt's view that a polis is not defined by geography, there will be no polis if there is not a natural world that supports life. If anything, the Anthropocene Age informs us that geography or habitat is the basis of the very possibility of speaking and acting together. While the polis is natural, in the sense of being a construction of human beings and a need for being human (persons), it is not separate from nature.[69] Distinction is not necessarily separation or exclusion. In brief, the natural world is the foundation of the very possibility of a polis.

There are several other aspects of the polis need mentioning. As noted, speaking and acting together requires interpersonal recognition,[70] which founds the individual and the collective sense of self-esteem, self-confidence, and self-respect in the public realm.[71] Put another way, to have political agency in the polis, to appear as a political agent, one must have affirmed one's sense of self-esteem, self-confidence, and self-respect. Instances of exclusion, such as slavery, and marginalization, such as racism, classism, and sexism, involve disciplinary regimes or apparatuses that deny personal recognition, which, in turn, accompany the collapse or attenuation of the space of appearances and the diminution of political agency. The apparatuses or disciplinary regimes that humiliate persons and groups depend on misrecognition, which undermines the self-esteem, self-confidence, and self-respect necessary for political agency in speaking and acting together. People who are marginalized or excluded, then, will be unable to discover or have affirmed their public-political self-esteem, self-confidence, and self-respect. A decent polis or *ekklesia*, by contrast, does not humiliate its residents or some group of residents, making possible shared esteem, respect, and confidence necessary for political agency, for speaking and acting together.[72]

---

69. We often hear people communicate as if human beings are separate from nature. Freud believed that civilization entails a fight over and against nature. Language like this reveals the illusion that human beings are distinct from nature, which often leads to separation. I will endeavor not to communicate in this way. Human beings are causing the extinctions of other species and if we become extinct ourselves, the extinction event will be one from nature, because we are part of nature.

70. Agamben would argue for the recognition of the individual's singularity or suchness, while Helmut Plessner refers to the principle of recognition as the individual's unfathomableness. Both, in my view, are connected to the notion of personal recognition, but Agamben extends singularity to other species and the earth. See Agamben, *Sovereign Power and Bare Life.* Plessner, *Political Anthropology.* For a discussion of personal recognition vis-à-vis the political realm see Macmurray, *Persons in Relation.*

71. Honneth, *The Struggle for Recognition.*

72. Margalit, *The Decent Society.*

It is important to stress that personal recognition in the polis has, as Nancy Fraser points out, very real effects on the distribution of resources.[73] In an indecent polis, those who are denied political agency or whose political agency is thwarted will not have the same access to resources as those who have full political agency and its corresponding sense of esteem, respect, and confidence. One need only point to the long history of slavery, racism, sexism, and classism in the United States to see this clearly. Also, when we consider that global warming will lead to the reduction of the resources needed for survival, we can imagine the likely possibility that recognition in the polis will become yoked to particular identities, leaving "lesser" identities (residents) in the polis to fend for themselves with less resources to cope. We already have clear evidence of this in Trump's draconian—barely hidden—white supremacist immigration policies and his comment that "Our country is full." It is also evident in environmental racism, which has negative effects on persons of color.[74] Clearly, then, social-political misrecognition is linked to the maldistribution of resources, and, in the Anthropocene, it will only get worse.[75]

Agency within the polis is also intertwined with civic faith. For cooperation to exist in the polis, for people to engage in speaking and acting together toward the common well-being of the polis' residents, there must be some semblance of shared civic faith—trust, fidelity, and hope.[76] We must have some semblance of trust and loyalty in the polis, if we are to risk appearing in our singularities. Even Hobbes' dismal leviathan enforces and allows for some degree of trust and fidelity between citizens, though it is dependent on the threat of punishment—political violence. One might say the leviathan poses a threat that enforces a minimal amount of cooperation vis-à-vis security and peace.[77] More positively, the polis that promotes mutual personal recognition also at the same time facilitates civic trust and loyalty for the sake of speaking and acting together toward common well-being.[78]

Included in the polis' civic faith is "the faculty to make and to keep promises."[79] To make and keep promises, Arendt argues, is necessary

---

73. Fraser, and Honneth, *Redistribution or Recognition?*

74. Santiago, "Environmental Racism Is Killing People of Color."

75. See Davenport, "Pentagon Signals Security Risks of Climate Change."

76. Niebuhr, *Faith on Earth*. Niebuhr argues that to be human is to have faith and that faith comprises three interrelated dialectical pairs, namely belief-disbelief, trust-distrust, and loyalty-disloyalty. I add another pair: hope-hopelessness.

77. Ryan, *On Politics*, 432–35.

78. The importance of civic faith can also be seen in Avishai Margalit's discussion of betrayal, treason, and politics. Margalit, *On Betrayal*.

79. Arendt, *The Human Condition*, 237.

given the uncertainties and insecurities of the future.[80] Yet, we also know that, as much as human beings are promise-making creatures, we are also promise-breaking beings. We are faithful and faithless, which, if the polis is to survive, requires the faculty of forgiveness. Arendt writes, "It is rather that forgiving attempts the seemingly impossible, to undo what has been done, and that it succeeds in making a new beginning where beginnings seemed to have become no longer possible."[81] In short, a decent polis would entail customs and institutions that would facilitate relational repairs due to broken promises.

Implicit in the notions of interpersonal recognition, political agency, and civic faith is civic care. Numerous feminist scholars and pastoral theologians have argued that care is a political concept.[82] While mentioned in a footnote above, care, in general, as a political concept refers to activities or practices that are aimed at meeting individuals' and families' vital biological needs, developing or maintaining "their basic capabilities, and avoid or alleviate unnecessary or unwanted pain and suffering, so that they can survive, develop, and function in society."[83] Even indecent or dystopian societies have a semblance of care among its members, though care may be reduced to the home or friendships. The television show *Deadwood*, for instance, portrayed moments of care amidst the violence of living in a Western territory that had no laws or government.

In light of the Anthropocene Age, we are invited to extend political agency/faith, care, esteem, confidence, and respect not only for all who reside in a geographical location, but for every resident of the earth. If this seems unlikely or even naïve, recall that Agamben considers this a possibility for human beings. Human beings can co-belong "without affirming an identity . . . without any representable condition of belonging."[84] I do not think that Agamben is suggesting that identity is not important. Rather, with regard to belonging, identity in the polis is not contingent on or determined by particular representations that legitimate participation. Put

80. Arendt, *The Human Condition*, 237.

81. Arendt, *The Promise of Politics*, 58.

82. See Bubeck, *Care, Gender, and Justice*; Engster, *The Heart of Justice*; Hamington, *Embodied Care*; Held, *The Ethics of Care*; Helsel, *Pastoral Power Beyond Psychology's Imagination*; Johnson, *Race, Religion, and Resilience in the Neoliberal Age*; LaMothe, *Care of Polis, Care of Persons*; Oliner and Oliner, *Toward a Caring Society*; Ramsay, "Compassionate Resistance"; Robinson, *Globalizing Care*; Robinson, *The Ethics of Care*; Rogers-Vaughn, *Caring for Souls in a Neoliberal Age*; Rumscheidt, *No Room for Grace*; Sevenhuijsen, *Citizenship and the Ethics of Care*; Tronto, *Moral Boundaries*; and Tronto, *Caring Democracy*.

83. Engster, *The Heart of Justice*, 28.

84. Agamben, *The Coming Community*, 85.

differently, particular representations vis-à-vis identity are inoperative in the polis. They are present, but not operative with regard to persons speaking and acting together. This paves the way for the idea that the polis, while local and having particular representations (narratives, rituals etc.), does not exclude others. If one believes this is not possible, consider the example of the Norwegian town Longyearbyen, which has over 50 nationalities among its 2,500 residents. It is a town where a visa is not required. As one resident remarked, "All are guests," which he understood to mean as guests of the island and its animal residents. Also, as guests, their specific nationalities are inoperative—present, but not operating vis-à-vis their speaking and acting together in this polis.

In terms of the Anthropocene Age, the political community comprises all human beings and nature. Does this imply a homogenous world? I am confident Agamben's idea of the coming community does not mean universal homogeneity or a global state government. It is possible to live like the residents of Longyearbyen amid diversity and plurality in speaking and acting together. Recognition of individuals' singularities is by definition an acknowledgement of plurality. Put differently, the singularity and suchness of individuals, then, is recognized and accepted, yet particular representations are not the basis of a particular political identity/agency that excludes others. We are all part of one habitat. We all have political-ecological agency amid diverse city-states that are dependent on one habitat. We are all guests of the earth.

Having defined and addressed some the characteristics of the polis and its relation to the Anthropocene Age, I turn briefly to the cognate concepts' "politics" and "political." Political philosopher Sheldon Wolin views the "political" as "an expression of the idea that a free society composed of diversities can nonetheless enjoy moments of commonality, when, through public deliberations, collective power is used to promote or protect the well-being of the collectivity."[85] He continues by saying "Politics refers to the legitimized and public contestation, primarily by organized and unequal social powers, over access to resources available to the public authorities of the collectivity. Politics is continuous, ceaseless, and endless."[86] These terms are obviously related for Wolin. He notes, "The political signifies the attempt to constitute the terms of politics so that struggles for power can be contained and so that it is possible to direct it for common ends, such as justice,

---

85. Wolin, *Fugitive Democracy*, 100. Wolin is arguing from the basis of the liberal political tradition as an ideal that informs his notions of politics and the political. However, Wolin recognizes that politics and the political also refer to various forms of tyranny or totalitarianism.

86. Wolin, *Fugitive Democracy*, 100.

equality, and cultural values."[87] Andrew Samuels holds a similar view. He argues that politics is "the concentrated arrangements and struggles within an institution, or in a single society, or between the countries of the world for the organization and distribution of resources and power . . . to maintain survival . . . or more positively enhance the quality of human life."[88] While I will say more about power below and in the chapters on sovereignty and change, both Samuels and Wolin view the political and politics in terms of discourse, contestation, and agency, all of which are aimed at living a life in common with the goal of common well-being. That is, both politics and the political emerge from the "shared concerns of human beings to take care of themselves and the part of the world they claim as their lot."[89] Politics, in short, represents agonistic relations of people struggling to speak and act together toward a vision of the good.

I quickly note here Wolin's view of the relation between care and these two terms—politics and political. Care, as indicated above, is central to the political and politics. It is difficult to imagine political arrangements surviving without some level of civic care and civic faith. Even totalitarian states that rely on violence and the threat of violence to quell political opposition require some basic level of civic care to keep the society from imploding. Another important point in Wolin's views is the importance of commonality vis-à-vis the political and politics. "The political," he argues, "is based on this possibility of commonality: our common capacity to share, to share memories and a common fate."[90] Lest one think that the term "common" is a code for exclusion of the uncommon or those in society who are included but excluded from common memories, Wolin believes that the "problem of the political is not to clear a space from which society is to be kept out but is rather to ground power in commonality while reverencing diversity—not simply respecting difference."[91] Unlike Hobbes, who feared human beings would return to the brutish state of nature, and Schmitt's friend-enemy distinction as the basis of politics and the political, Wolin founds the political in common care and a commonality that cherishes difference and diversity.

The idea of civic care and civic faith vis-à-vis living a life in common is connected to the process of the political. Agamben contends that politics is a means without end.[92] I understand this to mean two things. First,

87. Wolin, *Fugitive Democracy*, 298.
88. Samuels, *The Political Psyche*, 3.
89. Samuels, *The Political Psyche*, 248.
90. Samuels, *The Political Psyche*, 248.
91. Samuels, *The Political Psyche*, 249; see also Brown, *Regulating Aversion*.
92. Agamben, *Means without Ends*.

since human beings cannot, for Agamben, exhaust their potentiality, which indicates that a clearly defined end or telos would contradict the nature of being human.[93] Human beings, for Agamben, are defined as beings without an essence, unless we understand essence to be potentiality. Second, care vis-à-vis speaking and acting together in the polis, is the process by which potentiality becomes actual, which I will address in the chapter on political change. Care and attending personal recognition are means with no clear end or telos. Yes, the end is to live a life in common, but what that actually looks like is unclear and wildly diverse.

There is one other point that Hannah Arendt contributes to our understanding of the political. "Political activity," she contends, "is valued not because it may lead to agreement or to a shared conception of the good, but because it enables each citizen to exercise his or her powers of agency, to develop the capacities for judgment, and to attain by concerted actions some measure of political efficacy."[94] To return to Agamben, the political is humankind's "most proper dimension."[95] Arendt stresses that political activity—speaking and acting together in the polis—involves, like Wolin, diversity in the polis, which is not simply diverse singularities, but diverse visions of the good.[96] Again, what this "good" looks like is dependent on the means of care, which is without a determinative telos. Also, in my view, political activity/agency and care, as noted above, presupposes individual and shared, yet diverse, self-esteem, self-respect, and self-confidence, which are supported by public, political, and cultural institutions.

Neither Wolin nor Arendt associate politics and the political with government. To do so would limit these terms. They both acknowledge that the government or state is a creation of people speaking and acting together, which means that speaking and acting together precedes any notion or structure of government.[97] Moreover, for these theorists, politics is the lifeblood of society and constitutive for being human,[98] and not something simply and solely confined to those who are in the government. To be in

93. Colebrook and Maxwell, *Agamben*, 25.

94. In D'Entreves, *The Political Philosophy of Hannah Arendt*, 2.

95. Agamben, *The Kingdom and the Glory*, xiii.

96. See Arendt, *The Origins of Totalitarianism*, 275–90.

97. See also Macmurray, "The Conception of Society," 106. For Macmurray, "The State has no rights, no authority, for it is an instrument, not an agent; a network of organization, not a person." The state, Macmurray noted, "exists to make society possible, to provide mechanisms through which the sharing of human experience may be achieved."

98. As Agamben notes, politics is humanity's "most proper dimension." Agamben, *Kingdom and the Glory*, xiii.

society is to be engaged in the political and in politics. Even if one deliberately avoids voting and engaging in public-political discourse, they nevertheless remain part of the polis and are shaped by both politics and the
political.

It can be helpful to encapsulate the above by saying that, by the political,
I mean socially held and publicly used and expressed symbols, narratives,
and rituals that are embodied in a polis's institutions and social-symbolic
communicative spaces that function to:

a. organize persons' experiences and legitimate individuals' actions in the
   public realm.[99]

b. facilitate collective discourse and action in the public realm.[100]

c. distribute power and resources.[101]

d. legitimate authority and governance.

e. adjudicate claims and discipline and repair breeches of both social order and the laws governing social arrangements and the distribution
   of resources.

f. provide an overarching social-political identity that supports collective
   action and discourse, as well as provides for a shared sense of continuity and cohesion.

g. facilitate civic care and trust for cooperation vis-à-vis survival and
   flourishing.

The notion of politics, then, refers to groups of people, not necessarily
or always citizens, who are engaged in public action and discourse—speaking and acting together—pertaining to the common good and decisions being made with regard to a) who is allowed to participate in public-political
discourse (citizenship and identity), b) who should govern/rule and for how
long, c) what type of institution(s) should be the instrument of governing, d)
the kinds of policies and programs that administer and regulate economic
and social affairs, e) care of citizens and strangers, and f) the enactment and
adjudication of laws that order the society and repair social disruptions.

It is important to pause and stress that both concepts, political and
politics, are—as Arendt, Wolin, and any political philosopher or theologian
know—inextricably yoked to the issue of power. Indeed, some of the very

99. See Arendt, *The Human Condition*.

100. See D'Entreves, *The Political Philosophy of Hannah Arendt*; Young, *Justice and the Politics of Difference*.

101. See Ransom, *Foucault's Discipline*.

sources of problems in the polis and with politics is rooted in how power is understood and lived out. Agamben, for instance, contends there is inherent violence in law-making and law-preserving. Indeed, he asserts that what the "law can never tolerate . . . is the existence [of violence] outside the law."[102] While I will address this in subsequent chapters, for now I simply point out that, for Agamben and many others, violence is inextricably yoked to political power and to the political institutions that make and enforce the law.[103] Arendt offers a different view. Having lived in and later having fled Germany in the 1930s, Arendt was well acquainted with political "power" as force/coercion and violence. She differentiates between political violence and power, contending that political power "exists only in actualization . . . where word and deed have not parted company."[104] Positively stated, actualization of power refers to the space of appearances where residents of the polis are acting and speaking together—where they are politically engaged in varied ways—civic care and faith. As noted above, the metaphor, "space of appearances,"[105] denotes the mutual recognition and treatment of others as persons—unique, valued, inviolable, and responsive/agentic.[106] Individuals ideally appear in the political space as persons—unique, valued, inviolable, and agentic—and as having a voice, self-esteem, self-respect, and self-confidence, which founds their joining together in cooperative action. The mutual recognition and treatment of others as persons, which implies some level of social care and justice, are necessary for cooperation toward

102. Agamben, *State of Exception*, 53.

103. Let me stress that Agamben does not argue that human beings are determined by this view. He is arguing that in the West the political is inextricably a part of violence—bare life. It is possible, as I will endeavor to explain, his notion of inoperativity and its relation to the political suggest the possibility (potential) to think and be otherwise in the polis.

104. Arendt, *The Human Condition*, 200.

105. Arendt, *The Human Condition*, 179.

106. See Macmurray, *Persons in Relation*. The concept of person is, for Macmurray, not necessarily a legal concept, rather it is primarily a philosophical concept pointing to an ontological reality. This said, the notion of universal personhood accompanies the local realities of sexism, racism, and other forms of misrecognition, discrimination, and exploitation—realities that involve the denial of personhood. See Brown, *Politics Out of History*, 13–15. All of this suggests that personhood, as Macmurray recognized, is both a matter of fact and a matter of intention. In other words, human beings must continually create personhood in the face of the human tendency to deny personhood to those constructed as Other. I would mention here that recognition of Others as "persons" is beyond ascribing a particular identity. To be sure, particular identity is involved, but is not determinative of personal recognition. This is important because it points to the possibility of a polis and politics not based on or determined by recognition informed by the particular representations associated with identity. See Agamben, *The Coming Community*.

political aims—for shared speaking and acting together. In other words, *mutual personal recognition, which founds civic care and civic faith, is the basis for political power* (speaking and acting together), while political force and coercion represent the decline of political power, the attenuation of the space of appearances, the presence of misrecognition, and maldistribution.

The concepts "politics" and "political" take on special urgency given the present and future realities of global warming. There are many ways politics and the political are expressed and lived out across the globe. If we consider that in every country, politics and the political are sites of significant contestation, we can only imagine what this means when we zoom out to include international politics. International cooperation toward making any significant dent in reducing carbon emissions meets the seemingly impenetrable obstacles of global capitalism,[107] the rise of new imperialism,[108] and forms of xenophobic nationalism.[109] These are obstacles to acceptance of political diversity, to global political cooperation to reduce greenhouse gasses, and to the inclusion of nature. To be sure, there have been global summits where nations have drawn up plans to reduce global emissions,[110] but these treaties are weak in the sense of being unenforceable.

There are two points here. First, there is no escaping the political and politics. To be human, to become human, as Arendt posits, is to be part of the polis, which, in turn, means engaging in the political. Even for those who are excluded from the space of appearances—denied political agency—the very nature of their exclusion is political. The corollary is that the polis and its political life cannot be separated from the realities of other political organizations. This means that political cooperation among states is especially necessary given the stark realities of climate change. Second, while we tend to associate the political and politics with politicians and state apparatuses,

107. Part of the intractability of capitalism is not simply that it is a system of organizing societies, but that it has morphed into a religion that has no foundation or end. See, Cox, *The Market as God*; Frank, *One Market under God*; Agamben, "Capitalism as Religion."

108. Here I am thinking of the United States' imperialistic ambitions of retaining global hegemony, coupled with the rise of China and re-emergence of Russia as imperialistic nations.

109. Britain's Brexit vote and anti-immigration policies, Germany's Freedom Party, Hungary's Victor Orban, Italy's Five Star Movement, and Poland's Law and Justice Party are some examples of the rise of right-wing nationalist movements. Across the pond, the United States elected a president who clearly panders to nationalistic and white supremacist interests, with the slogans of "America First" and "Make America Great Again."

110. The first global summit was in 1979, the second in 1990, the third in 2009, and the most recent in 2019. The Trump Administration pulled out of the climate treaty, though it participated in the 2019 summit.

the people are the *arche*, the foundation of the polis and its political life. The corollary here is that the polis, political, and politics are ideally for the people and not for some segment of the population. The state and political leaders ideally function for the good of all people. They ideally serve the people. The people do not serve the political leaders or the state. If we widen the lens, given the Anthropocene Age, the political and politics is for the sake of the one habitat and its residents—human beings and otherwise. This view is reflected in the Roman Catholic Church's Vatican II document, wherein it states, "Because of the closer bonds of human interdependence . . . we are today witnessing a widening of the common good, which is the sum total of social conditions which allow people, either as groups or as individuals, to reach their fulfillment more fully and more easily . . . Every group must take into account the needs and legitimate aspirations of every other group, and still more of the human family as a whole."[111] We can include other creatures of the earth who also depend on a viable habitat for their well-being. To repeat, nature itself is the foundation of our polis, of our politics.

## Political Theology and the Anthropocene

Having provided some of the contours of polis and politics, I turn to the idea of political theology. The notion "political theology" dates back to Marcus Terentius Varro in the early second century. Hent de Vries writes that Varro speaks of the Stoic tripartition of theology, in which political theology is juxtaposed with mythical and cosmological theologies."[112] While the concept recedes in importance until the twentieth century with the publication of *Political Theology* by German (later Nazi) jurist Carl Schmitt in the 1920s,[113] it is clear that political theology is present in the works of Augustine, Aquinas, Luther, Calvin, and other prominent theologians. Indeed, one could argue that political theology is present in the Torah, as Jewish people assembled to figure out ways to live a life in common. It is clearly evident in the Israelites viewing God as their sovereign and later when the elders of Israel asked Samuel to "appoint for us a king to govern us like other nations" (1 Sam 8:5). We could add that a latent political theology is present in the formation of the early church communities, as evident in Acts. They addressed questions of who would lead/govern; how and who would live a life in common; how to distribute resources, etc. As Daniel Bell asserts,

111. "Gaudium et Spes," #26.

112. De Vries, "Introduction," 25.

113. Schmitt, *Political Theology*.

"theology is always already political."[114] De Vries makes a similar point, arguing that "the theologico-political problem is perceived and lived well before being theorized and named as such."[115]

While I contend that political theologizing has been going on since the moment the first Israelites gathered and self-consciously considered themselves a people living a life in common, political theology as a distinct concept and discipline did not emerge until the twentieth century. This is especially evident after World War II with the rise of 1) colonial peoples seeking to throw off the yoke of their colonial oppressors,[116] 2) second wave feminism[117] (and later womanist theologies), 3) black liberation movements in the United States[118] and South Africa,[119] Asian liberation theologies,[120] and LGBTQI movements.[121] This period of history ushered in an explosion of liberation theologies, which fall under the heading of political theologies.[122] In my view, the authors of these varied political theologies use or create concepts, located in particular theological *mythoi* and philosophical traditions, to address complex questions and problems associated with living a life in common (e.g., sovereignty, recognition/identity, organization of daily life, and distribution of resources) during a particular era and within a specific geography. There is, therefore, no definitive political theology for all people, in all places, for all times. Indeed, what we can expect is a vast diversity of political theologies, even when operating out of the same mythos.

Political theology, then, is the use of particular theological mythos and ethos to provide answers to questions about what it means to live a life in common; how are we to dwell together; who (and who decides who will live) lives in this assembly; who exercises political agency (citizenship); what political, social, and cultural institutions and practices found and support civic

---

114. Bell, "State and Civil Society," 423.

115. De Vries, "Introduction," 29.

116. Gutiérrez, *A Theology of Liberation*. Sobrino, *The True Church and the Poor*.

117. Daly, *Beyond God the Father*. Saiving, "The Human Situation: A Feminine View."

118. Cone, *A Black Theology of Liberation*.

119. Buthelezi, "Toward Indigenous Theology in South Africa." Boesak, "Coming in Out of the Wilderness."

120. Pieris, "Political Theologies in Asia," 256–69.

121. Greenough, *Queer Theologies*; and Moon, *God, Sex, and Politics.*.

122. There are also conservative political theologies that were interested in supporting and legitimating the status quo (e.g., Michael Novak) and more theocratic political theologies (Dominion Theologies and Christian Reconstructionism). See Novak, *The Spirit of Democratic Capitalism*; Novak, *Toward a Theology of the Corporation*. For an overview of a founder dominion theology, see "R. J. Rushdoony," in *Wikipedia*.

care, trust, and cooperation, as well as provide individual and collective self-esteem, self-confidence, and self-respect necessary for speaking and acting together (space of appearances); how are goods distributed so that residents can survive and thrive; what is the vision of the common good; who governs and how do they govern; what institutions are created to facilitate governance (laws, police, courts); what institutions and processes are established for justice and repair of social-political relations. To answer these questions might imply writing a political theological treatise (e.g., Augustine's *City of God*; Calvin's *Institutes*), but this, as stated above, is not my approach or aim. Instead, I am interested in sketching out a radical political theology (chapter 1) and pointing out and discussing various problems associated with political theologies and political philosophies. I have chosen this approach primarily because theological legitimation of sovereignty, even its democratic forms,[123] is fundamentally contradictory given the non-sovereignty of God. In other words, a radical political theology cannot legitimate any notion or permutation of sovereignty, because, as I make clear later, sovereignty is an entirely human issue (not a characteristic of God), and sovereignty depends on law-making and law-enforcing violence. Put differently, "Christianity pulls the rug out from under every political theology, because the trinitarian God of Christendom cannot be represented in any political order."[124] While a radical political theology cannot legitimate a particular form of sovereignty[125] or dominant political arrangement, it certainly can take a critical and constructive stance toward any iteration of sovereignty and its institutions and practices associated with citizenship (and residency), the common good, and distribution of resources by way of the concepts of care and justice,[126] which are, in part, understood vis-à-vis a particular, in this case, Christian mythos. That said, as Adam Kotsko notes "Political theology must seek out unexpected resources and connections elsewhere . . . if it is to reach its full potential as a critical discourse."[127] This is evident in my use of varied theologians, philosophers, and those engaged in the human sciences.

Given this, any radical political theology (or any theology) has to contend with the fact that it is not universal, since its religious mythos is particular to a group of people. To accept this means that a radical political

---

123. See for instance, Robbins, *Radical Democracy and Political Theology*; Eggemeier, *Against Empire*.

124. Hartwich, Assmann, and Assmann, "Afterword," 139.

125. Indeed, as indicated in chapter 3, sovereignty is a problem. Philosopher Jean-Luc Nancy writes that "The problem is not a matter of fixing up sovereignty: in essence, sovereignty is untreatable." Nancy, *Being Singular Plural*, 131.

126. Dickinson and Kotsko, *Agamben's Coming Philosophy*, 250.

127. Kotsko, "Genealogy and Political Theology," 164.

theology is both critical and confessional. Implicit here is the willingness to engage in conversations with diverse partners who hold different views and have different answers to the questions above. This said, I opt for Seyla Benhabib's view of interactive universalism. She writes:

> Interactive universalism acknowledges the plurality of modes of being human, and differences among humans, without endorsing all the pluralities and differences as morally or politically valid . . . Interactive universalism regards difference as a starting point for reflection and action. In this sense, "universality" is a regulative ideal that does not deny embodied and embedded identity, but aims at developing moral attitudes and encouraging political transformation that can yield a point of view acceptable to all.[128]

Interactive universalism posits, if not lauds, diversity, while positing the possibility of mutual engagement and agonistic contestation toward some degree of cooperation and agreement. I add here that interactive universalism can also embrace Agamben's coming community. As noted above, Agamben argues that we can dwell in the polis such that we "co-belong without any representable condition of belonging," "without affirming identity."[129] A radical political theology celebrates and includes a diversity of identities, which means being willing to do the work of understanding Others while being engaged in difficult, agonistic conversations.

The ideas of a constructive critical stance, interactive universalism, and the coming community are necessary for any political theology addressing questions, issues, and concerns in the Anthropocene Era. To care for the earth, for our one habitat, necessarily means caring for its residents, if there is to be any chance of stemming the tide of coming catastrophes (and even if there is little or no chance). There is, in fact, one polis, even as we live in its many neighborhoods. But this also means constructing a political theology of care that is not dependent on the realization of a future good or even a vision of the survival of humanity. Here I am reminded of Tillich's *Courage to Be*. He wrote, "Courage is the self-affirmation of being in spite of the fact of non-being. It is the act of the individual self in taking anxiety of nonbeing upon itself by affirming itself either as part of an embracing whole or in its individual selfhood."[130] While I will say more about this in the last chapter, for now I alter this and suggest that a political theology in the Anthropocene Era invites a radical courage to care in the present. It takes courage to

128. Benhabib, *Situating the Self*, 153.
129. Agamben, *The Coming Community*, 5.
130. Tillich, *Courage to Be*, p.155.

care when the extinction of human beings and millions of other creatures is likely. Put differently, the vision of the future is inoperative, which is not to say it is unimportant. This ideally means collective courage to care (means without ends) for the residents of this one polis and the earth upon which it depends despite a bleak future. That is, our care of Others and the earth is not contingent on the realization of a particular future, but rather on the theological and existential-political imperative to tend to our one habitat and its diverse residents. To end this section, there is indeed something unnamable, immeasurable, and indestructible about radical care in the face of the nonbeing of the Anthropocene Age.

## The Coming Chapters

Let me end this introductory chapter with a brief outline of the remaining chapters. Chapter 1 is concerned with first identifying some of the problems that attend political theologizing. This is necessary to highlight the limits of inquiry, as well as inherent limits in the creation and use of concepts and theories. Once this is accomplished, I identify and depict two theologies that are inextricably part of Judeo-Christian scripture, namely theologies of subjugation/subordination and theologies of vulnerability. Theologies of subjugation/subordination, which inadvertently spawn theologies of revolution and rebellion, have, by and large, served to ground political theologies and philosophies in the West. Theologies of subjugation/subordination, I argue, are problems because, while providing answers to political questions, these theologies and attending myths depend on excluded-included Others (human beings, other species, and the earth), which, in turn, leads to mimetic violence. From here shift to an existential and theological grounding of a radical political theology by first identifying and describing 1) primal acts of personal recognition and care revealed in parent-child spaces of speaking and acting together and 2) a theology of vulnerability that acknowledges the precarity, dependence, and vulnerability of life (human, other species, and the earth as a living system). The ontological-political imperative to care, I contend, is revealed in the non-sovereign God's indeterminate, infinite love/care in creation and of God's self-emptying and subsequent ministry and death of Jesus Christ. The remaining chapters serve to flesh out a radical political theology by addressing various dimensions and problems of political realities.

Given this chapter on sketching out a radical political theology, in chapter 2 I argue that the present and looming crises associated with climate change invite placing the issue of dwelling in the center of our political theorizing, as well as our thinking and being otherwise. The Anthropocene Age will be an era of millions upon millions of refugees seeking a home, not to mention the extinction or unhousing of millions of species. The figure of the refugee, against the backdrop of climate change, requires reimagining, as Agamben notes, our political philosophies, as well as our political theologies. The existential and theological question is how might we dwell together (human beings and more than human beings) in this place (earth) that is the primary condition of all dwelling? This chapter explores the issue of dwelling as it relates to political theology. This first entails addressing the notion of dwelling and identifying some of its attributes, which lays a foundation for discussing the problems of dwelling vis-à-vis political realities and the Anthropocene Age. From here I describe what I consider to be the existential roots of dwelling, namely the psychosocial, developmental experience of dwelling and the transition from this pre-political space to dwelling vis-à-vis the public political domain. This discussion provides the foundation for returning to a theology of vulnerability as it relates to the question of dwelling and its problems.

Dwelling, as it relates to the political, confronts the issue of sovereignty, especially in Western political theologies and philosophies. In chapter 3 I begin by providing some background on the concept of sovereignty and its attributes. This serves as a foundational step toward identifying and discussing some of the problems of sovereignty, not only with regard to other human beings, but also other species and the earth. In brief, I contend that sovereignty is not only a problem vis-à-vis human dwelling and the acceptance of the refugee, but also the dwelling of more-than-human beings and the earth as the dwelling place of all life. After addressing some of the problems of sovereignty vis-à-vis the Anthropocene Age, I shift to an existential and theological perspective of non-sovereign relations. I first depict an existential root of non-sovereign or anarchic relations, evident in good-enough parent-child interactions. What I claim here is that sovereignty, while a human issue, is not inevitably or irreducibly a fact of human relations. The "state of nature," if you will, reveals other-than sovereign relations as a condition of belonging or dwelling. I then shift to a radical political theology of a non-sovereign and non-privileging God and a non-sovereign humanity. I argue that Jesus Christ's vulnerability is, in part, a revelation of a non-sovereign, non-privileging God—a God of infinite, indeterminate love for creation. It is radical in the sense that it is the foundation or root of a political theology for the Anthropocene and radical in the sense of undermining and rejecting any theology or anthropology of human sovereignty (as well as anthropocentrism) over human beings and/or nature. That is, the revelation of the incarnation exposes the illusion of human sovereignty and privilege and exposes the theological and philosophical machines that aim to reproduce, legitimize, and maintain the illusions of sovereignty and invulnerability, which found relations of subjugation and exploitation.

Any discussion of human dwelling and sovereignty inevitably comes across the issue of human freedom, especially when we consider that human freedom is implicated in climate change. Though the issue freedom is a nettlesome and elusive political value, it nevertheless is key in addressing how we are to live and dwell given the present and future realities of the Anthropocene Age. For example, what will freedom look like as global resources diminish and there is a corresponding rise of fear and hatred? Will people sacrifice their freedom for the allure of national security and its promises of protection and stability? Will we freely circle the nationalistic wagons, ensuring that the exercise of freedom will foster exclusion and conflict, instead of inclusion, plurality, and cooperation? Will those specters of unfreedom—racism and classism (and other forms of marginalization)—become more virulent in an age of anxiety and scarcity? Will we continue to construct freedom to serve the interests of global capitalism at the expense of humanity, other species, and the earth? Will human beings recognize and acknowledge the material foundations of freedom—our dependence on the viability of the earth as a living system? Will we see, in other words, that all philosophies, theologies, and practices of freedom will turn to dust if human beings become extinct?

While these questions are daunting, a radical political theology must nevertheless undertake the effort to address freedom and political freedom, especially given that human freedom has played and continues to play a key role in climate change. Given this, in chapter 4 I endeavor to sketch out some of the contours or attributes of freedom and, in particular, political freedom. Toward this end, I begin with a definition of freedom, followed by a discussion of its attributes. In the next section, I describe some of the problems of political freedom given the realities of the Anthropocene Age. This sets the stage for depicting a radical political theology of freedom. As I have done in the previous chapters, this last section begins with an existential portrayal of freedom, which is followed by a theological framing of political freedom.

The topic of human freedom implies the movement from potentiality to actuality or simply change vis-à-vis human beings. The realities of climate change and the Anthropocene Age indicate that human activities have negatively impacted the earth, other species and many human beings. When we imagine the days, weeks and years ahead, we wonder about whether human beings will exercise their freedom to effect sufficient changes to alter the trajectory of climate destruction. There are already many individuals, groups, and states that have established programs, policies, and institutions that are aimed at addressing the effects of climate change. Change in the political realm is occurring. In chapter 5, my interest is to grasp some of the problems associated with political change, especially focusing on political violence as a method for change and for quelling change, and in so doing move toward a radical political theology of change. Toward this end, in this chapter, I begin with a brief depiction of some of the problems associated with change in the Anthropocene Age. From here, I focus on the problem of political violence, because it 1) has been a major mode of initiating change (and thwarting it) in history, 2) accompanies the political irrelevancy of nature, and 3) is fundamentally anti-political. In this section, I will also argue that political violence as a mode of change is completely unjustifiable not only because it is mimetically tragic in that it perpetuates alienation, but also because it undermines political dwelling vis-à-vis othered human beings, species, and the earth itself. This sets the stage for offering a radical political theology that does not depend on political violence to organize relations or effect change. I begin this section by arguing that from an existential developmental perspective, good-enough parents' caring actions are the foundation of developmental changes, which includes changes in relationships. I then shift from this existential perspective to the theological, arguing that God's care, evident in the incarnation and Jesus' forgiveness of perpetrators of political violence, is a redemptive invitation to eschew political violence as a method of change, which is not necessarily to advocate for pacifism, but rather for nonviolent political actions of defiance and resistance. More positively, the weak force of God's care is evident in political change that emerges from acts of inclusive care toward human beings, other species, and the earth.

The question of whether there will be sufficient changes to stem the gravitational pull of climate disaster raises the question of hope, which is apt for a concluding chapter. When it comes to the realities of the Anthropocene Age many of us ask what hope is there for human beings, other-than-human beings, and the earth? In what and in whom do we place our hope? Will we be able to alter course in time? A political theology could provide readers with a kind of radical hope based on the Judeo-Christian scripture, but this is not the aim of the last chapter. Instead, I believe that there are problems with hope when we consider what we are facing and will face in the Anthropocene Age. This does not mean I am against hope—Christian or otherwise—but given the problems of hope I offer a different question and answer. How will we care in the present for each other, other-than-human beings, and the earth? This question and its answers are political, not only because the question necessarily involves poleis, but also because it necessarily includes other species and the earth. The question of hope is in the background, not in the sense of being unimportant, but rather because it is not the source of motivation and action in addressing the realities of the Anthropocene Age. More specifically, a radical political theology grounded in care is an antidote to the temptation of illusory hopes, facile optimism, and despair, which arises when hopes are not realized or realizable.

To flesh out the argument in chapter 6, I first discuss, in general terms, what is meant by hope and its attributes. Since hope is always particular, it important to also outline briefly Christian hopes. From here, I identify some of the political problems with hope and Christian hope, such as anthropocentrism, narcissism, and megalomania. This sets the stage for framing a radical political theology in terms of existential and theological aspects of passionate and courageous care for each other, other species, and the earth, placing the issue and question of hope secondary to both motivation, action, and results. I also argue that a political theology for the Anthropocene is based on a radical Christianity that is not defined by or dependent on hope for survival and flourishing in the present or in some future ethereal realm. Possessing the courage to care in the face of hopelessness is a radical political act—an act we need to embrace in facing the challenges of the Anthropocene Age. In short, "This is our defiance—to practice love even in hopelessness."[131]

---

131. Kaur, *See No Stranger*, 241.

# 1

## *The Problem of Political Theology in the Anthropocene*

### A Sketch of a Radical Political Theology

———————

We need to experiment radically with new ways of thinking
and living, because the current paradigm is in a state of exhaustion,
depletion, and death.[1]

The face of vulnerable materiality, expressed within and beyond the
human, should guide human thinking, morality, and theology, as if
God were, within the infinite plural forms of Earth, pleading for nonviolence insofar as it is possible.[2]

We lack the strength to make ourselves weak.[3]

[W]e can understand nothing about the politics of the last 50 years if we
do not put the question of climate change and its denial front and center.[4]

———

1. Crockett, *Radical Political Theology*, 165.

2. Eaton, "Beyond Human Exceptionalism," 216.

3. Schell, "The Human Shadow," 17. I would add here that we lack both the strength
and courage to choose to be vulnerable.

4. Latour, *Down to Earth*, 2.

In 2016, the docudrama-fiction TV series *Mars* debuted, telling the story of an attempt to colonize Mars in 2033. At times, there would be flashbacks to 2016 or earlier, where real scientists and engineers would exclaim their excitement and enthusiasm for the possibility of interplanetary travel. There was one videoclip where Elon Musk remarked that human beings must become an interplanetary species if we are to survive. It is not simply that the realm of space and other planets spark the imagination of human exploration; it is that we must by necessity colonize other worlds or go extinct. Missing in this docudrama-fiction is the irony and tragedy of spending billions, if not trillions, of dollars to colonize inhospitable planets and moons, while living on the only hospitable orb in the solar system. Perhaps for Elon Musk and others, there is a sense that the earth has finite resources to extract and exploit, which impels us to seek other worlds, leaving this world in ruins for ourselves and other species.[5] Put more directly, we are moving toward the point where the earth is not enough to satisfy our profligate desires, at least for many in the West.

This said, let's continue for the moment with this fictional account of space travel and the colonization of moons and planets. Whether we find ways to live on Mars or elsewhere, I am absolutely confident we will continue to bring with us the social problems and political questions we face and have faced on the earth for millennia. Who will govern and for how long? What institutions will be constructed to facilitate cooperation, as well as deal with tears in the social fabric (injustice)? What will be the vision of the common good and who will elaborate this vision and corresponding

5. There are a couple of points here. First, while the idea of and work toward human space exploration and colonization are exciting, it is important to mention that there is an inherent issue of class, if not classism, at the attempts to colonize space, which means poor people will be left to deal with a degraded earth. The movie *Elysium* provides a stark illustration of this, where the wealthy and privileged are ensconced in a pristine world orbiting the planet. Also, the TV series re-make of *Lost in Space* tells the story of colonization of a planet in the Alpha Centauri star system. The people selected have to pass a series of challenging tests, suggesting, to me, that individuals who are deprived of resources and education are not chosen. Only the best and brightest are selected, which, in my view, is inextricably rooted in class. In his monumental work, Chris Harman notes that the issue of class (and classism) have been with us since human beings began gathering into larger, more complex living arrangements (Harman, *A People's History of the World*). A second point concerns the issue of ecological agency. As mentioned in the Introduction, the fact that we have caused climate change reveals we are a force of nature. We are ecological agents, which is largely informed by the ideology of having dominion over the earth. This means the earth is an object to be exploited and this idea, attitude, and behavior will accompany us to other worlds. As ecological agents, we first need to learn how to adapt to (not enhance, exploit, control—unless these benefit the earth and not simply human beings) the earth as a unique living system upon which we depend. See Wood, *Reoccupy the Earth*.

practices and institutions that aim toward realization of the vision? What stories and myths will inform our daily life, our social interactions in this extraterrestrial community? What stories and myths[6] will we rely on as we answer these questions, as well as inform the values of daily life—values necessary for dwelling together (human and other than human)? These questions are not new. They were evident in the colonization of the Americas where the answers to the questions left a wide and deep trail of suffering and exploitation of the people and lands. My point here is that while human beings may become an interplanetary species, we will bring with us our ways of being and all our problems that exist on this world.

While I enjoy science and science fiction, and, with qualifications, celebrate the human desire to explore, perhaps our main task is to re-imagine our living together—our political dwelling and cooperation—given our known and sole (currently) hospitable planet in the solar system. Can we keep our feet firmly planted on the earth, facing directly and clearly the challenges, problems, and questions of how we might dwell together to sustain the earth for ourselves and other species? More specifically, the bleak realities of climate change in the Anthropocene Era invite and challenge political theologians and other citizens/residents of the earth to construct responses to the problems posed by climate change with the aim of securing life on this planet for ourselves and other species. Can we direct our creative energies and resources to secure a viable habitat for future generations (and for other species)? This is not only a question for all of us; it is a question for political theologians facing the difficult challenges of living in the Anthropocene Age. Can political theologians provide helpful responses to the daunting realities we face now and in the future with the aim of thinking and being otherwise for the sake of caring for the earth and its residents?

To launch in this direction, it is first necessary to identify further a few problems that attend political theology. This is important because problems reveal some of the limits of inquiry, as well as inherent limits in the creation and use of concepts and theories. Once this is accomplished, I turn toward identifying and depicting two theologies, namely, theologies of subjugation/subordination and theologies of vulnerability—the latter theologies found a radical political theology. These theologies have distinct, yet related, *mythoi*

---

6. I will say more about myths below, but for now I wish to stress that while the hard sciences are in the foreground of the attempt to colonize Mars, it is a mistake to suggest that science and scientists are not without myths that inform their lives and behaviors. I state this because it is an illusion that somehow we can colonize another planet as if science is the only or even dominant framework informing living life together. As long as human beings live a life in common, there will be myths informing them on how to address the issues and questions of living in community.

of the Judeo-Christian traditions and are often intertwined in political theorizing. I contend that theologies of subjugation/subordination, which inadvertently spawn theologies of revolution and rebellion,[7] have, by and large, served to ground political theologies and philosophies in the West. Theologies of subjugation/subordination, I argue, are problems because, while providing answers to political questions, these theologies and their attending myths depend on excluded-included Others (human beings, other species, and the earth), which, in turn, leads to mimetic violence. From here, I sketch out a radical political theology that emerges from and depends on 1) primal acts of personal recognition revealed in parent-child spaces of speaking and acting together and 2) a theology of vulnerability that acknowledges the precarity, dependence, and vulnerability of life (human, other species, and the earth as a living system) and, consequently, the existential and ontological imperatives of care (and justice). This ontological imperative is revealed in the non-sovereign God's indeterminate, infinite love/care in creation and of God's self-emptying and subsequent ministry and death of Jesus Christ.

Before I begin, it is important to address briefly some caveats and clarifications. First, let me be clear that I do not view "problems" as negative issues seeking definitive solutions. Of course, some problems in life are negative and do need clear solutions. Other problems in human life are perennial because they emerge from the existential reality of being human. I view existential political problems as invitations for creative constructions/responses offered for shared consideration and deliberation, instead of definitive, sectarian answers to be promulgated. The former is out of a spirit of humility, cooperation, and conversation, while the latter is out of arrogance, coercion, and exclusion. Second, identifying two theologies of the Judeo-Christian scriptures is not meant to suggest that there are only two theologies or two types of theology. I identify the two strands mainly for heuristic reasons, as well as for succinctness and clarity. Third, while I provide a sketch of radical political theology in this chapter, the remaining chapters, which address other problems and issues, serve to deepen and expand on a radical theology for the Anthropocene Era. Fourth, while I recognize that theologies of vulnerability and the notion of a non-sovereign God may present challenges for addressing clear answers to political questions (e.g., governance), I believe and will demonstrate that theologies of vulnerability render inoperative 1) the grammar and apparatuses associated with theologies of subjugation, 2) the friend-enemy distinction in organizing political

7. Roland Boer points out that Ernst Bloch, who used Marxism as a lens for reading scripture, noted that there were myths of domination and rebellion in the Judeo-Christian traditions. Boer, *Criticism of Heaven*, 26–47.

life, and 3) the attending mimetic violence, making way for what Walter Benjamin calls the weak messianic force or slight adjustment that creates a space to think and be otherwise in the Anthropocene Era.

## Problems of Political Theology

All political theologies (and I would add political philosophies[8]) depend on *mythoi* in addressing political problems and questions. Moreover, "political myths can be a source of moral energy and enthusiasm."[9] Theologian Louis Bouyer argues that "myth is humanity's original conscious articulation of the unity-in-difference of reality . . . Myth gives us the world or cosmos, because it gives it to us as a unity reflecting a transcendent force."[10] In other words, myths, for Bouyer, "shed light on the meaning of being human and the cosmos."[11] Northrop Frye writes "myth is a form of imaginative and creative thinking,"[12] which emerges from the existential questions human beings have faced for millennia. Of course, mythic enunciation, while creative and imaginative, is for Claude Lévi-Strauss an illusion that we understand the universe.[13] While the belief that we understand the universe is illusory for Lévi-Strauss, mythic answers to existential questions are often latent ideologies, as Bruce Lincoln noted, arguing that myth is "an ideology in narrative form."[14] Ideologies are powerful in that they shape perceptions, dispositions, and behaviors. Indeed, as Stephen Larson notes, the "myths by which we live are empowering structures that affect our health, vitality, and psychological well-being. They can have positive and negative effects on our lives."[15] This is noted in a different way by Ernst Bloch, who argued that myths can be repressive or subversive and emancipatory.[16] Even myths

8. Claudio Baracchi writes, "What the Platonic texts unmistakably betray is the fundamental function of mythical enunciation in the philosophical inquiry . . . It reveals philosophical discourse as inherently mythical matters." Baracchi, *Of Myth, Life, and War in Plato's Republic*, 7, 10. Baracchi is not arguing that myth is the ground of philosophy, but rather that it is relevant to the philosophical enterprise.

9. Hunter, *To Change the World*, 171.

10. In Lemna, *The Apocalypse of Wisdom*, 61.

11. Lemna, *The Apocalypse of Wisdom*, 50.

12. Frye, *The Great Code*, 35.

13. Lévi-Strauss, *Myth and Meaning*, 17.

14. Lincoln, *Theorizing Myth*, 36.

15. Larsen, 13.

16. Boer, *In the Vale of Tears*, 82.

that are repressive, closing down moments of rebellion, can still preserve a strand of resistance within the myth itself, which will be illustrated below.[17]

What we glean from this is that myths represent a type of narrative knowing[18] that orients people to the world and the community/society. Myths, more specifically, provide political[19] answers to existential questions. Put differently, "politics is expressed through symbolism" and these symbols are rooted in myths that address existential concerns.[20] Who are we? What is our place in the world? Where do we come from and where are we headed? How are we to live our lives in common? Whom should we trust? To whom are we obliged to care? What is the meaning and value of our lives? While the answers can, as Lévi-Strauss noted, give us the illusion of understanding the world, they are also practical in the sense of providing a foundation for dwelling together, for both good and ill.

If indeed myths are the originary foundation of political theologies, we need to deal with the thorny issues of truth/illusion and universality. Paul Riceour accepted that myths are illusions, yet argued that they carry with them existential truths.[21] For instance, he explored the myth of original sin, indicating that there is a truth in the sense of babies being born into a world of finitude, wherein systems and structures limit life. Political myths, such as the Exodus story, contain, for example, the existential truths of human bondage and the desire for liberation. Of course, these truths can seem as if they are universal and timeless, especially if they endure. Yet, this overlooks the reality that myths are particular to a specific people and time. We may find, for example, the Greek myths interesting and that they do say something about being human, yet these myths and their pantheon of gods no longer form the basis of modern political philosophy and imagination.[22]

17. Boer, *In the Vale of Tears*, 105. Bloch, according to Roland Boer, Judeo-Christian myths "have an emancipatory-utopian dimension about them that cannot be separated so easily from deception and illusion." In this book, I am using the mythoi of the Judeo-Christian tradition not strictly for the aims of emancipation or attaining a utopian vision which would seem odd when juxtaposed with the dire realities of the Anthropocene Era. Instead, the *mythoi* undergird a theology of vulnerability and care, which make inoperative the theological and political apparatuses of subjugation, domination, and subordination. I add the premise that care founds emancipation and any positive vision of the future. Boer, *Political Myth*, 24.

18. See Polkinghorne, *Narrative Knowing and the Human Sciences*.

19. There are individual and family myths that are not political, yet address these questions as well. My focus is, of course, on the political—living a life in common.

20. Kertzer, *Ritual, Politics, and Power*, 2.

21. See Riceour, "Original Sin."

22. Of course, philosophers like Hannah Arendt rely heavily on Greek philosophy, which emerged within a culture of Greek myths. That said, she is framing her

Add to this that people ostensibly rely on the same myths to construct political theologies that are at odds with each other, revealing not only the inherent creativity of human beings, but also the plasticity of myths.[23] In using ancient religious myths, we often overlook those features of the myth that are inimical to the political theology we are constructing. If we do not overlook these anomalies, we find ways to smooth out the inconsistencies in the myth or our use of it. Some Latin American theologians, for instance, use the Exodus myth to construct theologies of liberation, overlooking the God-sanctioned brutality of Egyptians (and later, the inhabitants of the so-called promised land) and the subordination, if not subjugation, of women. All of this demonstrates the limits and issues of relying on Judeo-Christian myths for constructing a political theology.

There are two other related problems of political theology. First, the very construction of political theology in the present means we are shaped by the concerns and questions of the era, which today include the very survival of human beings and caring for the earth as the habitat that founds human survival and flourishing in the polis (as well as the survival and flourishing of other species). At the same time, in using the myths of scripture, we are also consciously and unconsciously shaped by the myths and/or ideologies of our culture and polis. For instance, Jeffery Robbins weaves theology and democracy together,[24] while some liberation theologians rely on the philosophy of Karl Marx as an interpretive framework for understanding Judeo-Christian myths. Robbins is influenced by the founding myths associated with the formation of a democratic society, while Marx relies on the Enlightenment myths of history and progress. In terms of this work, I live and operate out of an ostensibly democratic polis that has founding myths that supported the brutality toward native peoples and the use of Christian stories to support colonization and slavery, while upholding myths of equality and freedom. That said, I am not sketching out a radical political

---

philosophy in light of the twentieth-century philosophical thought that has links to early Greeks. Arendt, *The Human Condition*.

23. The range is significant. On the one end are Dominion theologies, advocating for a theocratic Christian state, and liberation theologies (black, feminist, womanist, Latinx, Asian, queer, etc.).

24. Robbins, *Radical Democracy and Political Theology*. By contrast, Clayton Crockett offers a radical political theology, wherein he attempts to think a political theology without religious myths, without God. To think of a radical political theology without God is quite paradoxical, raising the question of whether this includes jettisoning tradition because of its putative links to religious traditionalism or conservatism. One might wonder if Crockett is relying on philosophers whose philosophies are themselves "mythical." Crockett, *Radical Political Theology*. For discussion on radical political philosophy see, Gottlieb, *Radical Philosophy*.

theology to serve as a defense of a particular democratic polity, even though I am partial to genuine forms of democratic anarchy—a democracy without sovereignty. More to the point, I do not believe it is helpful to argue or suggest that Judeo-Christian myths support the idea of a democratic polis, especially given the inherent patriarchal substrate of these myths and the tendency to reify a particular construction of polity in God. That said, I am not suggesting that Judeo-Christian myths are without value in thinking a radical political theology, yet, as will become apparent, these myths must be problematized and reinterpreted if they are to serve as a foundation for a radical political theology.

A second challenge is that Judeo-Christian scriptures comprise numerable myths that reflect differing theologies. Indeed, some myths contain more than one theology, as will be pointed out below. So, when we ask ourselves what myths we rely on to construct a political theology, we also need to be cognizant that there may be more than one theology present and that these theologies may be interpreted and used differently depending on the historical and cultural contexts. It is not only that there are theologies in scripture, these theologies can also be intertwined even within the same story, making for contradictions, as well as hypocrisies. It is, then, not just a question of what myths undergird a political theology, but what theology or theologies are present in the myth we use.

Reminiscent of Leo Strauss, quoted in the Introduction, these problems of political theologizing do not impel us toward providing universal and concrete solutions or answers. Instead, I note that these problems are perennial, defying sectarian answers or self-certain solutions. More positively, these problems can serve as sources of creativity, as well as foster humility in offering responses in a complex, diverse world. Having said this, it is important to elaborate further about the theologies embedded in scripture, because in sketching out a radical political theology, I wish to be clear what theology I rely on as a response to political questions.

## Theologies of Subjugation/Subordination and the Political

The Torah is a political document. It contains stories of the origins of the Israelite people and how they organized themselves to live a life in common. There are stories of leadership, types of governance, and meting out justice in the polis. There are stories of who are deemed to be members of the society (and not—the excluded) and the distribution of resources. Similarly, Christian scriptures are political documents. We read numerous times about the kingdom of God, which at times is contrasted with political

realities of the Roman Empire. The gospels tell stories of the political execution of Jesus and the subsequent formation of *ekklesia*—an alternative
political community.[25] In this section, I wish to make a case that many of the
stories in Judeo-Christian scriptures are based on a theology(ies) of subju-
gation/subordination, which serve to ground answers to political questions
throughout Western history. Indeed, I suggest that these theologies are in
the background of Thomas Hobbes's[26] political philosophy that promotes
the necessity for a leviathan (a secular version of God), Hegel's notion of
the primal fight for recognition,[27] Carl Schmitt's notion that the political
is founded on a friend–enemy distinction (a secular version of the chosen
people versus Others),[28] and Heidegger's modern metaphysics and politics
that "renders possible the transformation of truth into certainty, in which
the human being . . . secures its unconditional dominion over the world by
means of techniques."[29] Here we see theologies and philosophies function
as anthropological-political machines that foster and legitimate anthropocentrism and narcissism and the concomitant exclusion and exploitation of
other species and the earth.[30]

To begin, it is necessary to define what is meant by the terms "subjugate" and "subordinate." The concept "subjugate" comes from the Latin
*jugus* (to bring under the yoke) and is defined as "to bring under control and
governance, to make submissive."[31] Synonyms include conquer, dominate,
subject, subordinate, overpower, and pacify. "Subordinate" means to make
subject or subservient, to treat as of less value or importance.[32] Each term
implies the presence of hierarchy, though "subjugate" is the stronger term,
meaning the hierarchical relation is established and maintained by violence,

25. See Horsley, *Jesus and Empire*.

26. Hobbes, *Leviathan*.

27. Kojéve, *Introduction to the Reading of Hegel*.

28. Schmitt, *The Concept of the Political*.

29. Agamben, *Opus Dei*, 61.

30. While the focus is on theologies of subjugation/subordination, I would be re-
miss not to mention that the history of science clearly demonstrates that science possesses myths and beliefs of subjugation. Consider Francis Bacon who wrote that "The
End of our Foundation is the knowledge of Causes and secret motion of things; and
the enlarging of the bounds of Human Empire, to effecting of all things possible." The
desire to control and dominate nature by way of science continues today in the debates
about climate change with some claiming that human beings are God species. Van den
Noortgaete, "Reconsidering the Anthropocene as Milieu," 156–57.

31. "Subjugate," in *Merriam Webster Dictionary*; https://www.merriam-webster.
com/dictionary/subjugate.

32. "Subordinate," in *Merriam Webster Dictionary*; https://www.merriam-webster.
com/dictionary/subordinate.

force, or coercion. "Subordination," on the other hand, refers to relations that are not overtly maintained by force or violence, yet these relations are hierarchical and unequal, usually with regard to political-social status and power/authority. This said, a cursory reading of scripture reveals numerous stories involving people being conquered, being brought under control and governance, and stories of Israelites subordinating themselves to God or to others within the community (women being subordinate to [and subjugated by] men). One of the founding political myths in the Torah is the Exodus story or stories, which is an apt starting point to illustrate the attributes of theologies of subjugation/subordination.

Many people are familiar with the Exodus story. The Israelites lived in Egypt and, during Joseph's lifetime, retained the favor of the Pharaoh, though they were obviously subordinate to the Pharaoh's rule. After the Pharaoh died, a new king was less inclined to favor the Israelites and more inclined to oppress and exploit them (Exod 1:8–15). Their situation worsened and eventually Moses and Aaron were chosen by God to confront the Pharaoh (Exod 6–7). Like most tyrants bent on subjugating a people, the Pharaoh was impervious to the demands for freedom, since he could easily exploit the Israelites without apparent cost or consequences. This required a response to reveal to the Pharaoh that he was not as powerful as he believed. We read that God sent plagues, poisoned water, destroyed crops and livestock, killed firstborn males, etc. all to make apparent the consequences of defying God's demand to free the Israelites. Eventually, the Pharaoh was brought under the yoke of God's crushing power/violence and agreed to let Moses and his people go. Soon after, the Pharaoh changed his mind, only to have his armies destroyed. Perhaps the powerful Pharaoh should have realized he was not in a fair fight with an omnipotent, sovereign God.

What is clear in this story are the parallel (and mimetic) themes of subjugation and subordination. The first Pharaoh is in a hierarchical relation with the Israelites. While they were subordinate to his rule, the Israelites were not subjugated, yet the presence of political violence was never far away. A new king changed the relations to one of subjugation. The Israelites lamented their suffering to God, who heard their cries. God demanded, through Moses, their freedom from the Pharaoh, which he rejected, leaving God to force the king and his people into submission. In the story, then, it is clear that enslaving the Israelites precipitated a desire for liberation, which led to the violent subjugation of the Pharaoh, his army, and his people in order to free the Israelites. The "miracles" demonstrated that the Egyptians and their king were subordinate to God's will, which led to the Israelites freedom. Failing to accept subordination resulted in violent subjugation.

Here we see a tragic formation of what René Girard called mimetic violence.[33] A subjugated people experience the suffering of bondage and desire liberation. In this case, liberation depended on God's violence to subjugate the Pharaoh and his people. Because the violence linked to liberation was done by God, there could be no question of whether it was just. Indeed, I have never heard this questioned in church or elsewhere. "Shall not the Judge of all the earth do right?" (Gen 18:25), we read. God's divine violence of subjugation evokes the return of the same. The Pharaoh pursues the fleeing Israelites, only to be crushed again by God's power. This is key, because this theology ontologically legitimates violence to subjugate Others for the sake of the Israelites (male) freedom. God's putative just violence,[34] in other words, serves later to legitimate violence toward the "enemies" of the Israelites. In brief, the violence of subjugation gives rise to liberative violence—a tragic mimesis.[35]

There is, of course, much more to the story. Once liberated from Egyptian oppression, the Israelites wandered for forty years in the desert before arriving at the borders of a land of milk and honey (3:17). The CliffsNotes version of this story is that God commanded the Israelites, who were apparently learning the arts of war and forging an army while in the desert, to conquer the peoples of this land and expropriate their land. The mimetic irony and tragedy here is that a people, who were once subjugated and oppressed by the Egyptians, later subjugate and oppress others without any apparent angst, misgiving or remorse. Of course, why should they have a grain of remorse? It is evident this theology of subjugation contained an

33. Girard, *Violence and the Sacred.* Colby Dickinson and Adam Kotsko, remarking on Agamben's use of Walter Benjamin's work, indicate that Agamben's anthropology includes the mimetic, which is based, in part, on humanity's attempts to ontologize the distinction between animals and human beings—to establish themselves as humans through violence. In my view, this is another example of an ontology of subordination that legitimizes subjugation of animals. This can also easily lead toward subjugation and subordination of other human beings. Dickinson and Kotsko, *Agamben's Coming Philosophy,* 53–58.

34. The issue of God's violence in this and other texts has long been discussed and used to justify violence of human beings toward others. This is why it is important to parse out myths that support theologies of violence. I am not suggesting we rid ourselves of these stories, perhaps snipping out sections of the bible to fit a new bible a la Thomas Jefferson. Instead, we need to be aware of how we create and use myths to justify human violence toward Others and the earth. My view is that myths say more about us and, more often than not, little about God. See, Dykstra, *Set Them Free,* 133–43.

35. Boer points out the Louis Althusser and Ernst Bloch identify the dynamic of liberation/resistance and subjugation evident in the stories of the bible. What I wish to stress is that these dynamics are intertwined, which Orlando Patterson depicts in his sociological history of freedom and its origins in slavery. Boer, *Criticism of Heaven*; Patterson, *Freedom in the Making of Western Culture.*

unquestionable command to the Israelites to subdue other peoples and ex-propriate their lands (which continues to this day in subduing the Palestin-ian people)—a command that legitimated violence toward Others and set aside any notion of universal justice.

The idea of the promised land and the desire for liberation have ap-peared throughout Christian history. Puritans, fleeing religious oppression in England, understandably turned to scripture to make sense of their expe-rience, to prepare for the journey to a new land, and to justify the disposses-sion of native peoples from their lands, as well as killing native peoples. John Winthrop and John Cotton, for instance, preached to their people about being the new chosen people and identified America as the new promised land.[36] Christian colonists, of course, used other theological rationalizations to expropriate land from native peoples. John Winthrop "created the excuse to take Indian land by declaring the area legally a 'vacuum.' The Indians, he said, had not 'subdued the land and therefore had only a 'natural' right to it, not a 'civil right.' A natural right did not have legal standing."[37] The scriptural referent here is the command by God for human beings to *subdue* the earth (Gen 1:28). Few, then and now, wring their hands over the religiously justi-fied ethnic cleansing of native peoples, revealing, to some extent, its theo-logical justification. This theological dictum has also appeared throughout U.S. history, justifying subjugation and subordination. For instance, in the nineteenth century, Harriet Beecher Stowe wrote, "Ere long colonies from these prosperous and Christian communities would go forth to shine as lights of the world, in all the now darkened nations. Thus, the Christian family and Christian neighborhood would become the grand ministry as they were designed to be, in training our whole race for heaven."[38] This fem-inine, genteel racist piety, cloaked a theology of subjugation/subordination and the legitimation of ruthless practices of subjugation. In the less genteel political realm, Senator Beveridge of Indiana, for example, believed that the U.S. had a moral "duty to bring Christianity and civilization to 'savage and senile peoples.'"[39] Of course, this, too, meant subjugating and subordinating native peoples.

There are four points here. First, theologies of subjugation/subordina-tion, which often originate in (and give rise to) the desire for freedom and liberation, legitimate violence toward and oppression and exploitation of Others (human beings, species, the earth). Second, these theologies become

36. Barry, *Roger Williams and the Creation of the American Soul*, 120–26.

37. Zinn, *A People's History of the United States*, 13–14.

38. Kaplan, *The Anarchy of Empire in the Making of U.S. Culture*, 32.

39. Johnson, *Sorrows of Empire*, 43.

not only a part of the long-term narratives a people uses to understand themselves and their place in the world, they also become part of the political milieu—a milieu of unquestioned and theologically rationalized entitlement with regard to freedom (for themselves), expropriated resources/lands, and subjugated/subordinate Others. Third, theologies of subjugation comprise narratives that are exclusionary, which function to silence any voices of Others that are deemed to threaten the relations of subordination/subjugation that privilege one group over another, either those within the polis (included-excluded Others) or those outside (merely excluded Others). The suffering of the Egyptian people and the peoples of ancient Palestine are instances where their narratives and experiences are absent or hidden. We see this as well in that the concerns, needs, and suffering of Native peoples who were and are, by and large, absent from the narratives of Puritan leaders and, when they are included, they are subordinate to the larger needs and desires of Euro-Americans. Fourth, these theologies cannot be effective without the theological and secular/political disciplinary regimes or apparatuses that enforce subordination and subjugation. For instance, the Israelites had an army to occupy the land and to force Others to abide by their rule.

It is important to pause here and indicate that many early liberation theologians[40] and religious activists (e.g., Martin Luther King Jr., Desmond Tutu) make use of the Exodus story (and other scriptural stories), but do not advocate liberation by means of violently subjugating their oppressors or by organizing political life through subjugating specific groups of people.[41] As I hope to make clear below, this is because, in most of these cases, we see a theology of vulnerability altering the metaphors and reframing the stories that support theologies of subjugation. The desire for liberation, coupled with theologies of vulnerability, provide the *possibility* of ending or, to use Agamben's[42] term, make inoperative, the mimetic cycle of violence through caring, nonviolent resistance.[43]

---

40. Cone, *A Theology of Black Liberation*; Gutiérrez, *A Theology of Liberation*; Moltmann, *The Gospel of Liberation*; Reuther, *Sexism and God-Talk*; Segundo, *The Liberation of Theology*.

41. It is necessary to mention that some liberation theologians use the Exodus story to justify violence. See Croatto, *Exodus*. What I am stressing is that theologies that justify subjugation also justify the violence needed to subjugate people, which leads to mimetic violence.

42. Agamben, *The Coming Community*.

43. Judith Butler argues for the force of nonviolent resistance which is based on the premises of human vulnerability and equality of life. I will say more about this in the chapter on political change and violence. Butler, *The Force of Nonviolence*.

Let me return to theologies of subjugation to tease out other points. Above I stated that theologies of subjugation become part of the political milieu, which, because of mimetic violence, can be a problem. Theologies of subjugation/liberation typically depend on the Other. The Pharaoh, as subjugator, was Other in the story. The Other is to be overcome, regardless of whether that is the oppressor or those, like the people in Palestine, who are to be killed or subjugated. These two instances indicate the Other is outside the community or, in some case, on the fringe of society (included-excluded Others) and is dealt with through violence or coercion. In constructing the Other as Other, there is a separation with regard to identity, empathy, and obligation. The Egyptians and people of Palestine are deemed to be Other than the Israelites, who are the chosen people. There is no identity shared and, when there is no sharing or partial sharing of identity, there is no empathy toward the Other and, of course, no moral obligation to care for them. Indeed, there is almost a ruthlessness and sociopathy toward those deemed as enemies or people to be ethnically cleansed.[44]

Of course, here I am talking about those who are Other outside the community or society. But what about those Others, those aliens, who exist within the society? Here we can turn to scriptures, where God commands the Israelites to treat resident aliens with respect: "You shall not oppress a resident alien; you know the heart of an alien, for you were aliens in the land of Egypt" (Exod 23:9). It is important to mention that this command comes after the command to empty the land. God's terror (Exod 23:27)— read Israelite armies—drove inhabitants out of the land, but those eventual "resident aliens" were to be treated with respect—as long as they did not interfere with God's laws. Here we begin to see the problem. A theology of subjugation can function to legitimate violence toward Others, but once the threat has been eliminated, how do you address and treat those Others who remain in the polis? If they are not subjugated, they must be subordinate to the Israelites, and this political subordination is legitimated ontologically. To mitigate the mimetic violence at the heart of theologies of subjugation, then, there must be commands to respect "resident aliens." We note instances of

44. Readers will recognize that there is also a later command to love your enemies, which would seem to counter the ruthlessness and sociopathy evident in these stories, but there is no evidence in the Judeo-Christian scriptures I am citing. Here is where we note the intersection of theologies of subjugation and those of vulnerability. What does it mean politically to love your enemies? Can one love one's enemies while violently subjugating them? Clearly people who have been and are violently subjugated (e.g., African Americans, Palestinians, etc.) certainly do not feel loved or cared for or about by those in positions to subjugate them. Perhaps this is a nearly impossible command, one that demands not attitudes and behaviors of subjugation, but attitudes and behaviors of vulnerability.

this within U.S. history, where ostensibly "good" U.S. Christians ignored this command in their treatment of Native peoples and in regard to slavery and Jim Crow laws. The "resident aliens" were to be subordinate, once they were subjugated. The result has been mimetic violence that lies at the core of U.S. society—the enmity of racism and the perennial desire to subjugate/subordinate "inferior" Others. The very existence of racism among Euro-Americans who were/are Christian means there is an accompanying (latent or manifest) presence of theologies of subjugation justifying the construction of Other residents as inferior.

Theologies of subordination also include those who are deemed members of the society, those who share a common identity. Israelite women and children were subordinated to male authority. Behaviors deemed to be egregious could result in stoning—the ultimate exclusion—a as well as the threat to subjugate any rebellious woman or child. For instance, a rebellious son can be stoned by the elders (Deut 21:18–21).[45] Theologies of subordination attend and justify disciplinary regimes and practices that ontologically legitimate subordination and communal practices that enforce subordinate relations within the polis. Of course, the subordinated Other in our midst is only one problem with a theology of subjugation that lies at the heart of the political community. If a theology of subjugation were to become the reigning theology in organizing a society, one would be left with a Hobbesian world grounded in the "primal act of recognition as enmity,"[46] which would require a leviathan to maintain order. This theology, then, can create problems within the community itself, requiring additional brakes and safeguards. Jubilee ordinances (Lev 25:1–7, 8–17; Deut 31:9–13), caring for widows and orphans (Exod 22:22; Deut 27:19), welcoming strangers, limits on enslaving foreigners (Deut 25:46), and constraints on treating servants (Exod 21:2–6; Deut 24:14) are some examples of modifying a theology of subjugation/subordination. In my view, these and other laws or commands were attempts to reduce the mimetic violence inherent in the theology of subjugation within the community of faith. At the same time, they served to theologically legitimate and leave unquestioned relations of subordination.

Naturally, Israelite women and children were not the only ones forced into subordinate roles. The Israelites, as people, were subordinate to God,

45. Alice Miller and Marcia Bunge explore social and theological representations of childhood and how they influenced child-rearing. Miller, in particular, notes the cruelty of these practices in caring for children. This cruelty is based, in my view, on theologies of subordination/subjugation, ontological legitimating forms of social-political violence toward children. Miller, *For Your Own Good*; Bunge, *The Child in Christian Thought*.

46. Wolin, *Politics and Vision*, 418.

which meant that men were subordinate to the leaders chosen by God, as well as to a patriarchal God. It is not clear that this arrangement sat well with some or maybe most men. Consider that the Israelites (read men), subordinate to God, were repeatedly called a stiff-necked people, usually by God (Exod 32:9; 33:3, 5; 34:9; Deut 9:6, 13; 10:16). Synonyms of stiff-necked are obstinate, headstrong, strong-willed, obdurate, and bull-headed. I suggest "stiff-necked" is an inevitable trait of people who are in a relationship where there is an enforced and not entirely happy dependency and one that exists between two unequal parties. Perhaps those stiff-necked male Israelites enjoyed the power and privilege of keeping other people in their community subordinate (e.g., women and children), but chafed at being subordinate to God and God's anointed.

Another illustration of this attempt to establish some degree of independence, and perhaps, freedom is noted in Israelite elders beseeching God to give them a king. Traditionally, leaders of the Israelites viewed God as their king or sovereign and not themselves, which I will address in greater detail in the third chapter.[47] But for now, we note the Israelites were to kill and steal only at God's command, and all Israelites were to obey a putative just and loving God—particularly just and loving to the Israelites. This arrangement, though, was unsatisfactory. After defeating the Midianites, the people asked Gideon to be their ruler. Gideon responded, "I will not rule over you, and my son will not rule over you; the Lord will rule over you" (Judg 8:23). Later we learn that the desire to be ruled over by a king continued. The elders of Israel asked Samuel to "appoint for us a king to govern us like other nations" (1 Sam 8:5). God commanded Samuel to go to the people and warn them of the consequences of having a human as their king. Samuel told them that:

> These will be the ways of the king who will reign over you: he will take your sons and appoint them to his chariots and be his horsemen, and to run before his chariots; and he will appoint for himself commanders of thousands and commanders of fifties, and some to plow his ground and to reap his harvest, and to make his implements of war and equipment of his chariots. He will take your daughters to be perfumers and cooks and bakers. He will take the best of your fields and vineyards and olive orchards and give them to his courtiers. He will take one-tenth of your grain and of your vineyards and give it to his officers and his courtiers. He will take your male and female slaves, and the best of your cattle and donkeys and put them to his work. He

47. Walzer, *In God's Shadow*, 53.

will take one-tenth of your flocks, and you shall be his slaves. (8:11–17)

Samuel was pointing out that a human leviathan eventually will rule through subordination and subjugation, but the elders were adamant. God accepted and fulfilled their request, leaving Israelites to discover the truths of his warning. In my view, the Israelite men/leaders bristled under their subordination to God, seeking to gain more independence and freedom for themselves by having their own king, only to discover more and greater chains of inequality.

Whether it is God or men who rule, theologies of subjugation/subordination establish relations that evoke a desire for liberation, evident in forms of resistance, insubordination, and/or revolutionary violence. What I wish to stress is that these theologies 1) can construct Others within or outside the society to be subjugated violently for the sake of liberation or occupation and 2) "govern" relations within society, whether that is between Israelites and resident aliens, wherein some group is deemed superior and others subordinate and inferior. For those who wished to color outside the patriarchal lines or who defied patriarchal authority, the consequences were severe—death, banishment, exile. The severe punishments of God could be seen as types of legitimate subjugation, forcing a people to re-subordinate themselves to God and the covenant.

Two other features of myths that found theologies of subjugation need to be mentioned. First, the exercise of power through subjugation, whether by God or by the Israelites, is the collective mythic belief that the Israelites are special—chosen to be God's people. Positively, this belief may attend a collective sense of esteem, which was likely important or even necessary during times of exile and oppression. Negatively, while not inevitable, this belief can be joined to a collective narcissistic arrogance, entitlement, self-righteousness, and sense of superiority that attend relations of subjugation and subordination. For instance, the chosen people are entitled to the land of milk and honey because God commands it. Because they are special, it is legitimate to kill and enslave "lesser" peoples and take and exploit their land. Because they are special, they are destined to rule over this land and its peoples. As mentioned above, this was evident in European Christians' justification of taking land from Native Americans, who were, more often than not, seen as lesser beings. We see a similar expression of this attribute today in conservative Israeli circles that claim God's promise of the land, while brutally subjugating Palestinians. Within the polis, the idea of the chosen people can mean that some people are more chosen than others (e.g., men, priests, etc.), which legitimates subordination of others in the polis.

When the idea of a chosen people becomes wedded to a theology of subjugation, the subjugated or subordinated Other functions psychologically to confirm the experience of being special, which is frequently linked to the beliefs in one's superiority and the Other's inferiority. This is part of the issue of mimesis. To feel special, to hold a belief in and experience of our superiority, requires subordinated and inferior Others. Of course, this necessitates the force and accompanying disciplinary regimes (e.g., army, police, legal-political-religious institutions) to make this happen. When it does, one can be assured that subjugated and subordinated Others will feel resentful, powerless, and desirous of liberation. A critic will point out that the Jews have been horribly oppressed numerous times throughout history, which would appear to undercut the idea that experiences of specialness are linked to the belief of superiority (and the inferiority of the Other). As stated earlier, the belief in being special can provide a necessary sense of individual and collective self-worth in the midst of bondage and *it does not inevitably* lead to arrogance and superiority. However, remove the oppression and offer the opportunity for power, and this theology of being chosen can easily produce a collective psychology of entitlement and privilege that accompanies beliefs in superiority of themselves and the inferiority of Others, which accompany political acts to subjugate and subordinate Others. For instance, it was understandable that many Jewish people desired a homeland after the social-political horrors of the Holocaust. Relying on a theology of subjugation, many Israelis, past and present, justify violently expropriating lands from Palestinians.[48] Entitlement, in these instances, is wedded to the belief in superiority, supported by the myth of the chosen people. Naturally, the Palestinians are not without their own prejudices and violence toward Israelis, but this simply proves the mimetic reality of theologies of subjugation. Put differently, exercising political power as subjugation involves psychological and material humiliation (inferiority), which are linked to the desire to experience being special/superior. Political humiliation breeds the desire to return the favor.[49]

What we have so far is that theologies of subjugation represent political relations of radically unequal power and status, which always accompanies maldistribution of resources. Human beings may be created in the image and likeness of God, but they obviously possess neither God's power nor status. Instead, human beings are fallible, dependent, finite creatures in relation to an omnipotent, infallible, omniscient, infinite, sovereign God. This

48. See Myre and Kaplow, "Seven Things to Know about Israeli Settlements"; Ozacky-Lazar, "Tackling Israeli Prejudice"; Remnick, "One-State Reality."
49. See Margalit, *The Decent Society.*

moves me to introduce another feature of a theology of subjugation/subordination, which is a complementary relation of vulnerability (exposure to being wounded) and invulnerability.[50] Systematic theologian Edward Farley[51] notes that human beings are vulnerable creatures, which raises their anxiety and often leads to making poor decisions that we might call sin—missing the mark.[52] Similarly, Judith Butler argues that we are "constituted politically in virtue of our bodies,"[53] which means being exposed to loss and violence. These views of vulnerability are evident in numerous stories of Jewish scriptures. Adam and Eve, Sarah, Abraham, and Isaac, Joseph, Israelites under the boot of the Egyptians and their sojourn in the desert, and the Babylonian captivity, are just some of religious stories that reveal human vulnerability. Many of these stories also reveal the vulnerability of those the Israelites defeated. The complement of vulnerability is God's invulnerability, which, as a people, Israel psychologically borrows by virtue of God's promise that they would never cease being God's chosen ones. This borrowed invulnerability can be helpful psychologically to defeat one's enemies (How could we lose, since God commanded it?) or to survive oppression (We will survive because we are God's chosen and God, in the end, cannot be defeated.).

To take this a bit further, if one is in a dependent relationship with an invulnerable omnipotent God, it is an open question whether one genuinely comes to term with existential vulnerability. Part of the mimetic dynamics of a theology of subjugation is to make Others vulnerable (defeating one's enemies, ruling over others) so that God's invulnerability can be confirmed and, in being God's chosen people, we might share in God's invulnerability, if only partially. Put differently, our invulnerable God cannot be defeated, and this means the Others must succumb to an all-powerful, invulnerable, sovereign God when so commanded. Of course, the violent or coercive political subjugation of Others creates intense experiences of vulnerability for Othered persons, which evokes a corresponding desire and action to end their vulnerability (liberation). On those occasions when the Israelites are

---

50. The next section deals with a theology of vulnerability. What I wish to stress here is that theologies of subjugation establish a rigid binary complementarity, wherein the subjugated other is made to experience vulnerability, while the subjugating Israelite obtains a sense of invulnerability by way of identification with an invulnerable God who legitimizes relations of subjugation. A theology of vulnerability, as will be seen below, eschews any notion of invulnerability and complementarity.

51. Farley, *Good and Evil*.

52. Dickinson argues that Agamben's philosophical and theological anthropology also begins with the vulnerability of human life. Dickinson, *Agamben and Theology*, 38.

53. Butler, *Precarious Life*, 20.

defeated by superior armies and become politically oppressed, their subjugation does not disconfirm God's invulnerability or power. It simply confirms their human failures to live out the covenant in the political sphere. But in the midst of defeat or oppression, they can rely on their belief that God's omnipotent invincibility and invulnerability will provide an individual and collective positive sense of self needed to survive. This is not mere survival, because it is coupled with a desire for God's liberative acts (once the Israelites politically recommit to the covenant), which in a theology of subjugation means defeating (making vulnerable) one's oppressors and, in the case of the Israelites, once freed from the oppressors one can subjugate and subordinate others. Vulnerability vis-à-vis a theology of subjugation, in short, is never directly faced and embraced, but rather displaced onto Others. Moreover, it exists in an eternal, mimetic complementarity.

In sum, theologies of subjugation[54] comprise four features, namely, omnipotent sovereignty (the ruler's power of exception), collective specialness or narcissism, enforced dependency, and the complementarity of invulnerability-vulnerability. These theologies emerge from and perpetuate a psychology and political relation characterized as master-slave, conqueror-or-conquered, perpetual parent-child, ruler-ruled. They contribute to anthropocentrism and political narcissism, which denies plurality and leads to vast inequalities and exclusions, if not extinctions. To be sure, the kinder, gentler version is the all-powerful, perfect, invulnerable, loving parent in relation to a vulnerable, finite, recalcitrant child—a child seemingly in need of constant correction. Even a kind and benevolent ruler remains a tyrant who refuses to be brought low. In my view, theologies of subjugation, in and of themselves, foster relations of subjugation/subordination, giving rise to mimetic violence or coercion.

## A Sketch of a Radical Political Theology

In this section, I sketch out a radical political theology, putting flesh on these bones in subsequent chapters. What I wish to claim is that the radical political theology discussed here is based on a theology of vulnerability, eschewing any theology/myth of subordination/subjugation and its attending complementarity of invulnerability.[55] That said, since I have opted for

---

54. While I have relied on Jewish scriptures in depicting theologies of subjugation, I am not in any way implying that theologies of vulnerability or, more importantly, theologies of subjugation are absent from Christian scriptures. As noted, these theologies are often intertwined.

55. This does not mean excising the Bible, because these theologies are intertwined.

the term "radical," which pertains to roots, I begin with a depiction of an existential, developmental view of good-enough parents' caring interactions with children. I indicate that this is a pre-political space that is inextricably joined with, yet distinct from, the public-political spaces wherein adults speak and act together. In so doing, I eschew Hobbes' negative view of the state of nature in constructing his political philosophy and Rousseau's positive view of the state of nature in his political philosophy. The problem with starting with the "state of nature" is that in both cases nature is perceived as something to overcome or recover. Both cases, "nature" is abstracted from present political life. Instead, by beginning with the commonplace or "natural origins" of any society, namely parent-children interactions of speaking and acting together, I place "nature" at the root of the political.[56] Put differently, I suggest "nature" is found in the developmental origins of any human life,[57] which is a pre-political space wherein good-enough parental care is ideally free of relations of subjugation or subordination. This pre-political space is, in short, a root of a radical political theology. From here, I turn to theology and, in particular, a brief discussion of the incarnation as a kenotic event, wherein God takes on human vulnerability, becoming an ontological vulnerary or remedy for relations of subjugation or subordination, which is the theological root for a radical political theology. Positively stated, Jesus, as a vulnerary, invites relations wherein speaking and acting together gives rise to experiences of singularity or suchness, which, in political terms, means relations that foster the self-esteem, self-respect, and self-confidence necessary for political agency, while making inoperative apparatuses of political humiliations and mimetic violence.

## Existential Roots of Care and Its Relation to the Political

We can begin to grasp the radical nature of care[58] for human survival and flourishing, as well as its relation to the political, by describing the attributes

---

Rather it involves being aware of these theologies when constructing a political theology, since as Carl Schmitt said, "all significant concepts of the modern theory of the state are secularized theological concepts." Brown, *Walled States, Waning Sovereignty*, 59.

56. Agamben argues that both politics and metaphysics in the West are founded on the exclusion of other than human life with particular focus on differentiating human beings from other animals—animals not considered to be part of the polis. See Whyte, *Catastrophe and Redemption*, 34, 78.

57. Using different language, Agamben argues that the "state of nature" is not in the distant past, but happens over and over in every speech act. See, Prozorov, 70.

58. I do not have the space to address the relation between care and justice. In my

and dynamics of care in good-enough parents' relations with their children—children who are psychologically and existentially vulnerable[59] and dependent.[60] I will argue that there is a correlation between the relational space, or space of appearances, between parents and children and the political space of the larger society.[61] Correlation does not mean identity. There are important differences, having to do with inequality, agency, dependency, exercise of power, sovereignty, and the prevalence of political, economic, and social institutions. This said, my focus will be to depict the correlation.

The foundational premise here is that good-enough parental care or attunement, as an action and disposition, is dependent on recognizing their children as persons—unique, valued, inviolable, and responsive/agentic

---

view, they are intertwined. For more discussion on the relation between care and justice, see LaMothe, *Care of Souls, Care of Polis*, 65–93; Held, *Justice and Care*; Kujawa-Holbrook and Montagno, *Injustice and the Care of Souls*.

59. Agamben uses the term "nudity" to connote our existential vulnerability and this vulnerability is our potentiality, which is connected with idea of excess. This can be seen in the infant, who is vulnerable and potential and it is the parent's care that facilitates, in my view, potentiality into actuality, yet the infant can never exhaust potentiality. See Dickinson and Kotsko, *Agamben's Coming Philosophy*, 33. It is also helpful to note that for Agamben "inoperativity is a mode of potentiality not exhausted in actuality." Like the idea of excess, inoperativity vis-à-vis potentiality reveals the kind of indeterminateness of life—an aspect of freedom that will be addressed in a later chapter. Kotsko and Salzani, *Agamben's Philosophical Lineage*, 142.

60. Daniel Engster argues that we are existentially obliged to care for Others because we are dependent creatures. I add here that human beings are existentially vulnerable, which is especially evident with regard to infants and infirm persons. It is this vulnerability (some chosen, some the result of a condition or state) that is the source of the existential and theological imperative to care for others, other-than-human beings, and the earth. Engster, *The Heart of Justice*.

61. Aristotle's work on politics addresses the differences between the household and the polis, yet Aristotle views these as connected in the sense that the care of children is a necessary feature of their development into citizens. In this article, I am arguing that there are parallels between parental care that creates a space of appearances and the space of appearances in the public-political realm, wherein individuals are recognized as citizens-persons. Barker, *The Politics of Aristotle*.

subjects.[62] Philosopher John Macmurray[63] argued that recognition of the Other as a person is a matter of intention and a matter of fact. This paradox points to Macmurray's desire to demonstrate that human beings create persons through their recognition and treatment of Others as persons, while at the same time positing the existential or ontological facticity of personhood. Giorgio Agamben, using different language, points to this ontological aspect of being a person:

> Assuming my being-such, my manner of being, is not assuming this or that quality, this or that character, virtue or vice, wealth or poverty. My qualities and my being-thus are not qualifications of a substance (of a subject) that remains behind them and that I would truly be. I am never *this* or *that*, but always *such, thus*.[64]

To be sure, parental recognition of their children as persons also means attending to their particular qualities, but personal recognition is not contingent on these. Personal recognition that founds care "is never directed toward this or that property of the loved one, but neither does it neglect the properties in favor of insipid generality (universal love)."[65] Oth-

62. Alexandre Kojéve's reading of Hegel points to the idea that the primal or foundational human encounter is a fight over the desire for recognition that leads to master-slave relations, which I briefly noted above. This is similar to a Hobbesian view of the foundation of the political, wherein there is a need for the leviathan to manage political life, lest it sink into the human nature, which is nasty, brutish, and short. While I agree that human beings are capable of violence, the "primal" relation is not one of a fight to the death over recognition. As I argue in this chapter, the primal relation is the infant-parent relation, where it is not a fight to the death. It is not characterized by subordination or subjugation, as evident in master-slave relations. Infants, to use Hegel's language, desire recognition, because their psychological and physical survival and flourishing depend on it. Good-enough parents are not challenged by this desire for recognition, but rather freely give it. Hegel's view is yet another illustration of political philosophy that has as its ground a theology/philosophy of subjugation/subordination. Kojéve, *Introduction to the Reading of Hegel*, 6–30.

63. Macmurray, like Kant, Hegel, Mounier, Lévinas, and others, located personal recognition as a central feature of his anthropology. Indeed, Macmurray argued that the question of personhood was the central question for the twentieth century, and the ancillary claim, for him, is that personhood emerges out of and in community. It is easy to see that Macmurray's anthropology fits well with Christian theologies and the emphasis on *imago dei*. Macmurray, *Persons in Relation*. See also, Polanyi, *Personal Knowledge*.

64. Agamben, *The Coming Community*, 96.

65. Agamben, *The Coming Community*, 2. It is important to note that Michael Hardt and Antonio Negri, in their book *Commonwealth*, argue that love is an essential concept for politics, because it is central in the establishment of what they call the common—the shared material and created resources. Hardt and Negri, *Commonwealth*, 179–88. Similarly, Terry Eagleton contends that love is a necessary political concept.

ers are persons in their suchness and, while possessing particular traits, personal recognition is not contingent on them.[66] This means that *there is an excess, something beyond or that exceeds the representations that comprise the individual.*[67] This also means that total strangers, which in one sense a newborn is, can be recognized as persons without having any awareness of or dependence on their qualities, characteristics, etc. In other words, care for the stranger is not contingent on particular representations or identity. An example of this is evident when caring for people who are in the last stages of Alzheimer's disease. Despite having lost many of their character or personality traits, we continue to construct and treat them as persons. That said, the foundation of parental acts of care is personal recognition/ knowing of their children.

Another way to understand this is through Agamben's use of the term "inoperativity,"[68] which will be key in the discussion below. For now, the idea of personal recognition/knowing as the basis of caring actions/dispositions includes the particular characteristics of the child, yet these are inoperative in that they do not *define* the child as a person or determine care. Put another way, dominant representations, while present, are not operative in recognizing the Other as person. It is important to stress that inoperativity

---

While I view love and care as related but distinct concepts, the focus will be on the more general term of care. Briefly, it may be helpful to say a few words about these two terms. Eagleton, *After Theory*, 168–70. Love includes care, but to care does not necessarily include love. I can care about people I have never met, while sending them aid. The Samaritan cared for the injured man, but I do not think he loved him. Some might try to make the case that he did love him, but this is love in the abstract. A physician or nurse can care for someone who she thinks is despicable. There is care, but no love. Care, then, from my perspective, is more a fundamental human reality and a more fundamental political concept. I believe, then, that developing and maintaining caring attitudes and behaviors in society are more realistic goals than love.

66. It is important to note here two aspects of "suchness" or "singularity." First, suchness implies plurality, not identity, in the sense of sameness. This will become important when discussing the problem of dwelling. For now, let say that suchness undergirds plurality that is necessary for living life together—a point evident in Hannah Arendt's political philosophy (Arendt, *The Human Condition*). A second point involves the difference between the experience of suchness and suchness itself, as an attitude, disposition, and action. The human experience of suchness can be understood as self-esteem, self-respect, and self-confidence that are necessary for speaking and acting together. When it comes to other than human beings and the earth suchness is not a resulting experience, but an attitude and disposition of respect for the inherent dignity and unfathomableness of the earth and its residents.

67. Sergei Prozorov that "there is an excess of living being that can never be subsumed under them [apparatuses or disciplinary regimes and their representations]. While the excess does not in itself constitute a political subject, it testifies to the fact that the apparatuses are never all there is." Prozorov, *Agamben and Politics*, 24.

68. Agamben, *Sovereign Power and Bare Life*.

is, for Agamben, not passive,[69] but is an action—in this case, recognition and treatment of the child as person. Indeed, the very notion of "person" conveys excess in the sense that the child cannot be entirely represented or captive to the cultural representations associated with the parents' narratives. The child as subject always exceeds whatever representations are present and, for Agamben, this means there is always an aspect of subjectivity that is ungovernable,[70] which will also be important to my discussion below regarding the political space of appearances and theology. Similarly, Emmanuel Lévinas argues that the irreducible singularity of each human being "is not reducible to the status of ultimate differences in a genus, for their singularity consists in each referring to itself."[71] Of course, parents, in caring for their children, recognize the numerous particular physical and psychological features of their children, which are, in part, linked to cultural representations, but these are secondary or inoperative in moments of personal recognition. Put differently, they are operative in that they are present and taken into account in moments of care. They are inoperative in that the loss of this or that quality does not make the child any less a person. "Seeing something," Agamben writes, "simply in its being-thus . . . is love,"[72] and while the qualities of the individual child are important, they are secondary to the recognition and reality of personhood.

In terms of parents' love/care for their children, this means that parents' attunements to infants' assertions are contingent on parents' personal knowing/recognition. It is this personal knowing and care creates a space for children to assert themselves, risking appearing in their suchness.[73] This space of appearances, to use Hannah Arendt's term for political space,[74] is a pre-political space of speaking and acting together, wherein parents' consistent personalizing attunement facilitates children's nascent trust and

69. Prozorov, *Agamben and Politics*, 134.

70. Prozorov, *Agamben and Politics*, 24. By ungovernable, Agamben is arguing that there is an excess vis-à-vis subjectivity that cannot be captured by the apparatuses of the society—apparatuses that produce and attempt to determine subjects that serve society and the state.

71. Lévinas, *Totality and Infinity*, 214.

72. Agamben, *The Coming Community*, 105. The same can be said of care.

73. Hannah Arendt used the term "space of appearances" when depicting life in the polis, wherein citizens ideally speak and act together. I am using it here to talk about the space between parents and children, which is a pre-political space, not in the sense of Aristotle's pre-political space of the household preparing (in this case, male) citizens to engage in public-political life. Instead, I see this pre-political space of care as having parallels to the political space, which I endeavor to explicate below. Arendt, *The Human Condition*.

74. Arendt, *The Human Condition*.

pre-representational[75] experiences of suchness. An experience of singularity or suchness can be further depicted as the child's nascent, pre-representational senses of self-esteem, self-respect, and self-confidence,[76] which are inextricably yoked to the children's budding agencies in asserting themselves in this space. To understand this further, I identify and discuss three dialectical pairs of personal knowing that found care and, by implication, the space of speaking and acting together.

Before I discuss the first dialectical pair, it is important to pause here and make two points. First, since the concept of vulnerability will be crucial when discussing a radical political theology, it is important to clarify this with regard to infant-parent relation. Newborns are, according to psychoanalyst Donald Winnicott, nearly absolutely dependent on the parent for physical and psychological survival.[77] From a different discipline, philosopher John Macmurray writes that the infant "is, in fact, 'adapted', so to speak paradoxically, to being unadapted, 'adapted to complete dependence . . . He can only live through other people."[78] In the child's unadapted, dependent state, she possesses an impulse or motivation to communicate—"the impulse to communicate is [her] sole adaptation to the world."[79] This early near complete dependence is also inextricably connected to vulnerability. Children are vulnerable because they lack capacities needed for self-protection and the capacities to act toward their own welfare. Indeed, they are dependent on their parents for both protection and nurture. Obviously, young children cannot choose to be vulnerable, since their sense of self and agency are nascent or potential. If all goes well enough in caring for children, they develop and internalize a sense of confidence and trust, as well as psychological capacities, to make decisions to be appropriately vulnerable with trusted Others. From another perspective, one could say that

75. Agamben explores the idea of infancy in relation to voice and language. Infancy is the state of wordlessness, but infant-parent researchers, while agreeing, nevertheless point to the fact that infants necessarily organize their experience, albeit pre-symbolically. Agamben *Infancy and History*. Mills, *The Philosophy of Agamben*, 24.

76. Philosopher Axel Honneth's political philosophy reimagines Hegelian recognition. Honneth posits that political recognition gives rise to and supports citizens' senses of self-esteem, self-respect, and self-confidence, which are necessary for a viable and vital political agency. I am suggesting here that a root of this is found in good-enough parents' personal recognition of and care for their children. Honneth, *The Struggle for Recognition*.

77. Winnicott, *Playing and Reality*. An important point here is that Winnicott did not view the infant as completely helpless or passive. Indeed, he posited that an infant's nascent agency was present in the birth process.

78. Macmurray, *Persons in Relation*, 48, 51.

79. Macmurray, *Persons in Relation*, 60.

good-enough parents, in caring for their children, serve as vulneraries—partial remedies—for the existential vulnerability of their children.

A second point involves the notion of suchness, since this will be important in subsequent chapters that deal with dwelling vis-à-vis the Anthropocene Age. The idea of suchness here is linked to personal knowing/recognition, which is further depicted in nascent experiences of self-esteem, self-respect, and self-confidence. But the idea of suchness also refers to recognition of animals and plant life, as well as material objects. This recognition does not result in an experience of suchness per se, but it does indicate a relation of respect for the integrity of the other-than-human animals and material objects. I am reminded of Martin Buber's notion of I-Thou relations and experiences.[80] What I wish to stress is that this relation and attitude subordinates, if present, instrumental knowing that objectifies the object for human use to a knowing that recognizes the inherent uniqueness and unfathomableness of the object or other-than-human animal (or the earth itself as a living organism/system).[81] Also, this knowing is without hierarchical valuations that place the object in positive or negative comparisons with other objects. This is important if we are to shift from the attitudes and practices of dominating nature to one of respect for the unfathomableness of nature.[82] As philosopher Helmut Plessner notes, "[U]nfathomability is the binding principle of human life and of the human comprehension of ·life."[83] In my view, this includes the unfathomableness of the earth and its other than human species.

In terms of parents' personal knowing/recognition, instrumental knowing and valuation are absent or if present, secondary. If instrumental knowing and hierarchic valuations are present, then the experiences of self-esteem, self-respect, and self-confidence become tied to and dependent on conditional hierarchical valuations. Parents who communicate to their children that they are better than other children have distorted children's experiences of suchness, because their children will link suchness with hierarchic valuation, making the children dependent on this for self-esteem,

80. Buber, *I and Thou.*

81. Philosopher David Wood makes a similar point arguing for recognizing the intrinsic value of nature, which points to a type of knowing and attitude that subordinates use-value. Wood, *Reoccupy the Earth*, 41–43.

82. The idea of the unfathomableness of nature does not mean we do not use science to understand nature, but it is to say that, even with all of science, we cannot fully grasp the "object" of study. This also does not mean that we do not ever use "nature" for our benefit, for humans have long possessed instrumental knowing in their use of nature. Instrumental knowing, however, can accompany a type of knowing that respects nature.

83. Plessner, *Political Anthropology*, 26.

self-confidence, and self-respect. The more egregious illustrations of this are seen in racism, where white supremacists are dependent on the illusion of white supremacy (and black inferiority) for a sense of self-esteem, respect, and confidence. In this scenario, there is no sense of unfathomableness and thus no genuine experience of suchness. With regard to other-than-human animals, the tendency of human beings to dominate and exploit nature indicates an absence of an attitude and knowing related to unfathomableness and the presence of instrumental knowing.

Now let's return to the dialectal pairs of personal knowing. The first dialectical pair is identification and disidentification.[84] Good-enough parental attunement includes identification—recognition that the child is like me. This parental identification has specific representations that are part of the parent's narratives, and these narratives comprise links to the parent's particular socio-cultural world. This is to say that any personal recognition/identification comprises representations that emerge from and are rooted in a specific age and milieu. Yet, these representations, as noted above, do not exhaust what "person" means. In caring acts, identification also includes disidentification—recognition that the child is not me. This "not-me" creates a space for children to risk appearing in their uniqueness—uniqueness as an experience of singularity or suchness. Negation, then, is necessary to preserve the alterity and singularity of the child, which, in other terms, makes possible the child's pre-representational senses of self-esteem, self-confidence, and self-respect.

The collapse of this dialectical tension represents a distortion or absence of care, resulting in both the attenuation or collapse of the space of appearances and the infliction of trauma. For example, if parents over-identify with children, they are projecting representations onto children and overtly or covertly forcing children to adopt these representations, which means children's experiences of themselves as unique (or in their suchness) will be obstructed. Over-identification is an attempt to deny the singularity and excess of a child *qua* person. If tension collapses toward the pole of disidentification, children become Other, which is seen in the objectification or depersonalization of children. In either case, care is lost or distorted, and the space of appearances is attenuated or collapses, undermining children's sense of agency (and concomitantly, self-esteem, respect, and confidence) and trust in asserting their needs and desires in this relational space of speaking and acting together. Put differently, the collapse toward one pole or the other forecloses the possibility of something new, something different,

84. Jessica Benjamin uses an analogous phrase to convey this dynamic—personal recognition involves difference in likeness and likeness in difference. Benjamin, "Sameness and Difference."

from appearing and being accepted in the relational space, which weakens children's nascent agency and gives rise to pre-representational experiences of distrust and hopelessness. Positively stated, care vis-à-vis the dialectical pair of identification-disidentification establishes nascent relational trust and hope for children to risk appearing in their suchness.

Before moving to the second dialectical pair, it is valuable to state that personal identification-disidentification and the space of appearances are part and parcel of our daily lives as adults in the polis. Indeed, a decent society, to use Avishai Margalit's[85] term, comprises spaces of speaking and acting together, wherein a dynamic tension exists between identification and disidentification, making possible routine moments of likeness in difference and difference in likeness in the polis. A woman recognizes a stranger as a person, while helping him through a door. A book club gathers together, and members identify with each other, while also recognizing their differences. These are common, even insignificant, moments of care wherein identification-disidentification fosters a space for the Other to risk appearing, to risk speaking and acting together. There are, then, countless daily caring actions in a decent society that create social-political spaces of appearance—spaces of speaking and acting together wherein individuals' agencies and experiences of singularity are affirmed. More tragic situations of indecent societies—societies that humiliate and oppress a group(s)—are seen, for instance, in racism, where those who believe in white supremacy disidentify with African Americans, while sharing in mutual identification with other white supremacists. This is tragic and destructive for at least two reasons. First, African Americans are objectified and forced by the dominant group's disciplinary regimes to adopt negative representations that undermine both political agency (as well as political-public sense of self-worth, respect, and confidence) and the space of appearance. African Americans become the excluded-included Others, forced to the fringe of the polis' space of appearances. Second, the foundation of white inclusion, participation, and political agency (esteem, respect, and confidence) are inflexibly tied to illusory identifications/beliefs. To be in this white group, all must adopt and live out of an identity grounded in illusive representations of white superiority and black inferiority. This undermines experiences of suchness, precisely because there is no "excess." Moreover, any sense of self-esteem, self-respect, and self-confidence depends on the illusion of white supremacy and associated representations, which means that white supremacists are unwittingly dependent on the continual creation of inferior Others. In terms of the space of appearances, between white supremacists

85. Margalit, *The Decent Society*.

and black persons, the space of appearances collapses, along with civic care and civic trust. An indecent polis, in short, is marred by depersonalization, carelessness, and perfidy.[86]

A second and related dialectical pair of personal recognition is determinate and indeterminate knowing.[87] Determinate knowing is parents' declarative representations of their children, which is necessary for attuning to children's assertions. Put another way, parents, in caring for their children, have explicit or definite representations regarding their children. "I know my child and why he is crying and what he needs." Determinate knowing, then, provides parents the confidence necessary for caring actions—actions that create, in part, a space of appearances. Also present in determinate knowing is instrumental knowing, which includes specific representations and utility/function.[88] There is, in other words, an aim in good-enough parents' caring for their children. A child cries out and the parent's particular representations of the child accompanies an aim to meet the specific need for the sake of the child's well-being.

As noted above, the parents' determinate knowing cannot entirely capture children as persons. Thus, determinate knowing of personal recognition accompanies indeterminate knowing. This is present because of a child's singularity, or what Plessner, as noted above, called the principle of unfathomability, or what one might call mystery. To repeat, the person's "own unfathomability is the binding principle of human life and of the human comprehension of life,"[89] which is necessary for caring actions whether in relation to other human beings or other-than-human beings. There are, then, no representations in personal-determinate knowing that can fully capture another human being—an excess that is equivalent to being unrepresentable. All determinate knowing, when it comes to other human beings,

86. Nancy Fraser and Axel Honneth recognize that failures in personal recognition in a polis are accompanied by undermining material conditions needed to survive and thrive. So, failures in personal recognition are not simply about the failure of an individual to care; it involves forms of social carelessness that accompany and are supported by institutions, collective narratives, and disciplinary regimes that deprive Othered people of the resources to thrive. Fraser and Honneth, *Redistribution or Recognition?*

87. Merleau-Ponty notes that "there is in human existence a principle of indeterminacy, and this indeterminacy is not only for us, it does not stem from some imperfection of our knowledge . . . Existence is indeterminate in itself, by reason of its fundamental structure." For Merleau-Ponty our very knowledge of the world is indeterminate, which I argue is necessary for accepting the Other, as well as for creativity. Put another way, ignorance is necessary for accepting and affirming the suchness and unfathomableness of the Other. Merleau-Ponty, *Phenomenology of Perception*, 169.

88. Polanyi, *Personal Knowledge*, 80.

89. Plessner, *Political Anthropology*, 26.

has a remainder. This remainder (or excess), this unfathomability with regard to the Other, opens a space for children to confidently assert themselves and for parents to recognize, welcome, embrace, and experience children's unfathomable uniqueness—suchness. For Agamben, "All true knowing," Colby Dickinson notes, "takes place on this level of the preservation of the object 'beyond or before its objective predicates.'"[90] This is an indeterminate knowing that founds the experience of suchness, free of hierarchies.

Negatively, we could say that indeterminate knowing involves accepting one's ignorance, one's not-knowing in the midst of knowing. There is, then, a gap in knowing. Positively, indeterminate knowing involves restraint of a parent's wealth of knowledge so as to acknowledge children's unfathomableness, such that a space is created for children to appear in their suchness, necessary for children's emerging agency and sense of self. Systematic theologian Thomas Gricoski, referring to the work of Edith Stein, argues that "The gap of knowledge appears not only as a defect of finite human understanding, but also a space of identity-in-difference in which alterity may relate itself to a person."[91] The gap of knowledge makes it possible for the singular, unfathomable alterity of the Other to appear. I add here that indeterminate knowing lacks instrumentality. There is no aim, no utility, no purpose in care/love as indeterminate knowing, which is noted in moments of parent-child being together, wherein there is no need to be met other than being together. It is also manifested in friendships. Theodor Adorno makes a similar claim, saying, "tenderness between people is nothing other than the awareness of the possibility of relations without purpose."[92]

The collapse of this dialectical pair toward one pole or the other diminishes the space of appearances. If it moves toward the determinate end, then the parent's confidence morphs into self-certainty, making it difficult or impossible to accept anything that does not fit the parent's schemas of the child. The parent, in other words, projects onto the child representations, expecting the child to adopt and conform to these representations, while denying or overlooking the child's uniqueness.[93] This self-certainty

90. Dickinson and Katsko, *Agamben's Coming Philosophy*, 34.

91. Gricoski, *Being Unfolded*, 223.

92. Waggoner, *Unhoused*, 82.

93. David Gauthier, in discussing Heidegger's philosophy, points out a term used by Heidegger (*Gestell*/enframement) to indicate how human beings "impose a framework on nature in order to force it to produce consumable material," which obstructs nature from appearing as it is or of its own accord. This establishes an adversarial attitude that is a type of violence. Enframement, then, would reflect the collapse of the dialectical tension between determinate and indeterminate knowing. Gauthier, *Martin Heidegger, Emmanuel Lévinas, and the Politics of Dwelling*, 8.

and instrumentality regarding children communicates to them that this is who they are and will be, which diminishes children's sense of trust and agency vis-à-vis asserting themselves in this relational space. We see this in adulthood. To return to racism, white supremacists operate out of determinate knowing when it comes to African American (and white supremacy), rejecting any principle of unfathomability, while demanding that people of color conform to the illusion of inferiority. This accompanies sheer instrumentality evident in the objectification of black and brown bodies. Understandably, persons of color will not trust this relational space to appear as they are, given the perfidy and lack of care of racists. In theological language, determinate knowing that involves the collapse of the space of appearances is reminiscent of idolatry, wherein individuals believe they not only have the truth, but all the truth there is. The idol is pure instrumentality—utility/ function.

The third dialectical pair of care's personal knowing is restraint-unrestraint. I have already mentioned restraint with regard to determinate knowing, but more needs to be said. Parents, in attuning to their children, necessarily exercise some restraint in their care, whether by holding back their own needs, feelings, and desires or by restraining from projecting their representations onto the child. This restraint is also necessary to create the space of appearances. Restraint clears a path, a space for children to appear as they are, in their suchness and not simply as the parent expects. For example, good-enough parents who get up at midnight to care for a sick child place their needs and feelings in the background. Busy parents exercise restraint in taking time to listen to their children's experiences of school. A simple example from adulthood illustrates routine restraint in caring. A young man takes time to help an elderly person with her groceries, illustrating a routine amount of restraint in her care.

Parental restraint can accompany and be in tension with a kind of unrestraint. Positively, this unrestraint is often seen in spontaneity or play, as well as in times of parental exuberance. Kay Redfield Jamison points to the importance of exuberance for intellectual curiosity, creativity, and playfulness, which we can note in the care of children, at least at times.[94] Parents' exuberance (unrestrainment, if you will) should correlate with a child's exuberance. That is, for exuberance to be connected to care, there must be some degree of mutuality. If a child is exuberant and the parent is not, the child will experience disconnection. The same is true if the situation is reversed. I add here that, even in parents' exuberance, there must be some degree of restraint so children are not overwhelmed or, positively, that there is a space

94. Redfield-Jamison, *Exuberance.*

for the children's assertions and for sharing their exuberance. When there is some degree of matching, the space of appearances is created, which is accompanied by a child's nascent agency and sense of suchness.

There is also a shadow side to being either restrained or unrestrained. Too much parental restraint can be experienced as relational and intrapsychic distance or disconnection. Parents who restrain themselves from being emotionally expressive or from being playful will attenuate care and the space of appearances. Children will learn that being emotionally expressive or playful is taboo, shameful, to be done in secret. On the other hand, parents who are unrestrained will dominate their children, foreclosing personal knowing and the space of appearances. A narcissistic parent, for instance, will have an exceptionally low threshold for restraint and a corresponding tendency for being unrestrained, both with respect to their desires and needs as well as projecting representations and expectations onto the child. Worse, a violent parent or individual does not exercise restraint. Moments of this type of unrestraint and the corresponding lack of care are noted in racism. To return to the parent-child relation, the result of the loss of dialectical tension between restrain and unrestraint represents a distortion of care, the collapse of the space of appearances and, correspondingly, the eclipse of the child's trust and experience of suchness.

In sketching this out, I am pointing to extremes. But it is true that all good-enough parents fail in various common or less extreme ways in caring for their children, which involves momentary misattunements and a corresponding attenuation of the space of appearances. This routine reality of human finitude and care invites parents to recognize their failures in identification-disidentification, determinate-indeterminate knowing, and restraint-unrestraint. Once relational disjunctions in care are recognized, good-enough parents can repair the relation/space.[95] These relational repairs are acts of care and, therefore, are crucial to children's pre-representational experiences of trust—trust to assert themselves in this space and cooperate in reparative actions.[96] In other words, children will have pre-representational, and later representational, trust/hope that relational failures can be repaired, restoring the space of speaking and acting together and concomitantly experiences of suchness, as well as self-esteem, self-confidence, and self-respect.

---

95. See Safron and Muran, "The Resolution of Ruptures in the Therapeutic Alliance." Schore, *Affect Regulation and the Repair of the Self.*

96. Arendt's political philosophy embraces the idea of repair vis-à-vis speaking and acting together, though this is expressed in terms of the importance of making promises and forgiveness, for those times when promises have been broken. Arendt, *The Promise of Politics.*

In the state of nature, by which I mean the nature of caring for children, acts of care, in brief, rest on personal recognition/knowing, which comprises three interrelated dialectical pairs, namely, identification-disidentification, determinate-indeterminate knowing, and restraint-unrestraint. When these dialectical pairs retain a dialectal tension, a space of appearances—a pre-political space of speaking and acting together—exists wherein children obtain sufficient relational trust to assert (nascent agency) their needs and desires—to appear in their suchness (e.g., pre-representational organizations of self-esteem, self-respect, and self-confidence). The implication here is that parental care is foundational for the emergence of children's subjectivity, agency, and sense of spontaneity/freedom.

In time, as children develop, these pre-representational subjective experiences become linked to the symbols and narratives used in the family and, later, the narratives, symbols, and rituals of the larger community and society.[97] Ideally, the self-worth, confidence, and respect garnered in the immediate relation between parents and children are extended to others in the family and later to the larger social-political world. That is, the parents' care establishes a space of appearances and trust wherein children construct experiences and obtain a sense of self-worth, confidence, and respect, which, if all goes well enough, will enable the child to discover and claim a positive self in the social-political world of speaking and acting together. Of course, the social-political world may lack both care and positive representations, which means that the social-political space of appearances is attenuated or absent. This can result in a painful, or even traumatic, split between the care experienced at home and the lack or absence of care in the social-political realm.[98] Put differently, the world of home and its attending experiences of esteem, confidence, and respect is split off from the larger world, which is marred by carelessness, perfidy, and distrust. Ideally, there should be a correlation between the dynamics of care in a good-enough family and the dynamics of care in the social-political world. A decent polis would not have a stark division between care in the home and care in the polis.

Another way to envision the radical nature of care and its consequences for subjectivity is through the metaphor of dwelling, which will

97. Agamben, who relies on Aristotle, distinguishes between *zoe* (merely the condition of being alive) and *bios* (life in the polis). The pre-political space, in my view, involves the process of introducing *zoe* into *bios*.

98. This painful realization is noted in the autobiographies of Malcolm X and Martin Luther King Jr., as well as in Ta-Nehisi Coates' book, *Between the World and Me*. This pain is present precisely because of the care experienced in their families, which can be a source of insurrection, revolution, and/or resistance, which will be discussed below. Haley, *The Autobiography of Malcolm X*; King, *The Autobiography of Martin Luther King, Jr.*; Coates, *Between the World and Me*.

be discussed in detail in the next chapter.[99] For now, I begin by saying that parental care establishes a space of appearances wherein children obtain an experience of embodied dwelling with an Other.[100] Let me come at this by way of Erik Erikson and John Bowlby. Erikson said the first developmental stage involved the parent-child couple handling trust-mistrust[101] and, if all goes well, this relation provides, to use Bowlby's term, a secure base.[102] Embodied trust and a secure base can be understood as children being in their bodies-with-another. To dwell in an embodied way with another depends on consistent care (including repairs), wherein children can trust themselves and Others—psychologically, socially, and bodily. Put differently, for Theodor Adorno, Matt Waggoner writes, dwelling "concerns the question of how the subject is able to reside in and with otherness,"[103] while obtaining and retaining an embodied, pre-representational sense of confidence, esteem, and respect. This suggests that parents are able to reside in and with the Otherness of their children, which is necessary for children to obtain an embodied sense of being with their parents who are Others. Dwelling in this pre-political space is an embodied suchness together.

99. I will address this in greater detail in the chapter on dwelling. For now, it may be helpful to provide a few remarks. David Gauthier addresses the notion of dwelling in the philosophies of Martin Heidegger and Emmanuel Lévinas. For Heidegger, human beings are thrown into the world and our anxiety reveals our sense of homelessness. Gauthier argues that Heidegger "interprets homelessness as a symptom of the abandonment of Being by beings." Philosophy, then, is an attempt to aid human beings "to become more at home in the world." By contrast, for Lévinas, homelessness is the "failure to meet [one's] obligation to the Other," which is an ethical not an ontological problem. Lévinas considers that "the home rises to the fullness of dignity when it is used as an instrument of welcome." From a psychological developmental view, it is feasible to consider the child's first experience of being unhoused through the process of birth, which could be deemed to be the experience of existential homelessness. However, I side more with Lévinas and suggest that parental care/welcome provides pre-representational experiences of dwelling in one's body with another. In other words, the root of parental care is welcome or hospitality so that Others can appear in their embodied suchness with Others. Gauthier, *Martin Heidegger, Emmanuel Lévinas, and the Politics of Dwelling*, 36, 129, 9, 11.

100. One could say that in the womb a child has a pre-representational embodiment that is not in relation to the Other. Before birth, there is no gap between need and the meeting of the need, which to my mind suggests there is no sense of the Other. After birth, after being unhoused, there is a gap, which accompanies a nascent consciousness of need and Other. A welcoming, caring parent provides the child with embodied experiences of being at home with the Other.

101. Erikson, *Childhood and Society*.

102. Bowlby, *A Secure Base*.

103. Waggoner, *Unhoused*.

Eventually, an embodied-relation of being at home or dwelling extends to the physical surroundings and, ideally, the larger world. If all goes well enough, we feel at home in our houses, with our friends, and in the world. By contrast, trauma or the collapse of the space of appearances heightens distrust and betrayal, which unhouses children psychologically and relationally.[104] Being unhoused by childhood trauma or by political trauma is painfully evident in adults who do not feel at home in their bodies or in their relationships or, often, in their homes or the world, which is accompanied by a devastating and perduring lack of self-esteem, confidence, and respect.

Let me return to the problem of racism to provide a negative illustration. Racism, which is a form of political carelessness, can be understood to eclipse the space of appearances (and its three dialectical pairs of personal recognition, namely, identification-disidentification, determinate-indeterminate knowing, and restraint-unrestraint) between white supremacists and people of color. This is accompanied by social, political, and economic disciplinary regimes that attempt to enforce the illusions of white superiority and black inferiority, while also enacting misrecognition/knowing and maldistribution of resources.[105] This enforcement (and enframement) involves mis- and non-recognition (depersonalization) of black people as persons, which accompanies social, political, and economic forms of carelessness and the absence of experiences of being-with Others. In a racist society, African American parents undertake care for their children, given the social, political, and economic realities that seek to undermine their children's sense of esteem, self-confidence, and self-respect, as well as their embodied experiences[106] of being at home with themselves and Others. If we consider the autobiography of Martin Luther King Jr., we can see that his parents provided sufficient care so that their son, Martin, developed confidence, esteem, respect and, I would surmise, an embodied sense of

104. LaMothe, "On Being at Home in the World."

105. Fraser and Honneth. *Redistribution or Recognition?*

106. The sense of disembodiment is discussed in King's biography and it is evident in the violence and threat of violence present when he was a child and later as an adult. Another more clearly portrayed disembodiment is seen in Ta-Nehisi Coates' book, *Between the World and Me.* He writes about the pervasive threat of violence that stems from racism and its impact on black bodies and psyches. For Coates, the presence of violence raises "the question of how one should live within a black body, within a country lost in the Dream . . . how do I live free in this black body?" Nakedness, disembodiment, body, and blood are terms used throughout the book. In my view, disembodiment means not only *not* feeling as if one dwells within one's own body, but also not dwelling in the larger social-political milieu. In addition, this attends a lack of self-esteem, self-confidence, and self-respect in the public sphere—a sphere fraught with all kinds of cruel carelessness.

being at home with Others, all of which is precisely why his experience of his white friend was so upsetting and disturbing. When Martin was 5 or 6, he experienced a painful blow, discovering that his white friend could no longer play with him because Martin was black. King's mother tried to counter this experience by saying that Martin must always remember he is a somebody and not to forget this when he was in the public world.[107] What he encountered in the public world of racism were the numerous ways he was denied a positive-embodied self in the social-political realm. Put differently, racism communicated to him that he could not dwell with white people, because he was recognized as inferior, as less than a person and, therefore, one who is denied care.

By sketching out the relation between parents' and children's space of speaking and acting together, I wish to posit that this pre-political space of appearances is a root of the polis. Instead, of imagining a state of nature to return to or avoid, I am suggesting that the state of nature is in and founds every society and that state of nature is the care good-enough parents provide their children. In positing this, I am following Giorgio Agamben's idea that political philosophy (and theology) should eschew splitting off nature from the polis, as has been done in Western philosophy for millennia. But before moving to the theological, I want to stress two points about the radical nature of this care.

In good-enough parental care there is an absence of subordination and subjugation. While infants are vulnerable and dependent, this does not necessarily mean they are subordinate to their invulnerable parents. Good-enough parental care does not, in my view, communicate subordination or subjugation. Indeed, parents, in caring for their children, do not have subordination in mind. It is not part of their knowing or acting. To return to the experience of suchness, there is an absence of any hierarchical evaluation (superior, inferior) in parents' personal knowing and acting, which means that experiences of self-esteem, self-respect, and self-confidence are not determined by and dependent on hierarchical valuations associated with relations of subordination and subjugation. Of course, as children develop, they may make use of cultural narratives that organize experience and relations in terms of hierarchy and subordination, which distorts not only suchness, but also the space of speaking and acting together. A second and related point is that good-enough parental care makes inoperative both the apparatuses that found self-esteem, self-confidence, and self-respect on hierarchical valuations and relations of mimetic violence that are inherent in subordination and subjugation. When parents seek to subordinate or

107. King, *The Autobiography of Martin Luther King Jr.*, 3–4.

subjugate their children, they inculcate a desire to rebel, to resist, and this desire is linked to the presence of an ungovernable self—a self not captive to or dependent on the apparatuses of society. Over the years, I have listened to countless adults who were subjugated as children, frequently traumatizing them. In most cases, people responded by adopting various forms of resistance, which sometimes led to returning the favor—subordinating or subjugating their parents, in fantasy and/or reality.

## A Theology of Vulnerability as a Foundation for a Radical Political Theology

I argue we must assiduously avoid, if not root out, theologies/myths of subjugation/subordination because they produce relations of superiority and inferiority, which "creates an abyss of inequality that is a great stumbling block in weighing the value of ourselves relative to nature. Our solitude in this respect places us at risk of arrogance that would be as fatal to ourselves as other species."[108] To construct a radical political theology for the Anthropocene Age gives rise to the question regarding what theological/myth foundation on which to rely for an ecologically minded approach.[109] In this section, I identify, albeit briefly, a theology of vulnerability that is evident in the stories regarding the life, ministry, and death of Jesus Christ. This is not to suggest that the gospels reveal only a theology of vulnerability.[110] Instead, this theology is understandably intertwined with Jewish scriptures and theologies of subjugation. My effort is to tease out and highlight a theology of vulnerability, which can be used to respond to perennial problems of political theological theorizing. Moreover, this theology which will serve as a foundation for a radical political theology.

There is one other point to make before beginning. In formal and informal theological discussions around climate change, one often hears

108. Schell, "Nature and Value," 9.

109. See also Keller, *Political Theology of the Earth*.

110. I am arguing in this chapter for a theology of vulnerability evident in scripture, as opposed to the notion of weak theology. This said, I find evidence for this view in the work of other theologians/philosophers, like Edith Stein, who offers a relational ontology, which can, in my view, be seen to parallel what I am doing. For instance, theologian Thomas Gricoski argues that Edith Stein's relational ontology "is not one of monarchial priority and subordination. I read the model for Steinian theory of being's inner self-relation as the co-constitutive and co-causal potency/act relationship. The potency/act relationship is characterized by co-originality, reciprocity, and mutual dependence." In this passage, while very abstract, we see the absence of subordination/ subjugation and a view of relationship that suggest the presence of vulnerability necessary for reciprocity. Gricoski, *Being Unfolded*, 52.

the term "stewardship" bandied about. For a sustainable earth, we must, as ecological agents, be good stewards of the earth. The problem with this concept is that it "remains a fundamentally theocratic and paternalistic model wherein responsibilities for nature are actually inseparable from subservience to God and potentially, depending on how directly or indirectly the relation to God is theologically envisaged, to God's (self-proclaimed) representatives on earth."[111] The theocratic and paternalistic model is part of the anthropological machine that proclaims humanity's sovereignty or dominion over other-than-human-beings and the earth. It is a theology of subjugation/subordination that screens human radical vulnerability.

The term "vulnerable" means being wounded or open/exposed to being wounded, which is derived from the Latin *vulnerābilis*, wound. A related term "vulnerary" means something used to promote the healing of wounds—remedy—which I will say more about later. For now, it is important to acknowledge that vulnerable is often associated with the adjective "weak." We can consider an infant as vulnerable and weak, lacking efficacy, physical potency, and mental strength. As stated above, children are vulnerable because of physiological and psychological dependence and a concomitant lack of psychosocial capacities. There are also numerous examples of adults being weak and, therefore, vulnerable. Older adults can be vulnerable because of a loss of cognitive and physical capacities. Of course, an adult *can be made* vulnerable, such as when an adult is robbed and beaten. In terms of adults or children, *circumstances and/or the conditions make a person vulnerable*, exposing the person to being wounded. In other words, an infant or elderly person does not choose to be vulnerable. The conditions of their physical-psychological being expose them to being hurt. By contrast, I am focusing on *vulnerability that is chosen*—an act of the will, an expression of agency, and a signifier of significant mental and spiritual resilience.[112]

Before unpacking the term "theology of vulnerability," it is important to begin briefly with my slight disagreement with John Caputo,[113] who ar-

---

111. Smith, *Against Ecological Sovereignty*, 14.

112. Sarah Bracke and other feminists (e.g., Susan Dodds, Caron Gentry, Anu Koivunen, Katariina Kyrölä and Ingrid Ryberg) have explored the issue of vulnerability and resistance in situations of marginalization and oppression. In general, these and other writers on vulnerability identify the problems of vulnerability, as well as its power vis-à-vis resisting trauma and oppression. In this chapter, I draw on the resistance aspects of vulnerability, recognizing that unchosen vulnerability in situations of political, economic, and social oppression tends toward the traumatic. Bracke, "Bouncing Back"; Dodds, "Dependence, Care, and Vulnerability"; Gentry, "Feminist Christian Realism"; Koivunen, Kyrölä, and Ryberg, *The Power of Vulnerability*.

113. Caputo, *The Weakness of God*. Caputo does recognize the power in weakness, recalling Paul's letters. So, it is clear that there is, for Caputo, strength or power in

gues for a weak theology, or what Walter Benjamin called "weak messianic power,"[114] as opposed to a strong theology, which in my view are theologies of subordination/subjugation. Let me quickly say that much of my depiction of a theology of vulnerability is informed by Caputo's work, as well as Richard A. Horsley[115] and John Dominic Crossan,[116] but the complementarity of weak and strong is problematic, for a couple of reasons. First and foremost, it suggests that weak and strong are opposed or in some binary relation. To be sure, Caputo, relying on Paul's letters, points to the paradox of the strength or power of weakness. This is a helpful rhetorical device, but one I wish to oppose because of the negative connotation of weakness, especially given the patriarchal context of scriptures, where weakness is negatively associated with women and children and my more immediate context of a militaristic, imperial nation like the United States, where weakness is associated with the absence of power and sovereignty. Second and relatedly, the adjective "weak" is woefully inadequate as a descriptor for the theology Caputo is addressing. In terms of defining the adjective, dictionaries use phrases like liable to yield, break, or collapse under pressure, lacking in bodily strength, lacking force, potency or efficacy, deficient in mental power. The definition and synonyms of weak, then, are not fitting when one considers Jesus' ministry and death. This is true when we consider that, for Caputo, Jesus "is the parable" of the kingdom of God, wherein the "power of the kingdom is the powerless power" that transforms people, but yet seems to lack efficacy with regard to larger institutions (e.g., the Roman Empire). Obviously, in relying on Paul, Caputo is saying that the life, ministry, and death of Jesus Christ are key for depicting weak theology. Yet, if we follow this, are we saying that Jesus showed mental deficiency in forgiving his tormentors? Did Jesus lack force and potency in his ministry and by enduring the suffering of torture and the cross? Did Jesus collapse under the pressure of imperial and religious authorities? The answers to these questions are, of course, a decisive no. But this does not mean I am endorsing the idea of Jesus being strong, at least in the sense of a "strong theology" that emphasizes dominance, subjugation, subordination, and the like. To do so, one would become trapped in a binary complementarity. Instead, I prefer the term "vulnerable," which I do not place in a complementary relation with invulnerability. To do that would be just another version of juxtaposing strength and weakness. In other words, the vulnerability, in terms of Jesus' ministry,

weakness.

114. Robbins, *Radical Democracy and Political Theology*, 177.
115. Horsley, *Jesus and Empire*; Horsely, *Jesus and the Power*.
116. Crossan, *Jesus*; Crossan, *God and Empire*.

is not in a complementary relation with the invulnerability of God. Instead, vulnerability is, in the case of Jesus, a *decision* made for the sake of Others.

To understand Jesus as the paradigmatic figure of a theology of vulnerability and as a vulnerary, I need to consider that Jesus possessed the courage, potency, and mental strength *to decide* to be vulnerable, which can be depicted in several ways. For instance, in Paul's letter to the Philippians, we read that Jesus, "though he was in the form of God, did not regard equality with God as something to be exploited, but emptied (*kenosis*) himself, taking the form of a slave, being born in human likeness. And being found in human form, He humbled himself and became obedient to the point of death—even death on a cross" (2:6–8). There are three key points here. First, Paul is depicting a decision Jesus made to open himself to the vulnerable realities of being human, which included torture and death on the cross. This is not the invulnerable God, but a God who chose to be open to being wounded, to be moved by the suffering of humanity, in general, and a subjugated people, in particular. Second, emptying Godself and taking on human form to dwell (to appear) among us were acts of God's care that can be understood in light of the dialectical pairs identified above. As Creator, God identifies with creation and, in particular, human beings, yet God is Other than human beings. Incarnation becomes an act of recognition and identification, but there remains disidentification in that Christ, as stated in our credal affirmations, is divine—Other than human. This Otherness is no less than the infinite, indeterminate love of God vis-à-vis the suchness of human beings. Also, to empty Godself is a moment of restraint—a judicious setting aside to be able to join with humanity, while creating a space for humanity's suchness, as well as a space of speaking and acting together—Jesus and the disciples. At the same time, we can understand God emptying Godself to be an act of God's infinite, indeterminate (and indeterminable) love/care manifested in a determinate being—Jesus. God's indeterminate love incarnated in Jesus is not bound to any human apparatuses. It is unconditional and unconditioned in the determinate being of Jesus Christ.

This can be further depicted in terms of *imago dei* or the sacredness of life. God becoming human affirms singularity or suchness of humanity, but also creation. It is a suchness beyond human apparatuses, which in my view means that the sacredness of life does not place human beings in hierarchical relations between human beings and other species or nature itself, as if human beings possess greater value. Any theological or philosophical suggestion that human suchness entails greater value merely indicates the anthropocentric narcissism of human beings and the accompanying perpetual impulse to create apparatuses that subordinate[117] and subjugate other human beings, other species, and nature itself. The sacredness of life manifested in the incarnation simply affirms the singularity or suchness of human beings and all of creation, which *by definition means the affirmation of plurality and difference that is constitutive to the notion of singularity.*[118] There is, in other words, not sameness linked to identity, but rather diversity, which fits well with Agamben's idea of human beings in terms of potentiality (and actuality) and excess. The sacred exceeds representations, as do human beings and indeed all creatures.

A third feature of this passage is seen when Paul states that God took on the form of a slave—the most humiliated state of being human in a polis. To be a slave presupposes sovereignty and a state of exception,[119] wherein other human beings are recognized and treated as slaves by the state. As property the slave's value is anchored in utility/function—there is no excess, no suchness. The slave is defined by and determined by representations sanctioned and enforced by the state and the "owner." The slave's identity, then, is objectified utility—a negative construction in that the slave is not deemed to be a citizen—an included-excluded Other. A citizen, on the other hand, is ideally a person who possesses a positive value and identity—legally and socially—that undergirds persons speaking and acting together. Slaves, then, are denied personal recognition/knowing in the polis' space of appearances and, therefore, are not allowed to dwell in it as persons. Now, God

117. In an otherwise fine book, John Howard Yoder argues that the social ethic of Jesus is manifested in his freely accepting his subordination to the social-political structures (Roman and Jewish), recognizing that these are passing. He goes on to suggest this ethic is evident in Paul's writings. I strongly disagree. His social ethic is what ensures that these structures are not resisted or undermined. He wrongly juxtaposes violence and subordination, refusing to see other alternatives than subjection and subordination. Yoder's social ethic is the ethic of a contented slave. Yoder, *The Politics of Jesus*, 185–89.

118. See Nancy, *Being Singular Plural*.

119. Carl Schmitt, a noted twentieth-century political jurist, argued that the sovereign is "he who decides on the exception." As a threshold figure, the sovereign "is both the sign of the rule and the jurisdiction of law, and supervenes the law." (See Brown, *Walled States, Waning Sovereignty*, 83, 59.) What is interesting and important here is that the sovereign possesses the supreme (legal) authority to set aside laws, because s/he is given the legal power to decide on the exception. Add to this the idea that the state of exception is at play in the very creation of the law itself. Put another way, the establishment of the law already reveals the state of exception. I stress here that the state of exception does not mean the law is invalid, but rather that in the exception, the law simply is not applicable. The law remains in effect, but is set aside. That is, "it is the sovereign who, insofar as he decides on the state of exception, has the power to decide which life may be killed without the commission of homicide." Slaves would be included in this category of exception. See Agamben, *Sovereign Power and Bare Life*, 83, 142.

taking the form of a slave made/makes inoperative any political notion of sovereignty and any political apparatuses or disciplinary regimes that seek to construct subjectivity in subjugated forms. Jesus Christ's status, in other words, was not founded in, produced by, or dependent on the state, and he is fundamentally ungovernable, though in the form of a slave. The form of a slave is not *being* a slave. One could suggest that Jesus, in taking on the form of the slave, was, of course, physically and psychologically vulnerable, yet his agency and sense of self-esteem, self-confidence, and self-respect were not dependent on the Roman or Jewish apparatuses that defined or produced subjects to be used by others—subjects without suchness or excess. These political apparatuses were inoperative. Inoperativity, for Agamben, does not mean that the princes and principalities are no longer functioning or having effect. They do, which is evident in the torture and death of Jesus. Yet, inoperativity meant Jesus' suchness was not dependent on the apparatuses that promulgated slavery, but instead was dependent on the indeterminate, unconditioned love of a non-sovereign God.[120] While I will say more about the issue of sovereignty in a following chapter, for now, Jesus' vulnerability in taking on the form of the slave makes inoperative sovereignty as such. "God," John Caputo writes, "is unconditional but without sovereignty,"[121] which means that Jesus is not the new sovereign. In terms of Agamben, Jesus as slave is ungovernable because of the indeterminate, infinite love of God. Briefly, in taking on being a slave, God communicates a radical care and vulnerability that makes inoperative sovereignties that depend on relations of subordination and/or subjugation. In this sense, Jesus is the ungovernable vulnerary—the remedy for relations of subordination/subjugation.

I wish to linger here for a moment to consider further the implications of vulnerability in light of Jesus taking on the form of a slave. Referring to the work of Agamben, Sergei Prozorov notes, "Beyond the apparatuses and forms of subjectivity they produce there is the excess of living being that can never be subsumed under them. While the excess does not itself constitute a political subject, it testifies to the fact that apparatuses are never all there is."[122] This excess vis-à-vis the subject, from a theological perspective, is evident in the story of God's infinite, indeterminate care manifested in the incarnation and in creation. Stated differently, God's care, which is the

---

120. Agamben argues that in Judaism and Christianity inoperativity is an attribute of God, though I would clarify this and indicate that inoperativity is an attribute of a theology of vulnerability, while theologies of subjugation/subordination function as anthropological machines that promote anthropocentrism. Agamben, *The Kingdom and the Glory*, 239. See also Wood, *Reoccupy the Earth*, 203–4.

121. Caputo, *The Weakness of God*, 12.

122. Prozorov, *Agamben and Politics*, 24.

ontological ground of the personal recognition of each human being[123] (and the singularity or suchness of all life), creates a space for the possibility of individuals' appearing in their suchness—a suchness that is ungovernable in the sense of not being ultimately defined or determined by subjugating, subordinating apparatuses.[124] God becoming incarnate in taking on the form of the slave is the event that reveals this existential reality of excess—an excess that founds the ungovernable self—a self not captive to society's apparatuses.

There is one other aspect I wish to tease out. God taking on the form of a slave—being human—means, in part, that while singular, identity itself becomes inoperative. For one, a slave has no particular identity. Slaves were slaves whether they resided in a Greek, Roman, or Jewish society. Stated differently, a slave's identity is negatively constructed by the apparatuses of the polis—not a citizen, which means having no rights, privileges, etc. In taking on the form and identity of a slave, Jesus is not only ungovernable vis-à-vis the human apparatuses that seek to determine and exploit some human beings, he also points to the possibility of inclusion that is not dependent on particular identity. A slave, as an included-excluded Other, is not seen as possessing a particular identity and certainly not an identity that would provide entrance into the polis' space of speaking and acting together. Of course, Jesus was born into a Jewish family and had an identity as a Jew, but this identity was inoperative in that it did not define Jesus as such. Just as God cannot be confined to a particular people, the event of the incarnation (taking on the form of a slave) makes inoperative the specificity associated with particular identities, which means there is an invitation and a possibility for all to live in the beloved community/polis. Let me return to my use of Agamben in the previous chapter. "For the State," he writes, "what is important is never the singularity as such, but only its inclusion in some identity, whatever identity (but the possibility of the whatever itself being taken up without an identity is a threat the State cannot come to terms with)."[125] Prozorov adds, "what is absolutely threatening to the state, what the state 'cannot tolerate in any way' is not any particular claim for identity, which can always be recognized and conceded, but rather the possibility of human beings co-belonging in the absence of any identity."[126] Here we also recall Galatians: "There is no longer Jew or Greek, there is no longer slave or free,

123. For a theological discussion of this in relation to community see Zizioulas, *Being as Communion*. Zizioulas, *Communion and Otherness*.

124. Prozorov, *Agamben and Politics*, 24.

125. Agamben, *The Coming Community*, 85.

126. Prozorov, *Agamben and Politics*, 79.

there is no longer male and female; for all of you are one in Christ" (3:28 NRSV). God's infinite, indeterminate love/care incarnated in Jesus Christ, then, makes inoperative identity, making possible beloved communities, wherein singularity is not contingent on the particularities of identity, yet these identities continue to exist. Put differently, the indeterminacy of God's care is possible in moments of human love/care that create spaces of appearances, wherein singularity or suchness is possible, while particularities are secondary to belonging—to being with one another. Ideally, parental care imperfectly incarnates God's infinite, indeterminate care, which suggests a correlation, not identity, between human and divine creation of the space of appearances.

It is not simply the decision to empty Godself where we see evidence of the decision to be vulnerable. In Luke chapter 9, there are two occasions when Jesus tells his disciples and others that he will be betrayed and die. Then in verse 51, we read that Jesus "set his face to go to Jerusalem." This means Jesus decided to move into greater vulnerability, likely knowing this was a more dangerous place to do his ministry. A momentary decision, though, was not set-in stone. There would be other times to affirm the decision, even as he hoped for a different outcome (e.g., in the Garden). Once Jesus was arrested, he was indeed wounded by torture and, even in the midst of this horrific occasion of Imperial Rome's terroristic practices, Jesus had the courage and fortitude to forgive his tormentors (Luke: 23:34). These are not illustrations of a weak person, but rather one demonstrating heroic spiritual and psychological courage and strength in the midst of choosing vulnerability.

We can deepen our comprehension of Jesus' vulnerability in terms of his being a vulnerary or remedy for the mimetic reality of the theologies of subjugation. First of all, Jesus upends or makes inoperative the complementarity of strong and weak that would prevail between Roman oppressors and subjugated peoples. Jesus is neither the "weak force of God," as Caputo[127] says, nor is he the strong force of God. The adjectives of weak and strong are more applicable to theologies of subjugation, wherein there are strong and weak actors. Let's return to the moments of Jesus' torture and the care he displayed in forgiving his torturers. From a theology of subjugation perspective, ostensibly strong Roman soldiers, acting for the Roman sovereign, possessed power over a weak person—a person weakened by torture [the absence of personal recognition and care]. We could even set up the complementary or binary relation in terms of vulnerability, wherein the guards are "invulnerable," and Jesus is vulnerable. But this would miss

127. Caputo, *The Weakness of God*, 38.

the point, because we would still be caught up in the mimesis that stems from theologies of subjugation. Instead, Jesus is the vulnerary or remedy in the sense that weak-strong, vulnerable-invulnerable binaries are not in the foreground. More strongly stated, to use Agamben's[128] notion, Jesus' care for his tormentors makes the complementarity of victimizer/subjugator and victim/subjugated inoperative. To reiterate, inoperative, for Agamben, means deactivating or neutralizing the apparatuses of power that subjugate, that form and determine subjectivities and identities, making possible the realization of other possibilities or potentialities.[129] Recall also that the notion "inoperative" is, for Agamben, not passive, but is an action.[130] Put another way, Agamben, Prozorov claims, does not "affirm inertia, inactivity or apraxia . . . but a form of praxis that is devoid of any telos or task, does not realize any essence and does not correspond to any nature."[131] In my view, Jesus' act of forgiving his torturers is a radical political caring action. Jesus' decision to be vulnerable and to forgive were inoperative in that they did not operate out of the grammar of subjugation and subordination of the Roman Empire or the subordination and subjugation of Jewish religious authorities, but rather out of the indeterminate, unconditional love of God. Indeed, in these acts, Jesus is the vulnerary with regard to the very apparatuses of subjugation that terrify, oppress, and wound subjugated peoples.

Since this is important to grasp, let me say more. The Roman apparatuses of subjugation, which were supported by Roman philosophies/theologies of subordination/subjugation, had no substantive meaning or power with regard to Jesus' decision to be vulnerable and to forgive the guards. Jesus' forgiveness rendered inoperative the complementarities of weak-strong, powerless-powerful, which are the basis of every theology of subjugation and subordination. What matters is the expression and embodiment, or incarnation, of God's infinite, indeterminate, non-sovereign[132] love/care

128. Agamben, *Sovereign Power and Bare Life*.

129. Prozorov, *Agamben and Politics*, 32–37. Prozorov states that inoperativity is not passivity. God emptying Godself is an action of indeterminate care. To amend Prozorov's comment, inoperativity vis-à-vis the incarnation or God emptying Godself is indeterminate care (like Adorno's tenderness) wherein telos or purpose are secondary.

130. Prozorov, *Agamben and Politics*, 134.

131. Prozorov, *Agamben and Politics*, 33.

132. I will say more about a non-sovereign God and radical political theology in chapter 3. For now, let me simply state that a non-sovereign care of God is reflected in Jesus' forgiveness of the soldiers and the idea that Jesus is not operating out of the apparatuses of Roman sovereignty or any other notion of sovereignty. Of course, one might point out the references to the kingdom of God or Jesus sitting at the right hand of God, signaling the ultimate sovereignty of God. In my view, these are evidence for theologies of subjugation that are woven into Christian scriptures—theologies that need to be

for all human beings in all contexts in this act of forgiveness, which affirms the singularity or suchness of the Roman soldiers and invites the possibility of communion beyond transgression. As Jürgen Moltmann argues, "the one who loves becomes vulnerable."[133] That is, God's love (for Caputo,[134] God as event) for humanity requires vulnerability and we see this truth in our human relationships wherein singularity is affirmed. To express and receive love/care necessitates vulnerability, which is why those human beings who have been so deeply wounded as children have difficulty as adults in being vulnerable enough to experience being loved.[135]

Let's linger here a moment longer. In the Gospel of John, Jesus responds to Pilate's query by saying that Jesus' "kingdom is not from this world. If my kingdom was from this world my followers would be fighting to keep me from being handed over to the Jews" (18:36). A thought experiment: Imagine Jesus' followers fighting to free him from imperial forces and their local lackeys. Liberation would depend on violence and we would again be caught up again in the mimetic reality of subjugation-liberation represented in strong theologies. Yet, Jesus has the temerity to choose a ministry of compassion and to forgive his torturers, which functions as a possible antidote (vulnerary) or, if you will, slight adjustment to the mimetic violence associated with a theology of subjugation that supported Roman exploitation of peoples. It is a slight adjustment in that Jesus' forgiveness of the Roman soldiers affirms the singularity or suchness of the Roman soldiers and *invites the possibility* of a relation of speaking and acting together—of the possibility of dwelling together. Of course, the Roman soldiers did not avail themselves of the experience of suchness or invitation, but this is, nevertheless, a radical political act because it offers a possibility of speaking and acting together determined by mutual personal recognition and care.

I add that if we accept the stories about Jesus with regard to vulnerability, then the theologies of subjugation/subordination extant in Judeo-Christian scriptures are inoperative as well, though they are nevertheless present. That is, theologies of vulnerability, which are *possible* remedies to mimetic violence, may subvert, while being intertwined with, theologies of subjugation/subordination. I mentioned Jesus' reference to his kingdom and the possible threat of warfare/rebellion, which is an illustration of the presence of a theology of subordination/subjugation. Also, in John 15:14–15, Jesus addresses his disciples: "You are my friends if you do what I command. I

avoided if we are to construct a radical political theology.

133. Moltmann, *The Crucified God*, 374.
134. Caputo, The Weakness of God, 88.
135. See Mogenson, *A Most Accursed Religion*.

no longer call you servants because a servant does not know his master's business. Instead, I have called you friends, for everything that I learned from my Father I have made known to you." The first sentence is arresting because John links friendship to obedience, which strikes me as a theology of subordination, even subjugation. Jesus' love and care for his "friends" are contingent on their doing what he says. This sounds less like friendship and more like a paternalistic relation between a superior who orders and a subordinate who obeys. Yet, in the second sentence, subordination no longer applies. Indeed, there is a kind of egalitarianism, reciprocity, and mutuality one would expect in friendship. Jesus is not the master, because he has shared all that he knows about God. The master-servant relationship no longer applies or is operative. What remains instead is friendship, which is free of subordination or subjugation. Put in different terms, Jesus is not only the vulnerary with regard to the wounds of mimetic violence in that he makes possible inoperativity with regard to theologies that support relations of subordination and subjugation, he also invites a slight adjustment through a ministry of caring for all people—as friends, as persons. I believe we get a glimpse of this in the early communities of faith in Acts, wherein we see a relative lack of relations of subjugation/subordination and mimetic violence. More positively, we note cooperation in sharing goods as people live a life in common—a life in common not determined by a dominant identity. Moreover, these early Christian communities can be seen as alter-communities in that they are other than the communities that are captive to or determined by the Roman apparatuses or communities that operate out of the theologies of subjugation/subordination evident in Jewish scriptures.

Of course, none of this means that Jesus, as vulnerary, was able to stop or undermine Roman force or the force of the client actors in the Jewish political apparatuses. If we are looking for subversion of political principalities when it comes to the inoperative vulnerary of Jesus, we will not only be disappointed, but also likely be operating out of criteria associated with theologies of subordination/liberation. Jesus was not a Jewish political revolutionary, at least not as many people understand this appellation.[136] That said, Jesus as a vulnerary and ungovernable self was nevertheless a threat to the political establishment. As a vulnerary, Jesus offers a slight adjustment, to use Agamben's term. That is, Jesus forgives and is later killed. Rome continued on for some centuries. Inoperativity means there is a possibility

---

136. Agamben is not suggesting the ungovernable self is necessarily a revolutionary subject. Of course, an ungovernable self may be a revolutionary subject and there are numerous examples of this in history. If not a revolutionary subject, ungovernable selves may simply live and work such that they resist the machinations of the dominant apparatuses of society. See Whyte, *Catastrophe and Redemption*, 160.

of something different. There may be only a slight adjustment, which suggests that with regard to theologies of vulnerability we are not measuring them by their effectiveness, efficiency, power, force, etc. Instead, I suggest theologies of vulnerability be evaluated based on the extent to which they are *not* operating out of the grammars of subordination/subjugation and, more positively, the criteria of care, forgiveness, compassion, and mercy.

Let's leave Jesus and fast forward to the twentieth century, wherein we have an example of a radical political theology and the weak messianic force of God. Martin Luther King Jr. and others sought emancipation from the chains of racism through nonviolent resistance. Briefly, King's (and others) nonviolent resistance was a form of deep care and chosen vulnerability, not only for African Americans suffering under the evils of racism, but a care and vulnerability or openness extended to white people (indeed, all human beings[137])—an indeterminate care not confined to particular qualities or identities.[138] This necessarily involved recognizing and treating human beings as persons, including people who were racist. That is, nonviolent resistance is a form of political caring that maintains the tension between identification and disidentification, which creates or invites a space of appearances. I say "invite" because the Other does not have to accept being recognized and treated as a person. Racists would not have accepted, for to accept this would mean mutuality vis-à-vis personal recognition. Nonviolent resistance can also be framed as a kind of public or civic care that does not operate out of the determinate logic and mimetic violence/alienation of racism. Instead, nonviolent resistance operates out of an indeterminate care vis-à-vis other human beings (and other-than-human beings). Of course, this did not mean that King did not struggle with his own hatred and desire for violence, but he chose not to *operate* out of the apparatuses that produced white supremacy and black inferiority, both of which operate out of disidentification and hatred. That is, he and others exercised courageous restraint—holding back their hatred and the desire for revenge. Their unrestraint was manifested in the gracious care offered to Others—a care associated with fostering a political space of speaking and acting together—shared experiences of suchness.

---

137. King's Riverside speech is a clear example of extending care to people of other lands, in particular the Vietnamese who were experiencing the brunt of American violence.

138. This is no way suggests King (and others) were not without limitations and biases. Shatema Threadcraft and Brandon Terry identify and critique King's (and other male leaders') masculine biases that resulted in the exclusion of women from being at the table with men making decisions. Threadcraft and Terry, "Gender Trouble."

Like Jesus, King and other nonviolent resisters manifested ungovernable selves. By deciding not to operate out of the political-economic apparatuses of racism, they revealed an excess vis-à-vis their singularities that were not dependent on and could not be captured by the apparatuses of hatred and division. For King, this excess, this ungovernable self, meant that self-esteem, self-worth, and self-confidence, which are necessary for political agency and civic trust, were not dependent on state apparatuses, but on the incarnate care/love of God. Of course, these decisions to care and resist made King and others vulnerable to the attacks of racists. These ungovernable selves, in this case, placed themselves in situations where they were vulnerable to harm and many times death. Yet, their vision of an inclusive community of diverse people speaking and acting together reflects, in my view, the radical theology of Jesus, wherein the defining characteristic of speaking and acting together is care and not relations of subordination, subjugation, or narrow conditions of established political-religious identities.

King's nonviolent resistance, then, is a form of care that invites the possibility of the arc of the universe bending toward justice. At the same time, it is an invitation to a possible relation of suchness not defined or determined by the particularities of identity. King's beloved community was not the Christian community, but fundamentally a community of human beings, which is, as Agamben points out, a threat to the state—the evidence for this is King's Riverside speech and the negative responses to it. The beloved community is a community of care, wherein the space of appearances and belonging are not defined or determined by particular identities, though identities are present and affirmed.

In brief, a radical political theology emerges from a theology of vulnerability represented in the event of the incarnation, which, like the act of creation, reveals the intersection of human care/love and God's love. Put differently, the indeterminacy of God's care is possible in moments of human love/care that create spaces of appearances, wherein singularity or suchness is possible (human beings and other-than-human beings), while particularities are secondary to belonging—to being with one another— speaking and acting together. Ideally, parental care imperfectly incarnates God's infinite, indeterminate care, which suggests a correlation, not identity, between human and divine creation of the space of appearances. In this space of appearances, mutual-personal recognition that founds caring relations contributes to experiences of singularity (self-esteem, self-respect, and self-confidence), which founds an ungovernable self—a self not dependent on or determined by society's apparatuses and one open to the suchness of nature. To shift to Jesus, as a vulnerary or remedy, he was ungovernable vis-à-vis the Roman and Jewish apparatuses, inviting the possibility of relations that depended on the love of God. As a vulnerary or remedy, Jesus made inoperative the theologies and politics of subordination and subjugation. Examples of this radical theology, this vulnerary to the mimetic violence of relations of subordination and subjugation, are seen in the thousands of people who nonviolently resisted (and resist) the apparatuses of racism.

Before concluding, I wish to connect this radical political theology to the issues of the Anthropocene Age, with the expectation that subsequent chapters will provide more flesh to these bones. As noted in the introduction, the Anthropocene Age will (and is) usher in significant upheavals and pervasive human suffering. We can sadly, but confidently, expect there will be more state violence and oppression. Regrettably, it is possible that the spaces of appearance will collapse or be attenuated, as people (and other species) are evicted from life-spaces or habitats in the face of scarce resources. In the midst of profound anxiety and fear, in the presence of violence, care becomes increasingly difficult, though even more necessary—care for other human beings, other species, and the earth as a living organism. In my view, a radical political theology(ies) will eschew any philosophical and theological perspectives and myths/stories that politically support and legitimate relations of subjugation and subordination, whether that is directed toward other human beings, other species, or the earth as a living system. More positively, a radical political theology will advocate and invite appropriate decisions of vulnerability, wherein Others (human and other-than-human creatures) are recognized and treated in their suchness. In so doing, prudent openness to and care for Others fosters a space of appearances—a space for Others to risk appearing in their suchness, while speaking and acting together. These ungovernable selves, in their acts of care, will make inoperative those political, social, religious, and economic apparatuses that promote relations of subjugation, whether we are referring to other human beings, species, or the earth. Referring to Agamben, Dickinson and Kotsko argue that the process of "rendering the anthropological machinery that generates our political, social, and religious representations inoperative allows us to strip away what has been foisted upon us and, thereby, perhaps to behold the naked 'whatever being' that stands in its precarious vulnerability and its absolute particularity."[139]

Someone may question, given the overwhelming realities of global warming, whether a radical political theology offers any realistic hope for effecting enough change to stem the coming tide of destruction. This is an important question that I will deal with in more detail in the last two chapters. For now, let me say that Jesus, in forgiving his torturers (as persons, not

139. Dickinson and Colby, "Conclusion," 246.

as torturers or Romans), offered a possibility of a new relation and ordering of the polis based on care and mutuality. Of course, we know that the guards did not take up the invitation. I do not think hope was primary in Jesus' act of care—an act that offered the possibility of a relation not based in subordination or subjugation. What was in the foreground was courageous care. If hope had been in the foreground, I suspect Jesus would have despaired. A radical political theology, in making inoperative the apparatuses that are ushering in the Anthropocene Age, does not mean these apparatuses will not and do not have effects. Jesus as a vulnerary is not a remedy for the human condition, but a remedy for relations of subjugation. As a remedy, this does not mean it is a remedy for the Anthropocene Age. A radical political theology is a remedy that offers a slight adjustment, revealing what Walter Benjamin called the weak messianic force of God. This messianic power/force of care "is 'weak' . . . because it is comparatively weaker than sovereign power . . . but it operates by weakening the latter without producing its own form of sovereignty."[140] Of course, whether this will be sufficient to reduce human violence and subjugation or make headway on reducing the effects of climate change is another question. The primary question is whether we choose to operate out of a theological and existential imperative to care for other human beings, other species, and for the earth as a living organism.

## Conclusion

Because of the existential threat of global warming and its consequences for human life as well as the lives of millions of other species, it is, I believe, necessary to express why we need a radical political theology. A radical political theology, I argue in this chapter and elsewhere in this book, is not simply about how human beings live life together, but how we live life with other species on this one living organism we call the earth. To answer the question about how we should or might live life together requires first depicting the problems that arise when relying on Judeo-Christian myths in constructing a political theology. Much of scripture, I argue, contains stories that support and justify relations of subordination and subjugation, which inevitably lead to mimetic violence. Yet, there are also stories that support attitudes and actions of vulnerability founded in caring relations, which make inoperative theologies and disciplinary regimes that support and legitimate subjugation. Before unpacking a theology of vulnerability, I also claimed that there is an existential root or foundation for a radical political theology and that is evident in the reality of care between good-enough

140. Prozorov, *Agamben and Politics*, 120.

parents and children—care as a state of nature evident in and foundational to all societies. Within these relations, the parents' good-enough care, which eschews subordinating and subjugating attitudes and relations, is founded on personal recognition/ knowing that invites children to assert and experience their suchness (self-esteem, self-confidence, self-respect) in this pre-political space of speaking and acting together. In time, children gain sufficient trust and agency to extend suchness to the larger polis, ideally finding and experiencing a positive self that can speak and act with others. Political agency and civic trust, I argued, have their roots, in part, in the pre-political space of parents and children speaking and acting together. A second root of a radical political theology is a theology of vulnerability founded on the stories of God's creation and the life and ministry of Jesus Christ. Here I argued that God's decision to empty Godself and take on the form of a slave reveals God's indeterminate care for and identification with human beings, which invites a determinate political space of speaking and acting together. God's care and taking on the form of a slave make inoperative the apparatuses that determine the "identity" of the slave and an included-excluded Other, which invites relations and spaces of appearances based on personal recognition or suchness—a radical space of speaking and acting together not founded on particular identities. I also indicated that Jesus' act of forgiveness of the Roman soldiers reveals a radical act in that forgiveness does not operate out of the grammar and machinations of Roman apparatuses of subordination/subjugation. Forgiveness, as an act of care, is a weak messianic force of God's care in that it invites a slight adjustment, which is the affirmation of singularity and the possibility of speaking and acting together founded on mutual personal recognition/care. A radical political theology, then, depicts a vulnerary—a remedy and slight adjustment to the mimetic violence inherent in relations of subjugation/subjugation, whether this regards human beings, other species, or the earth itself.

# 2

## *The Problem of Dwelling in the Anthropocene*

---

Being born is the first exile. To walk the earth
is an eternal diaspora.[1]

The privileged role of the home does not consist in being
the end of human activity but in being its condition.[2]

It is even possible that, if we want to be equal to the absolutely new
tasks ahead, we will have to abandon decidedly, without reservation,
the fundamental concepts through which we have so far represented
the subjects of the political (Man, the Citizen and its rights, but also
the sovereign people, the worker, and so forth) and build our political
philosophy anew starting from the one and only figure of the refugee.[3]

To be rooted is perhaps the most important
and least recognized need of the human soul.[4]

1. Jimenez-Vera in Danticat, *Everything Inside*, vii.
2. Lévinas, *Totality and Infinity*, 152.
3. Agamben, *Means without Ends*, 15.
4. Weil, *The Need for Roots*, 43.

To dwell is constitutive to the very condition of being alive, whether we are talking about human beings or any other species. In terms of human beings, one could argue that all theologies and philosophies are, in one sense or another, responses or answers to the question of what it means to dwell. The ancient Greek philosophers reflected on the *ethos*,[5] which meant abode or dwelling place, and the question of how we might live or dwell together. Aristotle's *Nicomachean Ethics*, for instance, precedes his *Politics* and together they form a unity—to dwell (ethos) is political. Millennia later, Martin Heidegger viewed dwelling as an existential need[6] and the ground of ethics.[7] Here we might note that ethos, which is in relation to the ethical, is also political and the political is fundamentally about dwelling. If we consider dwelling in terms of ethics, politics, and diversity, Emmanuel Kant recognized the problem of dwelling in a complex and diverse political world, arguing for cosmopolitanism—the etymological root means a world polis.[8] More recent philosophers, like Heidegger and Emmanuel Lévinas,[9] understand human beings to be existentially homeless, which for Heidegger meant the need for roots (e.g., place) and identity, and for Lévinas the importance of hospitality toward strangers. The discourse of Western philosophy is often concerned with questions of the relation between being and becoming, potentiality and actuality, or essence and existence, and one could say that all of this is inextricably connected to the fundamental question of human dwelling . . .

To turn to theology, myth, and the theme of homelessness, the story of Adam and Eve represents the first eviction from an original Edenic home, having failed to honor a clause in their rental agreement. Once summarily evicted, this pair had to learn to dwell in a more hostile, limited, and precarious world. The stories of Abraham, Noah, Joseph, and Moses are tales of migration and learning to dwell in other places and among other peoples. Of course, in many of these stories, there is also violence, evicting people from their homes or killing off the inhabitants of the new place to create space for Israelites to dwell—a theme sadly reminiscent of today's apartheid vis-à-vis the Palestinians. These ancient stories appear to corroborate the idea that human beings are existentially homeless, in which one might hear theological echoes in Augustine's prayer: "You have made us for yourself,

---

5. Gauthier, *Martin Heidegger, Emanuel Lévinas, and the Politics of Dwelling*, 90.
6. See Vogt, "Human as a Key Discipline of Environmental Ethics," 243.
7. Wood, *Reoccupy the Earth*, 56.
8. Kant, *Idea for a Universal History from a Cosmopolitan Point of View.*
9. See Gauthier, *Martin Heidegger, Emanuel Lévinas, and the Politics of Dwelling.*

and our hearts are restless until they can find peace in you."[10] Christians, Colby Dickinson notes, "from the earliest beginnings, considered themselves merely as 'sojourners' on earth, exiles amid a foreign people."[11] We may be a peripatetic species, but we still need to dwell wherever we go and, for religious folk, this includes God with us, indicating that God, becoming incarnate, dwells among us. Whether migratory or even homeless, God lives with us.[12]

Existential or theological reflections on being at home or homelessness can distract us from the very material realities and struggles of dwelling. Sociologists, like Mathew Desmond, depict the deeply painful and disturbing realities of people who are legally (but unjustly) and forcibly evicted from their homes, which often leads to homelessness in a country that has the resources to create homes for everyone.[13] Miriam Valverde details the draconian immigration policies of the Trump administration, where people are not only evicted from their homes, but also deported from this country.[14] Joe Soss et. al.,[15] and Loic Wacquant[16] provide comprehensive sociological analyses of the precarities of poverty, leaving millions of people food and housing insecure. Housing and food insecurity are linked to racism and classism, which are issues that undermine dwelling of the so-called lower classes. Georg Lukács,[17] Herbert Marcuse,[18] Dany-Robert Dufour,[19] Wendy

---

10. Augustine, *The Confessions of St. Augustine*, 17.

11. Dickinson, "Cur Deus Homo Sacer," 213.

12. One may question the theological idea of homelessness. Why would a good God create us to be homeless? Whenever questions about God arise, we can expect controversy and contestation. I am reluctant to make hypotheses about why or why not God did this or that. I think it is better to say that the ideas of homelessness and being at home reveal, in part, human existential experiences. What I will argue is that all creatures dwell, but not all creatures have the conscious experience of dwelling. Human beings, in particular, because of our agency, are able to shape our dwellings (structures, environment) and to provide hospitality for those in need of dwelling—physical, psychological, and spiritual. I would add that human beings are the only species I am aware of that have the agency to impact our global habitat, our global dwelling.

13. Desmond, *Evicted*.

14. Valverde, "Have Deportations Increased Under Donald Trump?"

15. Soss, Fording, and Schram, *Disciplining the Poor*.

16. Wacquant, *Punishing the Poor*.

17. Lukács, *History and Class Consciousness*.

18. Marcuse, *One-dimensional Man*.

19. Dufour, *The Art of Shrinking Heads*.

Brown,[20] Jerry Mander,[21] Sayak Valencia,[22] and others address political and economic realities that lead to psychological, political, and economic experiences of alienation. Political and economic alienation are implicated in dwelling—materially and socially. Add to this the violence committed when states unhouse their own people, as in the cases of evictions, ethnic cleansings, apartheid, as well as terroristic bombings of civilians.[23] Of course, there are the psychological traumas of physical and sexual abuse in every culture that leave people unhoused in their own bodies, as well as not feeling at home in their physical homes and in their relationships.

These tragic realities are routine, revealing that, as human beings, we do not need to depend on an ontology or theology of homelessness, because we are quite capable of furthering all kinds of homelessness for many people, while also fostering dwelling for select others. This anthropological fact takes on heightened seriousness in the Anthropocene Age. The Pentagon and CIA reports on global warming agree that the above tragedies will likely become more frequent as the effects of climate change deepen and broaden. Climate refugees[24] will impact every country. More to the point, the Anthropocene Age means that we are in real danger of making our one home uninhabitable for ourselves and millions of other species. Ironically and tragically, human beings, as ecological agents, are in the process of evicting ourselves from the very home on which we are dependent. In truth, human beings are vulnerable as a result of our collective actions, making the earth itself and other species vulnerable. If we are evicted, it will be the result of having failed to follow the existential rental agreement, which is to care for our only home.

The present and looming crises associated with climate change invite, if not demand, a radical political theology that places dwelling in the center of our thinking and being otherwise. More specifically, the Anthropocene Age will be an era of millions upon millions of refugees, not to mention the extinction or unhousing of millions of species. The figure of the refugee against the backdrop of climate change requires reimagining, as Agamben notes, our political philosophies, as well as our political theologies.[25] The

20. Brown, *Walled States, Waning Sovereignty*.

21. Mander, *The Capitalism Papers*.

22. Valencia, *Gore Capitalism*.

23. See Danner, *Stripping the Body Bare*.

24. The idea of the earth as our one home means that "there is no such thing as refugees" in the sense that there are people without a home. The earth is home to all. Of course, there are refugees in the sense that people have fled their home countries, seeking refuge in other lands.

25. It is worth mentioning that Agamben was familiar with Hannah Arendt's work,

existential and theological question is how might we dwell together (human beings and more-than-human beings) on this earth, which is the primary condition of all dwelling? In this chapter, I explore the issue of dwelling as it relates to political theology. I begin with some general comments about the topic of dwelling, briefly identifying some of its attributes. This is followed by a discussion of some of the problems of dwelling vis-à-vis political realities and the Anthropocene Age. From here I describe what I consider to be the existential roots of dwelling, namely, the psychosocial, developmental experiences of dwelling and the transition from this pre-political space to dwelling vis-à-vis the public political domain. This discussion provides the foundation for returning to a radical political theology as it relates to the question of dwelling and its problems. The aim in this last section is to further develop a radical political theology by relying on a theology of vulnerability.

A few comments are needed before beginning. One might wonder why begin with the topic of dwelling. Why not begin with sovereignty or freedom, since these are perennial topics in political theologies and philosophies? As indicated above, the premise in this chapter is that dwelling is constitutive to being human (as it is for other species). We initially dwell in the womb and with our caregivers, long before there is ever a question formulated about freedom, sovereignty or even what it means to dwell. The ethos is lived before we come to know it. And long before the first philosophers and priests toyed with the ideas of sovereignty and freedom, human beings found and created homes in various places. More importantly, our ethos, our dwelling in whatever forms, in whatever places, with whomever, depends on a viable earth. An uninhabitable earth means the question of dwelling is silent, vacant, voiding all other questions associated with the political. This is why dwelling precedes issues of sovereignty and freedom. I add here, and will say more in subsequent chapters, that the issues of sovereignty and freedom, having their own problems, are also about what it means to dwell. Second, as mentioned in the previous chapter, many scientists and others are working toward boosting human beings toward becoming an interplanetary species. If we are able to do this, it will mean creating earth-like conditions so that we can dwell in the inhospitable reality of space or on other planets or moons. It also will mean carrying with us the political questions of dwelling, since we will have to live life together—hence the need for a radical political theology.[26] Third, I wish to emphasize that if

which would include her views on refugees. See, Arendt, "We Refugees."

26. I am going to leave aside here the emerging technological revolution that may result in the integration of technology and biology—the evolution of Homo to Techno sapiens. Whether it is Homo or Techno sapiens, I suspect the political, social,

the fundamental premise is that dwelling is constitutive of being alive, then the ensuing premise is that embodied-relational and public-political forms of dwelling depend on care. Heidegger said, "Upon the earth and in it, the historical man grounds his dwelling, in the world."[27] The earth is indeed constitutive to our dwelling, but care is constitutive for ensuring a habitable earth that provides for the possibility of political dwelling. There is, in other words, an existential and theological imperative to care for the earth, each other, and other-than-human species *if* we are to continue to dwell. Finally, to do justice to the issue of dwelling would require a book, exploring its histories and numerous dimensions and attributes. My aim is to provide the contours of the notion of dwelling so that I can further develop a radical political theology for the Anthropocene Age.

## Dwelling

To dwell is a verb that means to live, reside, lodge, inhabit, or be domiciled. The verb presupposes the noun—home, house, (tents, trailers for those who are nomadic) etc. We do not simply live or dwell in houses, condos or apartments; we live in homes. Home, for many people, is more than a place; it evokes positive emotions and thoughts of belonging.[28] Home, then, is an experience of belonging in this place with these people. And yet, when asked, "Where is home?" it is not only a location, a place that we give, it is also linked to identity and ethos. Of course, the answer can refer to the present or the past, but, in any case, place accompanies identity and ethos. I grew up in Battle Creek, Michigan—a small, working-class city in the southernmost part of the state. Today I (we) make my home in Louisville, Kentucky— a larger city with southern and northern roots. While both are different homes, they are part of the U.S., which points to place and identity as an American citizen. My home, I answer when asked while traveling overseas, is the U.S. I can have, in other words, fond feelings and memories linked to all of these places of home. I might have ambivalent feelings about them as well. Let me quickly add that for people who are nomadic, home is an experience that may not be tied to a single place, but to a geographical region. Moreover, the experience of home may be more closely associated with the

---

and environmental issues of dwelling will remain, though likely in different forms. See Bingaman, *Pastoral and Spiritual Care in a Digital Age.*

27. Heidegger in Gauthier, *Martin Heidegger, Emanuel Lévinas, and the Politics of Dwelling,* 60.

28. Helmut Plessner writes that dwelling as "belonging to a people is an essential trait of the human, like being able to say I and You." Plessner, *Political Anthropology,* 86.

identity and ethos of the people than to a place.[29] This means dwelling is fundamentally a matter of belonging that is, nevertheless, tied to a place. Let me again stress that dwelling as the experience of belonging—as identity, ethos, and place—is completely dependent on a habitable earth.

There are two other interrelated features of dwelling as belonging. The first is that belonging necessarily means plurality.[30] Recall that the recognition of Others as persons means that there is an excess to the person's experience of suchness or singularity, which exceeds our ability to represent an individual.[31] The consequence of this is that every creature is unique and the corollary is that sameness is an illusion—a very dangerous illusion vis-à-vis dwelling.[32] Belonging, then, when referring to human beings and more-than-human beings, means diversity. An attending feature of diversity is that belonging accompanies contestation, not harmony. Even in loving families there are contestations, as people struggle to dwell together. The same is true for every group or polis, which is why Hannah Arendt argued that there must be opportunities for forgiveness or repair for an agonistic polis to thrive.[33] To belong, to dwell together fundamentally involves suchness/singularity, diversity, contestation, and repair.

Dwelling is much more complicated than our feelings or experiences of place and belonging. The physical sciences have a great deal to do with our dwelling. Engineers, architects, chemical engineers, electrical engineers, and others are needed for the construction and maintenance of houses (apartments, condos) that will be our homes, which includes the surrounding infrastructures. Naturally, we are not simply dependent on scientists and engineers for dwelling. There are bankers and lawyers who loan money and provide legal documents to own a home or condo.[34] Property laws are inter-

29. Richardson, *Place and Identity*, 77–79.

30. Karl Popper makes clear that a flourishing society depends on diversity or plurality. When belonging becomes connected to sameness (vis-à-vis ethos, identity), then we can be assured this is not an open society but one that will have one segment of the population flourishing at the expense of different Others. Popper, *The Open Society and Its Enemies*.

31. Dickinson, "On the Coming Philosophy," 34.

32. Aristotle, in criticizing Plato's polis, argued that unity based on sameness will result in the polis' demise. By contrast, a polis "by its nature is some sort of aggregation," comprising different kinds of people. This view is reminiscent of Agamben's and Arendt's contention that a polis flourishes because it is based on plurality. Barker, *The Politics of Aristotle*, 40–41.

33. Arendt, *The Promise of Politics*.

34. Katharina Pistor depicts how for centuries capital has been coded by lawyers to protect the wealthier. This is evident in the very notion of dwelling such that people are able to secure wealth through property, including houses, while those who are renting

twined with having a home, which was not always the case in history. For those who reside in apartments, there are rental agreements and payments, which, likewise, are based in property laws—laws that favor the owners and not the tenants.[35] To live in our homes, we need utilities, garbage pickup, streets, as well as supplies for food and other items so that we may dwell. Our homes are connected to other homes in our neighborhood, comprising a polis. If we are poor, the physical resources around our homes may not be conducive to exercise and engaging with our neighbors, which undermines our experiences of dwelling. Moreover, dwelling at home for poor people is harmed by anxiety about food insecurity or the possibility of being evicted. We may dwell in our homes, though our dwelling in the polis is diminished, because of a lack of political and economic rights. To dwell in a polis, we also need some level of physical security that is typically provided by the police. Yet, for some people, insecurity impedes the experience of dwelling, which can be the result of crime and excessive policing.[36] To dwell, then, reveals the intersections of science, politics (local, national, world), and economics, as well as our essential interdependency.

Implicit in the discussion above is the precarity of dwelling.[37] To dwell, to belong, is linked to human vulnerability and it is this vulnerability that establishes the existential motivation to dwell together and the existential imperative to care.[38] Vulnerability is an admission of one's need for the Other to dwell. Newborns leave the Edenic home of the womb and are thrust into a world that William James said is "one great blooming buzzing confusion."[39] While this is addressed in greater detail below, for now let me say that the infant is completely vulnerable and absolutely dependent on the caring ministrations of parents for experiences of being-at-home in this new and confusing place. The infant is like a turtle without a shell, and the parents

are unable to do so. In addition, it is important to mention that home is not identical to property, though since the rise of capitalism and what Piketty calls proprietarian societies property ownership has become nearly identical to dwelling. An entire chapter could be written on the relation between dwelling, capital, proprietarian societies, and inequality, but I do not have the space and time to address this in this book. Pistor, *The Code of Capital.* See also Piketty, *Capital and Ideology.*

35. See Thomas Piketty on ideology and property. Piketty, *Capital and Ideology.*

36. Goldberg, *The Threat of Race.*

37. Richardson, *Place and Identity,* 9.

38. Dickinson, in writing about Agamben's work, said it is poverty "that is also humanity's most natural state of dwelling." I understand this to mean that when we are born, we are impoverished in the sense of being in need and it is this vulnerableness or neediness that initiates the impulse to dwell with Others—Others who will meet those needs. Dickinson, "Immanence as Revelation," 100.

39. James, *Principles of Psychology,* vol.1, 488.

provide the protection the child needs to survive and thrive—to dwell. Even though we develop our psychosocial capacities, dwelling and experiences of dwelling are never completely assured. We see every year that natural (e.g., tornados, hurricanes) and human-made (e.g., fires) disasters can literally unhouse people. Wars unhouse people, creating waves of refugees seeking more secure places to dwell. Political and economic oppression can result in people being evicted from their homes and even deported. Diverse forms of interpersonal violence and exploitation contribute to trauma, which can be understood as psychological unhousing, wherein persons do not feel at home in their bodies or in relation to others. And, of course, dying and death are the great unhousing events in every life. Tragically, the Anthropocene Age signals the unhousing of millions of species and likely human beings as well. All creatures dwell and all are vulnerable to being unhoused.

Another associated attribute of the experience of dwelling is the issue of quality. It is not, in other words, a question of merely dwelling as survival, but also a question of whether our dwelling contributes to flourishing. There is, then, an evaluative feature of dwelling based on our perceptions and on material, political, and economic factors. A wealthy person can have a beautiful home, but be miserable and isolated. Dickens' Ebenezer Scrooge was a wealthy man and had a genuinely nice home, though not well cared for because of his miserliness. He was deeply miserable at home and with others. His poor, oft-berated clerk, Bob Cratchit, while poor, seemed to have positive experiences of dwelling with his family despite their precarity. This is not to say that poor people are likely to have more positive experiences of dwelling than wealthy people. Rather, the point is that our experiences of dwelling are largely contingent on the quality of our relationships and material well-being, though both are negatively impacted by poverty, racism, etc. This said, worsening material, political, and economic conditions undermine our perceptions and experiences of dwelling vis-à-vis our flourishing.[40]

Dwelling, as an experience and perception, is related to belonging as disposition. This can be understood in two ways. First, I may be ensconced in a nice house, but not, like Scrooge, be disposed to dwell there. Some people, for many reasons, may not be open to being at home. Scrooge certainly lived in his house, but it seemed to me he never really dwelt there. I recall, as a young lieutenant, living for six months in the cramped space of the Bachelor Officers Quarters (BOQ). I was grateful to have a place, though I was not disposed or open to dwelling there. It was merely a functional place

40. The political and economic exploitation of people undermine their physical homes as well as their experiences of psychosocial dwelling. For examples of this see Hedges and Sacco, *Days of Destruction, Days of Revolt*.

to reside until I moved to my first assignment, where I could make a home. It also may be the case that one is not disposed to dwell in one place versus another. Dave, for instance, lived in Germany for three years, but never tried to make it a home. He kept pining for his home in Iowa. Second, Lévinas, like Heidegger, believed that homelessness "is [humanity's] primordial condition,"[41] which, for him, is a reminder of man's failure to meet his obligations to the Other."[42] This feeling of homelessness, then, is universal for Lévinas and, while it is a reminder of our failure to welcome the Other, it is also the "impetus for human fraternity" or belonging.[43] Fraternity, for Lévinas, is not, like Heidegger, contingent on shared place, identity, and ethos, but rather on overcoming our rootedness and possessing the disposition of being hospitable or welcoming to Others, to Strangers in their singularity.[44] There is, then, the disposition to welcome and being welcomed, which Dave ignored and subsequently felt homesick. The disposition to welcome, to be hospitable to Others, is foundational for our dwelling together, which means accepting difference, embracing, not simply tolerating, diversity.[45] Indeed, the very first experience of dwelling rests on parents' disposition to welcome their children—children who are like and unlike their parents. The failure to do so leads to trauma, which means children will not experience dwelling, but rather the anxiety of being unhoused vis-à-vis being at home in their own bodies and being at home with others. The trauma of being unhoused can initiate a lifelong search for an experience of *being* at home.

While more is said below, there are two other attributes of dwelling, namely, care and faith. When we reside with others, there must be some basic level of care for us to have the perception and experience of dwelling. And for strangers to be welcomed, there must be some rudimentary level of care manifested in our recognition and treatment of the Other as a person or in our recognition of the suchness of other-than-human animals. This may be something that takes place in our own homes, as well as in the larger society that cares for and welcomes immigrants and travelers. A society that possesses sufficient care to welcome Others/refugees[46] also demonstrates

---

41. In Gauthier, *Martin Heidegger, Emmanuel Lévinas, and the Politics of Dwelling*, 113.

42. Gauthier, *Martin Heidegger, Emmanuel Lévinas, and the Politics of Dwelling*, 129.

43. Gauthier, *Martin Heidegger, Emmanuel Lévinas, and the Politics of Dwelling*, 114.

44. Lévinas, *Totality and Infinity*, 156.

45. Brown, *Regulating Aversion*.

46. Michael Northcott has a similar view, arguing that "the first duty of those with resources to tackle the growing climate crisis is to love the strangers who are already climate refugees." My only alteration would be to say we are to care. Love, it seems to me, is a pretty high bar. Northcott, "On Going Gently into the Anthropocene," 34.

civic care that founds people dwelling together. In every polis, in each *ekkle-sia*, foundational questions are asked and answered with varying levels of satisfaction: Is there sufficient civic care among the residents (citizens and all others) of the society to feel like they belong, to have a sense that they dwell with others together, and to have the disposition to welcome Others? In decent societies,[47] there is sufficient civic care among residents to provide a sense of dwelling together as a people, diverse as this society might be. By contrast, indecent societies oppress and marginalize groups of people (citizens and immigrants), undermining their sense of dwelling—both physical and psychosocial—while privileging the dwelling of people in power.[48]

The relational or civic care demonstrated to maintain a viable polis and experiences of dwelling is also connected to the material aspects of dwelling. We must necessarily care for the dwelling itself, whether this refers to my immediate dwelling place (house, condo, apartment, etc.) or my neighborhood, city, state, and, indeed, the larger world. But it is not simply my ability to care for my dwelling. It is also having access to the material resources that will enable us to care for our homes and our neighbors. The prevalence of classism and racism in the U.S. means that large segments of people do not have resources either to secure habitable dwellings or to maintain their dwellings.

This suggests that human beings, like other animals, have the capacity to make a home, which, in our case, can mean we also can contribute to undermining the habitat we need to dwell. Alfred North Whitehead remarked that "Any physical object which by its influence deteriorates its environment, commits suicide."[49] We can therefore make our homes uninhabitable because of our lack of care and, in the process, unhouse ourselves and others. A person, for instance, may not have the resources to care for the house he lives in, only to find that the city has condemned the house, forcing him and his family to find a new place to reside. There are also macro examples of human beings making places inhospitable for their own dwelling or the dwelling of other species (e.g., Chernobyl, Three Mile Island, vast dead zones like the Mississippi Delta). A lack of civic care also can degrade conditions in certain areas of the city or state (e.g., environmental racism),

47. Margalit, *The Decent Society*. Decent societies do not humiliate their citizens. As Nancy Fraser and Axel Honneth note, political misrecognition, which is often tied to humiliation, also is dependent on institutions that negatively impact distribution of resources. Fraser and Honneth, *Redistribution or Recognition?*

48. Racism and classism undermine persons' social-political experiences of dwelling. For instance, Alfred Lubrano writes of his experiences of not feeling at home in political-economic spaces associated with middle and upper classes. Lubrano, *Limbo*.

49. Whitehead, in Wood, *Reoccupy the Earth*, 65.

making it more difficult for some citizens to dwell because of the physical deterioration of the infrastructure or simply the lack of infrastructure.

Care, then, is constitutive to dwelling, which makes human beings incredibly interesting, but not superior, creatures. By this I mean, we seem to be a species that has the agency to care directly and deliberately for our surroundings and, by implication, the agency *not* to do so. Put another way, we are the only creature that can, through our agency, make the earth vulnerable to being uninhabitable and, in the process, make ourselves and other beings vulnerable to being unhoused. Given this, we might consider that instead of Sartre's claim that we are condemned to be free, we might say that we also are condemned and commanded (existential imperative) to care. Of course, the sad fact is that we have the dubious distinction of being the only species to be the cause of an extinction event. This is why there is an existential and theological imperative to care for the earth and its residents, because the failure to care will mean the loss of a habitable earth for ourselves and other species.[50] An uninhabitable earth means non-existence, non-dwelling vis-à-vis human beings and millions of other species. In addition, the imperative to care for other species and the earth, in my view, undermines the anthropocentric narcissism that undergirds much of the philosophical and theological premises that human beings have dominion over the earth and all other species.[51] Let me be absolutely clear; *the agency to care is not and has never been dominion, but rather one of collaboration and cooperation with other human beings and their environment.*

The other side of the notion of care is faith, which is another necessary attribute of dwelling. Faith, existentially understood, implies a relation founded on the dialectical pairs of belief-disbelief, trust-distrust, loyalty-disloyalty, and hope-hopelessness.[52] To dwell at home or in the polis, both as an experience, disposition, and a physical reality, requires a degree of trust, loyalty, and hope. A married couple dwells together as a result of their mutual trust and fidelity. Distrust and betrayal will result in them no longer

50. Gilles Deleuze and Felix Guattari argue that human beings must become animals if we are to heal the false split between humanity and nature. Alienation from nature will be evident in the discussion on sovereignty and the West's political philosophizing since Plato and Aristotle. There are other cultures, past and present, that do not depend on alienating nature for human belonging. Deleuze and Guattari, *A Thousand Plateaus*, chapter 10.

51. See Smith, *Against Ecological Sovereignty*, xii. See also, Wood, *Reoccupy the Earth*, 203f.

52. H. R. Niebuhr is the source of this view of the dynamics of faith, though I added the pair, hope-hopelessness. Niebuhr, *Faith on Earth*. For a more in-depth discussion of the relation between care and faith see LaMothe, *Care of Souls, Care of Polis*.

dwelling together as a couple, even under the same roof. They may live together, but not be at home with each other.

Faith and dwelling are also related to the polis. Often, as citizens, we take for granted the civic faith that is necessary for our residing together. The importance of civic faith becomes apparent in situations where groups of people are deemed to be untrustworthy and disloyal to the country and its people. Treason is a breach of this civic faith, and the punishment (exile, prison, death) reflects the degree to which treason has threatened to undermine our collective dwelling, which is founded on civic faith and care.

Civic or social faith includes having confidence and trust in our perceptions of the world and the polis, which are largely based on possessing a common symbol system. We unconsciously expect and trust that we share common beliefs and meanings, and we have confidence in their truth, which enables us to dwell together. The proliferation of lies, half-truths, and deceptions undermine our experiences of dwelling together. This can happen at the level of a married couple dwelling together or in the case of the larger society. For instance, most of us are familiar with the term "gaslighting," which is derived from the 1938 play *Gas Light*.[53] The term refers to an individual who sows seeds of doubt such that other persons question their perception, memory, experience, etc. Gaslighting is not only an example of relational alienation; it undermines a person's experience, perception of, and confidence in dwelling. This can happen at more macro levels, such as when an opportunistic, narcissistic leader consistently sows seeds of doubt about reality, leaving many citizens confused and uncertain about what is real or true and what is not. The leader fragments and polarizes, undermining our civic faith and experiences of dwelling together in the polis.

Implicit in civic faith is the importance of language, since it is integral to our individual and shared perceptions and experiences, which, in turn, is necessary for experiences of dwelling together,[54] as well as engaging in cooperative efforts to construct materially the structures necessary for dwelling. One might say that the tower of Babel was not completed because there was no shared language to found cooperation. From a different angle, in the earliest moments of life, parents are communicating to their infants in a language that infants cannot understand. These proto conversations involve speaking and acting together, which eventually results in children learning the language that grounds dwelling together. In one sense, language dwells within us and we dwell in the language of our people. Language, then, is

53. "Gas Light," on Wikipedia; https://en.wikipedia.org/wiki/Gas_Light.

54. Adam Kotsko argues that what is at stake in "language is not knowledge but ethics." Kotsko, "Perhaps Psychoanalysis," 139.

part of civic care and faith. We have confidence in it and to use it so that we might dwell together.

Of course, George Orwell,[55] among others, knew that language can corrupt a society, undermining civic care, civic faith, and collective dwelling. During his lifetime, Nazi Germany and the Soviet Union revealed the divisive and violent effects of politicians and others using language to completely manage dwelling and, in many cases, destroy dwelling of individuals and groups of people. Orwell was concerned with not only totalitarian regimes, but also with democracies. Today we have clear examples of profoundly corrupt and sociopathic politicians who undermine social faith and cooperation by using language that distort facts or worse present "social truths" that are blatant lies. The lies bind one group of people, while alienating others. The result is a fracturing of political dwelling.

While civic faith is important for dwelling together as a people, it is also important with regard to the physical realities of dwelling. When we do not care for the physical dwelling itself, we betray our responsibility to care for ourselves and others. We have demonstrated, in other words, that we are not trustworthy with regard to exercising our agency to care for dwelling. Let me offer a few short illustrations. Parents have an existential responsibility to care for their children, which necessarily includes ensuring that the physical dwelling is conducive to children's survival and flourishing. Raising a child in a meth house is not simply a demonstration of a lack of care for the children; it also is bad faith in relation to both the children and parental responsibility to care for the home and experiences of dwelling together. Of course, political, economic, and social realities can make it exceedingly difficult for some parents to provide safe homes for their children, which is not their breach of faith, but the larger society's breach of both civic faith and civic care because the society does not provide the necessary conditions for people to care for their children. If we extend the example to the earth as the dwelling place for human beings and all other species, we find that the realities of climate change reflect the betrayal of human beings (mostly wealthier nations) to exercise their agency in caring for the earth. This betrayal emerges out of the existential reality of human agency and limited freedom, which are inextricably joined to the existential, categorical (theological as well) imperative to care for the earth. We betray not simply this imperative, but ourselves and other species because our failure to care for our only dwelling threatens not simply our existence, but also the existence of millions of other species.

55. Orwell, *Politics and the English Language.*

In summary, to dwell is a verb that presupposes a noun (house, home, apartment, condo, etc.). Dwelling indicates that one resides in a particular physical place and locale with others, which implies a shared identity and ethos, but not always. There are occasions when strangers dwell with us. Whether we dwell with people we know or with strangers, the physical aspects of dwelling (houses, apartments, infrastructure, etc.) reveal the complex intersectional realities of human dwelling, as well as human interdependency and vulnerability. Physical and natural sciences, economics, politics, engineering, architecture, etc., play a role in our ability to dwell. I also pointed out that dwelling, as identity and place, is both a perception and experience, which further points to the reality of the quality of our dwelling—both as an experience and in terms of the physical locale. I also noted that dwelling is a matter of disposition. That is, the experience of dwelling depends on the disposition of openness with regard to being open to this place and people, as well as hospitality[56] to strangers (including other species), which includes other species. Dwelling, I noted further, is a matter of interpersonal and civic care and faith that are contingent on, but not completely determined by language. Both care and faith are also central in terms of the earth as the very foundation of our dwelling. An uninhabitable earth means the issue of dwelling is non-existent. As creatures endowed with agency and limited freedom, whether we like it or not, we have the existential imperative to care for the earth and its residents, which by all accounts we are in the process of betraying. Dwelling, in short, is a matter of survival and flourishing.

## Problems of Dwelling in the Polis

Before describing dwelling in light of a radical political theology, it is important to discuss some of the problems of dwelling, some of which have been alluded to above. These problems are perennial, even if we find solutions to address them, because human beings are variable creatures, capable of avoiding responsibilities to care. The aim is not to offer definitive solutions, but for us to consider acting and thinking otherwise. Toward this end, I identify what I consider to be a number of key problems associated with dwelling.

This may appear overly simplistic, but the most significant obstacle to dwelling on the earth for ourselves and other species is Us. We are the

56. I have mentioned the importance of a common language for dwelling to occur. It is also important to note that hospitality does not mean there is a common language. We can be hospitable to strangers, enabling them to dwell among us.

meteor that crashes into the earth, beginning a devastating, yet slow extinction event. To understand this, I begin with what I consider to be a founding (largely Western) problem of human dwelling on the earth, a problem that is linked to other obstacles that impede human and other species dwelling. For Giorgio Agamben, there is a "deep ontological rift . . . between animal and human"[57] and it is this rift, this alienation,[58] that has been a central theme in Western political philosophies and theologies. Agamben writes:

> It is as if determining the border between human and animal were not just one question among many discussed by philosophers and theologians, scientists and politicians, but rather a fundamental metaphysico-political operation in which alone something like 'man' can be decided upon and produced. If animal life and human life could be superimposed perfectly, then neither man nor animal—and, perhaps, not even the divine— would any longer be thinkable.[59]

This ongoing drive in the West to differentiate between human beings and animals, which is a project of philosophy, theology, and some of the sciences,[60] leads to "a radical and total discontinuity between human and nonhuman"[61] and, consequently, the privileging of human beings over all other species.[62] Human dwelling, then, is seemingly based on exclusion and alienation, which are supported by the illusions of anthropocentric narcissism, independence, superiority, and dominion. These illusions and radical alienation are continually produced by apparatuses or anthropological machines of domination or subjugation vis-à-vis animals, which are the necessary step for exploitation, slaughter, and extinction. In the previous chapter I discussed theologies of subjugation/subordination, which here I

57. Dickinson, "The Absence of Gender," 173.

58. See also Tully, "Life Sustains Life," 164–74.

59. Agamben, *The Open*, 21. Agamben also argues that if we can make these apparatuses of the anthropological machine inoperative, it will "show the central emptiness" of the proposition that human beings are superior and privileged beings. *The Open*, 92.

60. We can see this split in influential figures like Sigmund Freud. In one of his later writings, he contended that the aim of civilization is "to defend us against nature," as if "nature" is our enemy. Freud, *The Future of an Illusion*, 15.

61. Kompridis, "Nonhuman Agency and Human Normativity," 252.

62. Philosophers Deleuze and Guattari agree with Agamben's claim, arguing that "We make no distinction between man and nature . . . man and nature are not like two opposite terms confronting each other . . . rather they are one and the same essential reality." Deleuze and Guattari, *Anti-Oedipus*, 4–5.

am arguing are linked to our social constructions and subsequent treatment of "non-human" life, undermining their dwelling and eventually our own.[63]

The impact of what Agamben calls the anthropological machine with regard to dwelling is deep and broad in the Anthropocene Age. As mentioned earlier, it is expected that a million species will become extinct by 2050.[64] We not only have a history of displacing species from their habitats; we are also making their habitats uninhabitable. Someone might remark that this is fine because human beings have to survive. Land development for housing, cutting down forests and jungles for wood and for farming, mass production of animals for meat, eggs, cheese, etc., draining marsh areas for human cultivation, etc. results in the destruction of habitats and the exploitation of animals (if they survive), all based on the logic of human survival, as well as the logic of privileging human beings over all other creatures. In my reading of Agamben, all this is consciously and unconsciously justified because we construct human beings as superior and our survival is, therefore, privileged over all other beings. As Leland De La Durantaye states the biopolitical machine "serves to define human in it distance from animal,"[65] which is a prelude to objectifying other-than-human species. Fair enough, but some human beings are quickly learning that the earth is a living system and it is living precisely because of biodiversity. By destroying habitats and other species, we are diminishing the capacity of the earth to be a viable dwelling for human survival. The tragedy, for human beings, is that we will have unhoused ourselves because of the anthropocentric, narcissistic logic of the anthropological machine and the political philosophies and theologies of subjugation/subordination that support it.[66]

63. There are any of number of texts, including works by Agamben, that use the terms "non-man" or "non-human" to refer to animals. Identification of a sentient being or form of life through negation is not benign. There are all kinds of examples in history of dominant groups discussing other groups in terms of this negation (e.g., non-white, non-Catholic, non-European, etc.). While this negation does not always accompany violence, exploitation, and alienation, it does contribute to disidentification. A more positive appellation is other-than-human (or more-than-human), which, of course, can accompany disidentification, but my hope is less tilting toward the negative.

64. Leahy, "One Million Species at Risk of Extinction, UN Report Warns."

65. De La Durantaye, *Giorgio Agamben*, 334.

66. It is important to mention that not all philosophies and theologies exhibit the belief that there is an ontological rift (alienation) between human beings and animals. Some native cultures demonstrate the close relation between animals and humans, which leads to adaptation to the environment instead of exploitation. To be sure, native peoples kill animals for food and other necessities, but this is not because they see themselves as superior or that they are to exercise dominion over animals and the land. See Lévi-Strauss, *Totemism*. Also, Lévi-Strauss, *The Savage Mind*. I add, some theologies, as Agamben suggests, do not operate out of the anthropological machinery of

Sergei Prozorov notes that Agamben has a response to this exclusion of nature from the political. "What Agamben proposes instead," Prozorov writes, "could be termed 'unbecoming' both animal and man, ceasing the very process of becoming this or that but rather dwelling in the zone where humanity and animality are not separable and hence no difference between them is possible to mark."[67] In other words, "Agamben focuses on the possibilities of being-with on the basis of nothing but being-thus, a being together of man and animal."[68] I will say more about this later, but for the moment Agamben's perspective undercuts the anthropological machine that fosters the illusions of anthropocentrism and narcissism. Moreover, his view is that human agency is both acting in the polis and in nature, which, from my perspective, accompanies the responsibility to adhere to the existential imperative to care. Or, as Mick Smith argues, "In becoming political, nature is not eroded, but it too is recognized in its plurality and its natality. Acting into nature must, like acting into the political sphere, involve responsibility for others, concern about effects, and making choices."[69]

This problem of dwelling vis-à-vis the exclusion of nature is closely related to the political problems between and among human beings.[70] Human beings are valuing creatures, capable of constructing identities[71] and relations in terms of beliefs in superiority and inferiority, which become the basis of dwelling based on exclusion and alienation. Consider Edward Baptist's historical analysis of the brutal slave labor camps in the South during the height of slavery in the U.S.[72] Human beings were constructed as non-human, as animals to be exploited, because they were socially constructed as inferior beings. Their dwelling was in the service of masters and the apparatuses of white superiority. A slave was/is an excluded-included Other, who was/is not allowed to dwell in the civic world[73] and was/is precariously

subjugation/subordination and exclusion (e.g., St. Francis).

67. Prozorov, *Agamben and Politics*, 172. See also Nussbaum, *Political Emotions*, 159.

68. Prozorov, *Agamben and Politics*, 173

69. Smith, *Against Ecological Sovereignty*, 158.

70. Mauelshagen, "Bridging the Great Divide," 96–99.

71. Dickinson notes that Agamben argues that communal identifications, which are necessary for belonging, "take root in our ability to exclude others." I think another way to say this is that identification is necessarily based in disidentification, which I argued earlier is the basis for creating a space for the Other to appear. I think it is better to say that communal identifications are based in the dialectical tension between identification and disidentification, which does not necessarily mean exclusion. Dickinson, *Cur Deus Homo Sacer*, 202.

72. Baptist, *The Half Has Never Been Told*.

73. Patterson, *Slavery and Social Death*.

positioned to be unhoused, literally and figuratively. While slavery officially ended after the Civil War, African Americans continued to be constructed and recognized by most white people as less than human and, therefore, this justified, from a white racist perspective, decades of Jim Crow laws, lynching, rape, and economic mistreatment.[74] This human political tendency to construct others as inferior is evident also in classism, which is exacerbated by capitalism.[75] There are other occasions of misrecognition. Human beings who are seen as less than American citizens can be evicted and deported. Those who are citizens (e.g., the "homeless" and the chronically poor) can be constructed as having less value given their place in a market economy, which results in having less access to the material resources necessary for survival and flourishing.[76] Others who are civically unhoused are those caught in the grips of a carceral state.[77] Inequalities are largely the result of systemic misrecognitions, wherein some groups are deemed superior or more valued, while other groups are constructed as inferior. The society's disciplinary regimes perpetuate these inequalities. Constructing people as inferior impacts their psychological sense of dwelling. While I will say more below, negative societal attributions can lead people to feeling unhoused in their own bodies or the public, because of a lack of self-esteem, self-confidence, and self-respect.[78]

The dynamics of the anthropological machine (e.g., anthropocentrism) Agamben refers to parallels the apparatuses that are part of racism, classism, and sexism or any other symbol system that constructs one group of human beings as superior and legitimately privileged, while other groups are deemed inferior and "legitimately" exploited. This inevitably leads to political communities, wherein the dialectical tension between identification and disidentification collapses vis-à-vis Others (particular human beings or other than human beings), which means that these inhospitable communities are dependent for their dwelling on exclusion and the exploitation of included-excluded Others.[79] For Agamben, the fundamental

---

74. McGuire, *At the Dark End of the Street*.

75. See Sayer, *The Moral Significance of Class*; Lukács, *History and Class Consciousness*: Fussell, *Class*: Harmon, *A People's History of the World*.

76. See Fraser and Honneth, *Redistribution or Recognition?* These philosophers argue that misrecognition has negative impacts on the distribution of society's resources.

77. Taylor, *The Executed God*.

78. See Baldwin, *Notes of a Native Son*; Baldwin, *The Fire Next Time*; Coates, *Between the World and Me*. JanMohamed, *The Death-bound Subject*.

79. I wish to stress here that there is a key difference between Agamben's idea that communal identity is based on exclusion and what I am saying about the dialectical tension between identification and disidentification. Not all communities, not all

political task vis-à-vis dwelling is moving beyond "the logic of the excluded figure,"[80] hence the need for the figure of the refugee in reconceptualizing political philosophy.

One might ask whether the problem of dwelling vis-à-vis recognition is contingent on a more basic problem of dwelling, which, from Agamben's perspective, is exclusion. It appears that to dwell means that some people (and other than human creatures) cannot dwell with us, which also suggests that dwelling is inextricably tied to identity (my people) and place.[81] It seems logical that we must exclude some people from dwelling, because if everyone dwells here, we might lose our identity and place. The Israelites gained their dwelling place in the promised land through divine-sanctioned ethnic cleansing (Exod 23:20–33). Millennia later, Christians migrated to the shores of another continent, displacing and killing many of the native people who dwelled in and on this land for centuries. Those who survived became included-excluded Others, shunted to the side and sequestered on unfamiliar lands. So-called illegal immigrants in the U.S. are excluded-included Others, hiding on the fringe of society, misrecognized and denied basic services. For many Americans, immigrants are a threat to American dwelling—identity and place.

That recognition, identity, and place are aspects of dwelling and, more often than not, a perennial problem, does not mean we are determined by them or that human dwelling itself is necessarily based in exclusion. I want to address this in three ways before moving on to other problems. First, Lévinas constructed a philosophy that was based on the human capacity to welcome Others, to be hospitable to strangers. For Lévinas, "the home rises to the fullness of its dignity when it is used as an instrument of welcome."[82] Of course, many of us can recall times when we, as strangers, were welcomed or we welcomed strangers, but is this possible on a larger scale? Can a society be that open? In the eighteenth century, Emmanuel Kant believed that a city or state could be cosmopolitan, suggesting that identity is not necessarily contingent on place or dwelling.[83] A present-day illustration of this is Kwame Appiah's view of cosmopolitanism.[84] Yet, if we turn to

---

dwelling, is based on or dependent on exclusion, as he seems to suggest. See Agamben, *The Coming Community*.

80. Dickinson, "Gestures of Text and Violence," 59.

81. Exclusion for Agamben is a central feature of the anthropological machine and, in particular, the exclusion of nature or animals to make distinctions and to assert dominion. Agamben, *The Open*.

82. Gauthier, *Martin Heidegger, Emanuel Lévinas, and the Politics of Dwelling*, 11.

83. Kant, *Idea for a Universal History from a Cosmopolitan Point of View*.

84. Appiah, *Cosmopolitanism*.

Agamben, we see an underlying difficulty to cosmopolitanism. He argues "what the State cannot tolerate in any way . . . is that the singularities form a community without affirming an identity, that human beings co-belong (co-dwell) without any representable condition of belonging . . . For the State, therefore, what is important is never singularity as such, but only its inclusion in some identity."[85] Yet, this negative view accompanies an intriguing idea in Agamben. The coming community or inoperative community of "whatever singularities subtracts itself from the myriad of positive identities that divide its members and thus establishes itself as something new that is literally inaccessible to the apparatuses governing the situation and remains impervious to their grasp."[86] A cosmopolitan society or a coming community, where identity is not the sole criterion for dwelling, will be resisted by the State and its disciplinary regimes. But is it possible?

One might immediately recall the community in Acts, as being outside the Imperial apparatuses in establishing a coming community where identity or predicates were not the sole condition of dwelling together. Or in Galatians, where we read that the kingdom of God will not be based on identity or predicates. Do we have to wait for the kingdom to see glimpses of this political reality? No. A current secular example of this is a Norwegian town, Longyearbyen, where visas are not required and there are fifty nationalities among the population of over two thousand.[87] They have, in other words, found ways to welcome people with different languages and cultures in this one place, dwelling together amidst numerous identities and respecting the other-than-human beings who dwell on the island. I suspect the ethos of the people is that whoever comes and lives there belongs. Belonging is not contingent on one's identity. There is also the sense that everyone in this remote place is a guest, indicating that the animals are the first dwellers and are considered important and necessary, such that residents respect their suchness or singularity.

Related to this is a second point about identity and place with regard to dwelling. Understandably, human beings tend to be parochial in terms of identity and place. This is not necessarily a problem, but often is. If we confront the realities of the Anthropocene Age, as well as its attending anthropocentrism and narcissism, we might retain the particular (place, identity, and ethos), while embracing the universal. By this I mean recognizing that there is only one place to dwell and that is the earth. This fact

85. Agamben, *The Coming Community*, 85.

86. Prozorov, *Agamben and Politics*, 142.

87. Longyearbyen, Norway; https://en.visitsvalbard.com/visitor-information/destinations/longyearbyen.

means that every human being belongs and no one is a "refugee." We all dwell on this earth together and recognition of this should ideally lead to greater openness in welcoming those who seek to dwell "here" because they are climate refugees. As Lévinas remarked, "But he or she who emigrates is wholly human: the migration of man does not destroy, does not demolish the meaning of Being."[88] Nevertheless, we recognize that the "calamity of the rightless (refugee) is not that they are deprived of life, liberty, and the pursuit of happiness, or of equality before the law and freedom of opinion . . . but that they no longer belong to any community whatsoever."[89] Thinking and being otherwise means, in this instance, recognizing refugees as persons and as such they are welcomed, because they belong here. This said, I am not talking simply about privileging human beings. All creatures depend on the earth as a dwelling place. The challenge is to accept this and to find ways to adapt so that creatures can dwell in and on this one place.

Thirdly, the polis is not necessarily based on exclusion, even though this seems to be a problem with regard to dwelling. To reframe this, the problem of dwelling vis-à-vis exclusion is better understood in terms of the dialectical tension between identification and disidentification. Disidentification, not me, is linked to an indeterminate knowing that creates a space for the other to appear in their suchness. The collapse of this dialectical tension is evident in communities that are dependent on exclusion for their sense of belonging. In these communities, belonging is based on identification with other members and disidentification of Others (including nature)—exclusion and a concomitant loss of civic care and faith. By contrast, maintaining a dialectical tension means that Others can appear. My point here is analogous to Agamben's idea that the "only accurate representation was one that exposed its own inability to accurately portray what it tries to represent."[90] When this occurs, it is likely that the dialectical tension remains and there is sufficient space for other human beings and other-than-human beings to appear and to dwell with us in their suchness. The political community of Longyearbyen contributes to a sense of dwelling that is based on maintaining this dialectical tension, thereby avoiding the problem of exclusion (this includes nature) as the source of belonging together. It can be considered to be a polis "that rejects all legal-political determinations of identity."[91]

So far, I have identified problems of dwelling that, in my view, have been evident since human beings gathered together to form communities—at

88. Lévinas, *Totality and Infinity*, 11.

89. Arendt, *The Origins of Totalitarianism*, 295.

90. Dickinson, *Cur Deus Homo Sacer*, 204.

91. Zerbe, "On the Exigency of a Messianic Ecclesia," 270.

least most communities.[92] I want to touch briefly on three interrelated significant problems (and obstacles) with regard to dwelling in the Anthropocene Age, namely, capitalism, nationalism, and imperialism.[93] The origins of capitalism, Ellen Woods argues, is in sixteenth-century England, beginning with agrarian legislative "reforms" that eventually moved to Europe and elsewhere as a result of the European colonization of other peoples and lands.[94] The effect of these reforms in England (and elsewhere) led to the displacement of hundreds of thousands of people who desperately sought work and shelter in the cities.[95] Further displacements or unhousing and impoverishment of millions of people accelerated during the Industrial Revolution and later in the financialization of capitalism.[96] While many political changes reduced some of the harmful effects of laissez faire capitalism and later neoliberal capitalism,[97] we nevertheless see evictions, housing insecurity, and food insecurity in Western societies where there are increasing income and wealth gaps.[98] China, like the U.S., a major contributor to climate change and a capitalist economy, also has steep disparities in income and wealth,[99] while also having fewer protections for workers who are exploited by companies within and outside China. If we turn to the global south and so-called third world countries, we find even more dire conditions as a result of global capitalism.[100]

To be sure, capitalism has created vast amounts of wealth and many people live much better lives than were possible before capitalism. But this does not, as Marx knew, justify the exploitative relations that found

92. Mick Smith muses about the early cave art depicting the interconnection of human beings and animals, long before difference became associated with exclusion and superiority. The interconnection between human beings and more than human beings may still exist in some places on earth, but, by and large, human societies operate out of the anthropological regime. Smith, *Against Ecological Sovereignty*, 1–10.

93. See Mauelshagen, "Bridging the Great Divide," 92–100.

94. Wood, *Origin of Capitalism*.

95. Katharina Pistor argues it was not the political leaders who had the levers on the laws that undergirded capitalism and its proliferation, but lawyers who coded capital, protecting the wealth of the few over the many. Pistor, *The Code of Capital*.

96. See Harvey, *A Brief History of Neoliberalism*; Jones, *Masters of the Universe*; Piketty, *Capital in the Twenty-First Century*; Mann, *Disassembly Required*; Valencia, *Gore Capitalism*.

97. For an overview of neoliberal capitalism see Birch, *A Research Agenda for Neoliberalism*.

98. Mander, *The Capitalism Papers*; Stiglitz, *The Price of Inequality*; Stiglitz, *The Great Divide*.

99. World Inequality Database, "China."

100. See Valencia, *Gore Capitalism*.

capitalism or the devastating conditions of dwelling for large numbers of human beings, as well as more-than-human beings. Of course, it is not just that capitalism impacts the dwellings and experiences of dwelling with regard to human beings. It is also that capitalism, which human beings created, is responsible for climate change. Jason Moore argues that the current era we live in should be called the Capitalocene, because capitalism is the source of climate change.[101] His viewpoint suggests that capitalism is the source of the destruction of habitats, the unhousing or extinctions of species, and the likely future of the unhousing of human life on earth.[102] Capitalism is, therefore, a major problem with regard to millions of species, including human beings, being able to exist and, therefore, to dwell.

Capitalism, as Woods notes, expanded from England and into Europe and beyond. The expansion of capitalism was not "natural" or the result of people adopting the capitalistic machine because it provided for the common good. Yet, capitalism became a global phenomenon largely due to the imperialism of Western nations. The eighteenth, nineteenth, and twentieth centuries saw the world dominated by England, France, Spain, the United States, and other Western nations, all of which had adopted aspects of capitalism. The pursuit and control of markets were the concerns of imperialistic nations. The United States expanded from the east to the west coast, displacing and exploiting native peoples—legitimated by political-economic apparatuses that constructed native peoples as inferior. It also adopted doctrines (e.g., Monroe) and ideological-driven policies (e.g., Manifest Destiny) that legitimated or justified economic and political control of countries in Central and South America. American imperialistic, economic expansionism was the driving force in the War against Spain, and the colonization of Cuba, Philippines, Hawaii, and other Pacific territories.[103] Colonization, yoked to capitalism, displaced peoples from their homes, their lands, their cultures. Imperialism is by nature a system that negatively impacts the dwelling of

---

101. Moore, "Name the System!"

102. Gernot Wagner and Martin Weitzman argue that capitalism can actually adapt and become a change agent with regard to slowing the impact of climate change. They tend to link human creativity to capitalism and they overlook the long history of human exploitation and devastation linked to the expansion of capitalism throughout the world. James Speth also believes and hopes capitalism will be the answer to our present and future problems in the Anthropocene Age. I think their approaches are naïve in the extreme. Any cursory reading of the history of capitalism reveals massive inequalities and the exploitation of other human beings, other species, and the earth. Wagner and Weitzman, *Climate Shock*; Speth, *The Bridge at the Edge of the World*.

103. See Kaplan, *The Anarchy of Empire in the Making of U.S. Culture*. Kinzer, *Overthrow*; Zinn, *A People's History of the United States*.

most people who are being colonized, while privileging peoples' dwelling in the metropole.[104]

Of course, many people might believe that the bad old days of imperialism are gone. There are no more colonies. But this would overlook the changing nature of imperialism and capitalism. Geir Lundestad argued that an imperial nation like the U.S. is "a hierarchical system of political relationships with one power clearly being much stronger than any other."[105] Similarly, Julian Go defined "empire as a sociopolitical formation wherein a central political authority (a king, a metropole, or imperial state) exercises unequal influence and power over the political processes of a subordinate society, peoples, or space."[106] The power that is used to gain client-states or to gain influence over other nations is not merely political, but rather an amalgam of economic and military power. As Go noted, the "imperial state keeps these nominally independent territories in line or compels them to meet its interests, but does not declare sovereignty over them."[107] Given these definitions, we can see that the United States, China, and Russia are the current imperial hegemons that are bent on expanding their influence and control. China has interests in the East and in Africa and India. Russia is exerting its control of Crimea, parts of the Ukraine, and has interests in the Middle East. The U.S., by and large, is the most imperialistic with "approximately 725 known American military bases in over 38 foreign countries and over 254,000 military personnel in 153 countries."[108] The destruction to physical and bodily dwellings due to U.S. imperialistic adventures is morally disturbing, even with the specter of climate change. During the period of imperialism after WWII, Carl Boggs argued that "a rather conservative accounting of civilians killed by the U.S. military since 1945 would number in the vicinity of eight million,"[109] which does not include wounded persons and, of course, completely avoids unhousing with regard to other-than-human species.

But what do the current iterations of imperialism or empire have to do with dwelling in the Anthropocene? First of all, the metropoles are concerned about client-states to the degree that the needs and concerns of the metropole are met. Imperialistic nations, in other words, are not concerned

104. Naturally not all people of the metropole. Imperialistic capitalism benefited the dwelling of the upper classes.

105. Lundestad, The American "Empire," 37.

106. Go, Patterns of Empire, 7.

107. Go, Patterns of Empire, 11.

108. Johnson, Sorrows of Empire, 154.

109. Boggs, Crimes of Empire, 52.

about the well-being of client-states as such or their common good and will move to violence when client-states resist or rebel.[110] Worse, imperialism means that powerful nations, like the U.S., can intervene, destabilizing nations and their economies for the benefit of the U.S., which has a long sordid history of doing this.[111] These interventions have long-lasting material, psychological, and social effects on persons' dwelling on the peripheries of empires.[112] Second, imperial states are competing to expand their political-economic influence and control, which in the Anthropocene Age is deeply problematic, not only because it is based on a myopic premise of the ongoing existence of the imperial state, but also because these states are not cooperating to maintain the earth as a dwelling place for all human beings and other-than-human beings. Instead, they look for ways to cooperate, while also seeking to undermine the power of other imperial states. The pandemic of 2020 is an excellent, though sad, illustration of major global powers (e.g., U.S., Russia, and China) failing to cooperate for the benefit of themselves and the world and, as a result, unhousing untold numbers of people. In brief, these imperialistic nations and their client-states are huge problems with regard to human and other-than-human dwelling.

The third problem and obstacle to ensuring the dwelling of all is nationalism. Capitalism and imperialism are intertwined with nationalism in the U.S., China, and Russia. Yet, nationalism is also a fact of countries that are not imperialistic. The rise of modern nation-states has been attributed to the treaties of Westphalia in the seventeenth century, and this rise has been accompanied by the ideas of national sovereignty and national identity. Nationalism asserts that each nation should pursue its own self-interests, which, of course, may result in cooperating with other nations toward mutually shared interests. NATO, the Warsaw Pact, the Organization of American States, the G8, the United Nations, etc. are multinational organizations wherein nations have agreed to cooperate to meet shared goals. Moreover, there are international treaties or agreements that commit diverse nation-states to common goals (international treaties on climate change; Paris Agreement), though many of these treaties can be easily overturned or ignored when a nation deems them to be detrimental to nationalistic goals. Brexit and the U.S. departure from global climate change treaties are examples. While nationalism, with its focus on sovereignty and identity (read exclusion), does not, at first glance, appear to preclude the possibility

110. Go, *Patterns of Empire.*

111. See Klein, *Shock Doctrine.*

112. As an illustration, Frantz Fanon, a founding figure for post-colonial philosophy, depicts the material and psychological harms by imperial France. See Fanon, *Black Skin, White Masks.* See also Said, *Orientalism* and Said, *Culture and Imperialism.*

of global cooperation toward mitigating the effects of climate change, it is nevertheless an unpredictable, if not precarious, factor.

Consider that there has been a resurgence of nationalism, wherein people focus on their sovereignty and national identity, while lacking interest in the well-being of refugees (stateless persons) or lacking any idea of the common good for residents of the earth. We note that the immigration of large numbers of people from the Middle East and Africa to Europe over the last seven years, which has revived conservative nationalistic movements, aiming to deny residency to immigrants and seeking to focus exclusively on the needs of their citizens.[113] Marine Le Pen in France, Britain's Brexit, Matteo Salvini in Italy, the far-right Freedom Party in Austria, the conservative Law and Justice party in Poland are some examples of the rise of nationalism (and white supremacy) in Europe that undermine global cooperation. In the United States, millions of people support draconian anti-immigration policies and practices clothed in preserving national identity (again, read white supremacy). The forty-fifth president made it to the White House in large part because he fanned the nationalistic flames of America First, opting out of treaties that conservative nationalists deem to infringe on U.S. sovereignty (e.g., climate accords) or are seen to harm U.S. economic interests. Basically, "fuck" the rest of the world, we will go our own way is the message. I am not saying that nationalism is harmful in itself, because it has clearly resulted in benefits, such as countries freeing themselves from colonial rule. I am saying that, at its core, nationalism fosters a psychology of exclusion (e.g., Carl Schmitt's friend–enemy distinction) within one's own country and between countries, which is not only an obstacle to welcoming refugees in need of dwelling, but also an obstacle to the global cooperation needed to address the dire realities of climate change. This trinity of obstacles, which are founded on exclusion and exploitation (other human beings, other-than human beings, and the earth), may lead to the unhousing of us all.

The challenges and problems of human dwelling are perennial, but in the Anthropocene Age these problems reveal just how dire the situation is, not only for us, but for other species. Will we, as ecological and political agents, rise to the challenges of learning to dwell by caring for the earth, other species, and each other? Will we recognize that to dwell politically, while a local and particular reality, is necessarily global, including all human beings and species? Will we set aside the illusions of anthropocentrism and narcissism that undermine our dwelling with other-than-human species, let alone other human beings who are unhoused and deemed to be refugees? Will we release ourselves "from our desire for metaphysical mastery of the

113. BBC News, "Europe and Right-Wing Nationalism."

earth so that it might be reinhabited?"[114] Will we awake to the fact that there are no "refugees," because the earth is not only the foundation of all political realities, but also where we all reside? To return to Lévinas: "But he or she who emigrates is wholly human: the migration of man does not destroy, does not demolish the meaning of Being."[115]

## An Existential Root of Dwelling:
## From Psychosocial Dwelling to Dwelling in the Polis

Before depicting a radical political theology of dwelling, I wish to address the existential foundations or psychosocial roots of dwelling. As noted in chapter 1, while having decidedly different views of nature, Hobbes and Rousseau constructed their political theologies either hoping to avoid any return to the state of nature or to find some way to reclaim it. My view is that the "state of nature" vis-à-vis dwelling is evident in every birth. We are thrown from our ensconced dwelling in the womb into the world and without the welcoming disposition and care of good-enough parents, we would not be able to dwell. Put differently, birth initiates a vulnerability and separation where there is not exclusion, but rather a speaking and acting together that founds an embodied sense of suchness-in-belonging. In this section, I draw out some of the "natural" aspects of dwelling for human beings and their relation to the capacity for and experience of political dwelling. Included here is a discussion regarding events that unhouse people with regard to their embodied-relational experiences of dwelling and political-public dwelling.

Matt Waggoner notes in his discussion of Theodor Adorno's philosophy that "The human experience of dwelling begins with embodiment, with the fact that consciousness is inseparable from the somatic and sensorial."[116] "Embodied life," he points out, "contains within its phenomenology a template for what we have been calling dwelling. The necessity of corporeal beings to seek housing on a place and in relation with others is never purely subjective and cannot be individualized."[117] This perspective on embodied dwelling is perhaps most evident in the developmental task for both parents and children, wherein children learn to "inhabit the world in an embodied way" in relation to Others. This "means that [children] must also inhabit [their] essential sociality, since the contingencies of corporeal life are how

114. Wood, *Reoccupy the Earth*, 141.
115. Lévinas, *Totality and Infinity*, 11.
116. Waggoner, *Unhoused*, 105.
117. Waggoner, *Unhoused*, 105.

and why we are drawn into relations of interdependence with others."[118] Let me turn to depicting the developmental process of dwelling together.

In the late nineteenth century, William James, as noted above, posited that, to the newborn baby, the world is "one great blooming buzzing confusion."[119] Initially shielded in the warmth and dampened quiet of the womb where there are no needs,[120] the newborn is thrust into a sensorial complex world where there is a gap between need and the need being met, a gap which founds consciousness. A few decades later, using stronger language, Otto Rank argued that *"analysis turns out to be a belated accomplishment of the incompleted mastery of the birth trauma."*[121] Rank, I believe, indicates that the nascent, pre-birth ego is unable to "master" the experience of this new reality, hence his use of the term "trauma." It seems likely that a newborn is confused and overwhelmed by sensory input, yet infant-parent researchers have shown that a baby possesses preferences prior to birth.[122] This suggests not only that some level of psychic-semiotic organization of experience exists before our entry into a world of blooming buzzing confusion, but also that these organizations of experience may mitigate, to some degree, the strangeness of his new world. In other words, for Donald Winnicott, "The actual birth can easily be felt by the infant, in the normal case, to be a successful outcome of personal effort owing to the more or less accurate timing," which suggests the presence of a nascent ego organizing pre-representational experience.[123]

The "mastery" of this first unhousement is not simply a task for the infant. Winnicott remarked that the "beginning of ego emergence entails at first an almost absolute dependence on the supportive ego of the mother-figure and on her carefully graduated failure of adaptation."[124] All of this depends on good-enough parents' attunements to their children's assertions, which provide a space for children to dwell in and organize experience in

118. Waggoner, *Unhoused*, 107.

119. James, *The Principles of Psychology, vol. 1*, 488.

120. In the womb, there is no "need" because the need is met before it can be registered as a need. Because there are no "needs," there is no need for consciousness, though clearly there is a nascent awareness of the parent's voice. See DeCasper and Fifer, "Of Human Bonding."

121. Rank, *The Trauma of Birth*, 5

122. See DeCasper and Fifer, "Of Human Bonding"; DeCasper and Spence, "Prenatal Maternal Speech Influences Newborns"; Kumin, *Pre-Object Relatedness*; Beebe and Lachmann, "Representation and Internalization in Infancy"; Beebe and Lachmann, *Infant Research and Adult Treatment*.

123. Winnicott, *Through Paediatrics to Psychoanalysis*, 186.

124. Winnicott, *The Maturational Environment and the Facilitating Environment*, 9. Winnicott believed that care of children is not contingent on any particular gender.

this strange new world. To make use of Lévinas' views, the parents' ministrations can be understood as hospitality, a human welcome to infants' sense of confusion at not being at home (womb). Together, the parent and infant create a new home, a new sense of dwelling. That said, one reason I want to avoid terms like "trauma" and "mastery" is because the intersection of the infant's assertions and the parent's attunements can give rise to a new, nascently differentiated, embodied-relational experiences of dwelling. I would reserve the term "trauma" for situations of parental impingement and deprivation, making it impossible for infants to learn to dwell in themselves-with-others.

To explicate this process of dwelling further, I turn to an altered version of Christopher Bollas' notion of transformational objects/processes. Bollas, steeped in Winnicott's work, posits that before transitional objects, there are transformational objects, which are associated with the earliest period of infancy. Bollas, in brief, wishes "to identify the infant's first subjective experience of the object as a transformational object."[125] Of course, the "object" is the parent who "alters the infant's environment to meet [the infant's] needs."[126] The parent-object is not an object in the sense of the infant being able to differentiate between this or that object, but rather a "process of enviro-somatic caring."[127] More precisely, the parent-object is "a process that alters the infant's experience" or subjectivity.[128] This "object is 'known' not so much by putting it into an object-representation, but as a recurrent *experience of being*,"[129] which is contingent on good-enough, reliable attunement (and repair). From my perspective, the child's "experience of being" is understood as pre-representational organization of the embodied experience of dwelling, which precedes the child's representational capacities (e.g., language, symbolization, etc.). In other words, the infant's embodied-relational *experience of being* can be seen as the child's second experience of being at home—*dwelling in one's body-with-an-Other*. I add here that this early form of dwelling accompanies a nascent, pre-representational embodied sense of singularity and concomitantly self-esteem, self-respect, and self-confidence.[130] This early pre-representational sense of self, while

125. Bollas, *The Shadow of the Object*, 14.
126. Bollas, *The Shadow of the Object*, 15.
127. Bollas, *The Shadow of the Object*, 14.
128. Bollas, *The Shadow of the Object*, 13.
129. Bollas, *The Shadow of the Object*, 13 (emphasis mine).
130. I am taking these three experiences from political philosopher Axel Honneth. Honneth does not say anything about infancy vis-à-vis these terms. Instead, he argues that in a good-enough society, residents will obtain these experiences from their interactions. Moreover, these experiences are supported by social-political narratives,

not differentiated from the "object," is nevertheless inextricably tied to the "process of enviro-somatic caring"[131] that founds children's first pre-representational embodied-relational experiences of dwelling.

It is important to pause here and explain that this early embodied experience is not to be understood as if one is housed alone in one's body. In discussing Adorno's work on dwelling, Waggoner writes, "No one ever singularly inhabits a body because embodiment is not . . . a state of being, a self-sufficient thing. Its existence is inseparable from and can only be constituted as such within a matrix of contact and connectivity."[132] So, from the very first, embodiment is relational—embodied dwelling is belonging. Moreover, "The [nascent ego] is housed by extended realities that are material and social in nature."[133] In short, the experience of being is an embodied, pre-representational sense of being oneself-with-an-Other.

This pre-political space of embodied relational dwelling begs the question: how do infants move from this space to the world of animate and inanimate objects—to the public political world? Put differently, what is the process wherein children transition from embodied-relational dwelling to public-political dwelling? Winnicott's notion of transitional objects/phenomena (TO/TP) can be helpful in depicting this movement. To understand the child's transition from undifferentiated, embodied relation to engaging and using objects, Winnicott posits that a transitional object in early childhood is the first not-me possession, which involves infants' rudimentary ability to recognize an object as independent of themselves or as an external object.[134] In the act of omnipotently (in fantasy) possessing and using this object, infants both retain and partially hand over their belief in omnipotence.[135] This primary[136] TO is "not an internal object—it is a possession.

---

practices, and institutions. I place these here because they will be important in the discussion between child dwelling and dwelling in the political realm. For now, I simply mention that numerous African Americans (e.g., Frederick Douglass' speech about the 4th of July) have expressed the tension between feeling like an American but not feeling at home here because of racism. Honneth, "Recognition as Ideology."

131. Bollas, *The Shadow of the Object*, 14.

132. Waggoner, *Unhoused*, 107.

133. Waggoner, *Unhoused*, 109.

134. Winnicott, *Playing and Reality*, 3–4.

135. Winnicott, *Playing and Reality*, 9–11.

136. Winnicott did not differentiate between the transitional objects of childhood and those of adulthood, which raises all kinds of questions. The developmental achievements and complex psychological and relational realities that take place between infancy and adulthood are huge. This in itself would demand differentiation between types of objects. In this case, I designate the first transitional object as primary TO—an object that is associated with pre-symbolic modes of organizing experience. For critiques of

Yet, it is not (for the infant) an external object either."[137] Strictly speaking, the TO, for Winnicott, is neither an internal object nor an external object, and yet it is both, asking the readers to embrace paradox. Another related feature of TOs is that they must not be changed unless by the infant, because to do so would challenge the infant's sense of and belief in omnipotent control and, consequently, disrupt his experience of continuity or sense of going on being[138]—embodied-being-with-Other. Similarly, parents are not to challenge children's omnipotent selection and use of the primary transitional object, because this, too, would challenge children's *presymbolic* belief in and experience of omnipotence, which Winnicott contends is needed for children to have confidence in organizing their experience. That is, infants' omnipotent use of the TO may be understood, in part, as their creative and emerging ability (ego) to construct experience by way of and in relation to external objects, all of which is necessary for dwelling in the larger world.

Since the primary TO is not simply identified with either the external or internal world, a question is raised regarding the child's selection of the object and what the TO represents to the child. The object, which may be presented to the infant, is chosen by the infant and not shared.[139] This choice of a *primary* TO is in "accordance with its consistency, texture, size, volume, shape, and odor,"[140] which is psychologically joined to the "technique of mothering"[141]—the caregiver's handling, holding, comforting, and consoling of the infant. That is, the child unconsciously chooses a TO that represents the parent's care for the child, which permits the child to manage (regulate emotions) during times of separation from the parent. The TO also acts as "a resting place for the individual engaged in the perpetual human task of keeping inner and outer reality separate yet interrelated" and

---

Winnicott's theory of development, see Applegate, "The Transitional Object Reconsidered"; Brody, "Transitional objects: Idealization of a Phenomenon"; Flew, "Transitional Objects and Phenomena"; Litt, "Theories of Transitional Object Attachment."

137. Winnicott, *Playing and Reality*, 9.

138. Winnicott, *Playing and Reality*, 4.

139. Paul Pruyser suggests that the transitional object is shared to the extent that the object is often one that is "found" in the cultural realm of family life. Moreover, parents and siblings tolerate and accept the child's use of the object. While I agree with this view, it is clear that Winnicott does not believe that the earliest transitional objects or what I call primary transitional objects are shared or intersubjectively held, at least during infancy. Pruyser, *The Play of the Imagination*.

140. Kestenberg and Weinstein, "Transitional Objects and Body Image Formation," 89.

141. Winnicott, *Playing and Reality*, 11. Winnicott did not assign care simply to the mother. A mothering environment could be accomplished by fathers as well.

provides a sense of continuity (sense of going on being) during moments of separation and stress.[142]

All of this can be understood in terms of the experience of dwelling. This first object under the child's omnipotent control (belief) provides embodied soothing, rest, and continuity—pre-representational experiences of being-at-home-with-an-object in one's suchness. What I am suggesting is that children use the object to extend their experiences of being at home in the world of objects. The sense of dwelling, then, is expanded now to other objects, albeit, in this case, under the infants' omnipotent control. We see here also the growing sense of agency with regard to dwelling/belonging. The initial transformational object represents a nascent agency, but one where the object/process has the agency and power to alter one's subjective world of dwelling. The primary transitional object signifies the child's greater sense of agency and participation in the creation of dwelling in and with the world of objects. Put differently, the space of appearances, the space of speaking and acting together, is now under the infant's omnipotent (imaginative) control vis-à-vis the primary transitional object, which signifies an emerging agency with regard to creating and participating in the space of appearances with other objects. I add here that, in this presymbolic world, the infant is able to retain and share an embodied sense of self-esteem, self-respect, and self-confidence *with an object* at hand, which is a first step toward being at home outside the confines of the parent-child relationship.

I differentiate between primary and secondary transitional objects because there is a significant difference between the experience of dwelling vis-à-vis the proverbial blanket and the child's use of and dwelling with cultural objects. There is, in other words, a movement from presymbolic dwelling with objects to dwelling with animate objects (and later, persons). Perhaps one could say that the developmental question and task with regard to the secondary transitional object is how to dwell with others. A playful illustration of this is the comic strip *Calvin and Hobbes*. Calvin is a little boy who plays with his stuffed tiger, Hobbes. Together they create and inhabit a world together. Hobbes and Calvin embark on all kinds of adventures, they argue and make up, and they comfort each other when hurt or distressed. It is, in imagination, a mutual space of appearances, of speaking and acting

142. Winnicott, *Playing and Reality*, 2. One might wonder what happens to primary (and secondary) TOs as the child grows. In the course of human development Winnicott argued that the TO "is not forgotten and it is not mourned. It loses its meaning, and this is because transitional phenomena have become diffused: they have become spread out over the whole intermediate territory between 'inner psychic reality' and 'the external world as perceived by two persons in common,' that is to say, over the whole cultural field." Winnicott, *Playing and Reality*, 5.

together. The parents are present, but in the background and seemingly unimportant in their supporting roles. To Calvin, Hobbes is alive and not just alive, but a person who recognizes and treats Calvin as a person and vice-versa. In Calvin's imagination, there is, then, a sense of mutual singularity (self-esteem, self-confidence, and self-respect) that is derived from speaking and acting together, which includes shared repairs of conflict. While it is in Calvin's imagination, they together create a pre-political space of appearances wherein they reside—they dwell together. Calvin's and Hobbes' relationship represents more sophisticated experiences of care and repair associated with Calvin's and his parents' interactions. Moreover, Hobbes is not a mere blanket. He is instead a cultural object, signifying Calvin's entry into and use of cultural symbol systems and practices, wherein he learns to dwell with others. The secondary transitional object, in other words, represents more complex experiences of embodied-relational dwelling—complex because they include organizations of experience that rely on collectively held symbol systems. As a secondary transitional object, Hobbes serves as a process toward Calvin's learning to dwell-with-others.

Before continuing with this transition to political dwelling, it is important to point out again that, while this pre-political space between parents and children and children and secondary TO is distinct from the political-public spaces of speaking and acting together, political realities shape this space of dwelling together. Larger economic, social, and political apparatuses can enhance or undermine these pre-political spaces and, therefore, impact experiences of dwelling. A brief illustration will help here. Ta-Nehisi Coates wrote to his son about what it was like to grow up in a racist society.[143] For Coates, the reality of racism evokes "the sheer terror of disembodiment,"[144] which has its roots in the violent commodification of black bodies—"they transfigured our very bodies into sugar, tobacco, cotton, and gold."[145] "Disembodiment," he writes, "is a kind of terrorism, and the threat of it alters the orbit of all our lives and, like terrorism, this distortion is intentional."[146] Coates' question is how can I live free in this black body?

This fear of disembodiment emerged in the safety of his family. Coates tells his son of his first recollection of fear was when he was five, watching a street fight from his home.[147] He "heard the fear in the first music I ever

143. Coates, *Between the World and Me.*
144. Coates, *Between the World and Me,* 12.
145. Coates, *Between the World and Me,* 71.
146. Coates, *Between the World and Me,* 121.
147. Coates, *Between the World and Me,* 14.

knew . . . [and] in the visits to my Nana's home."[148] Then Coates moves to his father: "My father was so very afraid. I felt it in the sting of his black leather belt, which he applied with more anxiety than anger."[149] His father's physical discipline took place against the background of violence rooted in the sociopolitical machinery of racism. "Everyone," Coates writes, "has lost a child, somehow to the streets, to jail, to drugs, to guns."[150] Recalling his dad's voice, "Either I can beat him, or the police," Coates struggles with whether that saved him or not. "All I know," he writes, "is the violence rose from the fear like smoke from a fire, and I cannot say whether that violence, even administered in fear and love, sounded the alarm or choked us at the exit."[151] While his parents sought to protect and nurture their son, Coates' early experiences of dwelling were marred by the social-political realities of racism that seek to undermine the experiences of embodied-relational dwelling of African Americans. As James Baldwin notes, "Long before the Negro child perceives this difference [white superiority], and even longer before he understands it, he has begun to react to it, he has begun to be controlled by it."[152]

Like many other African Americans, Coates' movement or transition from experiences of dwelling at home to dwelling in the larger political-public world was fraught with challenges. Ideally, embodied-relational experiences of dwelling and accompanying representations of self-esteem, self-confidence, and self-respect—all of which are derived from good-enough speaking and acting together—find a place in the larger society. This transition for many children goes unmarked because these children are able to discover and have affirmed their embodied-relational sense of suchness. Put differently, children find and have affirmed their sense of self-esteem, self-confidence, and self-respect, because there is sufficient civic care and faith that found experiences of dwelling together in the political realm. They have a sense of dwelling in this place with these people. Of course, Coates and others provide illustrations of how this goes awry, leaving people un-housed in the sense of their own bodies and in larger society.

This said, when individuals of any oppressed and marginalized population discover that they are not allowed to dwell in the larger public-political realm, they are left to find other places to dwell: places to inhabit shared esteem, confidence, and respect; places of mutual care and fidelity;

148. Coates, *Between the World and Me*, 15.
149. Coates, *Between the World and Me*, 15
150. Coates, *Between the World and Me*, 16.
151. Coates, *Between the World and Me*, 16–17.
152. Baldwin, *Notes of a Native Son*, 26.

places of speaking and acting together. To return to Coates' book, he found an experience of being at home at Howard University. "My only Mecca," Coates writes, "was, is, and will always be Howard University."[153] Here he was surrounded by other African Americans engaged in study, including the study of African and African American history. While Mecca has religious connotations, Coates is using it as a metaphor that points to refuge, freedom, acceptance, and, of course, dwelling. "The Mecca," he writes, "is a machine, crafted to capture and concentrate the dark energy of all African peoples and inject it directly into the student body . . . The history, the location, the alumni combined to create The Mecca—the crossroads of the black diaspora."[154] Here is a home where he could experience his singularity, where he could speak and act with others, against the background of shared mutual personal recognition, mutual-personal trust/fidelity, and civic care. Howard University, for Coates, is not simply a sanctuary against the forces of racism that unhouse African Americans; it is also a cherished home to dwell with others.

Another example can aid us in seeing the relationship between the community of faith, as a dwelling place, and the political. Martin Luther King Jr.,[155] like Coates, struggled painfully as a child as he encountered racism. For King, a refuge was not only his family, but his religious community. As a young child, King experienced the mutual-personal recognition and emotional warmth within his Christian Baptist community—a political community. For Richard Horsley, the community of faith or *ekklesia* has a political character. He notes that the term *ekklesia* "referred to the assembly of citizens in a self-governing state city."[156] This suggests that, for King, his first forays into the public-political realm was this community, wherein he was welcomed in his singularity and where he learned to inhabit or dwell. More specifically, this community, which demonstrated mutual-personal faith and civic care among its members, provided a space of appearances, wherein King could discover, possess, and exercise a sense of self-esteem, self-confidence, and self-respect with others. Dwelling here meant speaking and acting together despite the background of political humiliation outside the confines of the church's walls. This community would later serve as a constant source of support as King (and others) faced the disciplinary regimes of systemic racism and the constant violent threats of being unhoused.

153. Coates, *Between the World and Me*, 39.
154. Coates, *Between the World and Me*, 40.
155. King, *The Autobiography of Martin Luther King, Jr.*
156. Horsley, *Covenant Economics*, 14.

The existential roots of dwelling are found in the earliest period of human life, wherein children's vulnerability and dependency are inextricably tied to existential imperatives of hospitality and care so that children can dwell at home and later in the larger public-political world. If we could imagine an invulnerable and independent child, we would find that this child does not need to dwell. Vulnerability, then, is the existential foundation of human dwelling. To summarize the above, children move from the dwelling of the womb to the buzzing confusion of this world. Good-enough parents provide the psychosocial matrix of speaking and acting together for pre-representational experiences of embodied-relational dwelling-with-Others. The primary transitional object represents these experiences of embodied suchness that children use to soothe their anxiety in the face of separation. That is, children assign or transfer their experiences of embodied-dwelling to the object, which is under their omnipotent control. In time, I argued, new capacities (e.g., symbolization) come online and the child uses a cultural object (secondary transitional object) to organize and manage psychosocial experiences of dwelling—again under their omnipotent control. Ideally, this provides a bridge for children to find and have affirmed their embodied-relational experiences of dwelling in the public-political world that demonstrates sufficient care and faith for experiences of being at home in the polis.

## Radical Political Theology and Dwelling on This One Earth

Having addressed what I consider to be the existential-political roots of dwelling, I shift to dwelling in terms of a radical political theology in the Anthropocene Age. Before doing so, it is important to indicate briefly how theologies of subjugation and subordination provide dwelling for the privileged, while undermining dwelling for the many, including nature.

Agamben uses the term "anthropological machines" to refer to political philosophies, theologies, and their apparatuses that establish distinctions between human beings and nature that are fundamentally exclusionary. Recall that Agamben argues that these machines have undergirded Western philosophical (and theological) traditions as they seek to establish differences between human beings and animals, which is a short step away from differentiating between groups of human beings. These differences are exclusionary and, in my view, based on the illusions of superiority (human beings) and inferiority, justifying and legitimating exploitation of so-called inferior others, whether that is other human beings, other species, or the earth itself. Theologies of subjugation/subordination are anthropological machines as well in that they rely on the illusions of superiority and inferiority to account for who can dwell and how they will dwell in the polis. Put another way, theologies of subjugation are fundamentally exclusionary. This can be explained in three ways. First, within the context of the political community, the Israelites, as the chosen people, dwell together, yet within this group, women are subordinate and therefore do not dwell equally in the political spaces of speaking and acting together. They are included-excluded Others with regard to speaking and acting together in the political space. Similarly, slaves are included-excluded Others who dwell in the polis, but their dwelling is more precarious because they are in relations of subjugation. Second, in relation to those outside the Israelite community of chosen people, there are more egregious illustrations of exclusion. Remember God's command to the Israelites to take possession of the promised land and to unhouse the inhabitants because they would "be as barbs in your eyes and thorns in your sides" (Num 33:55). This was not a command to subjugate the people who dwelled on this land, it was a command to unhouse them— to remove them either through killing or exile—the ultimate exclusion vis-à-vis dwelling. Third, nature becomes the excluded-included Other. For instance, theologies of subjugation point to humanity's "God given" dominion over nature, placing nature strictly in the service of human dwelling and ostensibly separated from the political. This means that nature can be politically and economically objectified, instrumentalized, and exploited, denying the suchness, vulnerability, and dependency of other species and the earth. All three explanations are theologically based, ontologically legitimating exclusion with regard to the dwelling of gods, persons, and nature and legitimating relations of domination. What is evident in theologies of subjugation is that dwelling is contingent on exclusion, privileging one group's dwelling over another, which accompanies forms of domination, exploitation, and forms of political violence.

The exclusionary feature of theologies of subjugation/subordination includes the denial of the existential reality of vulnerability and dependency, which impacts dwelling among human beings and nature. Theologies of subjugation, I contend, promote the illusion of invulnerability, autonomy, and determinate knowing, while projecting vulnerability and dependency onto "inferior" Others. That is, by making Others vulnerable, we can come away feeling *as if* we are protected from vulnerability and are independent. This is furthered by a belief in an invulnerable God. This dynamic results in undermining the dwelling of vulnerable "inferior" Others. For instance, the new Pharaoh undermines the dwelling of the Israelites who, in their vulnerability, dependency, and precarity, cry out to an omnipotent invulnerable

God. God, in turn, makes the Egyptians vulnerable by way of plagues, kill-ings, and starvation. The Israelites are freed under the aegis of an invul-nerable God. By subjugating the people of the promised land, the Israelites obtain a sense of power and invulnerability, supported by their beliefs in all-powerful God. If obeyed, their security vis-à-vis dwelling was assured. Disobedience resulted in their being made vulnerable though punishing acts of God. This mimetic dynamic continues not only in relation to an all-powerful God, but also in relation to other human beings.

I add here that this mimetic dynamic is evident in secular anthropo-logical machines (e.g., capitalism, imperialism, nationalism) that seek to dominate nature to secure the dwelling of human beings, as well as when those in positions of privilege, power, and authority use other human be-ings to secure their dwelling and their illusory, exclusionary sense of invul-nerability. For instance, classism reveals how the economic-political elite secure their experiences of dwelling by asserting their right or privilege to secure wealth at the expense of so-called lower classes. In another sense, the "lower" classes are needed for the elite to feel superior and less vulnerable in their dwelling in the world—physically and psychologically. The prophets, in one sense, emerged precisely because of the exploitation by and toward members of the community, which violated the covenant to care for all members of the community.[157] In short, the illusions of invulnerability and autonomy (and their apparatuses) are attempts to reject the existential and theological imperative to dwell in and with all of the plurality of life. The deeply tragic reality of these illusions is the fact that we are making not only ourselves, but other species, even more vulnerable.

To return to theologies of subjugation/subordination, it is clear that they are premised not simply on privilege and power, but also on the idea that citizenship as political dwelling is based in particular identities and places. To be sure, this is indeed part of all dwelling, but political dwelling itself is not necessarily contingent on a particular identity or ethos/place, which I will say more about below. Put another way, for theologies of subju-gation, dwelling is completely predicated on identity (and, often, place).[158] Those Others who dwell within the community of faith are not fully includ-ed—included-excluded Others, which includes other-than-human beings. Yes, they may dwell with us, but they are not of us and it is only a short step to exploiting or excluding them.

157. See Walzer, *In God's Shadow.*

158. After (and in some sense, at times, before) the diaspora, place vis-à-vis dwell-ing becomes secondary to identity as belonging. This is also similar to Christians and Muslims. While place is important to mark off the borders of dwelling, identity is primary.

The reason we must make these theologies inoperative is because they are fundamentally inadequate to the realities of the Anthropocene Age. I argue they are inadequate because dwelling based in exclusion, privilege, inequality, identity, and place overlook the reality that there is only one place to dwell—the earth—and that this dwelling is not privileged to human beings, but to all species. There is only one dwelling place, though its iterations are manifold. And human beings, from an existential point of view, have no existential or ontological privileged position with regard to other species or to the earth itself. This does not mean that human beings cannot construct narratives and practices that inform them of their superior privileged position vis-à-vis nature and other-than-human beings. But these are based entirely on human constructions, which means there is no external rater to confirm or deny this.[159]

In the previous chapter, I argued that a radical political theology rests on the issue of human (and other-than-human) vulnerability, using Jesus Christ's kenosis and forgiveness to illustrate the claims. While I am not going to repeat this here, I am framing vulnerability, kenosis, and forgiveness in terms of what this means for dwelling in the Anthropocene Age.

In terms of kenosis—God taking the form of a human being—there is a movement, a decision to be vulnerable with the aim of dwelling with human beings. "The 'flesh' of the *Logos*," Mathew Eaton writes, "then, refers not only to this instance of frailty and vulnerability, but also to the frail vulnerability of materiality itself."[160] Kenosis is taking on the vulnerability of dwelling. Also, one could say that, without emptying Godself, dwelling with and among human beings would have not been possible, because God as God is beyond both representation and experience. How, in other words, could human beings have an experience of dwelling with God when God is beyond the finite, beyond language and symbol, beyond the senses? For God to dwell means vulnerability was/is necessary for dwelling, which is a theological view of the existential claim that vulnerability and dependency are necessary facts of dwelling itself.

What is interesting and important is that this movement, this emptying Godself, included taking on the form of a slave. If God is to dwell among human beings, why take the form of a slave? Why not the identity of a Jew, Roman, Greek, etc.? Why not a citizen? A slave is universally and fundamentally an excluded-included Other, denied a place of speaking and

159. One could argue that God who gives dominion to human beings is the outside confirmation of human privilege, but this, too, is a human construction. It is possible that cockroaches may outlast humanity, suggesting that human superiority and privilege are illusions.

160. Eaton, "Beyond Human Exceptionalism," 204.

acting together in any polis. Put differently, the slave, like a refugee, has no political identity, yet dwells in the polis as an included-excluded Other—defined and determined by the predicates of the privileged and powerful. In addition, for human beings to be slaves, the apparatuses (law, philosophy, theology, etc.) of society must operate to construct and force individuals to be slaves—inferior included-excluded Others. God taking on the form of a slave meant operating within these systems, yet I would argue in so doing made these apparatuses inoperative vis-à-vis dwelling. Recall that, for Agamben, inoperative means deactivating or neutralizing the apparatuses of power that subjugate, that form and determine subjectivities and identities, making possible the realization of other possibilities or potentialities.[161] Also, inoperative is, for Agamben, not passive.[162] That is, inoperativity does not "affirm inertia, inactivity or apraxia . . . but [is] a form of praxis that is devoid of any telos or task, does not realize any essence and does not correspond to any nature."[163] Inoperativity means that, despite the apparatuses that determine dwelling vis-à-vis a slave, Jesus, in taking on the role of slave, retained his suchness or singularity, because his singularity was grounded in God and was not dependent on state apparatuses that are founded on exclusion and that promote illusions of superiority and inferiority with regard to Other human beings (and other-than-human beings). Jesus, in other words, was in the form of a slave, but not defined or determined by the predicates of domination extant in society. Jesus, then, could dwell among human beings as a "slave," making inoperative the state's focus on identity, place, and beliefs in inferiority and superiority vis-à-vis dwelling in the polis. To state this more strongly, the decision/act to empty Godself and to take on the form of a slave—a vulnerable and precarious subject—Jesus reveals a possibility of dwelling that is not dependent on political status, particular identity, or ethos. This possibility of dwelling is Agamben's coming community or inoperative community of "whatever singularities subtracts itself from the myriad of positive identities that divide its members and thus establishes itself as something new that is literally inaccessible to the apparatuses governing the situation and remains impervious to their grasp."[164] This type of dwelling is founded on the singularity or suchness of human beings (and other-than-human being) and not simply or solely on the representations associated with particular identities.

161. Prozorov, *Agamben and Politics*, 32–37.

162. Prozorov, *Agamben and Politics*, 134.

163. Prozorov, *Agamben and Politics*, 33.

164. Agamben, *The Coming Community*, 85.

A way to further understand taking on the form of the slave is to shift
to the political. The Roman and Jewish states were based on exclusion—
identity, place, and ethos—and, often, political violence. Political theologies
often replicate this. Even the political theology of the Jewish diaspora found
belonging and dwelling in identity. The act of taking on the form of a slave
is a radical political theology because it founds dwelling on suchness or singularity, which are not tied to predicates, whether they be place or identity.
Jesus as a "slave" cannot be defined by or confined to this role. Jesus dwells
with all, even those constructed as the "least," making inoperative anthropological machines that relegate some human beings (and other-than-human
creatures) to the inferior status of included-excluded (to simply excluded,
e.g., barbarians) Others to be exploited in a polis. Paul's letter to the Galatians points to the possibility of this new political dwelling, though I am not
sure Paul could have realized how radical this was: "There is no longer Jew
or Greek, there is no longer slave or free, there is no longer male and female;
for all of you are one in Christ."

Of course, a counter argument is that having an identity as a Christian marks the boundaries of the *ekklesia*. Is not this already exclusionary?
Inoperativity, though, does not mean that we are without identity, without
ethos, without beliefs—the refugee, for instance, belongs and, thus, dwells
with us. It simply means, in the case of dwelling, identity is not the criterion
for belonging. Instead, the existential and theological root of political dwelling is singularity or suchness, which, therefore, includes other-than-human
creatures. A radical political theology, then, is fundamentally and radically
welcoming, because it recognizes that the existential vulnerability of human
beings and other-than-human beings is requisite for dwelling itself. The
*ekklesia* is hospitable, welcoming not simply for the guest, but for people to
dwell in their suchness.

If we were to imagine God emptying Godself today, the role of the
slave would still to be apt, but perhaps more fitting would be God emptying
Godself to take on the form of a refugee—a human being without identity
or place or rights. At the start of this chapter, I quoted Agamben: "It is even
possible that, if we want to be equal to the absolutely new tasks ahead, we
will have to abandon decidedly, without reservation, the fundamental concepts through which we have so far represented the subjects of the political
(Man, the Citizen and its rights, but also the sovereign people, the worker,
and so forth) and build our political philosophy anew starting from the one
and only figure of the refugee."[165] Agamben adds that: "The refugee must
be considered for what he is: nothing less than a limit concept that radically

165. Agamben, *Means without Ends*, 15.

calls into question the fundamental categories of the nation-state . . . and thereby makes possible to clear the way for a long overdue renewal of categories in the service of a politics which bare life is no longer separated and excepted."[166] The Anthropocene Age, given the movement of peoples and their vulnerability and precarity,[167] is what determines the new tasks ahead, and that is welcoming refugees in the polis, not as refugees or any associated representation (e.g., immigrant), but in their suchness.[168] Lévinas echoes this when remarking that "he or she who emigrates is wholly human: the migration of man does not destroy, does not demolish the meaning of Being."[169] The refugee/immigrant is, first and foremost, a person; and as a person (suchness), the refugee/immigrant existentially and ontologically demands welcome as a resident of the one earth.

But it is not just refugees who are part of and dwell in the polis. A radical political theology affirms the suchness of all creatures and the earth itself as a living system, which means making inoperative disciplinary regimes of exclusion and their attending illusions of superiority and inferiority that legitimate apparatuses of exploitation and violence toward other-than-human beings. Existentially and theologically, to dwell in the world is to dwell with diverse individuals and the diversity of other-than-human creatures in their suchness. Our dwelling depends on their dwelling with us.

This means accepting our responsibility toward refugees, other-than-human beings, and the earth itself. This ecological responsibility is inherently political, which means that nature is not excluded from the political, but is the very basis for political dwelling itself. Moreover, ecological responsibility from a radical theological point of view eschews any

166. Agamben, *Sovereign Power and Bare Life*, 134. Agamben uses the term bare life to refer to the exclusion of *zoe* (to be alive) from *bios* (political/cultural life), which in reality means that human beings can be treated and managed as objects. The extreme of this is the Nazis treatment of the Jews. For Agamben, modern politics reflects this state of affairs, which has been debated by other scholars. See Prozorov, *Agamben and Politics*. I would add here that Agamben's notion of bare life is building on Hannah Arendt's research on totalitarianism. Arendt, *The Origins of Totalitarianism*.

167. John Lechte and Saul Newman depict "the barbaric treatment of stateless people" throughout the world, illustrating numerous examples of their deaths, incarceration, and surveillance. Lechte and Newman, *Agamben and the Politics of Human Rights*, 12–14.

168. Personal recognition or recognition of stateless people in their suchness necessarily means acknowledging their fundamental human rights. Hannah Arendt, who fled Nazi Germany, knew firsthand the plight of refugees. She wrote, "Their (refugees) plight is not that they are not equal before the law, but that no law exists for them." Arendt, *The Origins of Totalitarianism*, 295–96.

169. Lévinas, *Totality and Infinity*, 11.

idea of stewardship or domination,[170] both of which are founded in human privilege, superiority, and sovereignty. To return to Mick Smith's comment; "In becoming political, nature is not eroded, but it too is recognized in its plurality and its natality. Acting into nature must, like acting into the political sphere, involve responsibility for others, concern about effects, and making choices."[171] Theologically, the incarnation is dwelling not simply with human beings but with creation, and this has particular meaning for human beings in terms of our responsibility to dwell in and with creation. Of course, we know that human beings can eschew responsibility, shun the imperative to care, though in this case the result is tragic for ourselves, other species, and the earth itself.

There is one other point to consider with regard to a radical political theology of dwelling. In the previous chapter, I discussed Jesus' vulnerability in terms of his torture and death—being unhoused. In the moment of extreme vulnerability, Jesus forgave his tormentors, revealing that Jesus was not operating out of the Imperial Roman apparatuses of violence, control, and exclusion. That moment revealed a radical possibility of dwelling because Jesus recognized the Roman soldiers in their suchness—theologically, *imago dei*—and though forgiveness offered a *possibility* of dwelling together. Jesus' act of forgiveness made dwelling between himself and his tormentors a possibility. It was an act of inclusion, welcome, even though dwelling, in this case, did not become actual.

To carry this further, Hannah Arendt claimed that for a polis to survive and thrive there must be mechanisms for forgiveness.[172] A polis is not a utopia, but a place of contestation, disappointment, and disruption. The possibility of forgiveness means that dwelling in the polis will not be defined by conflict, but rather will embrace the realistic hope of forgiveness as a process of repairing our dwelling together so that we can welcome Others (including nature). A polis that lacks the grace of forgiveness among its residents will not be a polis that welcomes refugees. Jesus' act of forgiveness,

170. The notion of stewardship, as Christoph Baumgartner recognizes, is an ambiguous term in ecological literature, especially when linked to theology. Baumgartner attempts to recover the concept arguing that "A Christian understanding of stewardship can be defined as the God-given mandate of humanity to preserve the Earth for the future. The obligations of humanity in view of creation are direct obligations to God, who is understood as creator and owner of the Earth." While I appreciate the attempt, what remains in place is the sovereignty of God (and owner) and anthropocentrism. A radical political theology advocates a non-sovereign (non-owning) God and a non-sovereign humanity that is one species among millions dwelling on the earth. Baumgartner, "Transformations of Stewardship in the Anthropocene," 63.

171. Smith, *Against Ecological Sovereignty*, 158.

172. Arendt, *The Promise of Politics*.

in my view, was a radical act of creating the very possibility of dwelling in an agonistic polis. Even the alienating and horrific violence done by the Roman soldiers did not deter the possibility of dwelling with them, not as soldiers, not in terms of their deeds, but in terms of their suchness.

Perhaps we are realizing in the Anthropocene Age that human beings "are not only vulnerable to one another in nature, but nature is vulnerable as well."[173] The reality of our vulnerability is also the recognition of our dwelling together and the necessity of hospitality for refugees, as well as the ongoing task of forgiving those within the polis for the sake of dwelling together. Lest one think this is confined to a particular polis (it is), it refers to the world as polis. We are all residents; we are all citizens of one earth. And in this one polis, forgiveness makes exclusion inoperative and creates the possibility of cooperating with others for the common good of all, which includes the good of other-than-human creatures and the earth itself. Whether people will accept forgiveness is another question. The Roman guards apparently did not accept forgiveness, but that does not mean that Jesus' forgiveness was without meaning because it had no visible effect. A radical political theology of welcome and forgiveness is not contingent on results, though results would be welcomed. It is based on the possibility of thinking and being/dwelling otherwise. It is based on the possibility of a coming community, on dwelling together on this one earth.

## Conclusion

The problem and challenges of dwelling belong to all creatures, though human beings have exacerbated the problems due to our tendencies to exclude Others and nature. Yet, we know it is possible to dwell, not in spite of, but because of the immense plurality among living beings. A radical political theology must take note of and be critical toward anthropological machines, whether secular or theological apparatuses of subjugation/subordination, that base dwelling on exclusion and the illusions of inferiority and superiority. Positively stated, radical political theologies facilitate dwelling by aiding human beings to think and be otherwise, to accept vulnerability and dependency as the foundations for dwelling, to acknowledge and affirms suchness and plurality as necessary for experiences of dwelling, to claim responsibility for refugees, other-than-human beings, and the earth itself. In short, acknowledging our collective vulnerability is a recognition of the existential need for and dependence on diverse Others (including other-than-human

173. Davis, "Umwelt and Nature in Merleau-Ponty's Ontology," 125.

beings) for the possibility of dwelling and, more specifically, our political dwelling with nature.

# 3

# *The Problem of Sovereignty*

---

The original sin of sovereignty threatens to contaminate
the history which flows from it, and so must be suppressed.[1]

If we conquer nature, we will find ourselves among the defeated.[2]

A sovereign humanity will lay on the rubble of an unhoused earth.

The institutions of earthly sovereignty "of man over man" cannot
and must not represent the Messiah. The messianic cannot legitimate
real, existing political orders but can only make them irrelevant and
ultimately replace them.[3]

The real political task in a society such as ours is to criticize the workings of institutions which appear to be neutral and independent; to
criticize them in such a manner that the political violence which has
always exercised itself obscurely through them will be unmasked, so
that on can fight them.[4]

---

1. Eagleton, *Tragedy*, 101.

2. Schell, "The Human Shadow," 19. Alan Watts also points out the Western preoccupations with conquering nature, as if nature is an object to serve the needs of humanity. Watts, *The Way of Zen*, 174–75.

3. Hartwich, Assmann, and Assmann, "Afterword," 142.

4. Foucault in De La Torre, *Embracing Hopelessness*, 21.

Millenia ago, we read that the Israelites initially viewed God as their sovereign, which meant that leaders (e.g., Moses) appointed by God were subordinate to God and not sovereign themselves.[5] In terms of the divine state of exception, this meant that the Israelites could, without a tinge of remorse, slaughter the inhabitants of the promised land because a sovereign God ordered them to, thus connecting the tragic reality of dwelling with sovereignty.[6] Put another way, why should the Israelites feel guilt when ordered to kill, given that "the Judge of all the earth" can only "do right" (Gen 18:25)? This arrangement wherein God is THE sovereign went on for some time, ordering the life of the Israelites. Perhaps the first murmuring of dissatisfaction emerged during the time when Gideon was the leader. After defeating the Midianites, the "people"[7] asked Gideon to be their ruler. Gideon responded, "I will not rule over you, and my son will not rule over you; the Lord will rule over you" (Judg 8:23). Gideon was adhering to the traditional story that God is the only sovereign. I imagine that these men, dissatisfied with the response, went back to figure out another way to have their own appointed ruler. Later, the elders of Israel approached Samuel, asking him to beseech God to "appoint for us a king to govern us like other nations" (1 Sam 8:5). God commanded Samuel to go to the people and warn them of the consequences of having a human as their sovereign. Samuel told them that:

> These will be the ways of the king who will reign over you: he will take your sons and appoint them to his chariots and be his horsemen, and to run before his chariots; and he will appoint for himself commanders of thousands and commanders of fifties, and some to plow his ground and to reap his harvest, and to make his implements of war and equipment of his chariots. He will take your daughters to be perfumers and cooks and bakers. He will take the best of your fields and vineyards and olive orchards and give them to his courtiers. He will take one-tenth of your grain and of your vineyards and give it to his officers and his courtiers. He will take your male and female slaves, and the best of your cattle and donkeys and put them to his work. He will take one-tenth of your flocks, and you shall be his slaves. (8:11–17)

5. Walzer, *In God's Shadow*, 53.

6. From a psychological perspective, constructing a story in which God the sovereign orders one to commit murder is just a cover for human beings exercising the state of exception.

7. Since the Torah is a thoroughly patriarchal text, I am assuming that "people" refers to men who sought to gain from these changes.

Undeterred by the bleak warnings, the elders wanted a human ruler and God acquiesced, leaving one to wonder why—hopefully not to take pleasure in saying, "I told you so." As Samuel predicted, a human leviathan possesses the state of exception and rules through subordination and subjugation, taking what pleases him and ignoring the cries of the oppressed. Samuel's prophecies came true, which, in one sense, gave rise to the prophets who sought, in part, to bring the rulers into accountability, though, in my estimation, with little success because the fundamental structures of sovereignty remained firmly ensconced in Jewish (and later Christian) theology.

These early religious stories (and others[8]) may be said to begin the long tradition of ontologizing sovereignty,[9] which becomes, in my view, a strategy for the (political, religious) elite to legitimize, justify, and mystify various iterations of sovereignty and its "necessity" for human dwelling,[10] both in terms of privileging one group of human beings over other groups and privileging human beings over nature. Of course, it is not simply religious myths that ensconce sovereignty in ontology. Philosophers like Plato and Aristotle possessed their own ideas and stories about sovereignty and its roots in human nature and the transcendent, influencing much of the political and religious discourse on sovereignty in the West. Later, Hobbes and Rousseau, for instance, both used the myth of the state of nature to secure their ideas of sovereignty. For Hobbes, citizens ceded their individual

8. The Gilgamesh story, around 4000 years old, tells the tale and journey of a king who is initially quite bad, indicating that there were some shared views that the sovereign should be concerned about the needs of his people. What is also interesting in this story is an ecological warning regarding the exploitation of the land. For many scholars, this story precedes the stories in Jewish scriptures. See George, *The Epic of Gilgamesh*.

9. Agamben returns to the ancient Greeks in his criticism of sovereignty (split between *zoē* and *bios*) in the West. I however contend that the issue of sovereignty is steeped in scripture, which goes back at least as far and carries right through today in the claims of conservative religious Israelis' who use scripture to assert "sovereignty" over the land and Palestinians. The problem of sovereignty, in other words, does not simply fall to the Greeks, but to Judeo-Christian scriptures that ontologize a sovereign God. Agamben, *Sovereign Power and Bare Life*.

10. Agamben, in a later work (*The Kingdom and the Glory*), differentiates between sovereignty and government. While this is important, in this chapter I do not have time and space to address this, except to say that when I refer to the sovereign class, I am referring also to the governmental apparatuses that produce and enforce sovereignty. As Daniel McLoughlin writes, "the governmental machine is the practice of glorification (e.g., spectacle, acclamation), which celebrates the appearance of sovereignty and therefore binds the subjects of governmental activity to its power . . . In the society of the spectacle . . . the glorification gives legitimacy to the activity of governing." McLoughlin, "Agamben on the Post-Fordist Spectacle," 107. On the relation between sovereignty and governmentality see also Primera, *The Political Ontology of Giorgio Agamben*, 71–86.

sovereignty for the safety and security of the leviathan,[11] who seemed to be a secularized, but less loving and merciful, version of an omnipotent God.[12] Rousseau used the state of nature to defend human freedom and equality over and against a civilization that undermined both.[13] While different from Hobbes, Rousseau's more democratic sovereignty also had a tinge of the leviathan, which was the General Will. These and many other philosophers deliberated directly on the issue of sovereignty, but the notion of sovereignty also quietly crops up in both the hard and human sciences. For instance, many people are familiar with Freud's creative account of humanity in *Totem and Taboo*, which he used to buttress his idea of the Oedipal Complex as the foundation of psychosocial development—a myth masquerading as a theory.[14] In Freud's state of nature, he imagined a seemingly all-powerful father who led the tribe and possessed unfettered access to any female. His sons apparently resented their subordinate role and lack of salacious privileges, if you will, and plotted to kill the father. The revolution happened, but nothing changed. Patriarchal sovereignty remained, though with now having to deal with repressing guilt from having killed the father.[15] Freud (and others), in my view, unwittingly and not surprisingly, used a story to legitimize patriarchal sovereignty extant in his culture and religion. The issue of human sovereignty is also evident in the physical sciences as well. Today numerous safeguards are in place regarding science and the use of human subjects, revealing the past and present tendency for some scientists to have dominion over their subjects. If we consider science and the pervasiveness of animal testing, we see further evidence of human sovereignty over nature—animals are subject to human control and exploitation for human well-being. And there are climate scientists today who

---

11. Ryan, *On Politics*, 440–47.

12. Carl Schmitt claimed that "All significant concepts of the modern theory of the state are secularized theological concepts not only because of their historical development—in which they were transferred from theology to the theory of the state, whereby, for example, the omnipotent God became the omnipotent lawgiver—but also because of their systematic structure, the recognition of which is necessary for a sociological consideration of these concepts." Hobbes is a clear example of what Schmitt claims. Schmitt, *Political Theology*, 36.

13. Ryan, *On Politics*, 556–72.

14. Freud, "Totem and Taboo."

15. I do not have time to go further into this and it would divert my attention from other pressing matters with regard to sovereignty. But I would like to mention that Freud's story reveals the mimetic nature of sovereignty and its violence. It may also be that guilt is connected to the fact that to assert sovereignty is already to have committed violence, even in democracies, which will be clearer below.

argue for geoengineering of the planet, which suggests a kind of control and power associated with sovereignty.[16]

Theologies, philosophies, sciences, and other discourses on sovereignty seem to produce a sense that sovereignty is an unquestionable fact of human (and divine) nature. These anthropological machines and attending social-political apparatuses continually produce the "fact" of sovereignty. We are told in countless ways that, without sovereignty, there would be unimaginable violence and chaos, the loss of freedom, the obliteration of rights, stoking fears to accept the leviathan. Thus, with the fear and dread of Hobbes, let us kneel down and accept the sovereign leviathan, even as we see ourselves as sovereign over nature. But we should cast a hermeneutic eye of suspicion whenever we encounter the constant need to reproduce an idea and frighten people if they do not believe it, do not submit to it, or offer an alternative idea. Ideas that must constantly be reproduced and buttressed by "human nature" or the "divine," like racism, sexism, and, in this case, sovereignty, reveal not the reality but the illusion—albeit an illusion cloaked and mystified in "fact/truth," though, of course,[17] undergirded by powerful, very real apparatuses that have profound consequences.

Readers will have already picked up that I view sovereignty as a problem,[18] not simply for political philosophy and theology, but, as I will argue, for the Anthropocene Age. Sovereignty, having some benefits, always has been a problem in human dwelling, but with the arrival of the Anthropocene Age we can see more clearly how sovereignty, which is justified by dominion theologies and philosophies, is a cause of the devastating exploitation of the earth and other species (and othered human beings), leading to countless extinctions (and perhaps a tragic cause for human extinction). To refer to the quote at the beginning of the chapter, "If we conquer nature, we will find ourselves among the defeated." To proceed in my argument, I first

16. Smith, *Against Ecological Sovereignty.*

17. "Illusion" means misleading perception or mistaken belief. In this chapter and elsewhere I am using illusion to refer not to the belief in God (how could one prove or disprove this), but to beliefs that claim sovereignty is necessary for human existence, human belonging. While sovereignty clearly exists, it is a mistaken belief to say that it is necessary for human life, when clearly there are other ways of ordering communities and societies. To argue that this is an illusion with respect to God is more difficult. I would rather argue that human beings have tended to project sovereignty onto God to legitimate human manifestations of sovereignty and subsequent rule over other people and nature. The illusion is that human beings are indeed sovereign, which, ultimately, the Anthropocene Age reveals to be false.

18. Schmitt's second chapter of his book on political theology deals with the problem of sovereignty in terms of the legal decision, which I will say more about below. My understanding of the problems of sovereignty are more radical in that I (like others) question its very ontological existence. Schmitt, *Political Theology*, 16–35.

provide some background on the concept of sovereignty and its attributes. This serves as a foundational step toward identifying and discussing some of the problems of sovereignty, not only with regard to other human beings, but also other species. In other words, I contend that sovereignty is not only a problem vis-à-vis human dwelling and the acceptance of the refugee, but also problematic or the dwelling of other-than-human beings and the earth as the dwelling place of all life. The last section turns to a discussion of a radical political theology of a non-sovereign and non-privileging God and a non-sovereign humanity. Here I first turn to an existential root of non-sovereign or anarchic relations, evident in good-enough parent-child interactions. What I claim here is that sovereignty, while a human issue, is not inevitably or irreducibly a fact of human relations. The "state of nature," if you will, reveals other-than-sovereign relations in organizing society and relating to other species. I then turn to argue that the vulnerability of Jesus Christ is, in part, a revelation of a non-sovereign, non-privileging God—a God of infinite, indeterminate love for creation. It is radical in that it is the foundation or root of a political theology for the Anthropocene Age and radical in the sense of undermining and rejecting any theology or anthropology of human sovereignty over human beings and/or nature. That is, the revelation of the incarnation exposes the illusion of human sovereignty and privilege and exposes the theological and philosophical machines that aim to reproduce, legitimize, and maintain illusions of sovereignty and invulnerability/autonomy.

As is my habit, I would like to offer a few clarifications before beginning. As readers know, the topic of sovereignty is deeply complex and has been taken up in numerous volumes and articles. Indeed, the subject matter is daunting. While I make no claim to be an expert, I will endeavor to present, in a concise way, what sovereignty is and describe its attributes, recognizing that much more can be said, especially when we locate the issue of sovereignty in theological traditions. Second, the idea that sovereignty is an illusion, which is projected onto God (not an attribute of God), would appear to undercut much of scripture, not to mention much of Western philosophical and theological treatises. While this may border on hubris, if not heresy[19] for some, the Anthropocene Age invites a radical theology that

19. Heresy is a technical term and anyone familiar with Christian history will see its close connection to maintaining, often through violence, the sovereignty of dominant theological beliefs, if not the sovereignty of the rulers within the church. To say that sovereignty is an illusion does not mean that claims of God's sovereignty are heresy or a non-sovereign God is heretical. Just as many scholars believe the creation stories are myth, one could say that sovereignty of God is a myth—a human construction. Finally, instead of getting caught up in whether something is heretical or untrue, I find it more helpful to consider how one's beliefs give rise to a form of life. Then we can examine

"critiques the tradition from within so to suspend its authority and free it for a new use."[20] Or as Clayton Crockett contends, "We need to experiment radically with new ways of thinking and living, because the current paradigm is in a state of exhaustion, depletion, and death."[21] I would add, with further explanation below, those who vociferously advocate for sovereignty, divine or human, reveal the reality of classism, which is the base of claims of religious and secular sovereignty and its garnishment of power, privilege, and prestige at the expense of other human beings and nature. Any manifestation of sovereignty, in other words, will reveal social, political, and economic inequalities based on the privileging of one group over other groups.[22] Third, what I hope to make clear is that sovereignty is not a necessary and sufficient cause of human dwelling together, whether that refers to each other, other species, and the earth. In other words, I demonstrate that sovereignty is not an existential attribute of being human, and the evidence for this is not only in the "state of nature" of parent-child interactions, but in the numerous ways of living together that are not tied to or dependent on sovereignty. We see this in Acts and the early Christian communities struggling to dwell without Roman or Jewish forms of sovereignty. It is evident in some monastic communities (e.g., Benedictine), where the abbot leads and collaborates with the monks, but is not sovereign over them. As mentioned in the previous chapter, it is evident in the town of Longyearbyen, where the issue of sovereignty in terms of organizing society has no meaning or use. We also see glimpses of this in the works of philosophers like Agamben[23] and Hardt and Negri.[24] All of this is to say that where we find exceptions to living without sovereignty, we find evidence that sovereignty is not a necessary fact of human existence, but is instead a human construction that must be continually produced.

## Sovereignty: Definitions and Attributes

In the sixteenth century, Jean Bodin (1530–1596), a French jurist and political philosopher, sought to explain what sovereignty is, perhaps because

whether this form of life is, in the case of the Anthropocene Age, beneficial to others and the earth.

20. Kotsko, "Agamben's Messianic Nihilism," 123.
21. Crockett, *Radical Political Theology*, 165.
22. See Harman, *A People's History of the World*.
23. Agamben, *Sovereign Power and Bare Life* Agamben, *The Coming Community*.
24. Hardt and Negri, *Multitude*.

of the political instability resulting from the Protestant Reformation.[25] Of course, sovereignty and its varied forms had been discussed and argued since Plato and Aristotle, if not before,[26] but Bodin sought to identify its fundamental attributes. There are, for Bodin, four essential features of sovereignty, namely, supreme power (no superior), absolute, indivisible, and perpetual. One can easily imagine these traits fitting best in relation to God, but, for Bodin, they are also features of human sovereignty. The king has no superior (except God), is absolute in his rule, his power and rule cannot be divided, and his rule is perpetual, handed down to his sons (in rare cases, daughters). This pre-Enlightenment formulation of sovereignty was not completely abandoned following the Enlightenment, though it certainly had parallels in the work of Thomas Hobbes. Indeed, in the twentieth century, German jurist Carl Schmitt picks up on Bodin's work, pointing out that it is widely referenced in works on sovereignty,[27] though these works often ignore a core aspect of Bodin's thought. Schmitt writes:

> Bodin asked if the commitments of the prince to the states or people dissolve his sovereignty. He answered by referring to the case in which it becomes necessary to violate such commitments. To change laws or to suspend them entirely according to the requirements of a situation, a time, and a people. If in such cases the prince had to consult a senate or the people before he could act, he would have to be prepared to let his subjects dispense with him. Bodin considered this an absurdity because, according to him, the estates were not masters over the laws . . . Sovereignty would thus become a play between two parties.[28]

Sticking to his ideas regarding the attributes of sovereignty, Bodin considered the example above to violate at least three of the four attributes.

By the time Carl Schmitt (1888–1985) was writing, there had been a number of revolutions (e.g., American, French, and Russian), as well as a struggling democracy in Germany after World War I. Schmitt, in his study of law-making and law-preserving actions of the state, wished to reinterpret Bodin's work. Schmitt boldly states that the core feature of sovereignty is the state of exception. "The sovereign," he writes, "is he who decides on the state of exception."[29] He adds, "What characterizes an exception is principally unlimited authority, which means the suspension of the entire existing

25. Bodin, *On Sovereignty*.
26. See Grayling, *The History of Philosophy*, 35–39.
27. Schmitt, *Political Theology*, 8.
28. Schmitt, *Political Theology*, 9–10.
29. Schmitt, *Political Theology*, 5.

order. In such a situation it is clear that the state remains, whereas the law recedes."[30] The law and the state, in other words, are subordinate to the absolute authority of the sovereign.

Besides the fact that Schmitt carries forward the idea of sovereignty embodied in an ostensibly male person, there are two key points here. The sovereign possesses the absolute authority to make a decision that is beyond the law, which might awaken our memory of a democratically elected president who, after claiming he was the decider in chief, authorized torture and non-judicial confinement of so-called enemy combatants. The second and more complicated feature here is the state of exception. This phrase means that the sovereign, as we see in the quote above, can, because of absolute power/authority, decide to set aside laws according to the requirements of a given situation—*extremus necessitatis casus*.[31] Schmitt goes on to argue that a "sovereign produces and guarantees the situation in its totality. He has a monopoly over this last decision. Therein resides the essence of the state's sovereignty, which may be juristically defined correctly, not as a monopoly to coerce or to rule, but as a monopoly to decide."[32] Bodin's absolute power/authority is seen in Schmitt, though now framed as the state of exception. We might think of a state of emergency when the sovereign, for real or imagined reasons of security, has the power/authority to suspend the law. For Agamben, the state of exception has become the rule in modern states and especially in neoliberal capitalist regimes.[33]

It is important to mention that the power to exercise a decision on the state of exception does not mean the sovereign must exercise this power. According to Schmitt, power is inherent in sovereignty even if it is never exercised. This is why, in my view, he mentions the relation between miracles and the state of exception. Schmitt believed that "All significant concepts of the modern theory of the state are secularized theological concepts,"[34] which includes modern notions of sovereignty. So, if we turn to God, the occasional miracle is an example of the sovereign God's decision to suspend "natural laws." From Schmitt's perspective, God, as sovereign, and human beings as sovereigns, always have the potential to decide on the state of exception.[35]

30. Schmitt, *Political Theology*, 12.

31. Schmitt, *Political Theology*, 10.

32. Schmitt, *Political Theology*, 13.

33. Agamben, *State of Exception*.

34. Agamben, *State of Exception*, 36

35. Like Schmitt, Hannah Arendt, who is one of the key conversational figures in Agamben's work, argued that sovereignty "grew out of the Judeo-Christian theological notion of divine will, and survived, though in an inverted form, the transformation

For both Agamben and Schmitt, the "sovereign exception is . . . the condition for the possibility of the juridical order, for it is through the state of exception that sovereignty creates and guarantees the order the law needs for its own validity."[36] At the same time, "the state of exception exercises the law as force."[37] Agamben, then, takes on Schmitt's idea that the sovereign stands outside of, but belongs to, the juridical order, which is a paradox. The paradox is yoked to questions of the relations between sovereignty, the law, and violence. "The paradox of sovereignty," Agamben writes, "consists in the fact that the sovereign is, at the same time, outside and inside the juridical order."[38] As he states elsewhere, "the state of exception appears as the legal form of what cannot have legal form . . . if the law employs the state of exception—that is the suspension of the law itself."[39] Stated differently, "As a figure of necessity, the state of exception therefore appears as an 'illegal' but perfectly 'juridical and constitutional' measure."[40] Sovereignty, then, "is neither external nor internal to the juridical order."[41] While paradoxical, "The sovereign exception is, for both Schmitt and Agamben, the condition for the possibility of juridical order, for it is through the state of exception that the sovereign creates and guarantees the order the law needs for its own validity."[42] This stated, the paradoxical[43] nature of sovereignty is evident in

---

brought about in the modern world." Agamben sought to locate the notion of sovereignty in ancient Greece and Rome. In Kalyvas, "The Sovereign Weaver," 109. Andreas Kalyvas notes further that "Arendt and Schmitt underscore the inherent relationship between sovereignty and will" while "Agamben dispenses with questions of will, about which he is rather uninterested, to focus on a distinct set of issues involving the relationship between political power and life. Unlike Arendt, whose main concern was to rethink political freedom, by extricating it once and for all from Christian theological remnants of the will, Agamben explores the biopolitical nature of sovereign power." Kalyvas, "The Sovereign Weaver," 110.

36. DeCaroli, "Boundary Stones," 53.

37. Colebrook and Maxwell, *Agamben*, 54.

38. Agamben, *Sovereign Power and Bare Life*, 15.

39. Agamben, *State of Exception*, 1.

40. Agamben, *State of Exception*, 28.

41. Agamben, *State of Exception*, 23.

42. DeCaroli, "Boundary Stones," 54.

43. While I will focus on a couple of paradoxes of sovereignty, it is worth mentioning that Wendy Brown identifies six paradoxes of sovereignty: 1) Sovereignty is both a name for absolute power and a name for political freedom; 2) Sovereignty generates order through subordination and freedom through autonomy; 3) Sovereignty has no internal essence, but rather is completely dependent and relational, even as it stands for autonomy, self-presence, and self-sufficiency; 4) Sovereignty produces both internal hierarchy and external anarchy; 5) Sovereignty is both a sign of the rule and the jurisdiction of law and supervenes the law; 6) Sovereignty is both generated and generative.

that the "work of sovereignty precedes the law, creating a regular 'frame of life,' which the law preserves and codifies but does not instantiate."[44] One might imagine Freud's early tribal father and his rule over other men and women. As sovereign, his rule precedes the law, but it is later, as we see in patriarchal scriptures, laws and institutions are constructed to preserve the sovereign who, in turn, can suspend the laws. Theologically, we imagine God as sovereign of the universe. As sovereign, God precedes creation and the "laws of nature," but these very laws, which can be suspended (miracles), also preserve the majesty of God's sovereignty. This is evident in Job, where God falls back on creation as evidence of God's sovereignty that Job has no right to question.

Before turning to other key attributes of sovereignty, it is important to point out that sovereignty does not simply refer to *a person* exercising the decision about the state of exception. This can be understood in several ways. First, Agamben points out that "the police are always operating within a similar state of exception."[45] The police (and other security forces and institutions) can be understood as the arm of the sovereign's power vis-à-vis the state of exception. Moreover, the police, at least in the United States, often have power to make decisions to use deadly force. And we have seen that while police shootings are "reviewed," they rarely end up in convictions. That is, the "perpetrator" can be killed without it being considered a homicide (or sacrifice)—Agamben's term *homo sacer* fits here.[46] This means that the police stand with and belong to the juridical order, while also standing outside it. Second, it is not only the police who can exhibit the state of exception. In the United States, there is a long, sordid, racist history of terroristic lynching and raping African Americans.[47] These acts were outside the juridical order, yet done with tacit approval of the white juridical order in that African Americans could not obtain justice. White supremacists were within the legal order, but not subject to it during slavery and Jim Crow. In one sense, white supremacists decided on the state of exception when they terrorized African American citizens. African Americans were included-excluded Others—within the juridical order, but excluded from its protections. They could be killed or raped and, in both cases, these were not considered crimes. African Americans, then, existed outside the

Brown, *Walled Sovereignty*, 53–54.

44. Brown, *Walled Sovereignty*, 50.

45. Agamben, *State of Exception*, 103.

46. Agamben, *Sovereign Power and Bare Life*, 42.

47. See Alexander, *The New Jim Crow*; Anderson, *White Rage*; McGuire, *At the Dark End of the Street*; Wilkerson, *Caste*.

protection of human and divine law.[48] Agamben, I believe, would agree with this illustration, when he notes that it is the sovereign who "has the power to decide which life may be killed without the commission of a homicide."[49]

Third, when it comes to sovereignty as the state of exception, how does it pertain to democracies? The simple answer is that, in democracies, the issue of sovereignty becomes associated with the *demos*, the people. So, how is it that the decision on the state of exception can be possible if this falls to the *demos*? Is it not unlike Hobbes' leviathan, wherein the populace hands over their sovereignty to the leviathan for protection and security?[50] Or we could say that in representative democracies, elected officials, especially the chief executive, exercise sovereignty for a period of time. This includes governors, as we have seen during the recent pandemic when they declared states of emergency, closing non-essential businesses and confining people mainly to their homes. Governors and presidents, though, cannot exercise the decision for a state of exception without state apparatuses or disciplinary regimes to carry this out. As DeCaroli notes, "[S]overeign power ought not be envisioned as a force from outside, but rather as an integral part of the political field itself . . . Sovereignty is the embeddedness of authority within a field of application."[51]

Let me complicate this further. Many Americans believe we live in a democracy, but for Agamben, there is, despite many important differences, "an inner solidarity between democracy and totalitarianism,"[52] which is not far from Tocqueville's critique of American democracy (tyranny of the majority),[53] Hannah Arendt's views of the sources of totalitarianism,[54] and Sheldon Wolin's analysis of the U.S. as an inverted totalitarian system.[55] Commenting on Agamben's view, DeCaroli argues that "even if democratic regimes maintain safeguards designed to prevent many of the totalitarian excesses perpetrated against bare life,[56] they continue unwittingly to create

48. Agamben, *Sovereign Power and Bare Life*, 83.

49. Agamben, *Sovereign Power and Bare Life*, 142.

50. Ryan, *On Politics*, 418–20.

51. DeCaroli, "Boundary Stones," 48.

52. Agamben, *Sovereign Power and Bare Life*, 10.

53. De Tocqueville, *Democracy in America*. I would add that while Rousseau advocates for a kind of democracy, his notion of the General Will is frighteningly close to absolute power, revealing that the attributes of sovereignty make their way into discussions about democracy.

54. Arendt, *The Origins of Totalitarianism*.

55. Wolin, *Democracy Incorporated*.

56. To remind readers, bare life refers to the separation of *zoē* (physical life) and *bios* (political life), which results in the objectification and alienation of human beings.

the conditions of possibility for such consequences."[57] Another way of saying this is that democracies and totalitarian regimes, while demonstrably different, still operate out of and depend on the notion of the state of exception. To return to slavery and Jim Crow, both existed in an ostensibly democratic society, but both were clearly illustrations of totalitarianism existing within a democracy.

But this is only one side of the complication with regard to democracies and the state of exception. Sheldon Wolin used the term "inverted totalitarianism" to refer to the current conditions of sovereignty vis-à-vis democracies, like the United States. Wolin differentiated between classic state totalitarian systems (e.g., Nazi Germany, Soviet Union) and what he termed "inverted totalitarian systems." Inverted totalitarian systems project power inward by "combining with other forms of power, such as evangelical religion, and most notably encouraging a symbiotic relationship between traditional government and the system of 'private' governance represented by the modern corporation."[58] Wolin argued that inverted totalitarianism uses the state to legitimate its dominance, whereas in classic totalitarianism, the state uses business to achieve its aims of projecting power outwards. The accumulation of the various forms and nodes of power means that there is no clear leader/sovereign of the system, as there would be in a state totalitarian system.[59] In totalitarian states, there is a dictator or absolute sovereign, while in inverted totalitarian societies there are many leaders from different parts of society (e.g., political, economic, religious) who support and shape the inverted totalitarian system. This makes it difficult for citizens to identify who is responsible. Neoliberal capitalism, as a dominant social imaginary, functions as an inverted totalitarian system in which the state is used to legitimate and extend the power of the market, through legal privatization of previously public institutions and spaces, deregulation, austerity

---

Agamben uses the example of the Nazis, but closer to home we can see bare life vis-à-vis U.S. slavery and racism. Moreover, Agamben argues that bare life is the condition of the modern political realm and it is our task to bring these two together in the coming political community. Agamben's use of this term is connected to his reading of Arendt's *On the Origins of Totalitarianism*, wherein she indicates that in these regimes the life of citizens can become superfluous and when that happens they can be easily killed without it being considered homicide. Agamben takes this further, arguing that bare life today is the foundation of the political milieu and a seed embedded in Western notions of sovereignty. What Agamben tends to avoid are those instances of community or society where *zoē* and *bios* are united or when people resist and transgress the political machinery that leads to bare life. Agamben, *Sovereign Power and Bare Life*.

57. DeCaroli, "Boundary Stones," 172.

58. Wolin, *Democracy Incorporated*, xvi.

59. Wolin, *Democracy Incorporated*, 44.

measures, and the expansion of money in the political process—all examples of the state of exception and diffuse nodes of power. For instance, non-state institutions such as corporations, think tanks, lobbying groups, etc., work closely with the state in deregulating and privatizing public goods. Because there is no clear, single organization or person involved in using the state, it becomes impossible to locate the leaders who are responsible, heightening a sense of helplessness and futility among many citizens. I would add that while the center of power is difficult to locate, citizens may continue to believe that political power or sovereignty resides in traditional government institutions. This belief or illusion screens people from recognizing other real sources of power, as well as their own helplessness in acting toward that power.

A related feature of an inverted totalitarianism regime is that it constructs and "prefers a citizenry that is uncritically complicit rather than involved."[60] Henry Giroux similarly argued that the hegemony of neoliberal symbol systems contributes to the construction of acritical subjects who either rabidly support capitalism or who never think to question it.[61] Citizens or non-citizens (e.g., Pope Francis) who do question the system become marginalized or attacked as socialists, Marxists, communists, lefties, etc., which serves as a warning to others who might deviate from accepting the system as it is. An uncritical populace colludes with the inverted totalitarian system's exercise of sovereignty.

An acritical and passive citizenry can be achieved in a number of ways. In traditional totalitarian systems, the state uses police and military to instill compliance and to brutally repress dissent. Totalitarian states, at the same time, use patriotism to mobilize the masses and to squelch critique. As Wolin notes, inverted totalitarian systems, however, do not need the brutal tactics of police[62] and military oppression to keep citizens in line. Instead, it establishes itself as an unquestionable and pervasive reality. That is, inverted totalitarian systems, like the neoliberal capitalistic state, involves using the state (all three branches of government), groups (e.g., think tanks), and other power centers (e.g., media, religious communities and leaders) to legitimate, if not sacralize, the system, whereby it becomes an unquestionable fact of existence or a necessity. Margaret Thatcher's slogan, "There Is No Alternative," is an example. Besides the illusion of necessity, "Classical totalitarianism mobilizes its subjects; inverted totalitarianism . . . fragments

60. Wolin, *Democracy Incorporated*, 65.

61. Giroux, *Disposable Youth*.

62. It is important to mention that the police in the U.S. have often been used to "police" populations (African Americans) and squelch dissent.

them."[63] People "are encouraged to distrust their government and politicians; to concentrate upon their own interests; to begrudge their taxes; and to exchange active involvement for symbolic gratification of patriotism, collective self-righteousness, and military prowess."[64] An inverted totalitarian system at the heart of democracy maintains the illusion that sovereignty lies with the people, but in truth the oligarchs and plutocrats rule.[65]

When it comes to sovereignty and the state of exception vis-à-vis democracies, the troubling paradox above needs further attention. As Agamben and Schmitt point out, the paradox of the sovereign decision is that it is both within and outside the juridical order. Yet, in a democracy, it is believed that the people decide on the state of exception. There are several difficulties here. First, can we imagine that the *demos* deciding on the state of exception will be both within and outside the juridical order at the same time? This is not likely, since, as I will discuss below, the sovereign's decision denotes subordination and exclusion—those who do not have the power to decide. Second, sovereignty as the state of exception represents political hierarchy and power. The *demos* suggests the absence of political hierarchy and the presence of shared power, which in reality is an area of profound contestation. Third, and relatedly, can we actually imagine a society of adults acting as sovereigns, acting both inside and outside the juridical order? Perhaps Hobbes did, which may be why he opted for a leviathan. More to the point, philosopher Wendy Brown points out, "Sovereignty is inherently antidemocratic insofar as it must overcome the dispersed quality of power in a democracy, but democracy, to be politically viable, to be a (political) contender, appears to require the supplement of sovereignty."[66] There is, then, the complication and paradox of sovereignty vis-à-vis democracies, but also something we apparently "must" believe (necessary fiction?) and that is that sovereignty is inevitable or necessary, which Agamben will argue it is not.

Let's return to identifying several other related attributes of sovereignty. What is clear in the discussion above is that a foundational feature

63. Wolin, *Democracy Incorporated*, 196.

64. Wolin, *Democracy Incorporated*, 43.

65. A Princeton study by Martin Gilens and Benjamin Page reveals the harsh realities of an inverted totalitarian system and the toll of political irrelevancy in a so-called democratic nation. They note that "the preferences of the average American appear to have only a minuscule, near-zero, statistically non-significant impact on public policy." This point mirrors Wolin's in that the U.S. is not a democracy wherein the people are sovereign, but more of a plutocracy in which the political and economic elites are sovereign. Gilens and Page, "Testing Theories of American Politics," 575.

66. Brown, *Walled States, Waning Sovereignty*, 51–52.

of sovereignty is servitude or submission, associated with hierarchical relations.[67] From a theological perspective, God as the sovereign means that
human beings are to submit to God's rule. As mentioned above, God is both
inside and outside the laws of nature and God's own laws. We read, "Shall
not the Judge of all the earth do right?" (Gen 18:25), in light of killing Egyptians and orders to kill the inhabitants of Palestine. The sovereign God does
right regardless, because God is both outside and inside the law and can set
the law aside—as in the cases of miracles and orders to kill. God, in other
words, creates the ten commandments, but does not have to follow them. In
short, everything and everyone are subordinate to God's state of exception.

When the Israelites petitioned God to have their own sovereign, it soon
became clear that they continued to remain subordinate, if not at times subjugated, by their kings (and ruling class), perhaps leaving one to wonder if it
was better to be subservient to a sovereign God. This said, even the prophets
who railed against the injustices of political leaders never questioned their
subordination to the rule of God or to the rule of just kings. The prophets
critiqued how kings ruled in that they failed to keep the promises (social
contract) made to God, which included caring for their people. In democracies, we believe that the government is subordinate to the people, but in
actuality, the people are in many ways subordinate to the rule of law, which
they do not make themselves. In inverted totalitarian systems, citizens are
subordinate to, if not subjugated by, the rule of the market. The market is
the new sovereign god, to which we must submit on bended knee.[68] There is
also within the history of U.S. democracy the implicit sovereignty of white
men of means and, later, white men and women, and the subordination and
subjugation of Native peoples and African Americans. White male European "sovereignty," based on the illusion of white supremacy, subordinated,
subjugated, and killed[69] vast numbers of people within and outside the borders. Shall not the white people of all the earth do right—as they subjugate,
subordinate, and kill other peoples?

For Agamben, sovereignty as a relation of subordination is not simply
something that pertains to relations between and among human beings.

---

67. Lechte and Newman, *Agamben and the Politics of Human Rights*, 166.

68. Cox, *The Market as God*.

69. In his work, *Sovereign Power and Bare Life*, Agamben points out that the sovereign exception means that persons may be killed, but not be considered murdered
or their death considered to be homicide. They are also not deemed to be sacrificed.
These "people" are kept outside the law's protection, as well as outside divine law. The
murders of African Americans and Native Americans at the hands of white people are
illustrations of Agamben's *homo sacer*.

Subordination and submission extend to human beings' relation to nature.[70] Commenting on Agamben's work, Colby Dickinson writes that "the human subject, in order to appear as a 'human being,' must continuously distinguish itself from other animals, even if such distinctions become more and more difficult, or even impossible to make . . . language is what allows us as humans to declare ourselves as sovereign masters capable of naming, or signifying, the rest of the world around us."[71] We must not imagine that the idea or, more correctly, the illusion of dominion over nature simply falls within the province of Judeo-Christian theology (Gen 1:28).[72] Agamben is claiming that the idea of dominion is endemic to the capacity for signification. We see evidence of this in secular philosophies, the human sciences, and the physical sciences. In terms of the realities of climate change, we hear all manner of scientists (and others) arguing for control over nature. The scientist who is noted for coining the term "Anthropocene Age," Paul Crutzen, was a strong advocate of geoengineering. Michael Northcott writes that "Crutzen does not call for a moral and spiritual renewal to reduce humanity's impacts and tread more gently on the earth. Instead, his call is for a new intentionality in the human management of the Earth System, and for a significant ramping up of research and development by scientists and technologists of the technical means for intentional intervention in the Earth System, including active geoengineering of the atmosphere."[73] This view is a longstanding one in science, going back at least to Francis Bacon (1561–1626) who claimed that "the practical aim of improving humanity's lot [depended on] increased understanding and *control* of nature,"[74] which fits neatly with the scriptural command to subdue the earth and have dominion over all life. The underlying hubris is evident in human ideologies and actions to control and subjugate nature for our benefit, which is not [so far] for the benefit of other species and earth. As noted in the beginning of this chapter, a sovereign humanity will stand on the rubble of an unhoused earth.

70. See Agamben, *The Open.*

71. Dickinson, *Agamben and Theology,* 14–15. It is important to note that this does not mean we are fated to subordinate nature (or other human beings). Agamben explores aspects of monasticism and the Franciscan movement, indicating relations vis-à-vis other human beings and nature that are not based in subordination or sovereignty. Agamben, *The Highest Poverty.*

72. Jessica Whyte writes that "for 19th century philosopher Ludwig Feuerbach God is a projection, making nature 'merely a servant of his will and needs, and hence in thought also degrades it to a mere machine, a product of the will.'" Whyte, "Praxis and Production in Agamben and Marx," 81.

73. Northcott, "On Going Gently into the Anthropocene," 24; emphasis mine.

74. Grayling, *The History of Philosophy,* 197.

Relations of subordination and subjugation are connected to and dependent on violence, which is another key feature of sovereignty. John Lechte and Paul Newman, with Agamben and Benjamin, contend that the "law always articulates itself through violence which both preserves its boundaries and exceeds them, and violence always establishes a new law . . . violence is at the very origins and foundations of the law."[75] "Law," they point out, "is never free from violence."[76] This echoes Foucault's view the "The law is born of real battles, victories, massacres, and conquests, which can be dated and which have their horrific heroes; the law was born in burning towns and ravaged fields."[77] There is, however, a deeper connection than between law and violence. In DeCaroli's reading of Agamben, the "law is not the essential function of sovereignty."[78] "The work of sovereignty," he writes, "precedes the law, creating a regular 'frame of life,' which the law preserves and codifies but does not instantiate."[79] Nevertheless, the very emergence of a sovereign depends on violence and, while sovereignty precedes the law, it brings violence to law-making and law-preserving activities.

To suggest that violence is at the core of sovereignty and law-making and law-preserving actions may be understood in a couple of ways. First, we might imagine that the very origins of sovereignty as the state of exception meant one or more individuals violently exerted this privilege by establishing relations of subordination and subjugation. In my reading of Agamben, a reason why violence is at the core of sovereignty is that relations of subordination and subjugation require violence or the threat of violence/punishment. A cursory reading of the Jewish scripture reveals the divine violence "necessary" to subjugate enemies and to subordinate women and children, as well as those stiff-necked people who apparently were not sufficiently subordinate. Second and relatedly, for Agamben, relying, in part, on Aristotle, the definition or essence of being human is potentiality, which means that, ideally, human relations facilitate potentiality into actuality. While I will say more about this below, for now potentiality is related to the experience of suchness or singularity, which is, in my view, facilitated by caring relations. Relations of subordination and subjugation, by contrast, attempt to deny and diminish individuals' potentiality and suchness (freedom), which can be accomplished only through force and violence (or threat of). As Prozorov points out, "Sovereignty is . . . the force of actualization that exhausts

75. Lechte and Newman, *Agamben and the Politics of Human Rights*, 128.
76. Lechte and Newman, *Agamben and the Politics of Human Rights*, 173.
77. In Oksala, *Foucault, Politics, and Violence*, 40.
78. DeCaroli, "Boundary Stone," 50.
79. DeCaroli, "Boundary Stone," 50.

all potentiality."[80]Furthermore, *relations of subordination are not necessary to being human*, which indicates that these relations must be continually produced and reproduced by violence or the threat of violence. Even if we do not imagine a "state of nature," like Freud's or Hobbes', we know that sovereignty itself is maintained by the threat of violence and, at times, the exercise of violence. In short words, violence is a necessary condition for the emergence of and maintenance of sovereignty's relations of subordination and subjugation. It is important to stress that while violence establishes sovereignty, it does not always mean violence is used. Violence inheres in sovereignty and in its lack of use, it nevertheless remains a very real threat.

It is important to mention that violence is not always physical. Agamben writes that "If it is the sovereign who, insofar as he decides on the state of exception, has the power to decide which life may be killed without commission of homicide, in the age of biopolitics this power becomes emancipated from the state of exception and transformed into the power to decide the point at which life ceases to be politically relevant."[81] Agamben, then, extends violence to include the power to make individuals and groups politically irrelevant, which is a central feature in U.S. democracy's inverted totalitarian system. Individuals and groups cannot become politically irrelevant without apparatuses and disciplinary regimes that threaten and commit physical violence, while at the same time *violate* their political recognition as persons, as citizens.[82] To violate individuals' recognition and status as persons is already a form of exclusion and political irrelevancy, which accompanies material deprivation through failures in the adequate distribution of resources.[83] The reality of food deserts in the poorer sections of cities, food insecurity, inadequate housing, housing insecurity, dilapidated infrastructure, evictions, and policing the poor and people of color are examples of social-political apparatuses that violate, that threaten, that create political irrelevancy. The protest group "Black Lives Matter" is an example of the pushback that stems from decades of being forced into political irrelevancy. Similarly, The Poor Peoples Campaign is an attempt to give voice to the politically marginalized and oppressed.

Of course, the violence inherent in sovereignty is not something that relates simply to human beings. The belief that human beings have dominion or sovereignty over the earth is not simply religious; it is, as noted above,

---

80. Prozorov, "Agamben, Badiou and Affirmative Biopolitics," 175.

81. Agamben, *Sovereign Power and Bare Life*, 142.

82. See Wacquant, *Punishing the Poor*; Soss, Fording, and Schram, *Disciplining the Poor*.

83. See Fraser and Honneth, *Redistribution or Recognition?*

also secular, undergirding much of the sciences. Our belief in human dominion or sovereignty is evident in geoengineering the earth as a system, in the experimentation on animals for human "benefit," the vast capitalistic exploitation of animals for human consumption and use, the exploitation of natural resources, the concomitant destruction of habitats, and the extinction of species. These are all illustrations of the human belief in human sovereignty and the desire to dominate, which are supported, legitimated, or justified by anthropological machines—machines of anthropocentrism and narcissism. Nature (earth and other-than-human species), then, is, because of human sovereignty, outside of the law and its protections.[84] Put another way, *human sovereignty and the continual state of exception towards other-than-human species and the earth itself results in their politically irrelevancy—included-excluded others to serve the privileged sphere of humanity.*

The interrelated attributes of sovereignty discussed so far (state of exception, paradox, relations of subordination, violence) are also joined to the attribute of exclusion. Exclusion is a foundational feature of sovereignty. As Wendy Brown notes, sovereignty establishes a political identity and boundary.[85] Put differently, "Sovereign power," Jenny Edkins writes, "has to produce a homogenous and pure 'people' by the exclusion of all that do not count as people in its terms."[86] All of this can be recognized in terms of what Carl Schmitt, echoing Hobbes, considered to be the basis of sovereignty: the friend-enemy distinction.[87] This can be understood in three ways. First, friend-enemy distinction can refer to the shared identity within a particular sovereign territory over and against Others, who may or may not be enemies. For those external Others who are not enemies, they remain excluded either in terms of the boundary or within the state's boundary as resident aliens, since they do not share an identity. Second, within the geographical boundaries, sovereigns have power over their subjects, indicating a shared identity and the power to enforce that identity. Of course, even going back to early Greek experiments in democracy, those who reside in the polis did not all have the same access to political agency, even though they shared an identity. Women, children, and slaves, while not "enemies," were included-excluded others. They could participate in the life of the polis, but not in political life. There were also barbarians or those from other cities, who were included-excluded others, because they, too, were not part of the political life. They did not share the identity of, say, Athenian citizens—male. If we

84. De La Durantaye, *Giorgio Agamben*, 345.
85. Brown, *Walled States, Waning Sovereignty.*
86. Edkins, "Whatever Politics," 78.
87. Schmitt, *The Concept of the Political*, 26.

fast forward to the 19th and 20th centuries, slaves were included-excluded others who could be exploited and who could be killed without their deaths being deemed homicides.[88] They did not share in the identity of U.S. male citizens, though they were included within the geographic boundaries established by the state. The oppressions that took place after the Civil War up to today indicate that people of color are often constructed and treated as included-excluded others who are marginalized vis-à-vis their political relevancy, which protests seek to change. Finally, sovereignty's relations of subordination are exclusive in that they create an exclusion of those who do not share in the power, privileges, and prestige of the sovereign. Chris Harmon argues that, since the beginning of civilization, classism has been present in various forms and is based on the friend-enemy distinction or inclusion-exclusion. Maybe one could suggest that, since the beginning of the notion of sovereignty, classism has resulted between those included in power and privilege and those excluded (subordinated citizens). Today we could expand the notion of included-excluded others to other-than-human beings and the earth.

To say that sovereignty is based on exclusion is to say that human beings are preoccupied by signifying who shares identity, where the boundaries are (those outside), who adheres (obeys) to relations of subordination, who has power and privilege, etc. If we turn to Judeo-Christian scripture, innumerable passages tell who the enemies are, who are the chosen people, who within Israel is included, who are excluded-included others (e.g., slaves, women, children), who is a believer in Yahweh's sovereignty/power and who rebels, etc. In Christian scriptures, the sovereignty of God, at times, is noted as demarking the geographical-spiritual boundary between heaven and hell, which is the ultimate form of friend-enemy distinction and the privileging of some human beings (no animals) and the damnation of all others (no animals here either).

What is clear is that relations of subordination and subjugation, an inherent attribute of sovereignty, depends on exclusion and violence or the threat of violence/violation, which can take many forms. This segues into two other related features of sovereignty, namely, mystification and mimesis. William Connolly notes, "The aura of sovereignty is sustained through

---

88. It is important to point out that Agamben argues that "the fundamental categorical pair of Western politics is not that of friend/enemy but that of care life/political existence, zoē/bios, exclusion/inclusion." This is different from Schmitt because Schmitt makes no claim about the difference between bare life and political life. For my purposes, I am going to stay with what unites these two theorists and that is inclusion/exclusion. Agamben, *Sovereign Power and Bare Life*, 8.

the mystique of the sacred,"[89] which today is substituted by constitutions, which are secular, sacred objects associated with practices of acclamation that legitimate it and its origin story—fiction.[90] This "aura" can be further understood as the sovereign power's work (and attending apparatuses) "to produce (and reproduce) forms of subjectivity that consent to, and even defend, the conditions that make sovereignty, and the subordination it entails, possible."[91] This production of subjectivity takes place "beneath political mythologies sanctifying the 'right to rule,'"[92] providing an appearance of autonomy from the powers that created sovereignty and its institutions. Dickinson and Kotsko, commenting on Agamben's views on glory, argue that "politics today functions as a thinly veiled religious spectacle, complete with its own calls for glory."[93] Glory (democracies, spectacles of acclamation), which is produced by rituals and narratives, functions to legitimate (and constitute—perpetually reproduce) religious (and secular) sovereignty and its fictional origins, projecting an aura that sovereignty is ontologically necessary for human existence, for human belonging.[94] The aura of sovereignty shields the illusion of sovereignty's necessity.

In brief, the aura of sovereignty appears to be an unquestionable existential or even ontological fact of human life, which is produced and reproduced through various apparatuses that internalize these beliefs. We may protest, vote, and discuss the political state of affairs, but most of us never seem to question sovereignty itself. It is not unlike religious folks never questioning the existence of God. Many readers may recall the movie *The Wizard of Oz*. Dorothy, who desperately wishes to return home, is told to seek out the powerful wizard of Oz—an unquestioning and unquestionable sovereign. When she encounters the "wizard," there is a great and frightening spectacle (use of machines and deception—apparatuses) demonstrating his power, the threat of violence, and their subordination. They are initially captivated by the aura of power and possible violence of the sovereign of Oz, yet we espy a frail older gentleman, because Toto, Dorothy's dog, unmasks his "power," his sovereignty.[95] Dorothy and her friends are shocked and upset at being duped, only to discover she never needed the

---

89. Connolly, "'The Complexities of Sovereignty,'" 26?
90. See McLoughlin, "Agamben on Post-Fordist Spectacle," 99.
91. DeCaroli, "Boundary Stones," 45.
92. DeCaroli, "Boundary Stones," 45
93. Dickinson and Kotsko, *Agamben's Coming Philosophy*, 250.
94. McLoughlin, "Agamben on Post-Fordist Spectacle," 99.
95. I find it interesting that it is an animal that unmasks the illusion of the wizard's power. In the end, I think the exploitation and extinction of what human beings call animals reveal the bankruptcy of human sovereignty.

powerful sovereign to get home. In our reality, the apparatuses of society and the state repeatedly reproduce sovereignty, creating the illusion of its necessity for human dwelling though spectacle and glory. Belief in divine sovereignty, Rousseau's Wise Legislator, a constitution that stands for divine or unquestionable sovereignty, all are assumed "as being as necessary as the human subject of Western political thought, the state of exception and the rule of the sovereign reign unquestioned because they seem to better provide expansive answers to our most (undisclosed) pressing concerns."[96] Moreover, there is a continuous process of rearticulating and rejustifying its existence,[97] leaving most everyone accepting the belief that sovereignty is a necessary existential fact of human existence, which Agamben seeks to expose as an illusion so that we might envision different ways of dwelling and belonging with other human beings, other species, and the earth itself.

Connected to sovereignty's mystification is the tragedy of mimesis. Lechte and Newman write that Georges Bataille argued that "all conditions of servitude are only ever contingent, for the human *qua* human is the incarnation of freedom."[98] Similarly, Agamben argues that sovereignty is based on an anthropological machine that dismisses, denies, or overlooks the potentiality of human beings, which is the essence of human freedom. It is worthwhile to pause briefly and indicate what Agamben means by potentiality, before aligning it to sovereignty's mimetic structure. Agamben's philosophical anthropology is, Rasmus Ugilt argues, "centered on the notion of potentiality."[99] The notion of potentiality stems from Aristotle's work regarding the relation between potentiality (*dynamis*) and actualization (*energeia*). We do not need to delve too deeply into the complexities of Aristotle's philosophy to address how Agamben is using this concept. That said, it is important to point out that the Western philosophical tradition has largely "subordinated potentiality to actuality: so, we begin with the actual, speaking humans and their political and artistic productions, and we see potentiality at present as a capacity or skill that is defined by the final action. We see potentiality as secondary or accidental."[100] This is derived, in part, from Aristotle's notion that "actuality is prior to potentiality,"[101] though this does not mean that Aristotle believed that "potentiality exists

96. Dickinson, *Agamben and Theology*, 54.

97. Dickinson, *Agamben and Theology*, 57–58.

98. Lechte and Newman, *Agamben and the Politics of Human Rights*, 166.

99. Ugilt, *Giorgio Agamben*, 22.

100. Colebrook and Maxwell. *Agamben*, 188.

101. Ugilt, *Giorgio Agamben*, 26.

only in actuality."[102] From Agamben's perspective, there are two features of Aristotle's views. First is that "the very essence of humanity lies in a potentiality that is expressed when it does not unfold into actuality."[103] Here is where Agamben turns to illustrate potentiality in terms of impotentiality. He writes:

> Other living beings are capable only of their specific potentiality;
> they can only do this or that. But human beings are the animals
> who are capable of their own impotentiality. The greatness of hu-
> man potentiality is measured by the abyss of human impotential-
> ity. Here it is possible to see how the root of freedom is to be
> found in the abyss of potentiality. To be free is not simply to
> have the power to do this or that thing, nor is it simply to have
> the power to refuse to do this or that thing. To be free is . . . *to be
> capable of one's own impotentiality* . . .[104]

A second related idea Ugilt points out is "that potentiality is not exhausted in its own actualization."[105] Potentiality is never fully actualized. Potentiality is what marks all living beings, but human beings have the capacity to not actualize potential and, even in actualizing potentiality, never exhaust it.[106] In referencing Agamben's works, Ugilt notes that "Potentiality as such is a potentiality that relates only to potentiality itself; it is a potential potentiality . . . potentiality takes ontological priority over actuality."[107] While quite abstract, this means that human beings, for Agamben, are not defined or determined by a particular *telos*. We can say that human beings have ends, but these ends do not determine human beings because human beings *qua* human beings are defined by their potentiality. Put differently, "To say that something has potentiality is to say that it does not unfold like a programmed mechanism, and does not simply become what it already is."[108]

With this brief detour, let's shift to the relation between sovereignty and potentiality vis-à-vis mimesis. From Agamben's view, sovereignty makes actuality precede potentiality by threatening and demanding people submit

---

102. Agamben, *Potentialities*, 180.

103. Colebrook and Maxwell, *Agamben*, 289.

104. Agamben, *Potentialities*, 182–83.

105. Ugilt, *Giorgio Agamben*, 25.

106. For Agamben, his idea of potentiality/actuality refers to animals, as well. This is his way of attempting to avoid the Western tendency to separate human beings from animals. There are distinctions, but distinctions are not separation. Agamben, *The Open*.

107. Ugilt, *Giorgio Agamben*, 25.

108. Colebrook and Maxwell, *Agamben*, 37–38.

to relations of subordination.[109] Potentiality is the ground of actuality and is not diminished by it, though relations of subordination and subjugation propose that potentiality is exhausted by the actual reality of sovereignty itself. What Bataille and Agamben are pointing out is that sovereignty's relations of submission and subjugation, its dependence on violence and exclusion, create the very conditions of revolt, of revolution, of resistance by denying the essence of human potentiality—ungovernable selves. Even the most brutal totalitarian regimes, like the U.S. and slavery, could not and cannot eliminate or exhaust the potentiality of black persons. *This essence of potentiality is the seed of mimesis.* Consider the Israelites under the conditions of a sovereign God. They are repeatedly called a stiff-necked people, usually by God (Exod 32:9; 33:3, 5; 34:9; Deut 9:6, 13; 10:16). Synonyms of stiff-necked are obstinate, headstrong, strong-willed, obdurate, and bull-headed. I suggest "stiff-necked" is an inevitable trait of people who are in a relationship of enforced dependency and subordination, if not subjugation. They resist because they cannot be fully captive to a sovereign God or a king—*there remains an excess regardless of subordination and subjugation.* Human beings, in short, always exceed significations associated with sovereignty and its apparatuses. Consider that there have been countless revolutions in human history, where one group overthrows the sovereignty of the other group, only to enforce their own vision of sovereignty[110]—a perpetual mimetic, tragic reality of sovereignty's relations of subordination and violence,[111] relations that deny or attempt to undermine the potentiality and singularity of human beings (and other-than-human beings).

In summary, sovereignty is defined as the decision regarding the state of exception. The notion of the state of exception gives rise to a paradox, in that sovereignty precedes the law, yet depends on it. Sovereignty, in other words, is both within and outside the juridical order precisely because in the state of exception the law can be set aside. Besides the paradoxical nature of sovereignty, there are other key features, namely, violence, mystification, mimesis, and exclusion or friend-enemy distinction.

## Problems of Sovereignty

In providing the contours of sovereignty, I also alluded to some of the problems, such as violence, mystification, mimesis, and exclusion/classism, etc. I will not repeat these here. Instead, I will identify and describe several

109. Agamben, *Sovereign Power and Bare Life*, 44–47.

110. Prozorov, *Agamben and Politics*, 141.

111. See Mills, *The Philosophy of Agamben*, 76.

problems[112] of sovereignty, which is necessary for moving toward a radical political theology that seeks to avoid the shoals of sovereignty.

Iris Murdoch, in formulating her notion of the sovereignty of the good, remarked that human beings "are anxiety-ridden animals. Our minds are continually active, fabricating an anxious, usually self-preoccupied, often falsifying veil which partially conceals the world."[113] The most basic problem of sovereignty is that it is a fabrication—an existential illusion that masquerades as a necessary reality of human dwelling. I mentioned this above, but it is important to say more about why it is an illusion and why this is a problem. Illusions are defined as mistaken beliefs, which can take on the aura of unquestionable reality. I believe that a ghost is in my house, but this can be disconfirmed by many people who live with me. If I continue to believe it in the face of the absence of evidence, then we are moving into the area of delusion. But this gets more complicated when illusions are collectively held and believed to be real or true. Money, for instance, is an illusion shared by many, but taken as a reality. In one sense, of course, it is a reality that human beings construct the mechanisms that make money operative in the lives of individuals. Yet, it is a mistaken belief for two reasons. First, the ten dollars (piece of paper) in my hand is believed to have the actual value of ten dollars. In reality, it is simply a piece of paper that represents value to people in the larger society. When someone takes the ten dollars from me, I feel they have taken, not a piece of paper, but actual value. It is a fiction that feels real because it has real consequences. Second, this is also a mistaken belief because we believe these pieces of paper are necessary for human living in this society. How could we survive without money, we think? The belief that something is necessary for human living or being human when it is not is one criterion for determining whether a belief is an illusion. Human beings breathe, eat, defecate, sleep/dream. These are facts of being human, but all kinds of beliefs and values can attend them. These are necessary for

---

112. I have only the space to address what I consider are the fundamental problems of sovereignty, which means leaving out other issues, such as the problem of property and its relation to sovereignty. For a discussion of this see Bignall, "On Property and the Philosophy of Poverty." Also, some readers might argue that sovereignty has been responsible for much good throughout history. I do not dispute this, but it is analogous to claiming that the Roman Empire resulted in peace and security, connecting diverse cultures, and expanding commerce. But at what cost and to whom? Sovereignty, as I argue, creates more problems in ordering society than good and this is because of its foundational attributes. Moreover, while we have ordered societies for millennia by way of sovereignty, to continue to do so, as I will point out, will result in the demise of millions of species and perhaps ourselves.

113. Murdoch, *The Sovereignty of the Good*, 82.

human life and are not illusions. Money is not necessary for being human or for human dwelling.[114]

Another related piece of evidence that something is an illusion is that it must be produced and reproduced to keep it alive and maintain the aura of necessity for human life. To return to the illusion of money, the government prints money and also destroys old money. Banks, financial institutions, corporations, stores, etc. all have a role in producing and reproducing the illusion of money, and constructed disciplinary regimes ensure that transgressions are punished—transgressions that undermine the illusion of money and its practices. Try getting off the grid and refuse to live in this system. Stores do not barter, because they rely on "legal tender," which means I will not be able to purchase the food I need to survive. The IRS will take an interest in whether I am paying taxes and, if I am not, it has a great deal of power in insuring that I am brought back into the system of shared beliefs.

Sovereignty fits the criteria above for illusions. For millennia, religious storytellers, theologians, and philosophers have discussed and offered their views of sovereignty. These stories and theologies served and serve as anthropological machines or apparatuses that secure the "reality" of sovereignty, as if it is necessary for human life, for being human. Scripture, for instance, repeatedly affirms the sovereignty of God and, later, Jesus Christ, which becomes the basis of its reproduction in all kinds of theologies (and philosophies), leaving the question of sovereignty unthinkable and, if thought, punishable. But it is not just God who must have "his" sovereignty repeatedly affirmed in theological texts and rituals, it is also the sovereignty of some human beings over other human beings and all human beings over nature.[115] These apparatuses give us the sense that sovereignty is a necessary feature not simply of God, but of human beings, of human dwelling. The

114. Someone exclaims, "Try living without it." This points out just how powerful shared illusions can be in life. I certainly do not wish to try to live without money, but I also know that it is a human creation—a shared illusion.

115. A reader might wonder if I consider religious belief or belief in God to be an illusion. Freud, in his article *The Future of an Illusion*, certainly considered religion to be an illusion that was limiting human progress. In using the perspective in this chapter, I would argue that my belief in an infinite, indeterminate God is an illusion *only if* I believe that this belief is a necessary feature of being human and of human belonging. I do not believe that my premise about God is necessary for being human or for human dwelling. Many people have no belief in God and many others believe in a different God. Freud's mistake was twofold. First, there is no independent observer to say whether belief in God is an illusion or not. How could one prove God does or does not exist? The second mistake is he believed atheism was necessary for humankind's progress and religion its obstruction. Atheism, like religious belief, is not necessary for being human or for human belonging. Both can be obstacles to "progress" and both can spur "progress." Freud, *The Future of an Illusion*.

concept becomes unquestionable—a given. But sovereignty is not necessary for human belonging or in human relations with the nature and, as I will discuss below, it is not an attribute of God, but merely a preoccupation for many human beings—though not all. The evidence for this is seen in various communities today and in the past that have not or do not depend on sovereignty in organizing life together. Yes, these communities have varied types of leadership, but the leadership is not constructed in terms of sovereignty and relations of subjugation. The early Christian communities of Acts, Benedictine communities, utopian communities in the United States (e.g., Robert Owen in New Harmony, Indiana),[116] the Norwegian community of Longyearbyen, etc. are just a few illustrations of belonging that are not dependent on sovereignty as a form of organizing the group. Someone might point out that some of the examples were failures. The fact that a non-sovereign community may fail is not proof that sovereignty is necessary or a better choice. We need only scan history to see the numerous abject failures of various forms of sovereignty to counter this claim. In short, sovereignty is real in that it is being created and repeatedly produced by human beings, but the belief that sovereignty is necessary for human life or for being human is an illusion.

That sovereignty is an illusion is a problem because it involves the production of relations of subordination, subjugation, and servitude, and, correspondingly, the threat of violence, the realities of exclusion, and the specter of privilege (of the ruling class). Of course, sovereignty is not necessarily a problem for the ruling classes, but it is for everyone else, even if they obtain a measure of social stability and security. This said, consider any iteration of sovereignty and one will note politically irrelevant groups that lack political recognition and resources necessary for flourishing. Plato, Aristotle, Augustine, Hobbes, Rousseau and numerous other theologians and philosophers have proposed varied versions of sovereignty and they are all unsatisfactory because they accept the idea/illusion of sovereignty and its attributes, but they also further establish and enforce relations of subordination and the threat of violence, which benefits the sovereign class at the expense of the subordinate classes. Sovereignty, in short, comes with inequalities in power and resources.

To say that sovereignty is a problem does not mean that there are no benefits, such as social order and political security. But we also must ask who benefits and to what degree. In a democracy, where people believe they are sovereign, we find in reality there continues to be a ruling class(es) that aims to secure benefits for themselves at the expense of subordinate or

116. "Robert Owen," *Wikipedia.*

subjugated Others. The U.S. Constitution was written by the ruling class of white propertied men primarily for the ruling class. Women, freed blacks, native peoples, and poor white males were deemed politically irrelevant and, for slaves, worse, white sovereignty meant brutal exploitation and social death.[117] After over two centuries, women, African Americans, and people without property have the right to vote, but this does not mean all groups are politically relevant. As noted in the footnote above, the political and economic elites tend to ignore the interests of most Americans, while stockpiling political and economic power to benefit themselves. Further evidence is that women, African Americans, and Latinx persons are underrepresented in the ruling classes and overrepresented in poverty, lower education rates, lower wealth and income, higher mortality, etc.[118] And, of course, the most politically marginalized groups are the poor and immigrants/refugees. What, then, are the benefits people obtain from democratic sovereignty and how are these benefits distributed?

I suggest that safeguards have accompanied sovereignty, which point to its inherent problems. In scripture, God warned Israelite leaders that human sovereigns will exploit them. We also read that some prophets railed against the political elite for failing to adhere to the covenant and to care for God's people. Socrates and Thrasymachos argued about justice and the rule of the strong. Socrates believed that good rulers necessarily consider the interests of the people, while Thrasymachos had a more cynical, or perhaps more realistic, view of sovereignty that "justice is nothing but the advantage of the stronger."[119] Andreas Kalyvas notes that Plato, in part, linked care to sovereignty: "No other art could advance a stronger claim than that of sovereignty to be the art of caring for the entire community and ruling over humankind."[120] The Cynics understood that the sovereign is "selected by a god comes with an obligation, a mission, namely, to care for others. Taking care of others does not simply mean to lead the other through discourses or by offering an example of life, but to truly take care of them, even if this means sacrificing one's own life."[121] I am going to suggest that these attempts to establish the obligation of the sovereign to care for the interests of the people not only reproduce and reinforce the idea of sovereignty, but also seek to mitigate its inevitable problematic effects—effects that emerge from

117. See Patterson, *Slavery and Social Death.*

118. See Tuttle, "The Cost of Being Black"; Noël, "Race, Economics, and Social Status."

119. Plato, *The Great Dialogues of Plato*, Book I, 137.

120. Kalyvas, "The Sovereign Weaver," 122.

121. Lemm, "The Embodiment of Truth and the Politics of Community," 221–22.

the very attributes of sovereignty (e.g., subordination, servitude, violence, and the accrual of benefits for the sovereign class).

Of course, I am all for a caring sovereign, if we have to have sovereignty. It would be wonderful to have a sovereign who consistently addresses the material, psychological, political, and social needs of the people. Where is this evident in history? To be sure, there may have been a sovereign or two, but most types of sovereignty manifest problems vis-à-vis care precisely because the ruling classes are primarily interested in caring for their power, privileges, and prestige. This extends to how "sovereign" human beings treat other species and the earth, whereby we secure our interests and our privileges to the exclusion and exploitation of nature.

This suggests that sovereignty gives rise to a form(s) of life. As Andrew Norris writes "With the rise of sovereignty we witness the rise of a form of life that corresponds to it."[122] For Agamben, the form of life is bare life—the exclusion of *zoē* (life itself) from *bios* (political life). Agamben's view is helpful, but to my mind a bit strong, leaving out examples of forms of life that cannot be captured by sovereignty and its apparatuses. Instead of this view, I want to focus on the problem of sovereignty in that it distorts relations of care and faith—both of which are necessary for human dwelling. In other words, the form of life sovereignty fosters is a form of life that exhibits distortions of care and faith, which, in turn, accompany problems of speaking and acting together.

This said, let me explain what care as a problem vis-à-vis sovereignty means. In relations of sovereignty where one group is subordinate or even subjugated, the subordinate classes are to obey the sovereign and, in so doing, *may* obtain some benefits. But care, in this instance, is conditional on people supporting the sovereign. To transgress, to rebel, will insure the absence of care and the presence of violence or threat of violence. We just need to turn to scripture to see that Yahweh was demanding regarding obedience and quite punitive—sometimes brutally—when the Israelites failed. One might argue that punishment—a constant threat—was an act of care to get the people back on the track of obedience to the covenant, but punishment in these instances of deprivation, exile, and death seem more a reflection of maintaining God's sovereignty than actually caring for people. From my perspective, these stories have little to do with God and everything to do with cautionary tales told and retold to maintain a kind of human sovereignty, whether through the rule of men, the priests, or kings and the concomitant subordination/subjugation of women, other peoples, etc.

---

122. Norris, "Introduction," 9.

I want to stay with this and claim that sovereignty, because of its attributes, results in a distortion of political caring. The ruling classes, understandably in some ways, are primarily interested in caring about their collective status and the resulting material benefits that are often obtained at the expense of subordinate classes. Caring for subordinates is secondary and conditional—upon their obedience and support of the ruling class. I recall reading an article several years ago in which an extremely wealthy businessman argues that the current gaps of income and wealth are not sustainable, because eventually the people will grab their pitchforks and revolt against the political-economic elites. What I found interesting in this is that the businessman was not arguing from the point of view that the current system is unjust or that the system needs to change so that lower classes have the resources to care for themselves and others. No, he was primarily interested in saving the capitalistic system and, of course, his privileged status in the ruling economic and political elites. Care, in other words, was thoroughly conditional and primarily self-beneficial.

But we do not have to focus on an individual businessman. The rise of the neoliberal capitalistic state signifies a return to a kind of feudalistic sovereignty wherein the "subjects" appear not as persons—immeasurable, valued, unique subjects—but as beings in service to the overlords of the market and the ruling classes. This is a strong claim, especially when most citizens acknowledge that we live in a democracy. Clearly, many citizens hold democratic ideals, but the reality is that the United States functions as a mixed plutocratic/oligarchic democracy. This may seem oxymoronic, but it is not. We have democratic beliefs, practices, and political institutions, yet large corporations, which are hierarchical and non-democratic, and the wealthy hold a tremendous amount of political power on both sides of the political spectrum.[123] Groups like the American Legislative Exchange Council (ALEC), which represents the interests of large corporations, have, for decades, worked behind the scenes to influence and create legislation at state and national levels—outside the scrutiny of the American public—to further the interests of the wealthy. This kind of practice is endemic. Lisa Dugan, for instance, examines and highlights the numerous covert ways wealthy Republican and Democrat neoliberals have used social issues to screen political moves to privatize public sectors, such as public education, all of which cater to the interests of the wealthy.[124] Echoing Dugan's analysis, Nobel Prize winner in economics Joseph Stiglitz expressed concern that

123. See Gasparino, *Bought and Paid For*; Stiglitz, *The Price of Inequality*; Wolin, *Democracy Inc.*

124. Dugan, *The Twilight of Equality*.

huge disparities in economic inequality, which have been growing in the last three decades, threaten democracy.[125] Inequality threatens democratic sovereignty precisely because the plutocrats and oligarchs in a neoliberal economy are neither interested in the common good nor caring for citizens. They are instead interested in expanding their control of political-economic space to achieve what is "good" for them—greater wealth and political power—which is at the expense of the subordinate classes—classes that have unwittingly toiled to enrich the ruling classes. In brief, neoliberal capitalism is imbricated with the institutions of democratic sovereignty and foster relations of subordination wherein care is focused on the interests of the few and not the common good. That this is a problem is evidenced by increased depression among lower classes,[126] which is related to both a higher level of economic insecurity (including food insecurity, prevalence of evictions[127]) and feelings of helplessness among lower classes.[128] Economists, as well, have identified the psychosocial and material impacts of rampant capitalism and democratic sovereignty that ignores the many. Jerry Mander lists numerous studies that point to rising violence, anxiety, depression, and suicide in the United States,[129] which he attributes to the dominance of neoliberal capitalistic sovereignty. Citing studies from Jean Twenge, a psychologist, Mander notes that levels of anxiety (and depression) are at remarkably high rates compared to studies from forty to fifty years ago.[130] All of these are symptoms related to the type of sovereignty extant in the U.S.—a sovereignty that undermines civic care between ruling classes and the other residents. In my view, this problem in civic care is evident in all forms of sovereignty precisely because of the exclusion of many people from the sovereign class—from speaking and acting together in the political realm.

The problem of sovereignty vis-à-vis care also can be understood in terms of Agamben's view of potentiality and the unfolding of suchness or singularity. I briefly mentioned the problem of sovereignty vis-à-vis potentiality in terms of explaining how relations of subordination and subjugation undermine potentiality with regard to experiences of suchness and the mimetic violent aspects of sovereignty. Here I want to argue that the distortion

125. Stiglitz, *The Great Divide*.

126. Cvetkovich, *Depression*; see also Rogers-Vaughn, "Blessed Are Those Who Mourn."

127. Desmond, *Evicted*.

128. See Ehrenreich, *Bright-sided*.

129. Mander, *The Capitalism Papers*, 226–34; see also Hendricks, *The Universe Bends toward Justice*, 174–77.

130. Mander, *The Capitalism Papers*, 234.

of civic care in sovereignty undermines subordinated or subjugated Others from experiencing a sense of their singularity in the public-political realm. Subjugated and subordinate others are not recognized and treated as persons, and the apparatuses of sovereignty ensure that those who are not recognized as persons will not obtain the resources they need to flourish. Moreover, the sovereign classes' potentiality for singularity is similarly undermined because their "experiences" of singularity are dependent on apparatuses that produce and maintain subordinate classes. As will be discussed in greater detail below, the potentiality of singularity or suchness becomes actualized, in part, through relations of care—care that is free of subordination, subjugation, and illusions of superiority and inferiority. The problem of sovereignty, even the Cynics' and Plato's sovereign who cares, is that "care" in the political realm is always associated with power, dependency, and the threat of violence. From this, we can expect that in the civic-political realm experiences of singularity will be distorted, whether in relation to the ruling or the subordinate classes.

In arguing that sovereignty is a problem because it distorts social or civic relations of caring, I also contend it fundamentally distorts the civic faith that is necessary for cooperation—for speaking and acting together. When we consider the key attributes of sovereignty, such as subordination and violence, it is difficult to imagine much civic trust and fidelity between those in power and those who are required to submit. At best, it is a conditional faith, wherein those who obey and support (i.e., loyal) the sovereign class are trusted. Likewise, the lower class, as a result of their fealty, obtain some resources and security. This is not unlike the citizens of the leviathan. They are loyal to and trust the leviathan because the leviathan provides security through the threat of violence toward those who break the social contract. That is, those who question, transgress, resist, or rebel are deemed to be untrustworthy and the apparatuses of sovereignty may use humiliation, deprivation, and other forms of violence to stop these transgressions.

Consider an extreme, yet real, example. White male sovereignty over black slaves represents a horrific illustration of both the distortion and absence of civic care and faith vis-à-vis included-excluded Others living in subjugated relations. Orlando Patterson's notion of social death[131] and Agamben's notion of bare life[132] are terms that reveal the precarity of life for slaves. If they received any care, it was conditional on their utility for securing profit or their obedience in caring for their owners. To the extent that slaves were perceived to accept their conditions, they were warily trusted.

131. Patterson, *Slavery and Social Death*.
132. Agamben, *Sovereign Power and Bare Life*.

Any real or imagined transgression resulted in brutal punishment (sovereignty's violence) or death. I add that slaves, because they were included-excluded Others, were not due civic care or civic faith.

One may think that the horrors of white sovereignty are not fair illustrations of the distortion of care and faith in the political realm. Consider civic care and faith in forms of sovereignty that subjugate women, denying them full citizenship, which was noted by John Stuart Mill.[133] Were women treated as peers with regard to civic care and faith before they obtained the right to vote in the United States? Even after the 19th Amendment was adopted women are still underrepresented in positions of political and economic leadership. What about women in Saudi Arabia, with its monarchical sovereignty?[134] Women are cared for and trusted to the extent that they accept their subordinate (and subjugated) place in the kingdom. Step out of line and women can expect harsh responses by the sovereign male authorities.[135] Examine any type of sovereignty and there will be individuals and groups that are politically irrelevant and these groups will be denied civic care and faith.

The above is not to suggest that civic care and civic faith are completely absent from various types of sovereignty. It would be hard to imagine a viable society that did not have some measure of civic care and faith. What I am arguing is that the attributes of sovereignty give rise to forms of living that reflect aberrations in both civic care and faith, which is why, in part, the apparatuses of society must reproduce sovereignty, giving it the aura of necessity so that citizens will accept these distortions of care and faith, these forms of living, as inevitable.

Before moving to the next section, it is necessary to emphasize that the forms of life that sovereignty and its apparatuses produce have been taking place for millennia. We could imagine this continuing, but sovereignty is not simply a fundamental problem for human beings dwelling together. As Agamben notes,[136] Western philosophy and theology have supported the idea of human sovereignty over nature (the earth and all other species), which privileges human existence and flourishing over the earth and the dwelling of other-than-human species. The belief and practices of human sovereignty legitimate forms of life that exploit, dominate, and ruthlessly control nature, which is, as Agamben remarks, the included-excluded Other

133. Mill, *On Liberty and the Subjection of Women.*
134. See Human Rights Watch Report, "Saudia Arabia: 10 Reasons Why Women Flee."
135. BBC News, "Saudi Arabia Widens Crackdown on Women's Rights Activists."
136. Agamben, *The Open.*

in the polis. So, the distortion of care with regard to human beings extends to other species and the earth itself. At best, theologians, philosophers, and activists can promote a kind of stewardship in relation to nature that can establish caring relations with regard to some species. We might pick a particular animal to save, like whales, polar bears, bats, etc. Many people might echo Arthur Schopenhauer's view that compassion is "the immediate participation, independent of all ulterior motives, primarily in the suffering of another and thus in the prevention or elimination of it," whether it is directed toward human beings or any other living species.[137] The inclusion and care of other species into the political realm, into human belonging and dwelling, will be forever undermined as long as human beings produce the idea and live a form of life of human sovereignty with its anthropocentric superiority and narcissism.[138] This is *the* problem for the Anthropocene Age. If we continue to view humanity as sovereign over other species and nature, we will stand on the rubble of an unhoused earth, which will, in the end, serve as our tomb and reveal the illusion of human sovereignty.

## Radical Political Theology:
## A Non-Sovereign, Non-Privileging God and Humanity

Alexis de Tocqueville "acknowledged democracy as the political instantiation of the death of God."[139] This makes sense in that God had been used to support monarchal sovereignties for millennia, but with the rise of the idea that sovereignty lies with the people, then, as Sheldon "Wolin asks: What kind of God is suited to the democratic age."[140] But even this question seems to support the notion of both sovereignty and God—a God who can support or legitimize democratic sovereignty as God had previously been used to legitimize other forms of sovereignty. Interestingly, Tocqueville can pronounce, can imagine the death of God, but not the death of sovereignty. Indeed, Jeffery Robbins seeks, with some ambivalence, to retain God *and* the idea of democratic sovereignty, arguing for a political theology of democracy—"a political theology without sovereignty, as it were, or at least

137. Grayling, *The History of Philosophy*, 301.

138. Prozorov notes that Continental philosophers, including Agamben, have attacked philosophical and theological ideas of distinctions between humans and non-humans and sought to propose a post-anthropocentric world. Prozorov, *Agamben and Politics*, 150–58. See also Wood, *Reoccupy the Earth*, 202–18.

139. Robbins, *Radical Democracy and Political Theology*, 155.

140. Robbins, *Radical Democracy and Political Theology*, 163.

a new form of sovereignty."[141] Robbins uses Agamben's work and Caputo's weak theology of a non-sovereign God,[142] yet overlooks Agamben's and Caputo's more radical argument of getting rid of sovereignty altogether as necessary for human belonging.[143] What Robbins leaves intact is a notion of sovereignty[144] that continues the attributes of violence, exclusion, etc. vis-à-vis other species and nature. While there is much to appreciate about Robbins' work and others who support a radical democracy, I believe that Adam Kotsko is correct when he notes "the political-theological enterprise cannot content itself with a narrow focus on the problem of divine and human sovereignty. Political theology must seek out unexpected resources and connections elsewhere . . . if it is to reach its full potential as a critical discourse."[145] More to the point, a radical political theology argues not for the death of God, but the death of sovereignty as the principle for human belonging. But it is not only about human belonging. It is also about ridding sovereignty's relations of subjugation vis-à-vis other species and the earth.

While sovereignty has been a key feature of human dwelling for millennia, it is, because of its core attributes, untenable for the Anthropocene Age. As a result of the dire consequences of climate change, we now are invited to think and be otherwise. It is altogether another question whether we will have the courage to change. In this section, I am going to move toward a radical political theology of a non-sovereign, non-privileging God and a non-sovereign humanity. This is not a proposal for imagining specific ways of belonging or organizing political arrangements, though I will depict some general outlines for relations independent of sovereignty and its associated problems. Non-sovereign relations are evident in various political instantiations, which is not to say the non-sovereign relations of political communities are free of problems. This said, moving past sovereignty is, I argue, necessary if we are to find ways for individuals, groups, and societies to care for the earth and all of those species that depend on it for their dwelling. Toward this end, I begin with an existential, developmental view of non-sovereign human relations, which undermines the illusion that

141. Robbins, *Radical Democracy and Political Theology*, 182.

142. Caputo, *The Weakness of God*.

143. In a letter to Freud, Albert Einstein argued that the "quest for international security involves the unconditional surrender by every nation, in a certain measure, of its liberty of action, its sovereignty." This was written just years before the bloodiest war of sovereign nations. Quoted in Butler, *The Force of Nonviolence*, 176.

144. Note that Robbins embraces the paradox of a theology without sovereignty, while also supporting democratic sovereignty. Robbins, *Radical Democracy and Political Theology*.

145. Kotsko, "Genealogy and Political Theology," 164.

sovereignty is necessary for human belonging or for ordering human relations. Indeed, good-enough caring relations between parents and children
manifests an existential demand for a non-sovereign care, not only with
regard to human beings, but to other species. From here, I argue that Christianity's concept of the incarnation, taking on the form of human life, is a
revelation of a non-sovereign, non-privileging God. Sovereignty, I argue, is
a preoccupation of human beings and not a revealed characteristic of God.
Tocqueville's pronouncement is more aptly a call for the death of the illusion
of a sovereign God.

The previous chapters have, in different ways, elaborated on an existential developmental view. What I would like to do here is to depict an existential developmental perspective in light of the attributes of sovereignty.
Over the years, I have come across numerous good-enough parents and I
cannot recall ever hearing a parent tacitly or overtly express the view that
they were sovereigns over their children. By this, I mean that good-enough
parents do not see their children as subordinate or, worse, individuals to
be subjugated by parental demands. To be sure, parents well recognize and
acknowledge that their infants lack the capacities to care for themselves, but
this does not necessarily lead to the idea that children are subordinate or
that parents are sovereign—possessing absolute power over their children.
Of course, someone might point to religious references to sparing the rod,
spoiling the child, children being obedient,[146] etc. Yet, these and secular admonitions regarding children[147] often function as apparatuses to produce
a subjectivity that upholds the idea of sovereignty extant in society. When
this occurs, care becomes entwined with the attributes of sovereignty and is,
therefore, deeply distorted.

Let me come at this more positively. Good-enough parents' personal
recognition and attunement represent a kind of caring relation that creates
a space of speaking and acting together, wherein children develop sufficient
trust to assert their needs and desires, giving rise to their pre-representational (later representational), embodied experiences of suchness. This relation, this space of speaking and acting together is free of parental agency
that seeks to communicate subordination or, worse, subjugation to the
parents' needs. Of course, there are parents who do this, but their "care"

---

146. I do think that obedience has a place in caring relations between parents and
children, but obedience must be for the sake of children's well-being and not for shoring
up parents' sovereignty, power, etc.

147. See Bunge, *The Child in Christian Thought*. See also Miller, *For Your Own
Good*. Both of these authors, in different ways, provide illustrations of how parent-child
relations can be distorted by theological ideologies, which are connected to theocratic
or sovereign kinds of relating.

contributes to diverse forms and gradations of trauma. While relations of subjugation and subordination are forms of belonging, they are not evident in caring relations of good-enough parents. The form of belonging in good-enough relations involves speaking and acting together and children's experiences of singularity—fostering a sense of self-esteem, self-confidence, and self-respect.

As noted above, subordination, as an attribute of sovereignty, accompanies another attribute—violence. While some parents are violent,[148] good-enough parents are not. It is important to point out that there are numerous parental actions that, while not appearing to be violent, nevertheless can be impinging or depriving. A parent may deprive a child of affection as a way to control or punish. While this is not physical violence per se, it is a form of violation of the existential command to care for the child. What I am moving toward here is the idea that good-enough parental care is free of violence and violation. Naturally, there are numerous violations vis-à-vis care in any good relationship, but if these are minor, momentary, and repaired, the relationship and the child's sense of singularity is restored. In brief, good-enough parental relations with children are non-sovereign in that there is an absence of violence or the threat of violence and violation.

Another attribute of sovereignty that is absent in caring relations is exclusion. It is nearly unthinkable that a parent-child relation could be founded on Schmitt's friend-enemy distinction or included-excluded others. To be sure, some parents may view and treat their children as opponents, foes, etc., but these are not good-enough parents. To care for a child, to create a space of speaking and acting together, cannot be based on exclusion. An astute reader may recall that in chapter 1 I argued that there is a dialectical tension of identification and disidentification in personal knowing/care. Disidentification means recognizing that the Other is not me, but it is not in itself a form of exclusion. Instead, it is necessary to create and maintain a space for the appearance of the child's singularity. That said, disidentification surely can lead to included-excluded others, or the friend-enemy distinction. But in genuinely caring for another person/child, disidentification creates a space for children to appear and experience relational-embodied

148. If we turn to some biblical and religious references, some forms of violence are considered to be appropriate discipline (e.g., the rod, spanking). Some people may not consider these to be violence, but I do and they are evidence of relations of subordination, if not subjugation. The implicit idea is that children are to be subordinate to the all-powerful parent. Can I imagine an ethical example of violence toward a child? There may be the rare occasion when a parent exercises violence to protect the child, like violently grabbing a child from getting hit by a car. This form of violence is not for the sake of shoring up the parent's authority or power, but the parent's exercise of violence to save the child's life. As I said, these are rare instances and must be evaluated.

singularity with another. To care is inclusive and, in these instances, free of sovereignty and its attributes of subordination, violence, and exclusion.

Two other concepts (ungovernable selves and inoperativity) can further this discussion of non-sovereignty vis-à-vis good enough parental care for their children. Agamben contends that social-political apparatuses or disciplinary regimes produce forms of subjectivity or governable selves.[149] For instance, in terms of the political-economic realm, the apparatuses of neoliberal capitalism produce *homo oeconomicus*—subjects fitted to and for the market society.[150] *Homo oeconomicus* is a governed subject. By contrast, for Agamben, the ungovernable self *"could never assume the form of an oikonomia* [economy]."[151] Put differently, "Beyond the apparatuses [of sovereignty] and the forms of subjectivity that they produce there is an excess of living being that can never be subsumed under them. While the excess does not in itself constitute a political subject, it testifies to the fact that the apparatuses are never all there is."[152] This suggests that human beings are not condemned to be determined by disciplinary regimes of sovereignty for two intersecting reasons. First, the apparatuses of society cannot fully capture or produce subjectivity. There is always an excess that escapes or is beyond the control of the apparatuses. Second, Agamben, using the term "inoperativity," indicates that it is possible to deactivate the functioning of the apparatuses, which does not mean these apparatuses do not continue to operate or have effects.[153] Put another way, inoperativity vis-à-vis the subject means that she is not entirely captive to the grammar of the apparatuses, even if they continue to function. Frederick Douglass is an excellent example of inoperativity, excess, and an ungovernable self.[154] Slavery and northern racism aimed to produce humiliated subjects for the sake of serving the needs of white supremacists. Douglass, for numerous reasons, demonstrated an excess of subjectivity that could not be captured by the political apparatuses of racism and he did not, for the most part, operate out of the grammar of these apparatuses. This said, it is important to ask what a source of his excess of subjectivity, his ungovernable self—a form of life that is not dependent on sovereignty and its exclusive identity.

149. Prozorov, *Agamben and Politics*, 24.
150. See Brown, *Undoing the Demos*.
151. Whyte, *Catastrophe and Redemption*, 166.
152. Prozorov, *Agamben and Politics*, 24.
153. Prozorov, *Agamben and Politics*, 31–34.
154. Danjuma Gibson's excellent book on Frederick Douglass raises a similar question regarding how Douglass was able to overcome the traumas of slavocracy. For his answers, Gibson relies on emended psychoanalytic theories. Gibson, *Frederick Douglass*.

What I want to suggest is that *a* root of the ungovernable self as a form of life is found in the pre-political space of good-enough parent-children interactions. Parents' personal recognitions and attunements to their children, while shaped by larger systemic forces or disciplinary regimes, are not determined by them. Genuine care makes these apparatuses inoperative. To return to Prozorov's depiction of Agamben, "Beyond the apparatuses and forms of subjectivity they produce there is the excess of living being that can never be subsumed under them. While the excess does not itself constitute a political subject, it testifies to the fact that apparatuses are never all there is."[155] What I am arguing here is that the parents' care for their children is not captive to or operates out of the apparatuses of sovereignty and this gives rise to the excess or suchness of the ungovernable self. There is, in other words, something ungovernable about good-enough parents' care of their children. By ungovernable, I mean that good-enough parents, in situations of societal humiliation, seek to shield their children from these forces, while also, in time, trying to help them face the realities of an indecent society. That is, by recognizing and treating their children as persons, they make inoperative the grammar of sovereignty's violence, subordination, and exclusion. Inoperativity, as noted above, means deactivating or neutralizing the apparatuses of power that subjugate, that form and determine subjectivities and identities, making possible the realization of other possibilities or potentialities, which in this situation of care is children's experience of suchness.[156] It is important to stress that inoperativity, for Agamben, is not passive. That is, inoperativity does not "affirm inertia, inactivity or apraxia . . . but [is] a form of praxis that is devoid of any telos or task, does not realize any essence and does not correspond to any nature."[157] While Agamben does not elaborate on the praxis, in this case, I am saying that inoperativity is the caring action of parental attunement. Of course, Agamben knows well that that inoperativity does not mean that the apparatuses of society's sovereignty have no effect or impact. Any cursory reading of King's and Malcolm X's autobiographies, for example, indicate the negative impacts of racism (the rule of white supremacists) on their families and the impacts of racism on parental care. Agamben is saying that it is possible to act in such a way that one is not completely captive to or determined by the political-economic apparatuses of sovereignty, in this case, racist sovereignty in a so-called democracy.

155. Gibson, *Frederick Douglass*, 24.
156. Gibson, *Frederick Douglass*, 32–37.
157. Gibson, *Frederick Douglass*, 33.

To say that good-enough parents' ministrations are ungovernable, making inoperative the apparatuses of an indecent society, suggests that the result is the child's nascent ungovernable self,[158] wherein the experiences of suchness or singularity and the corresponding pre-symbolic experiences of self-esteem, self-respect, and self-confidence are not tied or captive to the grammar of humiliation and depersonalization of the larger society's disciplinary regimes or apparatuses. I contend that evidence of this is seen in the pain and confusion children experience when they encounter the public-political world that does not confirm their experiences of singularity they obtained from good-enough parental care. The self that emerged in speaking and acting together with the caring parent is at odds with the governed-humiliated self of an indecent society where, for instance, white supremacy is sovereign. An indecent society and its disciplinary regimes aim to control, govern, and determine the selves of the oppressed and marginalized group(s). A couple of illustrations will help here. In eighth grade, Malcolm X recalled a painful interaction. After class one afternoon, Mr. Ostrowski,[159] Malcolm's teacher, under the guise of caring about Malcolm, asked if he had considered a career. "The truth is I hadn't," Malcolm tells the reader. "I never have figured out why I told him, 'Well, yes sir, I've been thinking I'd like to be a lawyer.'"[160] Whether he wanted to be a lawyer is not the point. Malcolm chose a profession that was esteemed in the larger public-political world. Malcolm aspired to find a positive public-political self. His teacher replied, "Malcolm, one of life's first needs is for us to be realistic. Don't misunderstand me, now. We all here like you, you know that. But you've got to be realistic about being a nigger. A lawyer—that's no realistic goal for a nigger. You need to think about something you can be. You're good with your hands—making things. Everyone admires your carpentry shop work. Why don't you plan on carpentry?"[161] Mr. Ostrowski's "care" for Malcolm illustrates white supremacist sovereignty and the use of disciplinary regimes to humiliate and subjugate African Americans, forcing them to the fringes of public-political spaces of speaking and acting together and undermining

158. Agamben is not suggesting that the ungovernable self is necessarily a revolutionary subject. Of course, an ungovernable self may be a revolutionary subject and there are examples of this already mentioned. If not a revolutionary subject, ungovernable selves may simply live and work such that they resist the machinations of the dominant apparatuses of society. Whyte, *Catastrophe and Redemption*, 160.

159. Biographer Manning Marable indicates that the teacher's name was Richard Kaminska. Malcolm may have misremembered or altered the name, possibly for legal reasons. Since the autobiography uses a different name, I have decided to retain Malcolm's version. Marable, *Malcolm X*.

160. Haley, *The Autobiography of Malcolm X*, 38.

161. Haley, *The Autobiography of Malcolm X*, 38.

their political relevancy. Malcolm's understandable response was to draw "away from white people."[162] This painful memory, I suggest, represents the collision between Malcolm's ungovernable self and the dominant governed self of the larger indecent society. Let me add further that Malcolm's ungovernable self, which he obtained in the caring interactions of his family (and others),[163] became the seed and source of his resistance toward the racist sovereign apparatuses of white indecent society and, later, his resistance and resilience against the apparatuses of the Nation of Islam.

Agamben remarks that the "ungovernable . . . is the beginning and, at the same time, the vanishing point of every politics."[164] How I understand this is that ungovernable selves emerge within the context of caring relations that exist within the polis and, in the West, its particular forms of sovereignty. As Simone Bignall writes, "anarchy is the natural state of sociality."[165] Put differently, the "state of nature" is good-enough parental care, which is shaped by the apparatuses of sovereignty, but it is inoperative with regard to these apparatuses, thus creating a space for speaking and acting together, wherein children experience a sense of suchness that attends and is the source of ungovernable selves. This is why care and the ungovernable self are the vanishing points of every form of sovereignty that seeks to produce, through violence or threat of violence, relations of subordination and inclusion-exclusion and docile governed selves.

Caring and compassionate relations that do not operate out of the apparatuses of sovereignty are not simply and solely between human beings. St. Francis of Assisi, Arthur Schopenhauer, and George Washington Carver are examples of people who extended care to other-than-human species. There are also all kinds of examples today of individuals and groups that seek to protect species and their habitats (e.g., The Nature Conservancy,

---

162. Haley, *The Autobiography of Malcolm X*, 38.

163. I also recognize that Malcolm X's autobiography also details the disruptions within his parents' marriage and his family. But what I am contending is that he obtained sufficient care or good-enough care to develop an ungovernable self.

164. Agamben, *What Is an Apparatus?*, 24.

165. Bignall, "On Property and the Philosophy of Poverty," 56. The idea of anarchy is frightening to people because it evokes chaos, which echoes Hobbes' view of the state of nature. Indeed, fear of chaos is almost always used by the media and authorities to associate violence and chaos with anarchy. The concept actually means without a ruler. So, anarchy is not a democracy (rule of the people), plutocracy (rule of the wealthy), aristocracy (rule of the elite) or a monarchy (rule of a king/queen). But the absence of a "ruler" does not mean chaos, as Pierre-Joseph Proudhon strenuously stated in the nineteenth century. Anarchy, like the anarchy of parent-child interactions simply means there are other ways of ordering relations. In this case, caring and the accompanying speaking and acting together.

World Fund for Nature, Greenpeace, etc.). While some Christian groups view nature conservancy in terms of being good stewards of the earth (derived from the command of God to have dominion over the earth), they do not abandon the theologies that hold onto sovereignty and subordination. These groups are to be commended, but a political theology needs a more radical approach, which is to accept non-sovereign existential and ontological demands to care.

Having offered this brief existential view of care vis-à-vis sovereignty, I now turn to a theological perspective of a non-sovereign, non-privileging God—the ungovernable[166] and non-governing God. While the previous chapters have addressed, in part, a radical political theology, here I want to frame this in terms of the issue of sovereignty. Since a fundamental premise of the Abrahamic traditions is the belief that God is the creator of the universe, I begin with an analogy of creation in terms of a creator and the created. From here I move to the incarnation, focusing on *kenosis* and Jesus' forgiveness of the Roman soldiers as revelations of a rejection of sovereignty, whether in reference to God or humanity. I then turn briefly to the perspective of Jacob Taubes and his work on Pauline theology vis-à-vis the law, revealing what Agamben calls the coming community—a community of belonging and dwelling without sovereignty.

The artists I have read about or know do not refer to their work in terms of having sovereignty over the material. In the act of creating a work, they have a relation that is not characterized by violence, exclusion, or absolute power, but instead a kind of immanent caring. Like good-enough caring for children, to create, then, is not to be in a sovereign relationship. One way to think about God as creator is similar. God in the act of creating is not sovereign and is not in need of sovereignty to create. Indeed, sovereignty in the act of creation has no meaning or relevance.

Someone might remark that artists do have absolute power over their creation. They are in control and can even destroy the work of art, indicating a kind of sovereignty. And take note of God the creator destroying parts of God's creation (e.g., the flood, decimating Egypt). Most artists I am familiar with, however, say that they do not have absolute control over the material. We all have heard authors talk about their muses, about characters developing outside their control. Of course, it is their imagination, but they also are pointing out the experience of shared creation and the non-sovereignty of the relationship. In terms of theology, there is seemingly no end to acclamations of an all-powerful God creating the universe, which

---

166. I will say more about "non-governing" and ungovernable in relation to Jesus, but here it is important to say what I mean by ungovernable. There is nothing external to God that can govern God. By definition, God could not be governable.

is but one short step to claiming the sovereignty of God. But why does the power of creation depend on absolute power or the notion of sovereignty? For some theologians, sovereignty is necessarily an attribute of a creator God, but it is possible to argue the opposite. Human acts of creation do not depend on human sovereignty and, by analogy, God's power in creating the universe has nothing to do with sovereignty or governing, but rather an infinite, indeterminate care.

The creator of a work of art is also not sovereign in the sense of not establishing laws regarding the process or the artwork itself. Indeed, it would seem odd to think of artists this way. By analogy, God is non-governing in the sense of not creating "laws" for creation. Human beings create laws. What about natural laws (which are often attributed to God) or the Ten Commandments? To my mind, both are human creations aimed at ordering a particular people.[167] It is better to say that, in the ongoing act of creation, God creates patterns (e.g., orbits, gravity) that are not "laws." The term "law" connotes a juridical, sovereign source, which God as creator is not—at least not in a radical political theological perspective.

There is another important feature here. I think many religious people believe that creation was a one and done act by God who now sits back and observes creation. Yet, an alternative view is that God's creation is ongoing. Let me continue with the analogy. A human artist, in the act of creating, is intimately involved with the work/object. One could say the artist is immanent in the activity of creation and its object—within it and distinct from it. Moreover, the artist's immanence is in the act, as well as in relation to the object as a whole, which means the artist does not privilege one part of the object versus another. Put another way, the immanence of an artist's creation is their care for the relation and the object as a whole. A non-sovereign God's ongoing creation of the world suggests immanence and non-privileging care[168] vis-à-vis the universe itself. The unfolding creation of the universe reveals a non-privileging care, which is, no doubt, a narcissistic blow to religious beliefs that espouse human sovereignty and human

167. While I do not have the space to pursue this further, a cursory reading of natural laws, from psychological and sociological perspectives, reveals that these laws are created to establish social order and expectations. Moreover, when they are transgressed, they are enforced by social-political apparatuses. I suggest that the unconscious strategy of calling these "beliefs" laws is to legitimate and enforce them without remorse.

168. Non-privileging does not have anything to do with indifference. As I will touch on below, non-privileging means that God's care and grace is present throughout all of creation. Privileging care is the basis of injustice, whether we see this in human communities or the injustices perpetrated toward other-than-human beings and nature itself.

beings as privileged creatures. Put another way, many of us have confused the idea of *imago dei* (being sons and daughters of God) as being exclusive to human beings, when it can refer to creation in all of its plurality. Have we not also done the same for the promise "I will be with you until the ends of the earth"? Creation itself is heir, and God's promise is for creation itself. It is analogous to the artist saying, I will be with you until the end—the end of the creative enterprise, the end of creation.

Let me stay with this analogy to highlight one other point. In mentioning artists, I imagine that many readers think of created objects, like a painting, book, or song. But creation as we know it on earth is a dynamic, living system. Perhaps we can extend the analogy to good-enough parents as artists. Their care for their children is crucial to the child's well-being. Parents do not create the child, but they are involved in the creation of the child's developing self, body, and relating. The child as well is part of this creation process. Both parents and children are co-creators—relations without sovereignty as an ordering principle. To shift to a theological view, the universe and, in particular, the earth are living dynamic systems rather than mere objects. It is possible, then, to imagine that artists/parents are co-creators in God's ongoing creation.

I recognize that all analogies fail when it comes to God, but we have little choice. But if we consider analogies as representative of something important, not about God, but about creation, then we can say that this analogy has implications for human beings and other species. In the Anthropocene Age we need to think and be otherwise. If we think of ourselves as co-creators (like other species) involved with the act of creation itself, then we, too, are non-sovereign and we can be non-privileging in our care of other human beings, other species, and the earth itself. Whether we have the will and courage to do this is another question.

Another religious belief of Christians is the incarnation of God in the life and ministry of Jesus. As mentioned in previous chapters, we read that God empties Godself, taking on the form of a slave. The slave was the ultimate excluded-included Other. In other words, the slave is subject to sovereignty that uses the law and the threat of violence to enforce subordination and servitude. One could say that slaves—deemed completely politically irrelevant and denied speaking and acting together in the polis—are without sovereignty with regard to their very lives, which can be taken without, as Agamben notes, being considered a homicide.[169] In taking on the form of a slave, God reveals the inoperativity of sovereignty and, correspondingly, the presence of an ungovernable self.

169. Agamben, *Sovereign Power and Bare Life.*

Let me explicate this further by returning to Agamben and governable selves. Agamben contends that social-political apparatuses or disciplinary regimes produce forms of subjectivity or governable selves that accept the type of sovereignty of a particular society.[170] As mentioned above, in terms of the political-economic realm, the apparatuses of neoliberal capitalism produce *homo oeconomicus*—subjects fitted to and for the sovereignty of a market society.[171] *Homo oeconomicus* is a governed subject. By contrast, for Agamben, the ungovernable self *"could never assume the form of an oikonomia* [economy]."[172] By ungovernable, Agamben contends that while apparatuses produce forms of subjectivity, they are unable to fully capture human beings' potentiality. In short, the ungovernable self exceeds social-political representations and apparatuses of sovereignty, retaining suchness or singularity.[173]

In terms of Jesus taking on the form of a slave, we can see that Jesus is not defined by this form of life—a form constructed by the apparatuses of human sovereignty. Jesus' suchness does not reside in or depend on this role, this identity, and the apparatuses that produce and reproduce the slave (today—the refugee). Jesus' suchness instead resides in his relation to God the non-sovereign creator, though, of course, Jesus, in taking on the form of the slave, experienced the consequences of human sovereignty (e.g., torture and death). Nevertheless, Jesus, as an ungovernable self in the form of a slave, makes inoperative the Roman and Jewish apparatuses of sovereignty and law.[174] In this sense, Jesus taking on the form of a slave is a revelation, not simply of God being ungovernable and non-sovereign, but a revelation that human subjectivity bears an excess that cannot be captive to human apparatuses of sovereignty—human beings are essentially and potentially ungovernable. As a brief aside, I extend this to the idea that the incarnation

170. Prozorov, *Agamben and Politics*, 24.

171. See Brown, *Undoing the Demos*.

172. Whyte, *Catastrophe and Redemption*, 166.

173. While Agamben's notion of eternal life is pertinent here, I do not have time to delve into it. That said, Agamben understands eternal life to represent "the name of this inoperative center of the human, of this political 'substance' of the Occident that the machine of the economy and of glory ceaselessly attempts to capture within itself." Agamben, *The Kingdom and the Glory*, 251.

174. It is worth mentioning that John Howard Yoder is often credited with the shift to understanding Jesus in terms of the political, though, as mentioned in the introduction, Christian liberation theologians of various stripes have long been interested in framing political liberation in terms of Jesus Christ. Yoder, *The Politics of Jesus*. See also Crossan, *Jesus: A Revolutionary Biography*; Cone, *A Black Theology of Liberation*; Hendricks, *The Politics of Jesus*; Rieger, *Christ & Empire*; Rieger, "Christian Theology and Empire."

also means that human beings can never fully capture the suchness and excess of creation and its creatures. The universe (nature), despite human attempts at controlling it, is ungovernable in its suchness.

As a "slave," Jesus, like the unruly prophets, was not shy in confronting those in political leadership or the sovereign class. He warned the rich about their attachment to their wealth (Matt 19:23–24), he denounced the scribes and Pharisees (Matt 23; Mark 12:38), he cleansed the temple of money-changers (Mark 11:15–17), etc. This is a person who is not governable—an unruly man of compassion and justice. This ungovernable Jesus is ungovernable in relation to Roman and Jewish sovereignty, which begs the question: Did not Jesus mention, at times, the kingdom of heaven, suggesting the rule of God? First of all, Jesus overcame the temptation to exercise political sovereignty.[175] Second, it makes more sense to posit that the metaphor "kingdom of God" reveals a different ordering of political belonging—an ordering where there are no slaves and sovereigns, only the ordering of relations through care and compassion.

Another illustration of Jesus' ungovernable self is evident in his forgiving his Roman torturers and the rejecting violence as a response to sovereign violence. As mentioned in a previous chapter, the Roman soldiers served as a disciplinary arm of the sovereign in Rome. Torture and public execution were aimed at controlling/subjugating the population through terror. Jesus, from Agamben's perspective, could be killed by the state without it being considered homicide or a sacrifice (for Rome), thus putting Jesus outside both divine (as constructed by human beings) and human law. Jesus' forgiveness was a political act of repudiation of both Roman and Jewish sovereignty and law.[176] That is, in the act of forgiveness, Jesus was revealing that, as an ungovernable self, he was not defined by or dependent on the machinations of empire or religious authorities and their inclusive-exclusive ways of organizing relations, but he was defined by his care for (and forgiving) those who saw themselves as enemies. Moreover, Jesus, from my perspective, was not operating out of another sovereign authority to forgive. The slave (refugee) does not become the sovereign, but instead makes way for a new way of thinking and being otherwise—a way of relating that is not dependent on sovereignty and its relations of subordination and subjugation, but on care/love, compassion, and inclusion. More positively, Jesus' forgiveness involves recognition of the suchness of the soldiers, inviting the possibility of a relationship characterized by care, rather than the attributes

175. See Hunter, *To Change the World*, 157.

176. Agamben writes that "The only truly political action . . . is that which severs the nexus between violence and law." Jesus' forgiveness, then, is understood precisely in this way. Agamben, *State of Exception*, 88.

of sovereignty that deny singularity by enforcing a particular identity as the foundation of belonging. I add here that an ungovernable Jesus, in the act of forgiveness, breaks the mimetic chain of sovereignty's inherent violence.

Of course, we all know the end of the story. Despite Jesus' forgiveness, he was crucified and, according to Christian tradition, three days later rose from the dead. The cross was an ultimate symbol of Roman sovereignty and Jesus' execution was a repudiation, not of violence and death, but of sovereignty itself—sovereignty in all its forms. Given this line of thinking, the resurrection is a symbol of an ungovernable, non-sovereign God's care and the inability of human sovereignty to obliterate the singularity of Jesus, of human beings subject to sovereignty, and of creation itself.

Before turning to Pauline theology from Taubes' perspective, I offer a couple of other thoughts regarding the incarnation and its relevance for the Anthropocene Age. I think it is fair to say that most Christians consider the incarnation to be a singular event and exclusive to humanity. But what if we were to imagine that the incarnation is inextricably tied to creation itself. Thus, the incarnation could be seen as the embodied care of the immanent non-sovereign, non-privileging Creator, though Christians locate this in the life and ministry of Jesus. An implication is that this refers to creation itself and not simply or solely to human beings, which means the incarnation does not privilege human beings, but rather is the immanent expression of God's care for creation itself. This broader interpretation alters how we might conceive of God emptying Godself to take on the form of a slave. That is, the term "slave" represents not simply this particular form of life (or the life of the refugee), but how human sovereignty makes a slave of nature and other species. Human beings imagine having dominion over nature, which they can use and exploit to satisfy their desires and needs at the expense of nature. The revelation of a cosmic Christ eschews sovereignty and invites relations that regard the singularity of all life. A beloved community/ecclesia embraces the non-sovereign and non-privileging care for all members, for other-than-human beings, and for the earth.[177]

This view may lead to questions regarding salvation. Agamben uses the term "unsavable" that I am going to appropriate. Creation, both as object and process, is unsavable in the sense that it is not in need of salvation.

---

177. A type of beloved community is seen in some of the monastic traditions. DeCaroli writes that "Agamben finds in monasticism a community characterized by a refusal of authority, a refusal to recognize and thereby make inoperative the work of law and sovereignty. The monks' refusal to employ legal codes as a mechanism for binding the community was therefore neither the result of de facto illegality, nor a rebellious refusal to obey, but a form of life that rendered juridical authority inoperative." DeCaroli, "Giorgio Agamben and the Practice of Poverty," 214.

It already exists in its suchness. Human beings, however, can forget their suchness or singularity, as well as deny suchness to other human beings, other species, and nature itself. Indeed, the belief in human sovereignty, as noted above, is exactly this denial and undermining of singularity of some human beings and nature. There are all kinds of examples throughout history of human beings seeking sovereignty over others, violently oppressing, killing, and marginalizing Others for their own narcissistic gains. This said, human beings are "unsavable" in the sense that, despite all the apparatuses of sovereignty and its violence and exclusion, the suchness of being human, the excess of being human remains. That human beings need saving, especially in this age, is revealed in the incarnation. We need saving from relations defined and determined by sovereignty and its attributes. As John Yoder remarks, for God to save human beings, "Their sovereignty must be broken."[178] To think and be otherwise in the Anthropocene Age means we do not depend on the ordering of sovereignty, but instead on the immanent grace of God—grace that builds on nature, that builds on our capacity to belong without relations of subjugation, and that facilitates dwelling in the midst of plurality of suchness of all creation. To return to Agamben's notion of the coming community, the coming community or inoperative community is a way of belonging "without affirming an identity, that human beings co-belong without any representable condition of belonging."[179] One might immediately recall the community in Acts as being outside the Imperial apparatuses in establishing a coming community where identity or predicates are not the sole condition of dwelling together. More radically, this view would include, rather than exclude, nature from the political.[180] In this way, we could say that the coming community, in its partial expressions today and tomorrow, represents moments of salvation or healing of the rift between human beings and between human beings and nature. Put differently, a salvific event or moment reveals relations that eschew sovereignty as the principle of belonging and instead avows practices of non-sovereign, non-privileging care as the principle of belonging, of residing together on this one earth.[181]

---

178. Yoder, *The Politics of Jesus*, 147.

179. Agamben, *The Coming Community*, 85.

180. There are scholars and activists who advocate for nature being represented in politics. See Meijer, *When Animals Speak*. Meijer, *Animal Languages*. Rousseau, "In New Zealand, Lands and Rivers Can Be People Too (Legally Speaking)."

181. Theologian Catherine Keller makes a similar argument with regard to sovereignty and the need for a new public-political way of being, though she relies on different sources. See Keller, *Political Theology of the Earth*.

There is one last angle to pursue here. As discussed above, sovereignty and the law are interrelated and both have to do with ordering relations within society and between societies. For scholar Jacob Taubes,[182] Paul's theology addresses in different ways the challenges of the revelation of Jesus Christ and this revelation's impacts on both sovereignty and the law. Taubes stated that he "read the Epistle to the Romans as a legitimation and formation of a new social union-covenant, of developing an ecclesia against the Roman Empire, on the one hand, and, on the other hand, of the ethnic unity of the Jewish people."[183] His interpretation of Pauline theology led him to insights that were picked up by Agamben and others.[184] In summarizing some of Taubes' key ideas, Wolf-Daniel Hartwich, Aleida Assmann, and Jan Assmann write that the Epistle to the Romans was "directed against Rome and relativizes Rome's world imperialism . . . and directed against Jerusalem in that it relativizes the limits of Israel's self-definition, which are founded on *nomos* and *ethnos*."[185] Stated differently, Jesus "frees himself from the determination of ethnic ties and the Roman idea of empire,"[186] which can be seen as representing what Agamben calls the coming community. Hartwich et al. explain that Paul, from Taubes' perspective, "doesn't oppose a political theology of the Torah to the Roman nomos of the earth in order to establish a new national form of rule. He fundamentally negated the law as a force of political order. With this, *legitimacy is denied to all sovereigns of this world, be they imperatorial or theocratic.*"[187] The Epistle "undermines the function of the law as ordering power, be it in the context of political order, church order, or a natural order."[188] The messiah does not and cannot represent or legitimate institutions of earthly sovereignty, "but can only make them irrelevant and ultimately replace them."[189] This said, they point out that the "position of Paul doesn't imply any positive political form,"[190] however, the principles are identified. The "ecclesia understands itself, not as an autarchic polis that separates itself militantly from other communities, but as a

182. Taubes, *The Political Theology of Paul.*

183. Hartwich, Assmann, and Assmann, "Afterword," 117.

184. It is important to point out that there are other decidedly different interpretations of Paul and sovereignty. I am using Taubes because of the parallels to the work of Benjamin and Agamben with regard to sovereignty. Patterson, *Freedom in the Making of Western Culture*, 337–44.

185. Hartwich, Assmann, and Assmann, "Afterword," 117.

186. Hartwich, Assmann, and Assmann, "Afterword," 119.

187. Hartwich, Assmann, and Assmann, "Afterword," 121; italics mine.

188. Hartwich, Assmann, and Assmann, "Afterword," 122.

189. Hartwich, Assmann, and Assmann, "Afterword," 142.

190. Hartwich, Assmann, and Assmann, "Afterword," 121.

new universal world order."[191] "The new political order," they continue, "is constituted by love in its two forms: love of neighbor (inward love) and love of enemy (outward love)"[192] and I add care for other species and the earth.

The radical political theology of Jacob Taubes points to the possibility of a polis that does not separate *zoē* and *bios*; does not depend on relations of subjugation and servitude; does not rely on the illusions of superiority, inferiority, and human dominion; does not construct apparatuses that threaten violence; does not rely on sovereignty and law to order social-political life. More positively, a radical Christian political theology is rooted in a non-sovereign, non-privileging God of the incarnation that reveals a non-sovereign ordering of relations through care that recognizes and affirms the singularity (and by implication the vast plurality) of human beings and other species.

## Conclusion

We have for millennia largely depended on the notion and apparatuses of sovereignty to order life in society and our relations to other-than-human species and the earth. Theological and philosophical narratives and theories have affirmed and lauded various types of sovereignty and mystified the sovereign class, giving rise to the illusion that sovereignty and the sovereign class are necessary for human belonging. Today, massive population growth of human beings, coupled with industrialization, technological achievements, and capitalism, has led to changes in the climate and the beginning of the Anthropocene Age. Hopefully, we are learning that sovereignty not only unjustly privileges the sovereign and the sovereign class, but privileges human beings over other species and the earth itself. This anthropocentric, narcissistic belief in human sovereignty is a key obstacle in finding ways of living together that do not destroy the very habitat we and other species rely on for life. We need to expose the illusions, violence, and exclusion promulgated by theologies and philosophies of sovereignty and their attending apparatuses, whether they are evident in religious communities and organizations, societies, or other groups/systems (e.g., capitalism). We need to promote non-sovereign relations and practices within groups, communities, and societies, even as we do not yet know for sure what particular non-sovereign political forms will take. If we do not think and act otherwise, a sovereign humanity will lay on the rubble and ashes of an unhoused earth.

191. Hartwich, Assmann, and Assmann, "Afterword," 130.
192. Hartwich, Assmann, and Assmann, "Afterword," 130.

# 4

# *The Problem of Political Freedom*

---

Freedom is the defining character of human existence.
Our capacity for freedom makes us persons. But this capacity
has to be realized in the empirical experience of living
and in actual conditions.[1]

(W)e are human beings in the true sense
only in so far as we are free.[2]

The meaning of politics is freedom.[3]

Freedom is our nature. But our nature lies beyond us,
and has to be intended and achieved.[4]

To be free from convention is not to spurn it
but not to be deceived by it. It is to be able to use it
as an instrument instead of being used by it.[5]

1. Macmurray, *Conditions of Freedom*, 48.
2. Steiner, *The Philosophy of Freedom*, 141.
3. Arendt, *The Promise of Politics*, 108.
4. Macmurray, *Conditions of Freedom*, 79.
5. Watts, *The Way of Zen*, 11.

Who is against it, except perhaps would-be tyrants and slavers who privilege freedom for themselves, while denying it to others? Are we free to deny the freedom of others? Or does my freedom necessarily impinge on the freedom of others? While not a question for a determinist, how much freedom do human beings actually have? Nearly three centuries ago, Jean-Jacques Rousseau wrote that "Man is born free, and everywhere he is in chains,"[6] suggesting a tragic anthropological paradox, as well as a longing for a time long past. The juxtaposition between existential freedom and unfreedom also found its way into the philosophy of Jean Paul Sartre. Human beings, he wrote, are "condemned to be free,"[7] because they are responsible for everything they do, including our actions and inactions vis-à-vis climate change. While all are condemned to be free, some people bear more responsibility than others for climate change and, in the Anthropocene Age. Most of us in the West are all guilty. Perhaps the thorny questions around the complexity of freedom caused Wendy Brown to write: Freedom "is an eternally nettlesome political value as well as a matter of endless theoretical dispute."[8] It is, she continues, "historically, semiotically, and culturally protean, as well as politically elusive."[9]

The idea and practice of freedom are complex because they intersect with all aspects of human life, including the previous chapters' discussions of dwelling and sovereignty. Any political philosopher (including determinists) and theologian must address it, even though it is a nettlesome and elusive political value. This becomes even more important when we consider the present and future realities of the Anthropocene Age. What will freedom look like as global resources diminish and there is a corresponding rise of fear and hatred? Will people sacrifice their freedom for the allure of national security and its promises of protection and stability? Will we freely circle the nationalistic wagons, ensuring that the exercise of freedom will foster exclusion and conflict, instead of inclusion, plurality, and cooperation? Will those specters of unfreedom, racism and classism, become more virulent in an age of anxiety and scarcity? Will we continue to construct freedom to serve the interests of global capitalism at the expense of humanity, other species, and the earth? What does human freedom mean when we consider that over 1 million species will be extinct by 2050? Does human freedom mean we do not have a responsibility for the "freedom" of other species or for the well-being of the earth? Will human beings recognize and

6. Rousseau, *On the Social Contract*, 3.
7. Sartre, quoted in Grayling, *The History of Philosophy*, 490.
8. Brown, *States of Injury*, 4.
9. Brown, *States of Injury*, 5.

acknowledge the material foundations of freedom—our dependence on the viability of the earth as a living system? Will we see, in other words, that all philosophies, theologies, and practices of freedom will turn to dust if human beings become extinct?

The topic of freedom, in general, and political freedom, in particular, has filled the bookshelves of libraries for centuries. It is a daunting subject and one that we can sketch out but never fully grasp, whether in chapter or in book form. Nevertheless, a radical political theology must undertake the effort to address freedom and political freedom, especially given that human freedom has played and continues to play a key role in climate change. Moreover, like the notions of dwelling and sovereignty, discussions about freedom have largely excluded and continue to exclude other species and the earth—both as apparently politically irrelevant. If we are truly condemned to be free, then the Anthropocene Age reveals the tragic aspect of human freedom and a possibility to think about and practice freedom differently. Given this, in this chapter I endeavor to sketch out some of the contours or attributes of freedom and, in particular, political freedom. Toward this end, I begin with a definition of freedom, followed by a discussion of its attributes. In the next section, I describe some of the problems of political freedom given the realities of the Anthropocene Age. This sets the stage for depicting a radical political theology of freedom. As I have done in the previous chapters, this last section begins with an existential portrayal of freedom, which is followed by a theological framing of political freedom.

## Political Freedom and Its Attributes

In his intriguing book on the history of freedom, Orlando Patterson argues that Western conceptions about freedom were "generated from the experience of slavery."[10] "People," he wrote, "came to value freedom, to construct it as a powerful shared vision of life, as a result of their experience of, response to, slavery or its recombinant form, serfdom, in their roles as masters, slaves, and non-slaves."[11] We see evidence of Patterson's thesis when we turn to Greek antiquity, where the issue of slavery and political freedom obtained differing views.[12] For instance, in the sixth century BCE, Solon, an Athenian lawmaker, statesman, and poet, said "Whenever the poor are vulnerable to contracts that makes them potentially liable to be used or sold as slaves, they cannot be equal citizens, because they cannot be secure in their status

10. Patterson, *Freedom*, xiii.
11. Patterson, *Freedom*, xiii.
12. See De Dijn, *Freedom*, 15–68.

as citizens . . . They are in these circumstances always at risk of falling into some form of bondage."[13] To be a free Greek citizen meant one was equal[14] and had property;[15] to be in bondage meant unequal or non-equal (in that the notion of equality did not apply), which is related to material conditions and not simply an abstract notion of political equality.[16] A couple of centuries later, philosopher Alkidamas went further, arguing that "The deity gave liberty to all [human beings], and nature created no one a slave."[17] In this intriguing sentence, there is an ontological and existential or natural grounding of freedom. Human beings are given liberty by God, but in our freedom, we have constructed a form of life called slavery—an offense to God and nature. Aristotle, who criticized Alkidamas, had a different view, developing an anthropology that posited a belief that some human beings are naturally suited to be slaves (animate instruments that are property of their masters).[18]

Patterson's argument is not dependent on the disquisitions of Greek philosophers. We note that myths and religious stories have themes of freedom and slavery. I have used the Exodus story in the previous chapters, which reveals bondage and the longing for freedom. The Babylonian captivity is another tale of the loss of freedom and the freedom to return home. Jesus taking on the form of slave points to freedom beyond this form of life, which I will say more about later. Paul prayed to be released from the bondage of some physical torments, which is an example of how physical agony can impede one's experience of freedom. In short, the issues of human freedom and its loss are embedded in religious narratives of the Judeo-Christian tradition.

To add to Patterson's thesis, it seems to me the rise of concern about freedom also arose from the emergence of the idea of sovereignty as a way of ordering how people dwell in society. To be a slave in Greek society meant that there had to be a sovereign (and sovereign class) who makes a state of

13. Lane, *The Birth of Politics*, 34.

14. Ryan, *On Politics*, 92–97.

15. The relation between property and freedom is addressed in Jim Josefson's discussion of Hannah Arendt's political philosophy. This is a complicated and nuanced discussion that cannot be addressed in this chapter because it would take us far afield. Josefson, *Hannah Arendt's Aesthetic Politics*, 201–37.

16. De Dijn claims that "the Greeks can be said to have invented the concept of political freedom." While they may have invented the concept, the experience of political freedom is evident in religious myths that precede early Greek philosophers. De Dijn, *Freedom*, 18.

17. Lane, *The Birth of Politics*, 51. The reference to all men is probably accurate, since the Greek city-state did not include women under the banner of political freedom.

18. Barker, *The Politics of Aristotle*, 9–18.

exception such that some human beings are socially and legally constructed as slaves (or subordinate such as women)—denying freedom to some, while enhancing freedom for others. For example, the Pharaoh as sovereign made decrees that enslaved the Israelites. And the Israelites, at the command of an absolute sovereign, subjugated the peoples of the promised land. To construct a slave, to place a person in bondage, to deny their freedom, requires a sovereign—a sovereign less interested in the dwelling of the slave than in the well-being of the elect.

While the issue of freedom extends back to the dawn of civilization, it is not clear what freedom or political freedom means. Any definition will fall short and be subject to dispute, but we must nevertheless forge ahead and attempt to offer a definition, which can be further illuminated by identifying and addressing some of its attributes. In general, freedom is the power to act and speak without excessive restraints or hinderance.[19] This is a view heralded by Hobbes and his negative view of freedom. In his work, *Leviathan*, Hobbes writes "By liberty, is understood, according to the proper signification of the world, the absence of external impediments."[20] Hobbes' liberal or negative view of freedom "is guaranteed through a system of individual rights, which exist in order to ensure that individuals are subject to no other vision of the good life than their own."[21] Of course, to obtain this personal freedom, citizens would have to sacrifice some political freedom to the leviathan that insures political security and stability.

Philosopher Axel Honneth argues that Hobbes' negative view of freedom, which was later taken up by John Locke, emerged against the background of the English Civil War. "Hobbes sought to counter," Honneth writes, "the growing influence of Republicans . . . [by] proposing that freedom merely be understood as the externally unimpeded realization of human aims."[22] A similar view of negative freedom is evident in the work of John Macmurray, who argued that freedom "is simply the self's agency; its capacity to perform action and actualize an intention," which suggests a

19. This is typically understood as negative view of freedom which has its roots in Isaiah Berlin's famous essay "Two Concepts of Freedom." A negative view of freedom simply means being free from constraints (in order to act), which has a foundation in liberalism's construction of freedom and autonomy. Positive freedom has more to do with freedom to act toward one's self-realization. See also Berlin, *Four Essays on Freedom*.

20. Axel Honneth makes clear that Hobbes was more focused on external impediments to freedom than internal impediments. Theologians, like Augustine and Aquinas, would have viewed sin and vice as internal (and external) impediments. Honneth, *Freedom's Right*, 21.

21. Robinson, *The Ethics of Care*, 57.

22. Robinson, *The Ethics of Care*, 23.

minimum of constraints.[23] In terms of human agency, Honneth contends that "human actions can properly be called free only if they proceed from purposes that transcend mere causality and are instead anchored in self-posited or subjectively endorsed reasons."[24] Mere causality would refer to the biological constraints we experience as animals. But there are relational limits, as well, which Hobbes recognized.

In a comparable vein of negative freedom, Orlando Patterson argues that "Personal freedom, at its most elementary, gives a person the sense that one, on the one hand, is not being coerced or restrained by another person in doing something desired and, on the other hand, the conviction that one can do as one please within the limits of that person's desire to do the same."[25] Even here, we immediately run into a qualification. Consider the numerous examples of history when people have been constrained or hindered from speaking and acting, yet transgressed those limits on freedom. Nelson Mandela was imprisoned for twenty-seven years, being denied personal and political freedom, yet he spoke and acted in and from prison. Even in prison he had agency and carried out his intentions. Was he free? Yes and no. From a negative view of freedom, Mandela did not have freedom, yet in spite of the obstacles of the apartheid leviathan Mandela exercised personal and political freedom. If we turn to the prison guards, they ostensibly had personal and political freedom, yet were in bondage to the machinations of an apartheid racist state.[26] Who was freer, Mandela or prison officials? As Mariam Thalos writes, "Freedom . . . shows up not in the absence of a field of power; instead, freedom shows up only against a field of power working to counter a person's efforts. Freedom is the power to aspire-to-be over against what you are told-to-be."[27] This seems to contradict a negative, liberal view of freedom. Perhaps we can revise the definition to say that freedom is the power to act and speak often in spite of and, in some cases, because of restraints and hinderances.

There is another issue with this definition. What capacities are necessary to have the power to speak and act? A young child has some power to speak and act. Would we consider this child to be free? Perhaps in a limited way, but what defines these limits? A child's action has a motive and goal, which suggests some nascent capacity for reason (including the capacity for

23. Jeffko, "Introduction," ix.

24. Honneth in Genel and Deranty, eds., *Recognition or Disagreement*, 162–63.

25. Patterson, *Freedom*, 3.

26. Charles Taylor addresses internal obstacles to freedom, which would include one's psychological attachment to racist ideologies. In Warburton, *Freedom*, 120–22.

27. Thalos, *A Social Theory of Freedom*, 245.

judgment or deliberation), but we tend to believe that a 4-year-old is not free. Hannah Arendt can be helpful here. She argued that for an action "to be free [it] must be free of motive on one side, [and] from its intended goal as a predictable effect on the other. That is not to say that motives and aims are not important factors in every single act, but they are not its determining factors, and action is free to the extent that it is able to transcend them."[28] I understand her point using different language that will help distinguish freedom of a child from that of an adult. A "free" act is free to the extent that the person is not determined by or captive to motive and goal. Moreover, the free act is not determined by the motives and goals of others.[29] "Freedom," as Thalos contends, "is the ability to reject the judgments and expectations of others."[30] In other words, persons who possess a level of differentiated reason are free to the extent that they are not compelled to act on their motive or to demand a specific outcome *and* they are not compelled to act on the motives of significant others. Moreover, this includes resisting or even transgressing the identifications of significant Others. For a young child, the self is the act and the act is the motive and goal: there is little differentiation. In addition, young children tend to be motivated to act on the motives of people who care for them and to accept parental identifications, though as they continue to develop psychosocially they are able to resist or transgress the expectations and identifications of others. Yet, we can say that to thwart a child's motive and goal is to thwart the child's sense of self, which may be a reason why restraints in acting are taken personally. A child, in other words, has difficulty differentiating between self and emotions, actions, motives, etc. and the identifications of needed Others. Psychologically healthy adults recognize that their sense of who they are is differentiated from their acts, motives, and goals, as well as the expectations, motives, and identifications of Others. This differentiation gives them greater psychosocial flexibility or freedom in their actions. That said, adults also struggle with freedom whenever there is an issue of differentiation. Violence, addictions, absolute certainty or self-righteousness, and lack or absence of critical thinking

28. Josefson, *Hannah Arendt's Aesthetic Politics*, 89.

29. While I do have the time to address what some philosophers and theologians call moral freedom, it is important to note that the issue of differentiation applies here as well. Rudolf Steiner wrote that "An action is felt to be free in so far as the reasons spring from the ideal part of my individual being; every other part of an action, irrespective of whether it is carried out under the compulsion of nature or under the obligation of a moral standard, is felt to be *unfree*." Persons who are compelled to accede to a moral norm are not free, because they, in those moments, lack differentiation. Steiner, *The Philosophy of Freedom*, 138.

30. Thalos, *A Social Theory of Freedom*, 74.

(self-reflection) are examples of poor differentiation and a concomitant lack of individual freedom.

To return to the definition of freedom as the power to act and speak in spite of restraints, we can add that for the power to act to be relatively free means there must be differentiated *reason-emotion*,[31] wherein there is a distinction between the person acting and the motive and goal associated with the action. For instance, I have a motive to drive the car with the goal of arriving at the store to purchase groceries, which are connected to my power to act—to drive. If I am compelled by the motive and goal, then it is not a free action. "I" am determined by the motive and goal. Instead of having a motive and a goal, I am captive to both. If the motive and goal do not define the self (instead a part of the self), then the action is relatively free—given the normal constraints of human finitude.

Of course, I suspect that many readers have associated definitions of freedom with individuals, which is only partly true. Hannah Arendt, in reflecting on Greek philosophers, writes that "The realm of the polis was the sphere of freedom."[32] In a later work, she notes that "Freedom exists only in the unique intermediary space of politics."[33] And it is in this polis, that citizens "are held together not by a common will but by a common world."[34] In the polis the power to act refers to a group, in this case men, speaking and acting together in a common world and, at times, toward achieving common ends. "Power," then, for Arendt is in speaking and acting together vis-à-vis the polis' space of appearances. And it is this speaking and acting together that expresses and gives rise to freedom.[35] Power and freedom, in short, are relational and founded in the polis.

Naturally, this in no way implies that individuals do not have power to act, but that political power and political freedom are founded in speaking and acting together. What is important about Arendt's view is that it

31. There is a long philosophical history explaining the relation between reason and emotion, which has an impact on how people view freedom. If emotion is viewed as corrupting reason, we can expect that freedom depends on reason over emotion, which also has a gendered aspect. Twentieth-century philosopher John Macmurray argued that there is reason in emotion and emotion in reason. In terms of freedom, the notion of differentiation applies in the sense of being able to differentiate the self from one's emotions. If, for instance, I say, "I am angry," this indicates a struggle of differentiation because the self or "I" is the emotion. A more awkward phrase is "I have a feeling of anger." This is more differentiated because it connotes that the "I" is more than the feeling. Macmurray, *Reason and Emotion*.

32. Arendt, *The Human Condition*, 30–31.

33. Arendt, *The Promise of Politics*, 95.

34. In Josefson, *Hannah Arendt's Aesthetic Politics*, 200.

35. Josefson, *Hannah Arendt's Aesthetic Politics*, 199–207.

moves us from our preoccupation about individual freedom in terms of Isaiah Berlin's[36] egoistic notions of negative and positive freedom[37] to the relational attributes of personal[38] and political freedom/power. Put differently, in terms of the definition, *freedom, as the power to speak and act in spite of constraints, is founded in the existential and political relational space between human beings.*[39]

This relational feature of freedom needs greater elaboration since all other attributes of freedom flow from it. The attribute of relationality has long been recognized by numerous philosophers from Aristotle to Lévinas as central to human freedom. But "relation" does not yet inform us of the conditions necessary for freedom to be realized, albeit relatively. John Macmurray argued that "The primary condition of relative freedom . . . consists in the quality of our interpersonal relationships."[40] While I will address this in greater detail below, for now it is important to unpack what is meant by "quality of interpersonal relationships." First of all, Macmurray, following but altering Hegel, highlights the necessity of personal recognition for communication and freedom. As indicated in previous chapters, personal recognition involves recognizing (and treating) the Other as a unique, inviolable, valued, and responsive or agentic subject and that mutual-personal recognition is the foundation of civic care and civic faith. From Jean-Luc Nancy's and Giorgio Agamben's philosophical perspectives, this would include recognizing and respecting the singularity or suchness of the individual. In recognizing the Other as a person there is, in other words,

36. Axel Honneth notes that Berlin's negative freedom is a type of freedom "an individual is supposed to enjoy by virtue of being granted a circumscribed space for the unhindered pursuit of his goals." Positive freedom, on the other hand, "can properly be called free only [if it] proceeds from purposes that transcend mere natural causality and are instead anchored in self-posited or subjectively endorsed reasons." Honneth and Rancière, *Recognition of Disagreement*, 162–63. See also Warburton, *Freedom*, 5–23.

37. Positive freedom, simply stated, involves the capacity to act in realizing one's goal. It differs, in part, from negative freedom that focuses on obstacles to self-realization. See, Warburton, *Freedom*, 8–11.

38. Macmurray points out that personal freedom "can be achieved only in fellowship." This will become clearer when I discuss the existential roots of freedom. Macmurray, *Conditions of Freedom*, 48.

39. Socialism, as Axel Honneth notes, tends to regard "cooperation in the community as a necessary condition for freedom, but also as the sole way of exercising true freedom." Liberalism and, in particular, neoliberal capitalism, stresses the individual at the expense of the social. What liberalism fails to acknowledge is that, without freedom being rooted in the social, the project of liberalism would fail. Honneth, *The Idea of Socialism*, 24.

40. Macmurray, *Conditions of Freedom*, xv.

something unfathomable, an excess that "eludes thematization."[41] Using different language, Lévinas wrote that the "strangeness of the Other [is] his very freedom . . . Free beings alone can be strangers to one another."[42] Of course, in my view, strangers are recognized as persons who are invited into the space of appearances, the space of speaking and acting together.

For Macmurray, the flourishing of political relations depends on interpersonal recognition, which entails personal (and object[43]) knowing, and it is this personal knowing that undergirds personal and political freedom. In other words, for individuals to engage in the polis' space of speaking and acting together, there must be knowledge (and treatment) of them as persons, which accompanies individuals' sense of self-esteem, self-respect, and self-confidence necessary for political agency/freedom. This knowledge is supported and maintained by commonly held narratives, practices, and institutions. Axel Honneth, commenting on the work of Hegel, makes a similar claim: "he (Hegel) regards those social or institutional conditions that allow each individual subject to enter into communicative relationships that can be experienced as expression of their own freedom; for it is only in so far as they can participate in such social relationships that subjects are able without compulsion to realize their freedom in the external world."[44] To enter into communicative relationships depends on personal knowing and together they undergird personal and political freedom.

There are eight important features of personal knowing and its relation to freedom. First, personal knowing is different from what might be called factual or categorical knowing, such as 2+2=4. In factual (determinate) knowing, there is no freedom. This can be extended to knowledge that is proposed to be a fact when it is not. If I say with certainty that the earth is flat, then this "knowledge" indicates the absence of freedom because there can be no openness to a counterclaim or to proof. Another example would be individuals who claim with certainty that people of color are inferior and white people are superior. These "beliefs" are believed to be certain and this certainty reveals an absence of freedom. In religious language, idolatry

41. Lévinas, *Totality and Infinity*, 86.

42. Lévinas, *Totality and Infinity*, 73.

43. Macmurray differentiated between personal and object knowing, contending that object knowing appears first in development and is understood as the capacity to recognize and categorize objects in space. Object knowing is always connected to personal knowing in the sense that the other person is an object in space. When object knowing is dominant or supersedes personal knowing (and is not for the sake of the well-being of the Other, as in the case of a physician treating a patient), then there is objectification and depersonalization, which undermines interpersonal freedom. Macmurray, *Persons in Relation*.

44. Honneth, *The Pathologies of Individual Freedom*, 15.

represents a kind of "knowing" that is not free. Idolatry is the absence of doubt, which leaves little psychological space for not-knowing, for curiosity, for exploration. It also restricts the space of speaking and acting together for the unfree like-minded individuals. Personal knowing, by contrast, can aver with certainty that the Other is a person, but this accompanies an epistemological and spiritual openness to Others in their suchness.[45] Personal knowing, in other words, includes an indeterminate knowing that can never fully capture Others in terms of representations. Others always exceed personal knowing's ability to represent them. This creates an open relational space for persons to appear in and act out of their singularity—freedom to think, act, and be.

This space where the Other appears in their suchness points to a second feature of personal knowing and freedom. I have argued that personal knowing results in individuals' sense of self-esteem, self-respect, and self-confidence. To possess and act on one's freedom, as Miriam Thalos argues, one must have a self-concept, which is part of the capacities for reason, judgment, and motivation.[46] Of course, she is not arguing that any self-concept will do. Political and personal freedom depend on a positive self-concept. Two brief examples will illustrate this point. James Baldwin, writing about his father, said, "He was defeated long before he died because, at the bottom of his heart, *he really believed* what white people said about him."[47] His father's self-concept was obviously negative and his feeling defeated reveals the loss of personal and political freedom, having succumbed to the false identifications projected onto him by the larger white society and its apparatuses of unfreedom. Also, in my experience as a pastoral theologian and psychotherapist, I have seen many women and men, who having been terribly abused as children and adults, lack a sense of personal freedom precisely because they are captive to shame and concomitant negative identifications, which is how victimizers control victims. When victims of trauma obtain a positive self-concept, they correspondingly manifest greater personal and political freedom.

A third and related idea is that political freedom depends on plurality. Jim Josefson argues that for Hannah Arendt, freedom is connected to "love of the world and a commitment to actualizing the plurality within it."[48] To return to Macmurray, love or care entails the recognition of Others as

---

45. Thalos, *A Social Theory of Freedom*, 68.

46. Thalos, *A Social Theory of Freedom*, 44–46.

47. Baldwin, *The Fire Next Time*, 4.

48. Josefson, *Hannah Arendt's Aesthetic Politics*, 60.

persons, which means affirming their singularity[49] and, in so doing, necessarily affirms and intends the plurality of human beings (and I would add other species). Freedom by contrast is attenuated or absent in the face of sameness or the absence of plurality. We see examples of this in political and religious contexts where dogma must be adhered to by all, which reflects an attenuation of the freedom to think and act. It is interesting and ironic that religious liberty can be affirmed by the state, but religious liberty within religious denominations is often tenuous at best. If one does not hold to doctrine or dogma, then you are not considered to be part of the community. You are not free to think publicly, and if you do so you are asked to leave or are summarily expelled or excommunicated. To shift to the political realm, even in a so-called democratic society, there is a kind of religious preoccupation about patriotism, wherein people fear plurality and seek to deny freedom of thought and action by adhering to dogmatic patriotism (e.g., Love America or Leave It) or by their churlish, cultish following of a political figure. By contrast, freedom thrives when plurality is valued and achieved through speaking and acting together.

A fourth aspect of personal knowing and freedom is that the Other *qua* person is both the limit and foundation of my freedom. As Miriam Thalos notes, freedom exists within a field of power wherein one exercises freedom through resistance to the projections and expectations of others.[50] She writes that "Freedom is the power to aspire-to-be over against what you are told-to-be."[51] Agamben, in my view, has a different but similar perspective. He argues that inoperativity or Bartleby's "I would prefer not" is an expression of freedom in the face of the expectations and identifications of Others.[52] Personal knowing, then, does not suggest an absence of contestation or resistance in the field of speaking and acting together. Indeed, it is very much a part of and necessary to that field of communication and power, wherein others are the condition for and limit of freedom, which I will say more about below in the discussion on radical freedom. For now, I would point to the over seventy years women suffragists resisted the depersonalizing projections of and expectations of patriarchy and instead exercised their freedom to resist—acting on positive self-concepts that emerged in the interpersonal space of speaking and acting together. They resisted and transgressed cultural and political representations projected onto them.

49. Philosopher Gilles Deleuze contended that "all identities are effects of difference." This suggests that singularities likewise depend on difference and, in turn, found plurality. Grayling, *The History of Philosophy*, 501.

50. Thalos, *A Social Theory of Freedom*, 47.

51. Thalos, *A Social Theory of Freedom*, 245.

52. Agamben, *Potentialities*, 255–56.

They preferred not to live out of the demands of those who sought to keep women politically irrelevant and unfree. It was their shared speaking and acting together that founded the political freedom to transgress the limits of the political constraints of a patriarchal "democracy."

A fifth feature of personal knowing/relation vis-à-vis freedom is that persons obtain a sense of "being with oneself in the other."[53] Freedom from this perspective is never simply and solely individual or egoistic, which raises questions about liberalism's preoccupation about individual freedom that, in many ways, serves the interests of neoliberal capitalists.[54] More positively stated, forms of intersubjectivity such as friendship, as well as forms of political life where there is civic care and trust, involve degrees of freedom wherein "being with oneself in the other" is a necessary attribute. Intimately connected to this view is the sixth feature of personal knowing vis-à-vis freedom. While not always conscious, "each subject is able to perceive the liberty of the other as a prerequisite of his own self-realization."[55] Put another way, Honneth argues that the "'reality' of freedom is only given if we encounter each other in mutual recognition and can understand our actions as a condition for the fulfillment of others' aims."[56] Alain Badiou similarly notes, "What we learn is that otherness is immanent in all identity, which means I am only myself insofar as I am the Other of that Other for whom I am myself. There is no getting around this, and it is the real foundation of freedom . . . I am free only if I recognize the Other's freedom, so that is the foundation of freedom."[57] Yet, it is not simply the recognition that is important here. It is important to stress again that the quality of the relationship grounds the possibility of political and personal freedom. To return to John Macmurray, he claimed that "the primary condition of freedom, to which all other conditions are related, lies in the character and quality of human relations."[58] (p.15). This quality of human relations depends on mutual-personal recognition and treatment of the other as person—a unique, inviolable, valued, agentic subject. Hannah Arendt (1958), using different language, affirms this view, arguing that it is the polis' space of appearance where citizens are recognized and treated as persons, making self-realization or singularity possible.

53. Honneth, *The Pathologies of Individual Freedom*, 26.

54. Brown, *States of Injury*, 6.

55. Honneth, *The Pathologies of Individual Freedom*, 8.

56. Honneth, *Freedom's Right*, 124.

57. Badiou, *I Know There Are So Many of You*, 33–34.

58. Macmurray, *Conditions of Freedom*, 15.

In this relational view of freedom, there is a realization that my freedom is contingent on the liberty of others, which undermines the negative perspective that my freedom comes at the expense of others. Of course, we know that it can, but by denying the freedom of Others (which also means denying them recognition as persons) involves undermining my freedom. A Hobbesian or Schmittian society that is based on a friend-enemy distinction is not a society where political freedom or plurality flourishes, because the Other is not recognized as necessary to my own freedom or my self-realization and there is no acknowledgement of being with oneself in the other. Instead, there is only alienation and the exercise of freedom within one's own political enclave. But in the larger Schmittian society, there is no real freedom to think and act, because one is preoccupied about the enemy within and the enemy without.

What emerges from the recognition that the Other is a prerequisite of one's own self-realization points to a seventh aspect of personal knowing. In the first chapter, I indicated that a key feature of the space of speaking and acting together is the dialectical tension between restraint and unrestraint. For Nigel Warburton, there is a hint of this in Rousseau's political philosophy.[59] There are times when we restrain ourselves so as to create a space for the other's freedom and self-realization. More will be said about this below when I address the existential, developmental aspects of freedom.

The last attribute of personal knowing and freedom concerns equality. Honneth notes that, for Hannah Arendt, "political freedom both entails and realizes the equality of social participants."[60] In a Greek polis, male citizens were deemed to be equal and thus free, and this extended to the limits of the polis' boundaries. "Whoever leaves his polis," she writes, "or is banished from it loses not just his hometown or his fatherland; he also loses the only space in what he can be free—and he loses the society of his equals."[61] Equality, like politics, is a nettlesome issue, because it touches on topics of political rights, justice, distribution of resources, etc. These are important, but for my purposes I want to ground the equality associated with freedom with mutual personal recognition, which is further understood in terms of mutual appreciation of each other's singularity. Singularity accompanies mutual self-esteem, self-confidence, and self-respect that are necessary for the exercise of political agency. But this psychological and relational view of equality is also inextricably tied to the distribution of resources in a society. Equality does not necessarily mean equity in resources, but it does mean

59. Warburton, *Freedom*, 115.

60. Honneth in Genel and Deranty, eds., *Recognition or Disagreement*, 56.

61. Arendt, *The Promise of Politics*, 119.

sufficient distribution of material and political goods so that persons can exercise their capacities for freedom, for self-realization.

Let's consider a couple of illustrations to ground these points. Systemic racism entails political, economic, and social institutions; practices; rituals; and narratives that support and maintain depersonalizing (and idolatrous) forms of knowledge and treatment, as well as the maldistribution of goods within the society.[62] This systemic humiliation (and at times terror) and deprivation undermines political-public sense of self-esteem, self-respect, and self-confidence (positive public-political self-concept), which is accompanied by attempts to deny people of color political relevancy and freedom by marginalizing them from society's spaces of speaking and acting together.[63] In a racist society, the black Other is constructed as a threat to white freedom, which is dependent on the denial of black freedom. There is, in other words, no sense that white freedom is dependent on the freedom and well-being of African Americans, who are denied plurality and singularity. There is only alienation, which means persons do not experience being with oneself in the other. This said, depersonalized and marginalized persons can, and often do, form into communities or *poleis* that make inoperative these apparatuses by constructing their *poleis* in terms of interpersonal knowing and acting. In these communities, people have a greater chance of gaining the experience of being with oneself in the other, as well as recognizing that the liberty of the other is contingent on their own freedom and self-realization. There is, then, the exercise of freedom/power and plurality in this space, while it is denied in the larger public-political spaces. Moreover, there is a greater sharing of resources necessary to act on their freedoms within the community.

Those who seek to depersonalize Others for the sake of their privilege and freedom are not politically free. Recall above the comment by Arendt that "to be free [it] must be free of motive on one side, [and] from its intended goal as a predictable effect on the other."[64] When reason is captive to

62. Wendy Brown demonstrates how neoliberal capitalism has created enormous inequalities in income and wealth, undermining the freedoms of many citizens who are deprived of the resources to realize their freedoms. Brown, *Undoing the Demos*.

63. Michael Sawyer provides an excellent illustration of this in his depiction of the political philosophy of Malcom X. Sawyer argues that Malcolm X (and other African Americans) were politically irrelevant because white racists and their apparatuses denied them positive recognition (personal knowing) and subsequently tried to marginalize them. Malcolm had to establish a positive self-concept in spite of these negative attributions so that he could exercise his political agency in the face of attempts to marginalize him from the spaces of speaking and acting together. I would add to this that his community of faith was crucial to this self-concept. Sawyer, *Black Minded*.

64. Josefson, *Hannah Arendt's Aesthetic Politics*, 89.

emotion(s), identification, motive, and goal, personal and political freedom are diminished or absent. When people are captive, consciously or not, to knowledge based on beliefs (illusions) in inferiority and superiority, when people are in bondage to racism's depersonalization and marginalization of people of color, they are not free. Their collective conscious or unconscious motive is to maintain white supremacy (and black inferiority) for the goals of white self-esteem, self-confidence, and self-respect (and at the expense of constructing Others as inferior), as well as white identifications, privilege, and freedom (again at the expense of depersonalizing and depriving Others). Another reason why they are not free is because they are dependent on forever producing "inferior Others" (and "superior" white people) and will constantly be preoccupied about ensuring that inferior Others exist so white people can possess privilege and "freedom." Put differently, freedom is diminished when people are obsessively concerned with securing the space of speaking and acting together only for themselves (denial of plurality) and not for Others who live in the polis. Evidence for this lack of freedom and obsession with producing inferior Others is the white backlash and hatred/rage that occurs whenever African Americans achieve greater political and economic freedoms and rights.[65] The rage and hatred of whites toward African Americans signify the absence of freedom.

Implicit in the idea that the other person is both the limit and the foundation of my freedom points to accountability vis-à-vis personal and political freedom. Axel Honneth argues that "we should regard our individual freedom as a moral obligation we have toward all humans. We are ultimately only 'free' if we view ourselves as persons who impose laws on ourselves, which obligate us to respect all other humans."[66] The exercise of freedom "means taking part in a sphere of interaction that has emerged on the basis of shared and internalized knowledge—a sphere that is regulated by norms of mutual recognition."[67] Emmanuel Lévinas holds a similar view in that the face of the other entails our infinite responsibility for and to the Other, which comes "from the hither side of my freedom."[68] We are accountable for the freedom of the Other because "The other is in me and in the midst of my very identification."[69] More will be said about this below, but for now let me acknowledge that freedom accompanies accountability to and for each other, and failing this means a loss of freedom. Whenever we

---

65. See Alexander, *The New Jim Crow*; Anderson, *White Rage*; Wilkerson, *Caste*.

66. Honneth, *Freedom's Right*, 102.

67. Honneth, *Freedom's Right*, 105.

68. Lévinas, *Otherwise Than Being*, 10.

69. Lévinas, *Otherwise Than Being*, 125.

see the absence of social-political accountability with regard to a group of people, we can be confident that that group's freedom is diminished or curtailed. Racism, classism, and sexism (and other forms of marginalization) are examples where accountability is diminished toward the marginalized group and this always impacts the group's freedom of speaking and acting together in public-political spaces. The white conservative backlash against Black Lives Matter is a present-day example of the refusal to be accountable to and for African Americans. The anger and resistance to the Black Lives Matter movement represents a desire (if not action) to squelch their voices, their freedom. This is also seen in the animus toward people who immigrate. Expulsion from the geographic space is a refusal to be accountable toward immigrants and, concomitantly, a denial of their political freedom in the U.S.

This all-too-common state of affairs leads me to identify another feature of freedom. When one surveys history, we observe all types of political brutality, oppression, and the marginalization of millions of people. And yet, we also notice that, even in direr conditions of violent depersonalization and oppression, there are people who resist, who transgress. Yes, "Freedom is the defining character of human existence,"[70] but how can we understand not simply the desire for freedom but the existence of resistance when political plurality, personhood, self-esteem, agency, etc. are denied? Here I return to Agamben and his discussion of potentiality and actuality. The potentiality of human beings is the essence of human freedom. As noted in the previous chapter, Agamben's philosophical anthropology is, Rasmus Ugilt argues, "centered on the notion of potentiality."[71] "(T)he very essence of humanity," for Agamben, "lies in a potentiality that is expressed when it does not unfold into actuality."[72] In terms of potentiality's relation to freedom, Agamben writes, "*The greatness of human potentiality is measured by the abyss of human impotentiality.* Here it is possible to see how the root of freedom is to be found in the abyss of potentiality. To be free is not simply to have the power to do this or that thing, nor is it simply to have the power to refuse to do this or that thing. To be free is . . . *to be capable of one's own impotentiality*."[73] A second related point is "that potentiality is not exhausted in its own actualization."[74] Potentiality is never fully actualized. Potentiality is what marks all living beings, but human beings have the capacity to not

70. Macmurray, *Conditions of Freedom*, 48.

71. Ugilt, *Giorgio Agamben*, 22.

72. Colebrook and Maxwell. *Agamben*, 289.

73. Agamben, *Potentialities*, 182–83.

74. Ugilt, *Giorgio Agamben*, 25.

actualize potential and even in actualizing potentiality, never exhaust it.[75] This is why totalitarian regimes constantly employ violence or the threat of violence, because potentiality can never be exhausted or destroyed. People like Sojourner Truth, Frederick Douglass, W. E. B. Dubois, Fannie Lou Hamer, Rosa Parks, Malcolm X and numerous other African Americans revealed and reveal the inexhaustible potentiality through their acts of impotentiality (inoperativity toward the disciplinary regimes of racism).

This begs the question: if potentiality is a source of human freedom, how or in what ways is freedom actualized? In other words, what facilitates the actualization of the impotentiality of freedom? These are complicated questions and the discussion on an existential developmental view of freedom below will provide a partial answer. For now, though, let me address this in terms of the civic care and faith implied in mutual-personal recognition. When we consider persons like Malcolm X and Martin Luther King Jr. and their struggle to protest and change the social, political, and economic structures and forces that denied freedom to African Americans, we need to recognize that their acts of transgression and resistance (freedom) in the face of violence and the threat of death emerged, in part, by the civic care and trust exhibited in their respective communities of faith.[76] Civic care, as stated earlier, is based on mutual-personal recognition, which secures a mutual sense of trust and a positive self-concept necessary to speak and act with others. In terms of the larger society, where racism was (and is) rife, there is an eclipse of civic care toward African Americans. Even the care exhibited by government workers providing food for Malcolm and his family was marred by the public humiliation in labelling it "Not To Be Sold."[77] The government and its employees putatively cared for the children by putting Malcolm and his siblings in homes, while his mother was taken to a mental facility. "I truly believe," Malcolm X later wrote, "that if ever a state social

75. For Agamben, his idea of potentiality/actuality refers to animals, as well. This is his way of attempting to avoid the Western tendency to separate human beings from animals. There are distinctions, but distinctions are not separation. Agamben, *The Open*.

76. It is worth mentioning that Malcolm X's relation to the Nation of Islam (NOI) was troubled for some time before he left. He nevertheless retained support from many Black Muslims and formed another community after leaving NOI. Even though there was a lack of "civic" care and trust in NOI with regard to Malcolm X, there was a sufficient amount to buoy his acts of freedom. Similarly, toward the end of his short life, Martin Luther King Jr. had lost much of his support, especially after the Riverside speech. He nevertheless retained the care, support, and trust of his community of faith, as well as many other individuals. See Marable, *Malcolm X*.

77. Haley, *The Autobiography of Malcolm X*, 14. This example is also one of classism. Poor white people were given the same government-stamped food, marking them as dependent on the government, which was a social stigma.

agency destroyed a family, it destroyed ours."[78] The social-political humiliation of indecent societies represents a lack of civic care toward humiliated Others (often depersonalized), and we can be sure that the lack or absence of care accompanies a loss of freedom vis-à-vis humiliated Others.

A few words need to be said about civic faith, which can include the religious faith of a community. In chapter 2, I mentioned that faith comprises four interrelated dialectical pairs, namely, belief-disbelief, trust-distrust, loyalty-disloyalty, and hope-hopelessness.[79] We can see here that the dynamics of faith are social and, if the dialectical tension collapses toward one pole or the other, there is a corresponding loss or distortion of freedom. When the dialectical tension is present, there is freedom because there is an openness in terms of thinking/knowing, the social, and the future. For instance, in terms of thinking/knowing, the pole of disbelief qualifies the pole of belief, leaving a space for questions, possibilities, and curiosity. If one holds to an absolute belief, the individual is not free to think or know otherwise. Similarly, if one is overwhelmed with disbelief, there is a lack of freedom. It is difficult to act when one is plagued by uncertainty and disbelief. In terms of the social, absolute distrust in a relationship is not conducive to freedom between people. Schmitt's friend-enemy distinction in organizing the polis represents the presence of both distrust and lack of loyalty toward those constructed as enemies. There may be some semblance of freedom within the friend group, but there is no freedom between enemies, which confirms the poverty of Schmitt's political philosophy. A society constructed in terms of a friend-enemy distinction is not a free society. We see in the United States today the proliferation of friend-enemy distinction between political parties. The society is deeply polarized, and while we have "freedom," there is a lack of freedom in actuality because of the eclipse of speaking and acting together among plural groups. One might note that there has been contentiousness in politics since the beginning of the formation of the United States. It is not contentiousness that is the problem, because that itself is evidence of speaking and acting together, which requires some degree of trust, fidelity, and even care. Instead, it is the presence of vitriolic polarization where people huddle within their respective political enclaves, demonstrating a lack of trust and fidelity to those deemed to be enemies. There is, then, in this so-called democratic society, an attenuation of social-political freedom.[80]

78. Haley, *The Autobiography of Malcolm X*, 23.

79. Niebuhr, *Faith on Earth*.

80. I would add here that the United States has never been politically free. The depersonalization and violent removal of Native peoples, enslavement of Africans, Jim Crow, and ongoing racism reveals fault lines with respect to political freedom.

The presence of political polarization and its accompanying lack of trust and fidelity toward "enemies" also manifests a lack of openness to the future, which is another sign of the diminution of freedom. An openness to the future is an attribute of freedom, which does not mean persons do not have a vision or visions of the future. Instead, these visions do not determine the future, which creates a space for something new to emerge, as well as for openness and curiosity. Political polarization, on the other hand, represents people grasping onto their particular visions and working to enact those visions at the expense of speaking and acting together with those who hold other visions. Hobbes' leviathan, in my view, represents a bleak future of freedom because the future is always defined by the leviathan whose goal is to keep order and security.

In summary, relative freedom, political and personal, entails the ability to act in spite of the constraints of finitude and dwelling together. This ability to act takes place in a field of power, which entails the capacity to resist or transgress the constraints of Others' motives, identifications, and goals. Included in this capacity to act is a positive self-concept—self-representations of experiences of singularity. I argued further that the relational feature of freedom is founded on mutual-personal recognition/knowing and its attending attributes, namely, 1) indeterminate knowing that creates a space for the Other to act, 2) experiences of singularity, 3) plurality, 4) realization that the Other is both a limit and source of one's freedom, 5) a degree of restraint so others can realize their goals, 6) sense of being with oneself in the Other, 7) equality, and 8) acknowledgment that the freedom of the Other is a prerequisite of one's self-realization. Implicit in this formulation is our existential accountability for and to Others. Finally, I argued that civic care and civic trust found the possibility of political freedom.

## Some Problems of Political Freedom

In the discussion above, I have already tipped my hat to some of the problems of freedom. There are questions about the limits of reason, questions (and problems) about will and determinism,[81] questions about the criteria of harm vis-à-vis positive and negative freedom,[82] questions regarding the degree of restraint, issues of misrecognition and inequality and its relation to freedom, and issues about the relation between freedom and political and cultural institutions.[83] Hinted at, but not elaborated on, is how neoliberal-

81. Genel and Deranty, eds., *Recognition or Disagreement*, 164.

82. Mill, "On Liberty." See also Warburton, *Freedom*, 43–62.

83. See Dewey, *Freedom and Culture*; Honneth, *The Struggle of Recognition*.

ism and neoliberal capitalism foster inequality, alienation, and the illusion of political freedom.[84] Many scholars have explored these issues and questions in ways not possible in this chapter. That said, I am interested in addressing problems of political freedom that emerge from our dwelling in the Anthropocene Age. This is not meant to be exhaustive, but rather heuristic.

The first and foundational problem is evident in the discussion above. Nearly all philosophical and theological renderings of freedom are decidedly anthropocentric (and, more narrowly, freedom is understood to be an attribute of adult human beings). Like the issue of sovereignty in the previous chapter, discourses on freedom exclude other-than-human beings from consideration. One might remark that other species do not have the capacity for freedom and, therefore, it makes no sense to include them. They live out their existence largely determined to actualize what potentiality they have, which is determined by nature. They are scripted, if you will, while human beings have the capacity or potential to write the script within the constraints of human finitude. There is, I think, some truth to this, but it is nevertheless a problem for several reasons. First, discourses on freedom privilege human beings and this means privileging their existence and freedom over all other species. It is as if our putative "greater" freedom means we are superior to other species and, therefore, justifies our exploitation of other species and the earth itself. Of course, this is not logically necessary. In other words, the fact that I may have greater capacity for freedom than my child does not mean I am superior. Of course, I am "free" to believe this, but it would be an existentially and ontologically false belief, because within nature itself there is no valuation, except what human beings create and, not surprisingly, our "evaluations" place us on top. Similarly, my greater freedom vis-à-vis my pet or some other animal does not mean I am superior or sovereign or in a hierarchical relationship. Again, I can believe this and construct the relation to reflect this, but this belief is not an existential feature of this relationship. Instead, my valuing the belief in my superiority is my creation, my construction. It seems as if anthropocentric discourses on freedom, then, have superiority and hierarchy as tacit foundational or attending premises, which nearly always entail the privileging of human beings (or one group over and against an unfree Othered group) and, correspondingly, demands "inferior" Other species support human freedom,[85] and human dwelling.

84. See Brown, *Undoing the Demos*; Phillips, *Political Theology*; Wolin, *Democracy Incorporated*.

85. The horrid political, theological, and pseudo-scientific discourses regarding Africans (slave and free) in the United States (and elsewhere) constructed Africans as less than human—some lesser species—which justified the unimaginable brutality

Holding a different, though similar perspective, David Wood argues that the "value of freedom has become inseparable from the logic of sacrifice by those who claim to be promoting this value," which leads to the destruction of subordinate or subjugated human beings and other-than-human beings. The "project of human freedom," he continues, is "used to justify the mass destruction of other living species."[86] In brief, our belief in human superiority and the privileging of human life over all other life are inextricably yoked to discourses on freedom. Moreover, we freely create institutions/apparatuses that produce and "confirm" human superiority and attending political freedom. The result is the exploitation of other species and the earth itself.

I have avoided any comment about the freedom of other species other than to indicate that they are locked into enacting or actualizing their potentiality. While I do not believe that other species are capable of political freedom, this does not mean they: 1) do not have some nascent sense of freedom in being able to act; and 2) necessarily need to be excluded from considerations in political discourses.[87] Just as the welfare of infants is part of political discourses, so too the welfare of other species and the earth itself can be included in deliberations about freedom. This said, what I do know is that any possibility of "freedom" is lost when other species go extinct.

Second and relatedly, human constructions of freedom tend to view other-than-human beings as politically irrelevant. If other species are determined, then any discussion of them vis-à-vis freedom would appear to be ludicrous. What follows from this is that those engaged in discourses on freedom cannot see or acknowledge that human freedom is contingent on the plurality of other species or the realization of the lives of other species. Naturally, it does not seem to us that our freedom is contingent on the plurality of other species. We appear to have gotten along swimmingly without ever considering political freedom in terms of other species. In the cause of human freedom, we have exploited the earth and, in many cases (past, present, and future), decimated many species and lands (e.g., Amazon). So far, there have been no significant consequences with regard to this exercise of our freedom, at least for those of us who do not live in what Chris Hedges and Joe Sacco call sacrifice zones.[88] As the Anthropocene Age deepens and

---

against them. Not surprisingly, these discourses not only denied freedoms to Africans, but also bolstered the exercise of white privileges and freedoms. See, Kendi, *Stamped from the Beginning.*

86. Wood, *Reoccupy the Earth*, 40.

87. For a discussion of freedom vis-à-vis other-than-human species, see Bekoff and Pierce, *The Animals' Agenda*, 1–9.

88. Hedges and Sacco, *Days of Destruction, Days of Revolt.*

millions of species go extinct, the earth as a dynamic and living system will decline. In chapter 2, I indicated that this deterioration will undermine our dwelling and the dwelling of countless other-than-human beings, but it will also undermine our capacity for political freedom. Our very capacity for and exercise of freedom, politically and personally, is dependent on the biodiversity of the earth.

Someone might push back and say that we could have habitats on other moons or planets. These would be artificial environments, wherein people could exercise their freedom. I am willing to imagine that freedom in these non-biodiverse habitats can exist, but, in my view, they represent diminished forms of freedom. Persons are confined to these constructed buildings—cutoff from the earth and the richness and diversity of life. Of course, if we learn to live on other worlds and create, in an artificial environment that is a biodiverse habitat, then our personal and political freedom would be richer, but this would only prove my point that we are dependent on the habitableness of our environment.

A third problem of the exclusion of other species from discourses on freedom is that it accompanies a lack of accountability for and to other species and the earth. Civic care, freedom, and accountability extends only to the walls of one's particular polis. Implicit in any discourse on freedom is the issue of accountability, even in negative constructions of freedom that focus on lack of restraints there is accountability to others. John Stuart Mill,[89] for instance, argued that freedom is limited on the principle of not harming others, which suggests both restraint and that we are accountable to other human beings for, at the very least, not harming them. But constructions of negative or positive freedom and the issue of accountability and harm do not extend to other species. We can harm or destroy them with impunity because we are free, "superior," and sovereign. Many individuals believe we are accountable or obliged to care for other species, but, more often than not, this is not framed in terms of freedom. In other words, we are free and thus out of this freedom take accountability to care for other species (and the earth), but that does not mean that we see other species as politically relevant to our freedom.[90] If anything, the common understanding and exercise of freedom has eschewed any accountability and little restrain with regard to other species.

Before identifying other problems of freedom in the Anthropocene Age, it is helpful to say a few words about what it might look like to include

89. Mill, "On Liberty."

90. A notable example of freedom and our political accountability to and for other species is Eva Meijer's book, *When Animals Speak*.

other-than-human beings and the earth in our discourses about and practices of political freedom and accountability. How, in other words, do we
recognize other species and the earth as politically relevant? I mentioned in
the previous chapter that New Zealand has found ways to include the earth
and its species in political deliberations by assigning individuals to represent
(give voice) their needs in the government.[91] This involves an acknowledgement of our human responsibility to care for the survival and flourishing of
habitats and species. Currently, many NGOs seek to represent varied species
and habitats, but New Zealand is showing how we might have government
officials who are responsible for ensuring that these habitats and species are
taken into consideration in government policies and programs. In instances
like these, nature is not the excluded-included Other, but is instead politically relevant not only with regard to human survival and flourishing, but
also to the very exercise of personal and political freedom.

I wanted to begin this section by addressing the urgent issue of political freedom and the Anthropocene Age because it is a fundamental
challenge we must face. Now I turn to problems of political freedom that
impact human beings given the realities of climate change. As mentioned
in previous chapters, the consequences of climate change are often catastrophic, and in the future this will only increase. We can turn to history
to see that when anxiety and fear are rife, societal and political violence
increases and societies become destabilized.[92] As mentioned in a previous
chapter, the Pentagon[93] and CIA[94] are predicting that violence within and
between nations will rise as climate disasters increase. In the Anthropocene
Age, the destruction of habitats, declining arable land and habitable spaces,
food shortages, and lack of resources will heighten anxiety and fear, which,
for political authoritarian purposes,[95] are often transformed into hatred and
hostility toward Others. While not directly linked to climate change, the Republican presidential nominee in 2016 stoked fear, rage, and hatred toward
immigrants who were (and are) desperately seeking to survive by coming
to the United States. In one sense, immigrants were (and are) politically

91. Rousseau, "In New Zealand, Lands and Rivers Can Be People Too (Legally
Speaking)."

92. See Frazer and Hutchings, *Violence and Political Theory*; Ruggiero, *Visions of
Political Violence*.

93. US Department of Defense, "Climate Change Report, 2019."

94. Banerjee, "U.S. Intelligence Officials Warn Climate Change Is a Worldwide
Threat."

95. See Grady, "Panel: Rise of Authoritarian Governments Pose the Biggest Threat
to NATO"; Minakov, "The Authoritarian Belt in Europe's East; Appelbaum, *Twilight of
Democracy*; Norris and Inglehart, *Cultural Backlash*.

relevant in that they are constructed as a threat and used to advance, in this case, the political power of Republicans. Immigrants or refugees are deemed politically irrelevant in that they are denied access to spaces of speaking and acting together, and they are, at best, given the least amount of civic care and justice. These political tactics of division, humiliation, and violence are likely to increase as resources throughout the world decline and as states fail. In short, refugees will be and are on the move, and the problem of political freedom is the construction of refugees as a political threat to the personal and political freedoms enjoyed by many citizens.

But it is not only climate immigrants or refugees who will experience losses of political freedom. Within the borders of the United States, racism and classism intersect and will, in my view, increase as anxieties and fears associated with climate change and its consequences become more severe. We are already familiar with environmental classism/racism taking place in various parts of the country. In these zones, the well-being of citizens are undermined because of pollution, lack of medical care, poor housing, food deserts, etc. Whenever we see a decline in the well-being of a group of citizens, we can be confident that these citizens lack political relevancy and hence political freedom.[96] If history is any guide of the seemingly ineradicable social-political cancer of racism/classism in the United States,[97] we can expect in the Anthropocene Age that these ills will be exacerbated and used politically and economically by privileged groups.

There are three other threats to freedom looming in the future. The first is global capitalism, which, while lifting many out of poverty, has also been responsible (in societies dominated by neoliberal capitalism) for massive inequalities in income and wealth.[98] These disparities impact educational opportunities, which are crucial for exercising political freedom in so-called democratic societies. They impact access to medical care, healthy food, safe infrastructures for exercise, etc. One may ask how this impacts freedom and why we would expect it to get worse in the Anthropocene Age. First of all, poor people tend not to vote in comparison to people who are financially comfortable, at least in the United States.[99] And people who are well off financially are more likely to be represented in various levels of government. That is, neoliberal capitalism is intertwined with the political machinery of democracy and those who operate its levers. This means poor people, for various reasons, are politically irrelevant and this irrelevancy is linked to

96. See for instance Hedges and Sacco, *Days of Destruction, Days of Revolt.*
97. Porter, *American Poison.*
98. Piketty, *Capital in the Twenty-First Century.*
99. Akeel, "Voting and Income."

neoliberal capitalism.[100] The rise and pervasiveness of neoliberal capitalism, then, produces not more, but less, freedom for the so-called under-classes by impoverishing them and by their lack of representation at all levels of government.[101] It is not likely that capitalism, which is a major cause of climate change,[102] will end giving rise to more just ways of caring for citizens, other species, and the earth. As Frederic Jamison commented, "it is easier to imagine the end of the world than to imagine the end of capitalism."[103] In other words, there will be and is significant political resistance to ending capitalism, even as the dire realities of climate change worsen. The continuation of neoliberal capitalism in the Anthropocene Age, then, will lead to fewer political freedoms.

Democracy is often lauded as the engine of freedom,[104] but it is clear that capitalism has taken root and flowered in authoritarian regimes like China, Singapore, Vietnam, etc. Add to this the rise of populist authoritarian political figures in the United States, Europe, and Asia and we see a threat to political freedoms throughout the world. This rise of authoritarian governing classes has accompanied a rise in nationalism, wherein each nation is seen to compete with all other nations. To be sure, there are examples of international cooperation, but when authoritarian leaders, like the 45th president of the United States, focus on nationalistic interests, cooperation declines. This double rise is a threat to political freedoms not only because authoritarian nationalistic leaders seek to undermine the political relevancy of their enemies and correspondingly democratic institutions, but also because they undermine intranational and international cooperation toward reducing the effects of climate change. Put another way, long after these leaders are dead, the world will be less habitable for all and many human beings will be less free.

A related threat to political freedom, especially for poorer countries, is the re-emergence of global imperial powers vying to expand their military, political, and economic reach. These countries (U.S., China, Russia),

100. See Rogers-Vaughn, *Caring for Souls in a Neoliberal Age.*

101. One of the major evangelists for neoliberal capitalism was Hayek, who argued that capitalism is intertwined with freedom. Other systems like socialism and communism, for Hayek, undermine political and economic freedoms. From his high and privileged perch, Hayek (and other neoliberal capitalists) was unwilling to see or acknowledge, the brutal history of the rise of capitalism, wherein those on the lower end of the economic scale are made politically irrelevant in the face of governing authorities who code capital for their benefit. Hayek, *The Road to Serfdom.*

102. Moore, "Name the System! Anthropocene & the Capitalocene Alternative."

103. Ferguson and Petro, *After Capitalism,* 4.

104. See Hayek, *The Road to Serfdom*; Jones, *Masters of the Universe.*

especially the United States, are spending trillions of dollars on military and intelligence organizations, which deprive their populations (especially those deemed politically irrelevant) of the resources to foster more livable habitats. What is politically relevant in these countries is the military and intelligence industrial complexes, as well as the capitalist classes and machines that support both. Martin Luther King Jr. said that "war is the enemy of the poor." I would add that perpetual preparation for war is the enemy of the poor (and poor countries), and it is the poor and poor nations that are rendered politically irrelevant and less free. Add to this the notion that, as these global powers continue to compete for declining resources, we can be confident that there will be violent conflicts, if not wars. It is not simply that wars and preparing for war are environmental and human catastrophes; it is that global imperial competition undermines cooperation toward reducing climate change, while at the same time making politically irrelevant people who will be most affected by climate change. It is difficult to exercise political freedom when one is worried about where the next meal is coming from, when one is not assured of housing, when one is ill from disease and lack of health care, when one lacks water.

These problems or obstacles are daunting, but human beings are not necessarily determined by them. True, we may exercise our limited freedom to continue to construct institutions, practices, and narratives that privilege human existence over all other species and the earth itself. True, we may act in ways that collude with the machineries of authoritarianism, capitalism, nationalism, and imperialism, while insuring 1) the political freedoms of lower classes are undermined and 2) the political irrelevancy of other-than-human species and the earth. Of course, the results will be catastrophic. We will have authored ourselves out of existence, taking with us millions of other species. If this occurs, human freedom will have been a tragic failure.

## Radical Political Theology: Freedom for Others, Other Species, and the Earth

In moving toward theology, I am keenly aware that religions have a sordid history with regard to political freedoms. Judeo-Christian scripture is hardly a testament to political freedoms. Scriptural stories often read, at best, as witness to the political freedoms of one group over others. As mentioned in previous chapters, the Israelites' liberation from Egyptian bondage came at a steep price for the Egyptians. The Israelites' violent takeover of the promised land was certainly a case of denying personal and political freedoms of the residents of Palestine. Of course, scripture, as a whole, constructs, more often than not, women as politically irrelevant, which meant (and today, in some places means) the absence or minimization of personal and political freedom. Recall also that when the Israelite elders pleaded to God for a king, they did not realize that their limited political freedom would be at stake. Most theologies, understandably, are little different. "Good" Christian theologians used their theologies to justify the ethnic cleansing of Native peoples (in the U.S. and elsewhere), white superiority and slavery, colonization of other lands and peoples, and the denial of women's and African Americans' suffrage.[105] Lest one think all of this is in the past, some theologians and denominations use theology to justify the excesses of capitalism,[106] imperialistic wars,[107] and inaction in the face of the facts of climate change.[108] Of course, there are other decolonial and liberation theologians who advocate for political freedom for all peoples. My point is that I am aware that theology is quite plastic in its use to support or deny political freedoms—in the past and the present.

Naturally, this awareness and caveat will not deter me from offering a view of political freedom grounded in the stories around the incarnation. I am using these stories not to theologically legitimate my views. In other words, I am not saying anything about God and freedom. I want to avoid past and present human tendencies to legitimate their political views by invoking the name of God, as if they have some insight into God and therefore their insight legitimates whatever version of freedom (or sovereignty) they propose. As noted in the Introduction to this book, the only premise I associate with God is care for creation. I am not willing to make any claims about what God "thinks" about freedom or any other human feature of existence. Instead, I am using these stories to think about the possibility of radical freedom in and for the Anthropocene Age. That is, these stories "reveal" a possibility about human freedom.

Before moving to the theological, I continue the practice of beginning with the existential reality of freedom, which is connected to, but distinct from, political freedom. The radical nature of human freedom and its characteristics can be gleaned from the care of good-enough parents for their children. This care is the foundation of personal freedom. This depiction of radical freedom in psychosocial development includes political freedom,

105. See Barry, *Roger Williams and the Creation of the American Soul*; Kendi, *Stamped from the Beginning*.

106. An example of this is the prosperity gospel theologians and people like Michael Novak who are apologists for neoliberal capitalism. Novak, *Toward a Theology of the Corporation*; Novak, *The Spirit of Democratic Capitalism*.

107. Conroy-Krutz, *Christian Imperialism*.

108. Gander, "What Do Evangelical Christians Really Think About Climate Change?"

which children develop into, at least in those political situations where children and adults are recognized and treated as persons. As philosopher John Macmurray argued, "My care for you is moral if it includes the intention to preserve your freedom as an agent, which is your independence of me."[109] This lays the foundation for moving to theological renderings of human freedom as interpreted in the stories of the incarnation of God.

In the first chapter, I mentioned that parental care rests on personal recognition/knowing, which comprises three interrelated dialectical pairs, namely, identification-disidentification, determinate-indeterminate knowing, and restraint-unrestraint. Furthermore, retaining this dialectical tension fosters the space wherein children appear in their singularity or suchness, which is understood as a pre-representational (and later representational or symbolic) sense of self-esteem, self-respect, and self-confidence. If we shift to the topic of freedom, a question arises as to what all this means. Infants are not free in the sense that an adult is free, because infants have not yet developed the psychosocial capacities to exercise freedom. And yet, if we consider that infants have a nascent ego, and thus nascent agency, then it seems plausible to posit a proto capacity for and sense of freedom. At the same time, we need to acknowledge that the psychosocial foundations of adult freedom have roots in this early developmental period, which is evident when children, who have been traumatized, grow up and have challenges with regard to exercising their personal freedom. Put differently, recall from chapter 1 that infant-parent researchers have long recognized the cooperative elements of parent-infant interactions, which suggests rudimentary agency. When we consider early childhood traumas and their negative impacts on adult attachment and agency, it seems safe to say that the proto-agency and freedom of early childhood were interrupted or damaged, which later leads to diminished freedom as adults. This would suggest that freedom is a feature of human existence from the beginning and that it is fundamentally dependent on parental care. In other words, the very roots of existential or personal freedom lie in the good-enough parental care wherein infants obtain a sense of self-esteem, self-respect, and self-confidence that accompanies developing agency and parent-child cooperation. Care, then, is a foundational principle for the emergence of and exercise of personal freedom.

Given this overview, I elaborate further on the emergence of freedom and the transition from this relational-existential freedom to political freedom. Good-enough parents obviously possess more freedom (political and otherwise) than infants or children. It is the exercise of this freedom

109. Macmurray, *Persons in Relation*, 190.

in caring for their children that reveals something about the existential nature of care that undergirds political freedom. Above, I noted that negative freedom is the exercise of freedom without obstacles and positive freedom involves acting toward one's self-realization. If we consider parents' caring for children, these two understandings of freedom are inapt. Children are clearly obstacles to or constraints on parents' exercise of personal freedom, as any sleep-deprived parent knows. Similarly, while good-enough parents often find meaning and joy in having children, the numerous acts of caring for children are not aimed toward parents' self-realization. Instead, we find consistent decisions of parents to sacrifice their needs and desires for the sake of the well-being of their children. Indeed, parental restraint—a free act of care—with regard to their needs and desires, creates a space for children's partial and emerging self-realization. In another way, good-enough parents do not create inordinate or unnecessary obstacles to children's exercise of agency. So, from an existential developmental view, we note that the emergence of freedom depends on parents' exercise of freedom—a kind of freedom that involves caring restraint of one's desires and needs for the sake of their children's self-realization. From John Macmurray's perspective, a parent's care is "only moral if it includes the intention to preserve [the individual's] freedom as an agent."[110]

There is another feature of freedom that does not fit well with early psychosocial development. Hegel argued that "each subject is able to perceive the liberty of the other as a prerequisite of his own self-realization."[111] We find that this cannot be the case from the perspective of caring for children. Children cannot recognize that their parents' liberty is a prerequisite of their self-realization, though there may be a nascent recognition of dependence on the parent for their well-being. And it is doubtful that good-enough parents consider their children's liberty as requisite for their self-realization. On the contrary, good-enough parents' exercise of freedom involves care wherein they place restraints on their desires and needs to create a space for children's exercise of embryonic personal freedom. The paradox here is that parents freely choose to limit their freedom for the sake of the well-being and freedom of their children.

If I may make a slight detour here, we note a similar existential care and freedom when people take pains to care for the well-being of animals (and nature itself). Instead of seeing animals or nature as obstacles to our exercise of freedom or merely as the means of our self-realization, individuals (and groups) freely choose to limit or restrain themselves for the sake of

110. Macmurray, *Persons in Relation*, 190.
111. Honneth, *The Pathologies of Individual Freedom*, 8.

the well-being of other species and the earth. For instance, people in various countries have risked prison to protest climate change and others have long advocated for animal rights. Others have freely made personal sacrifices to reduce their carbon footprint. These and other examples reveal that the notions of negative and positive freedom are limited when it comes to the ideas of personal and political freedom. Paradoxically, these self-restraints are acts of freedom that limit one's negative and positive freedoms for the sake of the realization of the lives of other-than-human beings. Human beings, then, can freely limit their freedom and self-realization for the sake of caring for other human beings, other-than-human beings, and the earth itself. Let me add that human freedom—personal and political—is contingent on the well-being of other species and the earth, which is a good reason to limit our freedoms.

To return to an existential developmental view, a question emerges about children's movement from the kind of personal freedom experienced and exercised in relation to parents and political freedom. Ideally, as children move into the public-political sphere, they find and obtain a sense of self-esteem, self-confidence, and self-respect that is necessary for the exercise of political freedom/agency. That is, in these public-political spaces, children are able to exercise their personal freedom precisely because of the social apparatuses that secure and promote positive representations necessary for political agency. Of course, children do not exercise the right to vote or possess other adult freedoms, but they dwell in the polis' space of appearances, wherein there is mutual-personal recognition and cooperation toward common ends. Eventually, children become adults and, ideally, make use of their political and personal freedoms.

What I wish to press further here is that children's movement into political spaces of appearance depends on sufficient civic care and civic faith. It is not simply that the social-political sphere is a space of mutual-personal recognition. It is also one of care and faith. That is, in a decent society, citizens experience a sense of mutual care, wherein there is a recognition that one's self-realization is dependent on the self-realization of others. This is accompanied by a sufficient amount of mutual trust and fidelity. What I am claiming here is that the care necessary for a child's nascent freedom and self-realization is not something that is surpassed in the political world of adulthood. Rather, I am claiming that civic care and civic faith are the foundations of political freedom. This is noted in decent societies where public-political apparatuses uphold mutual personal-recognition (political self-esteem, self-confidence, and self-respect) and cooperation (necessitated by shared trust) in achieving common and individual ends. Dystopian or tyrannical societies represent the diminution of civic care and faith, which naturally accompanies a loss or attenuation of personal and political freedoms for those who are not in the privileged political-economic classes.

I take this further and contend that the exercise of political freedom, now and in the future, requires cooperative civic care and faith to restrain human desires and needs for the sake of creating a space for the inclusion of other species and the earth in our political deliberations. I am not suggesting that other-than-human species possess political agency or freedom. Instead, acts of political care and faith need to be inclusive of other-than-human species because they, like us, are dependent on the earth for our existence. That we have political freedom/agency means we can act to care for other species and the earth. I would go so far as to say it is a moral imperative that we do so, for the degradation of our habitat will result in the diminishment or even loss of personal and political freedom.

Let's return to the discussion of the polis and the relation between civic care and civic faith to political freedom. We can see problems in personal and political freedom when there is a loss or absence of civic care and civic faith vis-à-vis one or more groups in a society. Consider first the impact of the negation or diminution of political freedom with regard to the care of politically marginalized and oppressed parents. As mentioned in a previous chapter, the negative social-political recognition of a group of citizens has concrete implications with regard to the distribution of social, cultural, and economic resources.[112] The denial or restriction of resources is the outward sign of the lack of civic care toward people who are negatively constructed, and those who are negatively constructed, usually as inferior, understandably do not trust the political groups that are oppressing them and denying them resources. Add to this, the psychosocial toll of parents who have to deal with the daily social-political humiliations of an indecent society. This clearly has an impact on their freedom, as well as the care of their children. That so many parents living under oppressive conditions manifest courage and determination to care, in spite of political malfeasance, testifies to their resiliency and their freedom, even when it is limited by apparatuses of oppression. In addition, the social-political apparatuses that produce and maintain negative constructions of Othered persons and groups make it difficult for children to recognize and claim a positive political self in which to engage their agency in the polis' space of appearances. For instance, African American children growing up in a racist society do not have the sense that the society cares for them or that they are trusted in public political spaces. The exercise of their personal and political freedom is hampered by the apparatuses of the white dominant class. To say that their freedoms are

112. See Fraser and Honneth, *Redistribution or Recognition?*

hampered does not mean they are without freedom. The Civil Rights and Black Lives Matter movements, for instance, can be understood as emerging from the consistent lack of civic care and civic trust extended to African Americans. This and other groups politically express and assert their own care and faith and, in so doing, exercise their freedom in spite of the political machines that seek to undermine it.

Much more could be said about political freedom and caring relations, but it is time to shift to a political theological framework. We need to acknowledge at the outset that scripture while containing stories of bondage and liberation, is decidedly anthropocentric, as well as tending to privilege one group of human beings over others. Add to this the patriarchal foundations of scripture and much of theology in the West that has served as obstacles to the political freedoms of women. Moreover, scripture and theologies, as mentioned above, have been used to legitimate and justify undermining and denying freedoms to Othered peoples (e.g., Native peoples, Africans, etc.). Of course, as discussed in this and previous chapters, political theologies have largely privileged human beings to the detriment of the well-being of other species and the earth—included-excluded Others. Just as scripture and theologies have been used to deny freedoms, they also have been used to support liberative movements. All of this suggests that we must attend to the aims and impacts of political theologies vis-à-vis political freedoms.

Here I want to move to a discussion of political freedom in relation to scriptural stories regarding the incarnation and the life, ministry, and death of Jesus Christ. It is important to comment again that I am not using scripture to ground political freedom in God and the kingdom of God, as if the realization of political freedom lies in eternity, but rather how these stories reveal something about human freedom as such and, in particular, a radical political freedom that is inclusive and not dependent on apparatuses of the sovereign state. Also, as in the other chapters, I am not claiming that my interpretations are based on scholarly exegesis. Instead, I am using scripture to think and, hopefully, to act otherwise.

God, we read, emptied Godself to become human, taking on the form of a slave. This can be understood, in part, as an act of care (Divine empathy/compassion) wherein restraint creates a space for embodied-relational, mutual recognition. God enfleshed is by definition political,[113] because Jesus Christ lived and ministered in and among the people—a people oppressed by the Roman Empire. Even if Jesus had arrived during a time of peace and freedom, he would nevertheless have been limited by being human and thus experiencing all the challenges of freedom and political freedom of that

113. See Crossan, *God and Empire*.

time. Instead, Jesus was birthed into a society where the apparatuses of the Roman Empire (and the Jewish political authorities) clearly undermined the political freedoms of non-Roman citizens.[114] Becoming human, then, involved experiencing the political oppression and marginalization of the Jewish people and, at the same time, the incarnation made possible recognition of God dwelling with the people.

An aspect of the incarnation that I have turned to in other chapters is Jesus taking on the form of a slave, which I argue is a political act and a crucial feature with regard to political freedom. If there is a type or category of human being that is denied personal and political freedoms, an enslaved person has to be the apex. The political freedoms of the privileged group are used to fabricate laws, institutions, and practices that deny the personal freedoms of those constructed as slaves. Slaves are possessions who do not even possess their own bodies and lives. They are, as Orlando Patterson notes, faced with social death, which means that they have absolutely no political freedoms[115] and, worse, they can be brutalized or killed without it being considered a homicide.[116] Slaves embody the absence of freedom and thus are constructed as inhuman; as inferior; lacking political self-esteem, self-confidence, and self-respect; and thus, denied access to the polis' space of appearances. They are denied civic care and civic faith, while they are expected to care for and about their masters' well-being (and freedom). Any care directed toward slaves is instrumental and conditional, precisely because they are considered to be inferior beings. It is this social construction of inferiority—an ontological and existential illusion—that enables the politically privileged to produce slaves for the sake of the elites' well-being and freedoms. Of course, there is an inherent problem in all this, which is that slaves are human beings and thus capable of exercising personal and political freedoms. This underlying problem is dealt with through apparatuses that continually and incessantly produce and enforce slavery. So, in becoming human, Jesus takes on the most alienated and oppressed political figure. What, then, does this mean for political freedom?

In taking on the form of a slave, there is a paradox—being free to take on a form of an unfree slave. In this way, Jesus already exceeds any attempt by the state or privileged authorities to define him. Jesus' identity, his being as rooted in humanity and God, exceeds the category of slave (or any other appellation). Indeed, Jesus taking on the form of a slave makes

114. Of course, much if not most of the Mediterranean exhibited patriarchal forms of governance, which meant that women were denied political freedoms.

115. Patterson, *Slavery and Social Death*.

116. Agamben, *Sovereign Power and Bare Life*.

inoperative the very laws and apparatuses that seek to reduce human beings to the social death of slavery. In other words, the revelation of God's infinite, indeterminate care, manifested in the incarnation by taking on the form of a slave, means that even the most politically constructed individuals cannot be completely determined. All human beings are created in the image and likeness of God and thus exceed human constructions that ostensibly ground human capacities for personal and political freedoms. Put another way, in taking on the form of a slave, Jesus represents the fact that actuality does not exhaust potentiality, which means that the seed of freedom is in human potentiality that becomes partially actualized in care/love (in this case, God's indeterminate love), but is not exhausted by that actuality.

There is a liberative element here, but not in the sense of the violent liberation of the Israelites from the Egyptians or revolutionary violence that seeks freedom from oppression. This is a more profound or radical revelation of freedom, which can be understood in terms of inoperativity. Jesus did not operate out of the political grammars of the Roman Empire or Jewish religious leaders, which is not to say that he was not shaped by or affected by them. In the form of a slave, he not only exceeded the representations and constrictions imposed by the state, he also chose not to act out of them. This is evident in his ministry and perhaps most clearly seen in his forgiving his Roman tormentors and executioners. This act of forgiveness reveals a kind of freedom that was not bound to the machinations of Empire. To choose to forgive was a courageous and free act in the face of the Roman Empire's practices of terror that sought to keep populations unfree—captive to fear and/or hatred. Jesus' forgiveness, in other words, was an act and communication that revealed his freedom from bondage to terror, fear, and hatred. In saying that his tormentors did not know what they are doing, he, in my view, recognized that they were enslaved by the ideology of the Roman Empire; they were captive to the grammar of empire, such that they were blind to their own unfreedom. Jesus, however, was free of this grammar and thus able to forgive them.

A modern illustration of this kind of agonistic freedom is seen in the ministry of Martin Luther King Jr. and others who engaged in nonviolent resistance. Despite death threats and physical violence, King (and others) possessed a kind of political freedom that exceeded the democratic racist polity of the United States and the unfreedom of racists. This was evident in that he was not captive to the grammar of racist illusions of superiority and inferiority. He certainly experienced fear, hatred, and depression or hopelessness, but he was not captive to them and chose not to operate out of them. King's and many others' decisions to act nonviolently and to continue to care for the well-being of white people, including racists, revealed an in-operativity to the grammar and rubrics of racism.

I do not want to associate King's freedom simply with the exercise of his democratic rights. Just as Jesus' freedom exceeded the polities of his time, King's freedom surpassed the putative democratic polity of the United States. For instance, in his Riverside speech, he demonstrated a deep sense of care for the well-being of Vietnamese people who were suffering as a result of U.S. aggression, which also negatively impacted other peoples. For King, all human beings are created in the image and likeness of God and therefore inviolable. This is a kind of freedom that exceeds any polity, yet is linked to a polis. It is the kind of political freedom evident in caring for all people, regardless of their color, ethnicity, etc.—a political freedom not bound by geography and identity.[117] It is a political freedom of Agamben's coming community wherein belonging (civic care and faith) is not dependent on identity.[118] And yet, it is an agonistic freedom, because it is a response to the sufferings of those who are unfree, who are in relations of subjugation, those who are constructed as politically irrelevant, and those who are excluded from the polis. Jesus' and King's agonistic, political freedoms are acts of care in the midst of the machinations of empire, exploitation, racism, and other forms of human subjugation.

All of this is centered on human beings, but I think that we can imagi-natively extend the revelation of the incarnation to other species. Jesus, in taking on the form of an enslaved person, is the included-excluded Other who is subject to and subjugated by a master who is given license by the state to have dominion over a slave. As mentioned in the previous chap-ter, the Judeo-Christian tradition has a theological strand wherein human beings are understood to have been given dominion over the earth. This means that the earth and other-than-human species are subject to and sub-jugated by human beings—slaves to the needs and desires of human beings. In one sense, dominion theologies make slaves of the earth and other spe-cies. The incarnation is an existential and ontological rejection of dominion theologies/philosophies and a revelation of a kind of political freedom to care for the earth and its species. These free acts of care make inoperative

117. I suspect most readers will connect this to the theological notion "kingdom of God"—wherein there is a belonging that is not dependent on particular identity. The metaphor "kingdom of God" needs to be understood, in my view, not as referring to some state after life, but to the possibility of God's indeterminate care actualizing a political belonging and freedom that is independent of geography or identity.

118. Agamben, *The Coming Community*, 86. Agamben notes that the rejection of all identity as a condition of belonging is the principal enemy of the state, which might explain the threat Jesus and King posed to the state.

the political grammars of anthropocentricism, which means that freedom involves the inclusion of the earth's and other species' well-being in our political deliberations.

In summary, the radical nature of the revelation of the incarnation is that personal and political freedoms are not granted by political institutions that are created by human beings. To be sure, political institutions can contribute to freedom, but Jesus' freedom in making inoperative Roman and Jewish polities exceeds all polities. Let me explain this by shifting to the notion of friendship. Some philosophers going back to Aristotle remark that friendship represents an apex of human freedom. In friendship, there is an equality that grounds freedom. As Arendt noted, "Without those who are my equals, there is no freedom."[119] I think it is more than equality. The freedom inherent in friendship has to do with the mutual acts of care. Genuine care for others represents a freedom that is connected to but exceeds polity. Like good-enough parents caring for the well-being of their children, friendship is concerned about the well-being of one's friend. To return to the revelation of the incarnation, the care of God made flesh is a revelation of freedom linked to and dependent on care that is independent of sovereignty, polity, identity, etc., though it always exists within the particularities of a polity. Perhaps the incarnation today is a revelation of the freedom to care for the earth and other species. The kingdom of God, as a metaphor, is a polity without polity that radically extends the freedom to care to the earth and all creatures who dwell upon and in it.

## Conclusion

As we consider the decades ahead, the realities of global warming invite us to radically reimagine politics and political freedom. The very possibility of our dwelling and personal and political freedoms is dependent on a viable earth, which necessitates a rich and diverse system. To be sure, we carry into this Age the problems of political freedom that philosophers and theologians have discussed for millennia. And yet, to think and act otherwise, we need to problematize human freedom in relation to included-excluded others, such as other-than-human species and the earth. It is not simply that we are free and hence responsible to and for each other, but that we are politically and personally free to care for other species and the earth. To this end, the imperative includes reimagining the creation of political (and NGOs) institutions, cultural and religious narratives and rituals, and daily political practices that extend civic care and civic faith to all the residents

119. Arendt, *The Promise of Politics*, 117.

of the earth and to the earth itself as our only home. This imperative to care is the only hope of retaining personal and political freedom—a freedom to think and be otherwise for the sake of other human beings, other species, and the earth.

# 5

# *The Problems of Political Change and the Specter of Political Violence*

[T]he means used to achieve political goals are more often than not of greater relevance to the future world than the intended goals.[1]

Once the primal crime of nationhood is buried in the past, we can all come to be pleasantly oblivious of it. The violence which established the state in the first place is now sublimated into the military defense of it.[2]

The genuine history of [humankind] is the history of ideas. It is ideas that distinguish [human beings] from all other beings. Ideas engender social institutions, political changes, technological methods of production, and all that is called economic conditions.[3]

The philosophers have only *interpreted* the world, in various ways. The point, however, is to *change* it.[4]

The spirit of the times . . . is also about a renewed *will to kill* as opposed to the *will to care*, a will to sever all relationships as opposed

---

1. Arendt, *On Violence*, 4.
2. Eagleton, *Tragedy*, 102.
3. Von Mises, *Theory and History*, 187.
4. Marx, "Theses on Feuerbach," thesis 11.

to the will to engage in the exacting labor of repairing the ties that have been broken.[5]

Heraclitus, a pre-Socratic philosopher known as the Riddler,[6] was believed to have said that one could not step into the same river twice. Anthony Grayling points out that some commentators disagree with Plato's interpretation of this riddle as meaning everything is in flux. Instead, they believe "that things stay the same only by changing—as in the case of the river; its flux does not destroy its continuity as the same river, but in fact constitutes it."[7] Of course, this riddle appears to be talking about nature itself. Nature is continuous, yet always changing. Human beings, as part of nature and subject to its "laws," are like this river, in flux but able to maintain continuity. Put another way, human beings were subject to the forces of nature and, as such, in flux.

In one sense, the distinction between nature and humanity led to a division between human history and natural history. Human history represents the changes and continuity of the actions of individuals and groups and how these actions led to seen and unforeseen consequences. Natural history is about the laws of nature and the geological and biological changes over vast periods of time. Human history (and pre-history) is but a noticeably short chapter in the overall book of natural history. This picture is much more complicated when we consider the realities of the Anthropocene Age. The previous five extinction events were the result of forces of nature, whether that was the catastrophic impact of a meteor or large-scale volcanism. These forces of nature caused massive changes with regard to life. The sixth extinction event, unlike the previous events, is the result of human actions, which indicates that human beings, initially unwittingly, are a force of nature. During the last several centuries, human beings have organized themselves politically and economically to take advantage of advances in sciences and technology to enhance their dwelling,[8] which has included deliberate exploitation of and, at times, unintentional violence toward other

---

5. Mbembe, *Necro-Politics*, 107.

6. Grayling, *The History of Philosophy*, 27.

7. Grayling, *The History of Philosophy*, 29.

8. Of course, while the changes due to science and technology have improved the lives of many, it is important to point out that billions of human beings have and continue to benefit. This is an issue of classism and will continue to be a severe problem in the future as resources diminish for human dwelling. See Our World in Data, "Extreme Poverty."

species and the earth. The massive scientific and technological changes has led to many positive changes, while also accompanying changes in climate that is and will continue to have negative effects on human beings, other species, and the earth itself. For historian Dipesh Chakrabarty,[9] this means that the distinction between natural and human history no longer holds. Human beings are not simply subject to and subject of the laws of nature, we are also agents that repeatedly step into the river, altering its course, if not its existence. Of course, nature will almost certainly have the last word, but not before human beings as a force of nature cause the extinction of a million or more species.

I want to be clear here. Human dwelling and technology, in and of themselves, are not the issue with regard to changes in nature. For millennia, human beings have largely dwelt in and with nature, adapting to and coop- erating with the forces of nature. Indeed, many so-called primitive peoples continue to do so today. Certainly, in the past, human beings have changed nature in their various locales, such as irrigation projects, aqueducts, dams, bridges, buildings, etc. But human beings have never impacted nature on a global scale until modern times, with the rise of global capitalism, accom- panied by an explosion of technologies that depended and depend on the ruthless exploitation of human and natural resources. I add here that forms of political violence, as methods of change, have existed since the dawn of civilization and the rise of the notion of sovereignty. But when political violence became wedded to capitalism, militarism, and imperialism in the last four centuries, human beings (especially imperialistic nations) entered a trajectory of being a negative force of nature. If human beings are to be a positive force of nature, we will have to change this trajectory and the way we dwell—how we think and act politically. This said, some scientists and geoengineers have big plans for altering climate change through technology, which will mean we can continue to act politically and economically as we have before. Technology will not save us or other species, because currently technology is deeply intertwined with capitalism and the politics of impe- rialism. To think that technology will save us is to embrace the illusion that we need not alter the very conditions that have resulted in climate change. Can we change enough to be a less powerful force of nature? Can we change so as to cooperate with nature, instead of trying to control it for our own purposes? If we think and be otherwise, will it be enough to stave off the worse effects of global warming?

The answers to these questions, while important, are not the focus of this chapter. Instead, I attend to the problems associated with change

9. Chakrabarty, "The Climate of History."

vis-à-vis the Anthropocene Age. Naturally, it would be nice to have a detailed program for how we can adapt to the realities of global warming,
while also setting clear programmatic changes for reducing human impact
on the climate and on the habitats of other species. Already, many individuals, groups, and states have established programs, policies, and institutions
aimed at addressing the effects of climate change. Instead, my interest is
grasping some of the problems associated with political change and, in
so doing, move toward a radical political theology of change. Toward this
end, I begin with a brief depiction of some of the problems associated with
change in the Anthropocene Age. From here, I focus on the problem of
political violence, because it 1) has been a major mode of initiating change
(and thwarting it) in history, 2) accompanies the political irrelevancy of nature, and 3) is fundamentally anti-political. In this section, I will also argue
that political violence as a mode of change is completely unjustifiable, not
only because it is mimetically tragic in that it perpetuates alienation, but
also because it undermines political dwelling vis-à-vis othered human beings, species, and the earth itself. This sets the stage for offering a radical
political theology that does not depend on political violence to organize
relations or effect change. I begin this section by arguing that from an existential developmental perspective, good-enough parents' caring actions
are the foundation of developmental changes, which includes changes in
relationships. In one sense, care is inextricably joined to the "creation" of
children and their psychosocial development, while violence is inimical to
care and children's development. I indicate further that for children to join
public-political spaces of appearance, there must be sufficient civic care and
civic faith to engage in conversation and actions—speaking and acting together—aimed at political change. I then shift from this existential perspective to the theological, arguing that God's care, evident in the incarnation
and Jesus' forgiveness of perpetrators of political violence, is a redemptive
invitation to eschew political violence as a mode of change, which is not
necessarily to advocate for pacifism, but rather for nonviolent political actions of defiance and resistance.[10] More positively, the weak force of God's

---

10. I strongly reject John Howard Yoder's view that the social ethic of Jesus involves
accepting pacifism and rejecting political violence. Yoder believed Christians can accept their subordinated or subjected status vis-à-vis the political structures, knowing
these political structures will, in the end, fade as the kingdom of God is ushered in.
While I accept pacifism as a stance, Yoder's view tends to perpetuate systems and structures of oppression and there is an abundance of history to show that these systems and
structures continue to be present. This said, Yoder did not necessarily presume that
political change is ultimately irrelevant given the eschatological end—the kingdom of
God. He did accept nonviolent resistance and tactical alliance with other organizations.
However, a danger of his theological rendering of pacifism can serve as a soporific for

care is evident in political change that emerges from acts of inclusive care toward human beings, other species, and the earth.

## Problems of Change and the Anthropocene Age

Broadly speaking, change means to alter or modify or replace, which suggests that what has changed differs from its original state or status. Heraclitus' river is in flux because the water is constantly moving downstream, though the river *qua* river remains unaltered. A child growing up remains, in a sense, herself, but is changing all the time—physically and psychologically. We say that the United States is a democracy, but how democracy was/ is defined and lived out has changed since the time of the writing of the Constitution.

Of course, not all change is good and sometimes it is ambiguous, comprising positive and negative features. Moreover, clarity about whether change is good or bad (or some combination) may not be known until months, years, or decades later. Those Europeans who first stepped ashore, building villages and establishing forms of governance, believed these were good and necessary political and religious changes, but the changes incurred vis-à-vis native peoples were horrific. Native peoples were violently forced from their lands, faced numerous broken treaties, were deprived of their cultures, faced illnesses and death as a result of diseases brought by European immigrants, and experienced the systematic deprivation of resources by white immigrants. Change is also ambiguous when we consider technological changes. Many people welcomed and welcome the technological changes ushered in through science and the capitalism of the industrial revolution. These changes, for many people, improved the quality of their lives. Of course, not everyone has benefited from the emergence and rise of global capitalism and its accompanying technologies. Billions of people around the world are impoverished and in the United States poverty and inequality remain high, while the capitalist classes of varied countries rake in vast amounts of wealth for the betterment of their personal lives.[11]

---

those who are oppressed and a boon to people in positions of privilege and power. The issue is not a binary choice between political violence and pacifism. There are all kinds of nonviolent actions and nonviolent violent actions (e.g., destruction of property) that are aimed at political change. Moreover, my argument below that political violence is not justifiable does not mean that I am saying it should never be used to effect political change. In some cases, it is completely understandable. However, by saying it is unjustifiable means taking responsibility for the harm caused and feeling remorse. Yoder, *The Politics of Jesus*, 185–92. See also Yoder, *Pacifist Way of Knowing*.

11. See Piketty, *Capital and Ideology*.

Even if we could imagine that the industrial age and the age of capitalism have helped 90% of the world's population (it hasn't), we would still have to face the resulting negative changes to the climate, the earth (exploitation of resources), and other species (extinctions and exploitation of animals). To continue with the theme of technological change, we are learning that recent technological innovations associated with communications technologies are having negative effects on human development and relationships, even as they represent possibilities for other people.[12] Even more interesting and frightening, human beings are on the cusp of changing themselves through technology. There is the possibility of genetic manipulations as well as using technology to enhance human capacities. For instance, technologies are being developed "to augment cognitive and memory function with patients diagnosed with Alzheimer's or Parkinson disease."[13] These improvements are certainly welcomed, but we are also in the process of creating what Kirk Bingaman calls techno sapiens.[14] There are advantages to this, no doubt, but these changes are likely to lead to extremely negative outcomes. It is not difficult to imagine, for instance, that poor people will be excluded from these advances, leaving me to predict an even greater class divide.

The ambiguous nature of changes incurred by human beings indicates that we are not able to predict with much if any precision the short-term and long-term effects of the changes—political, economic, social, or technological—we introduce in the world. Gregory Bateson coined the term "schismogenesis" to refer to changes and unforeseen consequences that result from human interactions with themselves and the environment. A simple example is the introduction of the effective pesticide DDT, which increased crop yield, but had devastating effects on animal life. Scientists only later realized how impactful the introduction of this pesticide was. Perhaps the ultimate illustration of schismogenesis is the proliferation of capitalism and the explosion of scientific advancements. No one could have predicted in the early nineteenth century that capitalism coupled with scientific advancements would lead to the devastating effects of global warming. Schismogenesis is true as well when we consider political and economic changes that are introduced for good "reasons," yet in the end have unpredicted negative effects. William Easterly, for instance, details the negative effects of well-meaning philanthropists and their policy experts in Africa (and other places).[15] This is true of well-meaning politicians who seek to develop

---

12. See Hamman, *Growing Down.*
13. Bingaman, *Pastoral and Spiritual Care in a Digital Age,* 18.
14. Bingaman, *Pastoral and Spiritual Care in a Digital Age,* 16.
15. Easterly, *The Tyranny of Experts.*

policies, programs, and laws that are, in their view, aimed at helping people and improving society. President Bill Clinton's so-called welfare reforms, for example, were aimed at reducing poverty, but in the end did little to help poor people.[16]

Since I have turned to the political, it is worth mentioning that there is a continuum of well-meaning persons consciously or unconsciously seeking change to secure more power, privilege, and prestige. When it comes to human beings and change, our conscious or stated motivations may be one thing, but the unstated or unconscious motivations are often much more powerful with regard to the consequences. In the U.S., well-meaning Christian people sought to "civilize" native peoples, and in the process furthered the illusions of white supremacy and U.S. exceptionalism. In the nineteenth century, for example, Catherine Beecher believed that the mission of the United States was to demonstrate "to the world the beneficent influences of Christianity, when carried into every social, civil, and political institution."[17] The white Euro arrogance of this view had destructive consequences to people in Cuba, Philippines, Central America, etc.[18] Ibram Kendi provides numerous examples in U.S. history of white politicians, consciously and/or unconsciously motivated by the belief in white supremacy, devising laws, policies, and programs that undermined and undermines the well-being of African Americans and other people of color.[19] So, when we consider social, political, and economic changes, the problem of human motivation arises.

There is another point to be made here. Most of the time, I suspect, we associate change with progress. A modernist belief holds that history reveals human progress, which is positive. This can include evolution in that evolution is one of progressive change. This is a problem because it suggests that human beings are the teleological pinnacle of evolution or that human beings of today are more advanced than human beings from millennia past. To be sure, we can point to advances and changes in technology, but that does not mean human beings have changed for the better or that the changes that have accompanied human "progress" have created a better world.

Change is not simply a matter of motivation, agency, and opportunity. Change also occurs naturally. By this, I mean two things. First, human beings adapt to their environment, at times changing their practices, culture, and language to ensure their survival and flourishing. We are also learning

16. Tanner, "How Did Bill Clinton's Welfare Reform Turnout?"

17. Kaplan, *The Anarchy of Empire in the Making of U.S. Culture*, 29.

18. Johnson, *Blowback*; Johnson, *Sorrows of Empire*.

19. Kendi, *Stamped from the Beginning*; see also Anderson, *White Rage*; Alexander, *The New Jim Crow*.

ways to adapt to an environment that we are also changing. The tragic irony is that we must adapt to an environment that we have (at least decades ago) unwittingly changed. For instance, some cities are altering their architecture and infrastructure to adapt to warmer temperatures.[20] Other cities are finding ways to promote ecological awareness and practices among residents.[21] Second, change occurs "naturally" in the sense that language and culture change over time. This is due to, I believe, part chance and part human creativity. The British understand Shakespeare, but certainly no longer speak Elizabethan English. What is meaningful in one generation may not have relevance in subsequent generations. The criteria used to discern beautiful art today may change decades or centuries later.

"Natural" changes are often ambiguous as well. People may decry the changes to the English language, fearing its corruption, while others are content with or celebrate the changes. Traditional artists may lament the changes introduced by modernists, though modernists take a different view. Human intelligence and creativity have been part of the advance of science for centuries, though a cursory glance at the use of science in human history can hardly be lauded given the bloody wake of human experimentation on and exploitation of othered human beings and other species.

One problem with regard to "natural" changes is that human beings may become extinct because we cannot adapt to the changes we have incurred. Scientists note that there have been five previous mass extinction events, having various natural causes. These events introduced massive changes in the environment, resulting in the extinction of some creatures and the evolution of other beings. Human beings are relatively new creatures, given the ecological timeline on earth. We are, of course, part of nature and, as part of nature, we have introduced sufficient changes to give rise to another extinction event. This is certainly a change that is a problem for ourselves and for many other species, but perhaps not for cockroaches. We certainly can lament the passing of human and other species, but the changes human beings have introduced may give rise to other evolutionary changes. Who knows, other creatures may emerge, which is good for them, not so much for us.

20. Walsh, "The Facts about Architecture and Climate Change."
21. Miller, "The Most Environmentally Friendly Cities in the U.S."

## The Problem of Political Violence as a Method of Change in the Anthropocene Age

I want to shift from a general discussion of change vis-à-vis the Anthropocene Age to focus more specifically on political violence as a means of change for three reasons. First, a cursory reading of history reveals that political violence is more often than not the preferred method for inciting political change, as well as quelling it. Indeed, as noted in a previous chapter on sovereignty, political violence is the basis of the emergence of the idea and practice of sovereignty (and law) and, not surprisingly, more often than not the very source of revolutionary political violence that is directed against instantiated sovereign powers. Of course, political violence can appear to be efficient,[22] resulting in victory, "but the price," Hannah Arendt remarked, "is very high; for it is not only paid by the vanquished, it is also paid by the victor."[23] Given the impending crises associated with climate change, we can anticipate more, not less, political violence in the future as powerful states scramble to secure more resources and as political and economic elites seek to protect themselves from the effects of climate change, fostering more desperate conditions for those without political and economic resources. Second and relatedly, political violence possesses a tragic mimetic strain, at least among human beings.[24] Political violence begets more violence vis-à-vis other human beings[25] or, as Judith Butler remarks, political violence "does not exhaust itself in the realization of a just end; rather, it renews itself in directions that exceed both deliberate intention and instrumental schemes."[26] Of course, other species and the earth are also forced to endure political violence. This suggests that with regard to change, political violence leads to a vicious cycle that is destructive to human beings, other species, and the earth as our one home. Third and relatedly, political violence has been primarily understood in terms of the consequences to human beings, which means that other species and the earth itself are constructed as politically irrelevant and thus ignored or exploited for political aims. Indeed, the Anthropocene Age can be understood in terms of the forms of political violence associated with and used by global capitalism and imperialism/nationalism, leading to climate change, the demise of habitats, and the

22. Oksala, *Foucault, Politics, and Violence*, 109.

23. Arendt, *On Violence*, 53.

24. See Mills, *The Philosophy of Agamben*, 76. See also Balibar, *Violence and Civility*, 118.

25. See Arendt, *On Violence*, 80.

26. Butler, *The Force of Nonviolence*, 20.

extinction of other species. In other words, the Anthropocene Age reveals the bankruptcy of Western political philosophies and theologies that view political violence as a key feature of being human or something uneliminable and, in many cases, justifiable, while constructing nature and other species as politically irrelevant and subordinate.

Given this, I intend to argue that the varied forms and aims of political violence are fundamentally problematic and that a radical political theology not only needs to explicate why this is so, but also seeks to think and be otherwise vis-à-vis political violence and change. More specifically, if we are to consider change in light of the political and the realities of the Anthropocene Age, we need to be clear about why forms of political violence as methods of change are unjustifiable and anti-political, even if and when they are understandable and, perhaps, even necessary.[27] This will be done in three moves. First, I explain what is meant by political violence, addressing its types, aims, and consequences. Second, this is necessary to set the stage for arguing that political violence as a method of change is anti-political and morally unjustifiable by portraying how political violence is typically explicated. For instance, as Johanna Oksala points out, "Thinkers from Plato to Hobbes, Machiavelli, Sorel, Clausewitz, and Schmitt have built their understanding of the political on the recognition of the irreducibility of violence in human affairs. More recently scholars such as Chantal Mouffe and Slavoj Žižek have emphasized the ineliminability of violence from the political domain."[28] At best, in these views, we can limit violence or find constructive, justifiable ways to use it, because it is a part of human nature.[29] While political violence is present throughout history, it is not necessarily clear that it is irreducibly part of the political or ineliminable from politics. In other words, one can argue that there is a proclivity of human beings with regard to violence without arguing it is irreducible to being human or ineliminable from political relations. More to the point, if we are to proceed toward a radical political theology that includes other human beings and nature, we need to find ways to think and be otherwise with regard to using political violence as a method of change, precisely because it is unjustifiable and anti-political. Given this, the third move is to argue that political

27. Frantz Fanon argued that political violence, in the case of liberation from colonization, was necessary. His context was the brutal oppression of France in Algeria. Something may be necessary, but necessity is not, as I will argue, a reason to justify political violence. Mbembe, *Necro-politics*, 129–30.

28. Oksala, *Foucault, Politics, and Violence*, 3.

29. Charles Bellinger explores the works of Ernest Becker and Søren Kierkegaard to explicate the roots of political violence, suggesting that political violence is inextricably part of being human. Bellinger, *The Unrepentant Crowd*.

violence is never justified not only because it is at its phenomenological core anti-political vis-à-vis human beings,[30] but also because it constructs and treats other species and the earth as politically irrelevant (and inferior)—ripe for exploitation, marginalization, and destruction. What I believe we are learning—though not fast enough—is that political violence is not something to be understood merely in its impact on human beings, but also its impact on the very nature of dwelling for all life. Political violence is a problem vis-à-vis change, because in the end it has and will continue to undermine our capacity to dwell, to live on this one earth.

Elizabeth Frazer and Kimberly Hutchings note that "The concept of violence and the concept of politics are vague and contested."[31] Many people often think that violence is direct physical harm to individuals, but there are also indirect forms of political violence,[32] such as environmental racism and classism that lead to illnesses and shortened lifespans. There is also the indirect (also direct[33]) violence of neoliberal capitalism with its maldistribution of resources such that the rich garner vast amounts of wealth at the expense of the so-called lower classes, undermining their well-being.[34] Johanna Oksala, using the work of Foucault, argues that political violence "is inherent to the rationality of neoliberal governing" and, worse, "it effectively depoliticizes violence by turning it into an essentially economic rather than a political or moral issue."[35] We then elide neoliberal capitalism from its attending forms of political violence. All of this suggests, then, that there are diverse forms of both direct and indirect political violence.

From this it is necessary to note that direct and indirect forms of political violence must be grasped in terms of their relation to and dependence on the forms of knowledge, narratives, practices, and institutions used to justify and prosecute violence.[36] These forms of knowledge and institutions or apparatuses reveal the functions and aims of the varied types of political violence. Given this, I offer a general definition of political violence: political violence, which is justified by the use of a group's narratives, is the use or the threat of force[37] by varied state and/or non-state apparatuses to secure

30. See Arendt, *On Violence*. Frazer and Hutchings, *Violence and Political Theory*, 76–86.

31. Frazer and Hutchings, *Violence and Political Theory*, 2.

32. Frazer and Hutchings, *Violence and Political Theory*, 2.

33. Zinn, *A People's History of the United States*, 253–95.

34. See Piketty, *Capital in the Twenty-First Century*. Klein, Naomi. *Shock Doctrine*; Valencia, *Gore Capitalism*.

35. Oksala, *Foucault, Politics, and Violence*, 136.

36. See Brown, *Undoing the Demos*.

37. Hannah Arendt distinguishes between power and violence. Power is associated

or safeguard political, economic, social, and/or cultural goods (e.g., identity, resources, privileges) within a polis or between poleis. To further understand political violence, I identify some of its types and features.

Perhaps the most obvious feature of political violence is the direct violence seen between states. The use of the varied branches of the military to defend borders against the incursions of other states and to extend borders and influence over other states are rife in history. Wars, proxy wars, and military skirmishes are forms of direct political violence, which seemingly confirm Clausewitz's famous dictum that war is the continuation of politics by other means. This is not something we find only in secular political states. Judeo-Christian scripture, for instance, is packed with stories of wars and battles between states/peoples as well as the cosmological (political) violence seen in the Book of Revelation. These stories have, throughout Judeo-Christian history, been used to justify political violence by any who invoke the name of God,[38] freeing the victors from remorse. Wars and the threat of wars are examples of direct political violence that pursue real and imagined changes.[39]

There are also indirect forms of violence prosecuted by states, especially imperialistic states. This can take the form of threatening to use direct violence, such as U.S. involvement in Iraq when securing a no-fly zone. It can also include sanctions on governments to insure or enforce compliance. These, too, are forms of political violence not only because of the threat of violence, but also because sanctions harm the citizens of the targeted country. For instance, U.S.-led sanctions against Iraq in the 1990s resulted in the deaths of approximately 300,000 to 500,000 Iraqi children, which apparently was justifiable for Secretary of State Madeline Albright,[40] because the U.S. is apparently "an indispensable nation . . . and we see further than other countries into the future."[41] The sheer arrogance of that rationalization of political violence was and is common among citizens who espouse the exceptionalism of the American Empire. Sadly, we could also list numerous

---

with people speaking and acting together, while force is a synonym for violence, which is characterized by its instrumental nature. She writes "Power is indeed the essence of all government, but violence is not. Violence is by nature instrumental." Arendt, *On Violence*, 51.

38. This is what Walter Benjamin refers to as mythic violence, which in intertwined with law-making. Frazer and Hutchings, *Violence and Political Theory*, 72.

39. As an example, Mark Danner provides a detailed account of the political violence waged by the United States against other countries and their peoples—for real and imagined reasons and justifications. Danner, *Stripping Bare the Body*.

40. Zinn, *A People's History of the United States*, 659.

41. Eggemeier, *Against Empire*, 32.

U.S. imperialistic "nonviolent" political interventions in Central and South America and their devastating effects on the lives of millions of people.

Indirect political violence between states can also have deleterious effects on their respective peoples. For instance, during the Cold War, the U.S. and U.S.S.R. were spending hundreds of billions of dollars on nuclear arsenals and military equipment and training. The rationale was the doctrine of Mutually Assured Destruction (MAD) as a way of deterring outright war. Indirect political violence is evident in the vast amounts of money and resources that were rendered unavailable to address the needs of poor persons, whether within the U.S., the Soviet Union, or so-called third world countries, which were often used for proxy wars between the U.S. and the Soviet Union. The intent was not necessarily political violence toward citizens, but the effect was a kind of political violence of deprivation vis-à-vis poorer citizens and their needs.

Indirect political violence can take on sinister forms in the sense of marginalizing and oppressing people, whether that is within a state or directed toward persons living in other states. Persons who are marginalized are usually written out of the dominant narratives of the ruling classes. If they are present, they are usually captive to the imaginations of the ruling classes, which means that oppressed and marginalized Others are misrepresented,[42] if they are represented at all. All of this cannot be accomplished without the aid of political, economic, and cultural apparatuses. As Miguel De La Torre writes, "To be written out of the story becomes a terrorist act, in which the memory of the marginalized is replaced by the fictitious story of their oppressors, robbing them of identity, of centeredness, of authentic being. Such a terrorist act is more insidious than physical harm, for it devastates the soul, the spirit, the mind, the very essence of a people."[43]

As mentioned above, the direct and indirect political violence directed by states against other states always excludes other species and the earth from consideration. To be sure, animals have long been used in a state's use of political violence against other states (and within states), but these animals are mere instruments, possessing no political relevancy. If we consider De La Torre's comment above, other species are largely written out of the political stories of human beings, leaving them, at best, as footnotes and, at worse, exploitable. Moreover, the damage to the earth in the prosecution of wars or in the exploitation of land is rarely a consideration vis-à-vis those who are advocates of political violence by states.[44] Environmental de-

---

42. See Saïd, *Orientalism*; Saïd, *Culture and Imperialism*.

43. De La Torre, *Embracing Hopelessness*, 32.

44. Crawford, "Pentagon Fuel Use, Climate Change, and the Costs of War."

struction is not merely the result of political violence of states waging war. Destruction to the earth includes preparations for war, especially among powerful military states and organizations (U.S., China, Russia, NATO).[45]

Political violence—direct and indirect—can also take place within states, in the forms of state-sanctioned violence (or threats of violence), as well as insurrections and revolutions. Hobbes' leviathan wields violence and the threat of violence to insure cooperation among the populace. Here the state is given license to commit direct and indirect forms of political violence to ensure security and stability for citizens. While Hobbes believed that the threat of political violence for the sake of security and stability benefited all citizens in their pursuit of private aims, it almost always is deployed to insure the power, privileges, and positions of political and economic elites. The threat or use of political violence for the sake of civic stability includes the use of police [and on occasion military] to discipline citizens especially those constructed as unruly or dangerous. In U.S. history, there are innumerable illustrations of state-sanctioned violence against residents, such as ethnic cleansings of Native peoples, slavery, terroristic practices of Jim Crow, police brutality toward people of color, etc. There is also indirect political violence toward citizens noted in environmental racism wherein people of color experience higher rates of illness and death because of the areas where they live.[46] Laws and policies are constructed and enforced such that people of color and poor white people are corralled into living in areas that are polluted, while people of privilege live in areas protected from environmental degradation. Indirect violence, as mentioned above, is also evident in a society's maldistribution of resources due to neoliberal capitalism,[47] as well as racism, classism, sexism, and other forms of political and economic marginalization of residents. Maldistribution of a society's resources is a form of indirect political violence because it undermines the well-being of marginalized residents. Judith Butler's discussion of violence furthers this view. She writes that "violence operates as an intensification of social inequality."[48] Social inequality is not simply the result of the negative social constructions of those deemed lesser and thus not grievable; it is also the result of systemic direct and indirect violence that undermines "lesser Others" from having access to resources for their well-being. A clear illustration of this is Malcolm X's autobiography, where he describes how

45. IPB, "The Military's Impact on the Environment; Webb, "The U.S. Military Is the World's Biggest Polluter."

46. Newkirk, "Trump's EPA Concludes Environmental Racism Is Real."

47. See, Desmond, *Evicted*; Silva, *Coming Up Short*.

48. Butler, *The Force of Nonviolence*, 142.

the state was implicated in the demise of his mother's ability to care for her family.[49] The current interest in microaggressions can also fall under the heading of indirect political violence, which can be subtle (e.g., maldistribution of resources) or overt (policing marginalized communities) in its consequences.[50] These microaggressions are part and parcel of systemic forms of marginalization and oppression, which are founded by types of knowledge and institutions that justify indirect political violence. Together, state-supported political violence is, more often than not, aimed at preventing political changes that would be seen as giving advantages to people of color, while removing privileges from whites and ruling elites.

The presence of state apparatuses and attending direct and indirect political violence often gives rise to the political violence of revolutions[51] and insurrections.[52] History is rife with stories of violent insurrections, revolutions, and rebellions. The foundation of the U.S. depended on the revolutionary violence against England. Though once established as an independent nation, the U.S. resorted to political violence to thwart a number of violent insurrections of enslaved persons and to quell violent rebellions against companies by workers in the nineteenth century. More recently, there have numerous peaceful protests in 2020 regarding the treatment of people of color at the hands of police. At times, violence broke out, usually labelled as rioting, but, in my view, it is more accurately called rebellion—a form of political violence toward powerful state and non-state apparatuses. The U.S. has also used indirect and direct forms of violence to maintain colonial rule and to undermine insurrections and revolutions in other countries. The U.S. tortured and killed untold number of Filipino insurrectionists in the early twentieth century.[53] There are numerous other instances where the U.S. actively supported other states (e.g., Iran, Nicaragua, Philippines, Israel, to name only a few) in their use of police, secret police, and

49. Haley, *The Autobiography of Malcolm X.*

50. Pérez-Huber and Solórzano, *Racial Microaggressions*; Spanierman and Wing, *Microaggressions in Everyday Life.*

51. Raymond Williams stresses that "we need not identify revolution with violence or with the sudden capture of state power." This is echoed by Sheldon Wolin, who calls for the creation of forms of life and organizations that resist the political violence of nationalism and empire. They are, in my view, both correct, but historically political revolutions more often than not depend on violence as the method for effecting change. That said, I agree, as argued below, that political change need not depend on violence and there are examples of this with nonviolent resistance seen in the Civil Rights Movement. Williams, *The Long Revolution*, x. Wolin, "What Revolutionary Action Means Today."

52. For example, see Sorel, *Reflections on Violence*; Morris, *Bakunin.*

53. Zinn, *A People's History of the United States*, 312–20.

military forces to crush those deemed to be rebels, dissenters, etc. Add to this the political violence fostered by the U.S. with the aim of overthrowing elected governments.[54]

Of course, not all revolutions, insurrections or rebellions result in the achievement of political goals. Indeed, there are many times when the state doubles down on the use of direct and indirect forms of political violence toward revolutionaries, insurrectionists, and rebels. Southern states were brutal in their crackdowns on slaves who rebelled and on enslaved people in general.[55] Terroristic forms of political violence after the Civil War were aimed at keeping Black persons subjugated and terrified of rebelling. Overall, the United States has a long history of government and non-governmental groups using direct political violence against varied groups of citizens. The ethnic cleansing of Native peoples, slavery, lynching, police brutality, and killings of African Americans are just some examples of state-sanctioned violence wielded against those who are constructed as threats to the established order of privilege and power.

In this general overview of direct and indirect political violence, we can discern basic types of violence. For instance, Johan Galtung identified and described structural violence in relation to the political.[56] Structural or systemic violence is evident in the social, political, and economic institutions (apparatuses or disciplinary regimes) that, along with socially held narratives and policies, legitimate and justify the practices of or threats of violence in society toward particular groups.[57] For instance, the rise of the Black Lives Matter movement is a response to the structural violence directed at African Americans by the police,[58] which is supported by local, state, and national laws that serve to shield police officers from responsibility for the consequences of their violent (and intimidation, which is a form of violence) actions. To add to this, environmental racism depends on structural violence, forcing impoverished communities of color to live in conditions that violate their health and lead to higher rates of illness and early death. There is structural violence in neoliberal capitalism, which is supported and promulgated by state and non-state apparatuses that legitimate theft of workers' pay and benefits, increasing their precarity. Put

54. Naomi Klein details the political violence fostered by the U.S. in the overthrow of Chile's elected leader. Klein, *Shock Doctrine*. Stephen Kinzer also details other occasions where the U.S. instigated political violence in the overthrow of governments. Kinzer, *Overthrow*.

55. Kendi, *Stamped from the Beginning*.

56. Galtung, "Structural and Direct Violence."

57. Ruggiero, *Visions of Political Violence*, 17–28.

58. Soss, Fording, and Schram, *Disciplining the Poor*; Goldberg, *The Threat of Race*.

another way, structural violence, often indirectly, establishes and maintains classism, as well as the growing disparities in wealth and income, which are the result of the maldistribution of resources.[59] This is accompanied by structural problems in obtaining adequate healthcare and education, which undermines (violates) the well-being of poor persons. Structural violence is also evident in social and political institutions that deny or restrict people from participating in the polis' space of appearances. Voter suppression laws and policies are examples.

These subtle and overt forms of structural violence are legitimated and justified by socially held narratives, institutions like the media, and discourses of political and economic elites. For instance, the rise of neo-liberal capitalism in the West was initially promulgated by intellectuals and their thinktanks, before making its way into the minds and hearts of governmental elites.[60] Foucault's work on the intersection of knowledge and power and its connection to the workings of neoliberalism has been helpful in highlighting how structural violence quietly deforms the subjectivities of individuals.[61] Jennifer Silva's[62] work on how neoliberal ideology and its accompanying discourses have deleterious effects on the psyches of so-called lower class individuals is a more recent illustration of socially held and legitimated narratives, policies, etc., that undermine the well-being of residents.

Structural violence is attended and supported by symbolic or epistemic violence. Epistemic forms of violence "damage people through a process of denigration and exclusion."[63] According to Hannah Arendt, epistemic violence entails the systemic misrecognition or nonrecognition of some residents such that they are marginalized from participating in the space of appearances—speaking and acting together. Moreover, epistemic violence, which depends on narratives and practices that construct Others as inferior, results in public-political spaces devoid of self-esteem, self-respect, and self-confidence (political agency). This has long been true with regard to women in the West and whose equality has been denied, through coercion, threat of violence and violence, and restricted access to public, political, and economic spaces. Someone might suggest that this is not necessarily political violence, but this would be incorrect for two reasons. First, to subordinate or subjugate persons (e.g., women, people of color) and to deny them civic

59. Piketty, *Capital in the Twenty-First Century*. See also Soss, Fording, and Schram, *Disciplining the Poor*.

60. See Jones, *Masters of the Universe*.

61. See Foucault, *Power/Knowledge*; Foucault, *The Birth of Biopolitics*.

62. Silva, *Coming up Short*.

63. Frazer and Hutchings, *Violence and Political Theory*, 3.

agency, while also denying them access to resources to actualize their potential, is accomplished by forms of political violence. Epistemic violence depends on structural violence that, in the case of women, violates their ability to actualize their potential. Second, a cursory glance at the 70 plus years of women agitating for the right to vote in the U.S. (1848–1920) reveals the violence and the threat of violence used to undermine women activists. Epistemic violence is also evident in the long sordid history of racism in the U.S., wherein African Americans and other people of color (Latinx, Chinese, etc.) have been and are discriminated against, as they face political violence in daily forms of humiliation as well as terroristic practices such as lynching.[64] Both structural and symbolic or epistemic violence depend on the dominant narratives that involve negatively constructing Others as inferior, which "justify" political violence. As mentioned above, this can take the form of indirect violence wherein targeted groups are denied access to political spaces, as well as denied resources to care for themselves, their families, and communities.[65]

The aims of political violence are varied. States pursue political violence to maintain sovereignty, identity, and territory. Imperial states can also engage in forms of political violence to expand economic power and territory. Groups in positions of power within a state seek to maintain their power, wealth, and privileges through the use of direct and indirect forms of political violence. Those who suffer under the heel of political oppression may use political violence to overturn the government. Others may use political violence to change unjust institutions and practices. Persons on any point of the political spectrum may resort to political violence out of fear of losing cherished moral, theological, or philosophical traditions. There are also instances of political violence that emerge out of despair, with the aim of causing malignant destruction.[66] Of course, many of these aims overlap. As the realities of climate change worsen, we can safely predict that the varied forms and aims of political violence will be used by those seeking change and those seeking to remain ensconced in the soporific embrace of neoliberal capitalism, nationalism, and imperialism.

---

64. Cone, *The Cross and the Lynching Tree*.

65. See Trepagnier, *Silent Racism*.

66. Jonathan Lear describes the differences between the Crow and Sioux people in facing the hegemony of white Euro-American political violence. The Sioux leaders decided to fight to the death, instead of learning to live with White people. Without making a positive or negative judgment on that decision, it is to my mind understandably based on despair. That is, the political violence of insurrections can be based in despair. Lear, *Radical Hope*.

Now I want to shift directions, arguing that political violence is a problem because it is not justifiable. In addition, I argue that political violence is unjustifiable because it is inherently anti-political or anti-dwelling. Let me begin by saying that there are many arguments for justifying political violence, including the vast literature on just war theory. More often than not, the arguments justifying political violence are consequentialist, though other arguments are based on rights—human, sovereign, etc.—as well as distinguishing between good and bad violence.[67] Consequentialist views tend to focus on the outcomes of political violence, whether that is security or stability, freedom (however understood), or justice, etc. There are also justifications based on good and bad violence,[68] but one can be immediately suspicious of who is arguing for good violence, while ignoring the experiences and voices of those (including other species) who undergo "good" violence. One may wonder why so much ink is devoted to justifying political violence. Besides the obvious answers that people committing acts of political violence seek permission or legitimacy and do not wish to experience remorse for their actions or be emotionally moved by the suffering of those who they have killed or harmed, there is, I contend, a more existential answer. Political violence is fundamentally anti-political; it contradicts existential dwelling together and undermines the dwelling of other species who are constructed as politically irrelevant. Justifications of political violence, in other words, are akin to the existential illusions of racism—they must continually be produced because they are existentially and ontologically false when it comes to the polis—human nature. That human beings can be violent is true. It is also true that violence has been and is used to attain political goals, which is not the same as saying that human beings by nature are violent or that violence is integral to the polis.

Before elaborating further, it is important to acknowledge that the idea that political violence is not justifiable[69] has been put forward by some feminist theorists, as well as by Hannah Arendt. Elizabeth Frazer and Kimberly Hutchings, for example, explore political violence from a phenomenological perspective that focuses on the relation that violence

---

67. Frazer and Hutchings, *Can Political Violence Ever Be Justified*, 113–14.

68. Frazer and Hutchings, *Can Political Violence Ever Be Justified*, 113–14.

69. Giorgio Agamben, in discussing the work of Walter Benjamin, writes, "the end is sole criterion to determine the justice of the means. Benjamin correctly noted that, while such a framework can justify the application of violence, it fails to justify the principle of violence itself." Benjamin wanted to debunk the legitimacy and justification of political violence, though he did this by introducing the notion of divine violence. In this paper I am steering clear of associating violence with the divine. Agamben, "On the Limits of Violence," 234.

produces.[70] They view political violence as instantiating relations of hierarchy and exclusion.[71] What is notable is their focus on understanding political violence as a relation, and this relation is fundamentally alienating.[72] Political violence, they argue, "builds edifices and structures of inequality, rejection and estrangement."[73] It "constructs a world of hierarchical, zero-sum distinctions between warriors and non-warriors, between aggressors and victims,"[74] wherein some lives are grievable (valued), while other lives are not.[75] Frazer and Hutchings are not positing "purist pacifism." They write: "The claim that political violence can never be justified does not mean that violence is always (if ever) evaded, or that violence is always retrospectively condemned. Rather, we rest our case on the claim that the experience, intersubjective relations, and effects of political violence qua violence are certainly pain, trauma, hierarchy, and exclusion."[76] They contend further that feminist analyses of violence "have shown how modes of justification themselves are complicit with the conditions that enable political violence to flourish . . . These are the conditions for producing subjects who will find it acceptable to reduce others—the enemy, foreigner, the ruling class, the colonized, the colonizer, the racialized and feminized subject—to nothing."[77] This view echoes a previous chapter's discussion on relations of subordination and subjugation and forms of misrecognition, wherein force or the threat of force or violence is used to retain dominance and privilege,[78] while also aiming to undermine or destroy the political agency (self-esteem, self-confidence, and self-respect) of Othered persons, which attends the attenuation of the space of appearances.[79] Add to this the notion that sovereignty depends on relations of exclusion and subordination, which are

70. For a similar analysis see Butler, *The Force of Nonviolence*.

71. Frazer and Hutchings, *Can Political Violence Ever Be Justified*, 119.

72. Frazer and Hutchings, *Violence and Political Theory*.

73. Frazer and Hutchings, *Can Political Violence Ever Be Justified*, 119. See also Judith Butler, who argues that equality is a principle that must undergird nonviolence. The implication is that political violence is relationally based on inequality in terms of whose lives are valued, whose lives matter. Butler, *The Force of Nonviolence*.

74. Frazer and Hutchings, *Can Political Violence Ever Be Justified*, 119.

75. Butler, *The Force of Nonviolence*, 28.

76. Frazer and Hutchings, *Can Political Violence Ever Be Justified*, 115.

77. Frazer and Hutchings, *Can Political Violence Ever Be Justified*, 121.

78. Judith Butler argues that nonviolence is predicated on equality and freedom, while violence is based on relations of inequality and restriction of freedom. While I do not spend much time on the issues of inequality, the idea of equality is imbedded in discussions of care and mutual-personal recognition. Butler, *The Force of Nonviolence*.

79. Oksala, *Foucault, Politics, and Violence*, 67–71.

maintained by political violence or the threat of political violence. As James Martel notes, it is the political violence of archism or sovereignty that fears, if you will, the nonviolence of cooperative anarchism.[80]

While Frazer, Hutchings, and Martel are speaking mainly about human beings, we can easily connect this to other species and the earth. Political violence relegates the earth and other species as inferior and subordinate so as to serve the political dwelling of human beings. Nature is Othered, and the stance toward other species and the earth is one of utility or instrumentality. As a result, a hierarchical relation of exclusion, marginalization, and exploitation perdures. It is important to stress that political violence is not only unjustifiable with regard to human beings but nature itself. Why is this so? First, I contend, perhaps channeling Schopenhauer, that political violence toward nature is unjustifiable because it is instrumental and objectifying vis-à-vis nature, ignoring the singularities and needs of other species. Second, political violence toward nature is anti-political because it undermines, in the long run, the very material foundations of the polis, of dwelling and is, therefore, not justifiable. Thus, from my perspective political violence is unjustifiable and that it remains narcissistic and self-serving to try to justify it. This is not to suggest that I reject all violence vis-à-vis nature. For instance, a hunter kills a deer so she can feed her family and recognizes that she has killed a sentient being. This is understandable and ethical when it is free of illusions of dominance and superiority. I am arguing that political violence is not justifiable because of its wholesale exploitation of nature.[81]

Now I turn to Hannah Arendt's political philosophy and her views on violence to extend our understanding of why political violence is not justifiable and why it is anti-political. Arendt's views on political violence demonstrate that violence, while political, is, at its core, anti-political. Arendt distinguished between power and force when discussing the polis. Power is associated with people speaking and acting together, while force is a synonym for violence, which is characterized by its instrumental nature.[82] "Power and violence," she writes, "are opposites; where one rules absolutely,

80. Martel, "The Anarchist Life We Are Already Living," 187–90.

81. Someone may ask about the killing of mosquitoes because they bring various forms of deadly diseases (e.g., malaria, Dengue fever, West Nile Virus), resulting in a great deal of suffering to people around the world. It is completely understandable that political communities would seek to eliminate mosquitos, but we also do not know the consequences to other species. A collapse of the mosquito population would be a loss of food source for many animals, which in turn would impact those animals that rely on them as a source of food. Perhaps it would be better to find ways to live with mosquitoes, annoying as they are, while finding ways to protect people from these illnesses.

82. Arendt, *On Violence*, 44–46.

the other is absent . . . This implies that it is not correct to think of the opposite of violence as nonviolence; to speak of nonviolent power is actually redundant. Violence can destroy power; it is utterly incapable of creating it."[83] She goes on to remark that "Power is indeed the essence of all government, but violence is not. Violence is by nature instrumental."[84] Of course, violence can be efficient and result in a political victory, "but the price is very high; for it is not only paid by the vanquished, it is also paid by the victor."[85] The cost of political violence is that it results in a mimetic and tragic relation of alienation and, concomitantly, the absence of speaking and acting together. Of course, Arendt recognizes that violence "is undeniably part of politics because it can be used as a means of pursuing various political goals and causes but, critically, it is ontologically apolitical. As a mere means it always needs justification through the political end or cause it espouses."[86]

For Arendt, then, violence and power are opposites. Power emerges from people speaking and acting together, which presupposes mutual-personal recognition. Moreover, this includes shared political agency derived from shared self-esteem, self-respect, and self-confidence, all of which are necessary for a viable polis. Political violence, on the other hand, destroys or is inimical to the space of appearances. Put another way, political violence is anti-political because it aims to undermine or eliminate mutual-personal recognition, as well as the attending sense of self-esteem, self-respect, and self, confidence of Othered persons. Recall also, for Arendt, violence "is utterly incapable of creating" power.[87] While violence changes the world, "the most probable change is a more violent world,"[88] hence the mimetic nature of political violence and its anti-political nature. In Arendt's view, then, political violence as a means of change cannot create a polis (though it may maintain a polis-Hobbes' leviathan) and is therefore not justifiable.[89] I

83. Arendt, *On Violence*, 56.

84. Arendt, *On Violence*, 51.

85. Arendt, *On Violence*, 53.

86. Oksala, *Foucault, Politics, and Violence*, 84–85.

87. Arendt, *On Violence*, 56.

88. Arendt, *On Violence*, 80.

89. A reader may point out that revolutionary violence produces a polis, identifying the United States as an illustration, or colonial revolutions after World War II. I think Arendt would agree that these states were established through forms of political violence and could be seen as understandable responses to the violence of colonial powers. However, to use political violence to establish a polis means that the "enemy" or colonizer is excluded from spaces of speaking and acting together. The danger is that once employed, political violence can be used to justify fracturing within a polis, establishing enclaves that are disconnected or alienated from each other. Consider the former Soviet Union, which used various forms of political violence to maintain political control of

imagine Arendt would have agreed with Stanley Hauerwas, who argued that "All genuine politics—that is, politics in the sense of conversation necessary for a people to discover the good they have in common—are nonviolent."[90]

There is another sense in which political violence is anti-political. The foundation of the polis, of the political, as mentioned in chapter 1, is exposure, vulnerability, and dependency of human beings.[91] All life is precarious, exposed, vulnerable, but we are not turtles who are independent of their parents after birth. They are precocial. Instead, we and other species are altricial, which means our exposure and vulnerability are dependent on the care of others. For apes, this means existing within the social network of the group. For human beings, it means being born into a polis, wherein there is sufficient care to develop, to appear, not in spite of our vulnerability and dependency, but because of it. Political violence is a rejection of this founding reality of the polis. It is a rejection of our vulnerability by making Others vulnerable. It is a rejection of dependency by making Others (colonized Others) dependent or annihilating the dependency of the enemy. It is a rejection of exposure by exposing Others to precarity and even death. Political violence is anti-human, even though it is conducted by human beings. It is essentially anti-political because it rejects, denies, overlooks the very foundations of what it means to be human.

I want to add to this view by returning to the relations between the space of appearances, civic care, and civic faith. The space of appearances or the space of speaking and acting together is the foundation of a viable polis. To be sure, this space is agonistic with people contesting various views, but it nevertheless has a level of mutual-personal recognition, civic care (including forgiveness[92]), and civic faith that keeps the space of appearances from imploding or fracturing into competing alienated groups. The types of knowledge and practices associated with political violence are inimical to mutual-personal recognition, civic care, and civic faith. In other words, the instrumentality of political violence involves the construction of the Other as an enemy to be defeated, and this Other is not due personal recognition, care, or trust. Political violence, then, produces relations of carelessness, infidelity, and depersonalization whereby "enemies" are not included in the space of appearances. Any society that is based on Schmitt's friend-enemy distinction will be a society fractured by varied forms of political violence.

---

varied regions within the Soviet Union and client states. Eventually it collapsed and the result was a fracturing of this political entity.

90. In Eggemeier, *Against Empire*, 169.

91. See Mbembe, *Necro-politics*; Butler, *The Force of Nonviolence*.

92. Arendt, *The Promise of Politics*.

This kind of polis will contain a fundamental contradiction; the stability of the polis will be based on anti-political forms of relating—carelessness and distrust. In short, political violence, while at times understandable, is not justifiable because it is anti-political, undermining the civic care and trust necessary for speaking and acting together.

There is another contradiction to highlight. Giorgio Agamben and others have argued that political philosophy and theology in the West have excluded nature from political theorizing and discourse. Ironically[93] and tragically, nature, then, has been deemed politically irrelevant or seen in an instrumental way—existing to support human beings. Nature as politically irrelevant or to be exploited has depended on forms of knowledge that embrace the Judeo-Christian beliefs that humans have dominion over nature and are superior. Together these beliefs establish hierarchical relations of exclusion and violent exploitation of other species and the earth. The problem with this, as noted above, is that our very political existence, our dwelling together, depends on a biodiverse earth, which we are in the process of making uninhabitable for other species and ourselves. Political violence, then, includes violent actions toward or neglect of the well-being of other species and the earth—the absence of care. It is not simply the inter-human dynamics of political violence that demonstrate it is unjustifiable; it is also the consequences of human-caused extinctions of other species and likely us. We have relied on political violence vis-à-vis nature to maintain our dwelling, which in the end undermines this very dwelling on which the polis depends—hence political violence vis-à-vis nature is not justifiable and anti-political.

In summary, political violence as a means of change is deeply problematic and unjustifiable. It is a problem because it produces and maintains hierarchical, exclusionary, and instrumental relations between human beings and between human beings and nature. Political violence is the opposite of power, which establishes the polis' agonistic spaces of speaking and acting together. In this sense, political violence is anti-political, even as it is used to attain political goals, because it undermines the space of speaking and acting together vis-à-vis the Other. The very problems associated with political violence as a method of change also point to it not being justifiable, whether we are talking about human beings, other species, and the earth. The latter is especially evident in the forms of political violence that undermine the very material conditions of the polis in the Anthropocene Age.

93. It is ironic because human beings are part of nature, yet in the West we often see nature as something decidedly different.

## Political Change:
### Existential and Theological Perspectives
### on Thinking and Being Otherwise

If political violence is unjustifiable as a means of change, what methods of change are justifiable? To move away from our reliance on political violence to promote or suppress change requires us to think and be otherwise in the Anthropocene Age, where the temptation of political violence rises as resources dwindle. In this section, I propose ways of understanding change from existential and theological perspectives, recognizing that scripture and the history of theology are imbued with political violence and its justifications. Indeed, theological justifications of political violence are particularly pernicious because they leave little opening for being interrogated. Who can question the legitimacy or justification of political violence when done by or sanctioned by God? Well, anyone can question, but who will listen? In this section, I begin with a brief discussion about the use of political violence as a means of change in scripture, suggesting that if we are to move into imagining something other than political violence, we will need first to problematize scripture.[94] I then shift to an existential view of change as it relates to good-enough parent-child interactions. Here I argue that while human beings can be violent, they are not inherently so. Moreover, the very foundation of change in human life vis-à-vis survival and flourishing is contingent on caring relations. I then return to a discussion of Jesus Christ and the incarnation of an infinite, indeterminate care of God as founding creation. More particularly, I argue that Jesus' refusal to engage in political violence as a means of change is evident in his taking on the form of a slave and in his forgiveness of those perpetrating political violence on him in the name of Rome.

In the previous chapters, I have discussed the Exodus story from various angles. Here I want to view the story in terms of political violence as a means of change. The laments of the Israelites are heard by God, who then sends all kinds of havoc to persuade the Pharaoh to free the Israelites. Clearly, to oppress the Israelites, the political authorities must have employed varied forms of political violence. Similarly, to free the Israelites,

---

94. In his exploration of political violence and religion, William Cavanaugh writes that "There is no reason to suppose that so-called secular ideologies such as nationalism, patriotism, capitalism, Marxism, and liberalism are any less prone to be absolutist, divisive, and irrational than belief in, for example, the biblical God." While I am focusing on Judeo-Christian myths and political violence, it should be clear that, from Cavanaugh's perspective, political violence is justified by way of other secular ideologies. Cavanaugh, *The Myth of Religious Violence*, 55.

political (divine) violence was used—violence that caused great suffering among the Egyptians. Once free of the clutches of the Pharaoh's decimated army, the Israelites began to form their own army, which they used to defeat Amalek (Exod 17:8–15), to kill the inhabitants of the promised land, and then to subjugate survivors—all with the blessing and command of a demographic God of profound partiality. And there are numerous other narratives where Israelites are commanded to kill and steal. But it is not "enemies" or included-excluded Others (e.g., Israelites as residents of Egypt) are the targets of divine political violence;[95] it is also some of God's chosen people.[96] To re-establish order, God commands Moses to kill those Israelites who had rebelled by fashioning a golden calf (Exod 32:25–29). And then God sent a plague on those who made the calf. Like the plagues against the Egyptians, this plague is also an act of political violence directed toward those who had turned from God—the Sovereign. It is an act of political violence because its aim is to secure adherence from members of the community.

Recall in chapter 1 the discussion regarding a shift from the sole sovereignty of God to a human sovereign. The elders wanted God to "appoint for us a king to govern us like other nations" (1 Sam 8:5). Samuel was told by God to warn the elders of the implications of their request:

> These will be the ways of the king who will reign over you: he will take your sons and appoint them to his chariots and be his horsemen, and to run before his chariots; and he will appoint for himself commanders of thousands and commanders of fifties, and some to plow his ground and to reap his harvest, and to make his implements of war and equipment of his chariots. He will take your daughters to be perfumers and cooks and bakers. He will take the best of your fields and vineyards and olive orchards and give them to his courtiers. He will take one-tenth of your grain and of your vineyards and give it to his officers and his courtiers. He will take your male and female slaves, and the best of your cattle and donkeys and put them to his work. He

95. Walter Benjamin distinguishes between mythic violence (violence associated with law-making and law-preserving) and "divine violence," which refers to pure violence that is outside the political violence of the law and sovereignty. Divine violence is beyond violence—a kind of nonviolent violence. I will not use this term, because it still links God to political violence. A view of God as non-sovereign necessarily eschews any connection to political violence, though clearly scriptures link the sovereignty of God with God's use of violence to achieve political ends. Perhaps this is why it is easier for people to imagine the end of the world, but not the end of sovereignty and political violence. See Oksala, *Foucault, Politics, and Violence*, 148–56.

96. I add here that in scripture God also legitimates political violence as a method for securing the community's stability (e.g., Exod 21:12–26).

will take one-tenth of your flocks, and you shall be his slaves. (8:11–17)

The human sovereign will legitimize theft from the people, using political violence to secure his power, privilege, and prestige. To force people to be soldiers, to take sons and daughters to serve the sovereign, to demand and take income from residents, and to make a people into slaves can be done only through varied forms of political violence and the threat of violence. The sovereign can never do this alone, instead relying on apparatuses of political violence to ensure compliance and legitimate both violence and its attending aims.

Lest we believe that Jewish scriptures alone legitimate political violence, Christian scriptures (and theologies) also contain stories of political violence. For instance, in Matthew, Jesus says, "Do not think I came to bring peace to the earth; I came to bring, not peace, but a sword. For I came to cause division, with a man against his father, and a daughter against her mother, and daughter-in-law against her mother-in-law" (Matt 10:34–36). Perhaps this is a bit of hyperbole, especially when placed in the context of other passages where Jesus eschews violence. Nevertheless, it is suggestive of political violence. Political violence also occurs during the founding of the first "Christian" community, when Ananias and Sapphira were struck dead for having lied about the selling of their property. We then we read that "a great fear seized all who heard of it" (Acts 5:5). I would interpret the deaths as acts of "divine" political violence meant to instill fear so that people would fully share what they possessed. Even if these events did not happen, but were instead stories told to compel people to be forthright about what they were contributing to the community, it remains as a threat of political violence. And there is, of course, the gratuitous orgy of cosmic political violence found in the book Revelation that establishes the thousand-year reign of Christ (Rev 20)—a reign founded on bloody exclusion.

These and other passages in Judeo-Christian scripture reveal direct and indirect, structural and epistemic forms of political violence used to establish political changes (e.g., liberation) or, in other cases, to prevent political change. There are, in my view, a number of problems with violence vis-à-vis scripture. First, scripture is used to justify and legitimate political violence within the state and between states (and other peoples). The history of Christian leaders and theologians legitimating political violence by way of scripture and God is depressingly long and not possible or necessary to detail here. And yet, others have cited scripture to argue for pacifism or nonviolent resistance. Consider John Howard Yoder's work on Christian pacifism, for instance. His view of nonviolence was based "in the character of God and the work of Jesus Christ" such that "the triumph of God comes through resurrection and not through effective sovereignty or assured survival."[97] More particularly, Yoder used the terms "revolutionary subordination" and "servanthood" to ground his view of political nonviolence.[98] Thus, we can "freely" submit to the political violence of the sovereign because somehow we supposedly know "the structure . . . is passing away."[99] This pacifist view rejects political violence at the expense of accepting the present world as it is, which includes the present realities of political violence—religious and otherwise. According to Yoder, political change apparently occurs during the end times when structures of political violence pass away. Indeed, Yoder even mentioned how a Christian wife can submit to her husband, no doubt in the "hope" that the patriarchal structures of political violence will one day magically disappear in the end times. Yoder's use of scripture to argue against political violence is a boon to those who use political violence in the present to establish unjust and unequal relations. In contrast, other religious leaders (e.g., Martin Luther King Jr.[100]), scholars,[101] and scientists[102] have advocated for nonviolent resistance in the face of the varied forms of political violence arrayed against them. This said, a cursory glance at Judeo-Christian history reveals a mountain of discourse legitimating all kinds of political violence.

Another problem with scripture is that political violence is ontologized. By this I mean it becomes an eliminable feature of being human in that "divine" political violence becomes the premise for organizing human relations in the polis/ecclesia. This is a problem because people think that political violence is an ineliminable feature of being human (and apparently God), and the only responses are to accept political violence, find ways to use it to our advantage, or find ways to reduce it. Ontologizing political violence impoverishes our capacity to imagine and work toward a polis that does not rely on political violence as a method of change or as a method or organizing relations. Unfortunately, it becomes easier to imagine the end of

97. Yoder, *The Politics of Jesus*, 239.

98. Yoder, *The Politics of Jesus*, 186.

99. Yoder, *The Politics of Jesus*, 186.

100. King's belief in and practice of nonviolent resistance served to negate the mimetic dynamics of political violence. See Moody-Adams, "The Path of Conscientious Citizenship."

101. For example, see Butler, *The Force of Nonviolence*; Mantena, "The Showdown for Nonviolence"; Nussbaum, "From Anger to Love"; Wonhee, *Heart of the Cross*; Hauerwas, *Performing the Faith*.

102. Albert Einstein described himself as a militant pacifist. See Butler, *The Force of Nonviolence*, 181.

the world (Book of Revelation) than it is to imagine a world not dependent on political violence.

A third and related problem is the tragic mimetic nature of political violence. Scriptural stories of political violence reveal its mimetic nature. The Pharaoh violently oppresses the Israelites only to have violence returned in spades. There are wars that Israel started and won, and wars they lost. The Book of Revelation promises a time when there is an end to violence, but only after God violently crushes Satan and his followers. Ontologizing political violence—theologically or philosophically—only ensures a tragic mimesis in human life because the achievement of political ends through the use of violence does not exhaust violence.

A final problem of political violence in scripture is that it tacitly affirms either instrumental relations toward other species and nature and/or the complete political irrelevance of the earth and other species. Animals can be used in the prosecution of war. The needs of other species and nature are not taken into the political consideration when committing violence. As an example, the myriad wars (and threats of war) the U.S. has been involved in could not have taken place without the support and justification of Christian leaders (and followers) who justified war without considering the impacts of violence on people constructed as enemies, other species, and the earth. Indeed, the Christian justification of the development and use of nuclear weapons reveals, as some Christian leaders have noted,[103] a stunning lack of sensitivity to the environmental costs of making these weapons as well as employing them. But it is not simply the planning and execution of war that represents political violence toward Othered individuals, species, and the earth. As stated above, varied forms of capitalism are examples of direct and indirect political violence. In the U.S., neoliberal capitalism is lauded by many Christians who are followers of the prosperity gospel as they deny, overlook, or minimize not only the harms done to other human beings, but also the vast ecological destruction that results from apparatuses of capitalism.[104] And finally, the scriptural (or philosophical) justification of political violence means the objects of violence do not merit grief, leaving the perpetrators (God or those commanded by God) of violence to be free of remorse and to be free to forget.[105]

Given these problems, I first shift to an existential view of change. As in previous chapters, I begin with the space of speaking and acting together

103. See https://www.usccb.org/issues-and-action/human-life-and-dignity/war-and-peace/nuclear-weapons/upload/statement-the-challenge-of-peace-1983-05-03.pdf.

104. Klein, *This Changes Everything*.

105. See Butler, *Precarious Life*, 33–34.

between parents and children. In chapter 1, I noted that acts of parental care rest on personal recognition/knowing, which comprises three interrelated dialectical pairs, namely, identification-disidentification, determinate-indeterminate knowing, and restraint-unrestraint, which are necessary for creating a space for infants to risk appearing, to risk asserting their needs and desires. Infants, then, are dependent and vulnerable, needing the good-enough caring attunements of parents (and others) to develop, to change, to survive, and to flourish. The biological and psychosocial (e.g., language acquisition, self-reflection/mentalization) changes children undergo are incredible in the first years of life. These changes continue and would not occur without the caring attunements (including repair) of parents and others. The absence of care (deprivation, neglect, violence) undermines these changes and, worse, leads to death. Acts of care are the means of change that are not determinate, though the direction is toward the good of the child. By indeterminate, I mean that parental care, while aimed at the good of the child, is not captive to the parent's specific vision for the child, which creates a space for the child to appear, to unfold.

Of course, parental care can be instrumentalized wherein acts of care are aimed less at the child's singularity or suchness and more at what the child can do for the parent. A parent who cares for a child because he wants the child to fulfill the dream the parent failed to achieve is an example. Care in this situation, while present, is distorted by its determinacy. Another example is a parent caring for children in order to get the affection and attention they are not receiving from their partners. When this happens, children develop, change, yet they are often psychologically or emotionally harmed. So, parental acts of care are not simply the means to biological changes, but also psychosocial changes in children. The distortion of care impedes those changes toward human flourishing.

There is another way to depict parental indeterminate care and changes in psychosocial development. Agamben, relying on Aristotle, indicates that potentiality vis-à-vis human beings is not exhausted by actualizing their potential.[106] In my view, it is the parent's care that facilitates the movement from potentiality into actuality, yet children never exhaust their potentiality. Here we see that care is the method for change, for children's moving from potentiality to actuality (e.g., language, self-reflection, narrative, etc.). In more concrete terms, parental care facilitates the actualization of children's capacities for speaking and acting together, which includes agency and self-esteem, self-confidence, and self-respect. The absence or attenuation

106. See Dickinson and Kotsko, *Agamben's Coming Philosophy*, 33. It is also helpful to note that for Agamben "inoperativity is a mode of potentiality not exhausted in actuality." Kotsko and Salzani, *Agamben's Philosophical Lineage*, 142.

of care impedes potentiality from becoming actual—undermining agency, freedom, and self-worth.

Donald Winnicott argued that for parents to care for their children, they need to be cared for as well by the larger community and society.[107] Parents, in other words, cannot provide effective care without the civic care of the larger society. We can observe this by way of negative illustrations.[108] As mentioned in other chapters, systemic racism, classism, sexism, and other forms of marginalization and oppression instantiate varied apparatuses of direct and indirect political violence,[109] which negatively impact the distribution of resources necessary for parents to care for their children. Malcolm X's story of his early life reveals the pervasive, pernicious effects of racism on his parents and family. Add to this, the apparatuses of oppression that systematically deny social-political self-esteem, self-confidence, and self-respect, which are necessary for political agency vis-à-vis speaking and acting together. This naturally impacts (but does not determine) parents and their ability to provide the care their children need. James Baldwin, for instance, wrote about his father, saying, "He was defeated long before he died because, at the bottom of his heart, *he really believed* what white people said about him."[110] This clearly had an impression on the young James. Indeed, Baldwin noted, "Long before the Negro child perceives this difference [white superiority], and even longer before he understands it, he has begun to react to it, he has begun to be controlled by it."[111] Ta-Nehisi Coates also provides a painful illustration of the impact of systemic racism on his parents and their care. He writes, "My father was so very afraid. I felt it in the sting of his black leather belt, which he applied with more anxiety than anger."[112] Later in his book, Coates writes that "it was a loving house, even as it was besieged by its country, but it was *hard*."[113] Parental care is essential for positive developmental changes to occur, and civic care vis-à-vis the parents is also a crucial factor in facilitating parents to care for their children. Indecent societies rely on apparatuses or disciplinary regimes of political violence that undermine civic care for some parents, depriving

107. Winnicott, *Playing and Reality.*

108. See Howard, "US Ranks Lower than 38 Other Countries When It Comes to Children's Wellbeing, New Report Says."

109. These forms of oppression intersect with types of capitalism, which has negative impacts on the so-called lower classes. See Zaretsky, *Capitalism, the Family, and Personal Life.*

110. Baldwin, *The Fire Next Time*, 4.

111. Baldwin, *Notes from a Native Son*, 26.

112. Coates, *Between the World and Me*, 15.

113. Coates, *Between the World and Me*, 126.

them of material, psychological, and political resources that can undermine their abilities to care.[114]

There is, then, a correlation between care of and in the polis and care provided by parents. To illuminate that correlation, a brief detour is needed regarding care as a political concept.[115] As noted in a previous chapter, feminist scholars[116] and, recently, theologians[117] have argued that care is a political concept. It is helpful and necessary to briefly say a few words about care as a political concept. Feminist scholar Joan Tronto argues that care "is a species of activity that includes anything we do to maintain, continue, and repair our 'world' so that we can live in it as well as possible. That world includes our bodies, ourselves, and our environment."[118] Like any general definition, this covers a large swath of human activity, ranging from a nurse tending to an infant to public policies that make health care affordable and available to all. Building on and critiquing Tronto's definition, Daniel Engster suggests that care is "everything we do to help individuals meet their vital biological needs, develop or maintain their basic capabilities, and avoid or alleviate unnecessary or unwanted pain and suffering, so that they can survive, develop, and function in society."[119] I add to his perspective, arguing that "Care is everything we do to help individuals, families, communities, and societies to 1) meet the vital biological, psychosocial, and existential or spiritual needs of individuals, families, and communities, 2) develop or maintain basic capabilities with the aim of human flourishing, 3) facilitate participation in the polis, and 4) maintain a habitable environment for all."[120] In addition, care as a political concept involves shared critical and constructive reflection on how the structures (and their accompanying narratives and practices) of the state, governing authorities, and non-state organizations (e.g., businesses, labor unions, religious and secular communities, etc.) and actors meet or fail to insure the stability of the space

---

114. Even under the most oppressive circumstances, parents can provide the necessary care needed for their children to survive and flourish, but the obstacles they face are manifold. The point here is that while the political sphere is correlated to parental care, parents are not determined by it.

115. This was mentioned in the introductory chapter, n17.

116. For feminist views of care as a political concept see Hamington, *Embodied Care*; Noddings, *Caring*; Robinson, *Globalizing Care*; Robinson, *The Ethics of Care*.

117. See Helsel, *Pastoral Power Beyond Psychology's Imagination*; LaMothe, *Care of Souls, Care of Polis*; Rogers-Vaughn, *Caring for Souls in a Neoliberal Age*.

118. Tronto, *Moral Boundaries*, 103; see also Tronto, *Caring Democracy*.

119. Engster, *The Heart of Justice*, 28.

120. LaMothe, *Pastoral Reflections on Global Citizenship*, 8.

of speaking and acting together so that residents of the polis/ecclesia can survive and flourish.[121]

The underlying premise here is that *acts of care are means to political change and stability.* More specifically, the organizing principle of the polis, of people speaking and acting together, is caring relations. Civic care entails mutual-personal recognition that makes actual individuals' singularity—their sense of self-esteem, self-confidence, and self-respect that are necessary for political agency. Civic care is necessary for the survival and flourishing of an agonistic polis. As previously mentioned, the agonistic aspect of politics necessarily includes forgiveness—an act of care—that repairs the space of appearances.

The polis' space of speaking and acting together includes the creation of institutions and practices and, if the polis is to be viable, these institutions foster civic care and civic faith. Negative examples illustrate the importance of care in founding and maintaining the polis. For instance, systemic racism and its apparatuses of political violence undermine the space of speaking and acting together between Whites and Blacks, which, in turn, is accompanied by a poverty of civic care and faith toward those constructed as inferior. Political violence is inimical to and obliterates civic care and, as a result, obstructs positive political change from occurring.[122] Of course, political violence could not and cannot stop the care among African Americans who organize caring communities and develop ways to resist white supremacy. More importantly, instances of care that inform practices of resistance can also be a locus of political change. For instance, Martin Luther King was cared for by his parents and his church, which founded, in part, his (and others') political practice of nonviolent resistance,[123] leading to positive political changes, as seen during the Civil Rights Movement. I would add that Malcolm X relied on the care of his community of faith to resist racism.[124] Of course, white supremacy is malignantly resilient and what followed the advances in civil rights was new Jim and Jane Crow laws.[125] Today, nonvio-

121. LaMothe, *Pastoral Reflections on Global Citizenship,* 8.

122. Thomas Piketty's recent tome identifies ideologies of inequality and how they are legitimated and supported by apparatuses, which I would contend reflect forms of political violence. He points out that actions leading to greater equality have beneficial effects for the people of the polis and the polis itself. Piketty, *Capital and Ideology.*

123. Étienne Balibar prefers the term "antiviolence" to suggest a more active stance against political violence. Balibar, *Violence and Civility.*

124. Of course, it is important to point out the political violence that was directed at Malcolm from the Nation of Islam. But Malcolm was able to find support from the larger Muslim community and the religious community he formed in the U.S. See Marable, *Malcolm X.*

125. Alexander, *The New Jim Crow.*

lent Black Lives Matter protesters seek justice for people of color harmed by the apparatuses of white supremacy. These acts of nonviolent resistance represent a means to change that involve care for people of color, but also civic care for those who stand against them. This said, the illusions of white supremacy and the apparatuses that maintain it are large obstacles to civic care and, consequently, political change, because they foster political violence and carelessness. This is evident in Eduardo Porter's detailed examination of the negative effects on how racism's political violence (absence of care) has undermined the well-being of the entire nation.[126] Racism and its apparatuses of direct and indirect violence snuff out civic care and stifle political change.

Naturally, in a polis, a group can demonstrate care for its members while demonstrating indifference or hostility toward another group—racism is a clear illustration of this. When Avishai Margalit discusses an indecent society that humiliates a group(s) with the society,[127] he is, in my view, demonstrating that, in indecent societies, there is an absence of care vis-à-vis humiliated Others. An indecent society remains stable as long as there is the consistent presence or threat of political violence, which reinforces care within and for the dominant group, while promoting indifference, carelessness, and violence toward the demeaned group. The lack or absence of civic care is anti-political because it undermines mutual-personal recognition vis-à-vis Othered people, which undercuts self-esteem, self-respect, and self-confidence (political agency). All of this accompanies marginalization from the polis' space of speaking and acting together, which accompanies maldistribution of resources. In my view, the U.S. is an indecent society that has a long history of demonstrating a lack of civic care for the well-being of Native peoples, African Americans, the poor, and Othered peoples (e.g., colonized Others). A true democracy is not simply one where members speak and act together; it is one in which there is sufficient civic care for all residents to survive and flourish. Civic care, which founds the space of speaking an acting together, is a means of political change that is, at its best, inclusive and non-hierarchical (non-sovereign), making it more likely the polis' potentiality is actualized, though not exhausted.

As a means to change, civic care, unlike political violence, is always justifiable. There are libraries full of books defending, rationalizing, legitimating, and justifying varied forms of political violence as a means for political change or thwarting political change. This suggests that there is an existential flaw with regard to political violence as a means of change, which, as

126. Porter, *American Poison.*
127. Margalit, *The Decent Society.*

noted above, lends weight to the idea that political violence is unjustifiable. That which must be continually defended, in other words, reveals its existential falsehood. In other words, like white supremacy, political violence is an existential falsehood that requires advocates who rationalize, ontologize, and moralize its necessity. By contrast, what argument can be laid against civic care as a means of political change? Care is an existential reality in that it brings into being human beings, and this takes place in the polis. As Agamben argues, politics is humankind's "most proper dimension,"[128] and it is care that makes this proper potential dimension actual, while political violence prevents it. Civic care is an existential fact that does not require constant justification. Unlike political violence, care is its own justification. It is only its absence or attenuation that demands to be justified.

Of course, arguing that care founds the polis confronts the reality of human freedom and finitude. The previous chapter dealt with some of the problems with regard to freedom, but here I simply mention that human beings possess sufficient freedom to not care. If care is an existential imperative to the realization of a polis and for being human, human beings, as history shows time and again, can choose to defy this imperative. We, as human beings, in other words, can obstruct our own potentiality from being actualized, and political violence and the Anthropocene Age are paradigmatic examples. Add to this that we can choose to care for one group, while denying care to Othered persons, to other species, and to the earth itself. Put another way, we can choose to engage directly or indirectly in political violence as a means to achieve political-economic aims, while choosing to care only for the members of one's group. The political can exist in relation to the anti-political.

This existential view of care and the polis must be extended to nature and other species. At the most basic level, caring for nature facilitates its flourishing—its actualization. Even the simplest act of tending to one's garden illustrates the relation between acts of care and nature's unfolding. The same can be said about caring for animals. To be sure, human beings can and often do tend to vegetable gardens and animals in instrumental ways. We need to eat and have dwellings. But the industrialization of farming crops and animals has led to significant environmental harms and here we see instrumentality or objectification of nature at its worse. The rise of sustainable farming[129] and care for animals that will be "humanely" killed for consumption is a direct response to the mass industrialization of agriculture. My point here is that care, even if instrumental, *can* include nature

128. Agamben, *The Kingdom and the Glory*, xiii.
129. See Bialik and Walker, "Organic Farming is on the Rise in the U.S."

and other species and necessarily needs to do so if human beings are to dwell on this one habitat.

I recognize that many Christians have argued that we are to care for the earth and its residents because we are, as God commands, to be stewards of creation.[130] Christoph Baumgartner points out that "the religious notion of stewardship has not always been free of instrumental and anthropocentric attitudes of humanity toward nature."[131] When stewardship is connected to the religious idea of God giving human beings dominion over the earth, we can be sure of an anthropocentric attitude and belief in human superiority. Even when dominion and stewardship are accompanied by care, one can be sure political violence vis-à-vis nature follows in its wake. While I think the Judeo-Christian idea of stewardship is salvageable in the Anthropocene Age, it can be so only when it sheds it anthropocentric, narcissistic view that human beings are superior to nature (and somehow distinct from nature) and thus justified in exploiting other species and the earth. If we are to retain a religious version of stewardship, we must recognize that the command to care for creation means we are vulnerable and dependent on the earth, as are all other species. Moreover, stewardship is political in the sense that there is a recognition that the very existential facticity of the polis is dependent on a viable earth.

Given this, I now turn to providing a theological grounding of care as a political concept and method of political change, while also arguing that political violence is not theologically justifiable. Recall again Paul's letter to the Philippians wherein we read that Jesus, "though he was in the form of God, did not regard equality with God as something to be exploited, but emptied (*kenosis*) himself, taking the form of a slave, being born in human likeness. And being found in human form, he humbled himself and became obedient to the point of death—even death on a cross" (2:6–8). The incarnation as a kenotic event represents the infinite, indeterminate care of God for human beings (and all creation). It was an act of care aimed at all human beings equally. Add to this that taking on the form of an enslaved human being can be understood as a political act in that enslaved people are outside the space of appearances, though they reside in the polis as included-excluded Others. To construct a slave *qua* slave requires forms of political violence and threats of violence. Human beings do not willingly become or remain slaves (politically irrelevant) without the use and threat of political violence. Yet, why take on the form of a slave? Why would this be an act of political

130. See Hescox and Douglas, *Caring for Creation*; Miller, *God, Creation, and Climate Change*; Jorgenson and Hayhoe, *Ecotheology*.

131. Baumgartner, "Transformations of Stewardship in the Anthropocene," 57.

care, let alone a method of change? Yet, God taking on the form of a slave is a political act that defies the forms of political violence that creates and sustains enslaved persons.

Here I turn to Giorgio Agamben's notion of inoperativity to explicate this further. Agamben contends that social-political-economic apparatuses or disciplinary regimes produce forms of subjectivity or governable selves that are deprived of their singularity or suchness.[132] Enslaved individuals are produced and denied their singularity or personhood by virtue of the varied apparatuses that rely on political violence to enforce slavery. Jesus, in taking on the form of a slave, makes these apparatuses inoperative vis-à-vis his singularity. Inoperativity is a concept that indicates it is possible to de-activate the functioning of the apparatuses, which does not mean that these apparatuses do not continue to operate or do not continue to have negative effects.[133] Put differently, inoperativity means that Jesus was not captive to the grammar of the Roman apparatuses and their attending political violence. It is important to stress that, for Agamben, inoperativity is not passive. That is, inoperativity does not "affirm inertia, inactivity or apraxia . . . but a form of praxis that is devoid of any telos or task, does not realize any essence and does not correspond to any nature."[134] Jesus' actions of care (includes taking on the form of a slave) represent the indeterminate, unconditioned love of a non-sovereign God.[135] Put differently, taking on the form of a slave was a political act in that Jesus made inoperative the apparatuses of political violence aimed at the most politically marginalized group and as a result restores the *possibility* of the space of speaking and acting together, restores the *possibility* self-esteem, self-respect, and self-confidence for any and all Othered individuals and communities. This is the inbreaking of the kingdom of God that is without a sovereign, without political violence, and where acts of care are radically inclusive, founding the possibility of a polis not based on the organizing principle of violence. Jesus taking on the form of a slave makes *inoperative the ontologizing of political violence* as the organizing principle of the polis and instead reveals the *ontological premise of care* as the organizing principle of any polis.

We can extend this perspective to nature. To enslave human beings means to construct them as inferior and to treat them instrumentally.[136]

132. Prozorov, *Agamben and Politics*, 24.

133. Prozorov, *Agamben and Politics*, 31–34.

134. Prozorov, *Agamben and Politics*, 33.

135. See Caputo, *The Weakness of God*.

136. Martin Buber's distinction between I–Thou and I–It relations is reminiscent of what I am talking about. In the West, most neoliberal Christians have an I–It relation to nature and other species. Buber, *I and Thou*.

They, as included-excluded Others, are constructed to serve the needs of their masters and their value is seen in how well they do this. This attitude and relation extends to nature. More often than not, human beings treat nature as solely existing to serve our needs—exclusively—as if nature as a whole and other species do not have their own singularity or suchness. To think and be otherwise in the Anthropocene Age, we need to broaden the revelation of God's indeterminate and infinite care manifested in the incarnation. We need to profess and act on the revelation of Jesus taking on the form of a slave making inoperative all relations (and attending apparatuses of political-economic violence) of domination, subjugation, and instrumentalization. In so doing, nature becomes part of the polis, not as a servant or a slave to meet the needs of human masters, but rather as an integral part of dwelling.

There is another act of political care that is inoperative and that further illuminates the non-sovereignty of God and the absence of political violence as a means of organizing the polis/ecclesia. In the Gospel of Luke (23:34), Jesus, after being tortured and crucified, forgives his tormentors. This is not Yoder's act of revolutionary subordination, but rather an act of care that makes inoperative the grammar of Roman political violence. It is an act that invites the *possibility* of a space of speaking and acting together in the present and not some magical future. It is an act that reveals that care—in this instance embodied in the act of forgiveness—is the organizing principle of the ekklesia, eschewing the political violence of empire. It is a nonviolent act that refuses to submit or be subordinate to the machinations of Roman political violence. It is more than simply resistance. Better, it makes inoperative the apparatuses of political violence, though of course not their effects.

The early Christian community seen in Acts can be seen as an attempt to make inoperative apparatuses of political violence that found a polis through relations of exclusion and subjugation. Instead, an ekklesia is a political assembly that is organized around inclusive caring relations[137] and, because the ekklesia is an agonistic space, there is the need for forgiveness to repair relations and restore the space of speaking and acting together.[138]

137. A number of Christian scholars advocate for a radical democracy, finding support (and problems) in reinterpreting scripture. I find I am sympathetic to many of these efforts because they advocate equality, inclusion, liberation, as well as nonviolent methods of change. My only quibble is that democracy presupposes sovereignty, though in this case it is the sovereignty of the people. I have already explicated a number of problems with the notion of human or divine sovereignty. The direction of these chapters lean toward anarchic forms of organizing the polis. See Eggemeier, *Against Empire*.

138. Hannah Arendt makes clear that the practice of forgiveness is necessary for a viable and flourishing polis. Arendt, *The Promise of Politics*.

The ekklesia reveals the possibility of a polis that does not rely on the political violence of sovereignty. Indeed, the revelation of the indeterminate, infinite care of God for humanity in the ministry of Jesus is a testament to the unjustifiable nature of political violence, whether in organizing a polis or rebelling against a sovereign,[139] and a testament to the forms of resistance to apparatuses that undermine acts of care. Finally, this ekklesia can offer a possibility for relating to nature, not in terms of subordination, domination, or instrumentality, but out of care for the earth as the material foundation of not only life, but also the ekklesia. Human beings need the earth to survive; the earth does not need human beings for its survival.

I have been arguing from an existential and theological perspective that care is the method for change. To be sure, political violence can result in changes or prevent changes, but it is, I argue, anti-political and also not justifiable. To care for each other and the earth does not mean that the sixth extinction will end. Just as we do not always know the consequences of political violence, we do not know the future of our acts of care. When we think of Jesus caring for people and for those who tormented him, we can readily see that there were no radical political changes that resulted. Instead, the Roman Empire continued chugging along for centuries. Moreover, Christianity eventually became institutionalized and political in its identification with the state, often initiating and supporting diverse forms of political violence toward Othered human beings and other species. The radical revelation of Christianity may have been overlooked and denied in favor of the expediency and pleasure of political violence, especially when Christianity fell under the seduction of Constantinian sovereignty. Nevertheless, the ontological and existential necessity of care for and in the polis (including nature) remains. Regardless of what future lies ahead, care is and remains a categorical imperative and a method of political change that is inclusive and non-hierarchical. Let me add that if we are to engage in political change given the new realities of the Anthropocene Age, we will need to think and be otherwise than Christians (traditionally understood). Change will involve a Christianity of a non-sovereign God; a Christianity without hierarchy and exclusion; a Christianity that makes inoperative the Christianity of history so as to imagine a realistic future on earth—a radical change based in inclusive care of othered human beings, othered species, and the earth.

139. Let me stress that rebellions and revolutions may have very understandable and justifiable motivations for emancipation, which does not mean that the use of political violence to attain political goals is justifiable.

## Conclusion

A radical political theology must interrogate methods associated with political change. Political violence seems to be a common method for engaging in political change, and I have argued it is morally bankrupt, both with regard to organizing the polis and toward nature itself. I certainly understand that desperate, oppressed people may view violent revolution as the only way to achieve liberation. There are many instances in history of political violence being used to achieve freedom. I also understand that some climate activists may resort to political violence to try to achieve their goals of a better climate and a viable earth. Despite these positive ends, the means are not justifiable because of the relations political violence instantiates. As Johanna Oksala writes, "In the realm of politics anything is possible, even the end of violence."[140] The end of violence or to make political violence inoperative, a worthy goal, can only be brought about by care—care of other human beings, other species, and the earth. This, it seems to me, is a key feature of the incarnation, but whether care as a political method will bring about sufficient change to alter the trajectory of climate change is another question and one that raises the question of hope.

---

140. Oksala, *Foucault, Politics, and Violence*, 156.

# 6

## *The Problem of Hope*
## *in the Anthropocene Age*

---

Disaster overtakes disaster, the whole land is laid waste . . . I looked
on the earth, and lo, it was waste and void; and to the heavens, and
they had no light. I looked to the mountains, and lo, they were quak-
ing, and all the hills moved to and fro. I looked, and lo, there was no
one at all, and all the birds of the air had fled. I looked, and lo, the
fruitful land was a desert, and all the cities were laid in ruins.
(Jer 4:20, 23–24)

To hope is to bury one's head in the sands of peace, making
us useless to meet the inevitable struggle that is coming.[1]

Hope is a feeling that waxes and wanes, sometimes brilliant and
luminous, sometimes a faint sliver in the sky, sometimes gone completely. No matter how hopeful or hopeless we feel, we can choose
to return to the labor anyway. Sometimes we receive the gift of our
labor. Sometimes we do not. But it does not matter. Because when we
labor in love, labor is not only a means but an end in itself.[2]

This is our defiance—to practice love even in hopelessness.[3]

1. De La Torre, *Embracing Hopelessness*, 96.

2. Kaur, *See No Stranger*, 241.

3. Kaur, *See No Stranger*, 243.

In the end, do we have the courage to care without hope?[4]

Two scenes have stayed with me years after watching director James Cameron's film *Titanic*. In one scene, it is clear to many passengers and crew that the ship is sinking and there are not enough lifeboats—why have sufficient lifeboats when the ship is unsinkable? In the frigid darkness, a number of people gather on the upper deck and play music, until such time the slant of the deck becomes too steep, leaving the musicians to slide into the waiting icy waters. The other scene is of an elderly couple who realize that they will not be able to get off the ship. Even now, I remember them calmly and tenderly holding each other in their cabin. The musicians' and the couple's actions were not based on hope, but neither did their actions emerge from despair. To be sure, there was fear and dread, yet these powerful emotions did not deter their acts of care.

The story of the Titanic is, in part, an apt analogy given the realities of climate change. There was the hubris of engineers who believed they had built an unsinkable ship and the hubris of the captain who rejected the typical nautical caution when plying the waters of the North Atlantic at night. With regard to climate change though, we are not in the early evening when a captain decides whether or not to slow down and be wary of icebergs. Instead, we already have hit the iceberg of climate change. Like the passengers and crew who hoped the ship would not sink and later hoped to be rescued, many people today have the temerity to believe and hope that science alone will save us from the grim realities of climate change, while others hope for becoming an interplanetary species, escaping an unhabitable earth. In another way, the story is fitting in that the Titanic represents a polis, with the captain as the sovereign, the crew representing governmentality, and the passengers dwelling with the crew on the ship. The unelected leader made a tragic decision and the crew carried it out. Perhaps we could say it is a story where the illusion of sovereignty and its apparatuses failed, sinking to the depths of the sea. Today, we might wonder about the hubris, greed, and opportunism of elected and unelected leaders—leaders who are failing to commit to actions aimed at mitigating the effects of climate change. Of course, the failure of leaders does not let the rest of us off the hook of accountability with regard to contributing to climate change, as well as our responsibility to act individually and collectively to make changes. The story, however, does not fit because it overlooks nature and the fact that

4. The author.

millions of species will become extinct, having had no access to a lifeboat; it is also inapt in that it is not likely that help will arrive to save the privileged remnant who happen to secure a lifeboat.

When it comes to the realities and future consequences of climate change, many of us ask: what hope is there for human beings, other-than-human beings, and the earth as the foundation of all dwelling? In what and in whom do we place our hope? Will we be able to alter course in time? One can sense the anxiety, fear, and dread that give rise to the question of hope when facing the dire realities of the Anthropocene Age. A political theology may provide readers with a kind of radical hope based on the Judeo-Christian scripture, but this is not the aim of this chapter. Instead, I believe there are problems with hope and Christian hope in particular, when we consider what we are facing and will face in the Anthropocene Age. This does not mean I am against hope—Christian or otherwise—but given the problems of hope, I offer a different question and answer. How will we care in the present for each other, other-than-human beings, and the earth given present and future climate disasters? This question and its answers are political, not only because they necessarily involve poleis, but also because they necessarily include other species and the earth. The question of hope is in the background, not in the sense of being unimportant, but rather because it is not the source of motivation and action in addressing the realities of the Anthropocene Age. More specifically, a radical political theology grounded in care is an antidote to the temptations of illusory hope, facile optimism, and despair, which arise when hope is not realized or realizable.

To flesh out the argument, I begin by discussing, in general terms, what is meant by hope and its attributes. Since hope is always particular, it important to outline briefly hope from a Christian perspective. From here, I identify some of the political problems with hope and Christian hope, such as anthropocentrism, narcissism, and megalomania. This sets the stage for framing a radical political theology in terms of existential and theological aspects of passionate and courageous care for each other, other species, and the earth, placing the issue and question of hope secondary to motivation, action, and results. In this section, I also argue that a political theology for the Anthropocene is based on a radical Christianity that is not defined by or dependent on hope for survival and flourishing in the present or in some future ethereal realm.

Before beginning, I wish to offer a few comments to further clarify my interest here. In the last 10 to 20 years, a great deal of ink has been spilled on topics like eco-anxiety, eco-melancholia, eco-mourning, eco-guilt, eco-despair, and eco-denial. These are understandable emotional responses as people become aware of and experience the impact of climate change. In one sense, I see these responses as, in some ways, emerging from answers to the existential question of hope—hope primarily for human beings. We are anxious because of an unknown future for ourselves and our children. Facing the devastation of the earth, we mourn for ourselves, other creatures, and for the loss of the beauty of the earth. In our mourning, which is mixed with guilt, we question whether hope is possible. Dare we hope? Rather than face the present and coming disasters, many refuse this question and instead pursue a strategy of denial and ignorance, secretly fearing not simply the future, but also enervating depression and despair. I add that these emotional responses take place within the context of and in response to varied political milieus and how various poleis respond to the threats of climate change. The question of hope, then, also seems to arise in light of a political (and ecclesial) milieu. That said, by exploring the problems of hope, we can arrive at a place where hope is not the basis for our action and change. Instead, we may come to rely on passionate and courageous care—an existential imperative to care in the present even in the face of hopelessness. A second caveat and clarification concerns how much has been said about hope in Christian theological literature[5] and, in particular, theologies that address climate change.[6] As one can imagine, the literature is vast and deep, leaving one with a sense that hope is integral to Christianity. Perhaps it is, but to delve into this literature would take me astray from the task at hand. Instead, I rely on various texts in my discussion on the contours of hope and in the discussion on some of the problems of hope. It will be clear, I hope, that a radical political theology embraces a Christianity that is not dependent on hope, especially an anthropocentric hope, but rather is grounded in the ontological imperative to care for others, other species, and the earth even in the face of human extinction.

## Hope and Its Attributes

Some years ago, while chatting with a student during a break, I mentioned some situations in ministry when there is no hope. Before I had a chance to explain what I meant, another student, sitting across the room, who had apparently overheard, responded with alacrity and passion, "There is always hope!" Apparently, my comment had struck a chord, a chord of anxiety and anger. The very idea of a hopeless was obviously disturbing. If I had said

5. See Henriksen, "Hope"; Moltmann, *Theology of Hope*; Moltmann, *The Spirit of Hope*; Campbell, *Paul and the Hope of Glory*; Brown-Crawford, *Hope in the Holler*.

6. See Poole, *Christianity in a Time of Climate Change*; Floyd, *Down to Earth*; Doran, *Hope in the Age of Climate Change*; Keller, *Political Theology of the Earth*.

that there are occasions in ministry when there is no love, no care, devoid of anything just, I am confident there would have been agreement. What was intolerable was the idea that a person and situation could be without hope. Who would have thought that a seemingly simple four-letter word would evoke so much emotional energy and so much spilt ink over the centuries? In this, I briefly offer some thoughts about this four-letter word, discussing some of its attributes, as well as its relation to agency.

One of the first things we notice about hope is that it is often seen as a feeling or emotion. Even infants have an inchoate or pre-representational feeling of hope evident in their crying out. Their crying can be understood as an expression of the hope that a parent (the world) will respond. I cannot remember where I read this, but during the Nazi bombings of England there were many children and infants who survived when their parents did not. The resources to care for these children were understandably stretched thin during this precarious period. Infants were placed in capacious rooms where one nurse was assigned per room. What they discovered was that within two weeks the rooms were silent. I suspect the infants lost hope that anyone would respond to their cries of need. Infant-parent researcher Daniel Stern uses a term "vitality affects" to refer to infants' pre-symbolic affects that provide a child with a sense of being alive.[7] Hope may be said to be one of those early global affects.

A pre-representational or pre-symbolic construction of hope accompanies what Erik Erikson called the first task of development, namely trust-mistrust.[8] To return to the orphaned babies, the lack of timely responses to their cries gave rise to a lack of trust in the environment or what Winnicott called the environmental mother,[9] which accompanies the feeling of hopelessness. Recall from earlier chapters that trust-distrust is one of the dialectical aspects of faith (the others being belief-disbelief and loyalty-disloyalty), which suggests that hope is not simply a feeling; it is also a part of relational faith and, in this case, a pre-representational relational faith vis-à-vis one's parents. Ideally, then, a child develops a feeling of hope in speaking and acting together with a parent who attunes to their child's assertions. While I will say more about this below, it is clear, given the example of the British children, that *caring actions provide the foundation for pre-representational experiences of trust and feelings of hope.*

To play with this further, we could say that the infants in those rooms began with a disposition to trust that someone would hear their cries and

---

7. Stern, *The Interpersonal World of the Infant.*
8. Erikson, *Childhood and Society.*
9. Winnicott, *Playing and Reality.*

respond to comfort them and meet their needs. Over time, the children became silent, suggesting that they did not possess enough hope to act—to cry out. So, we could say, at this point, hope involves a *disposition* that initiates an action. Edward Farley writes that "my hopeful disposition, so orients me to action that my future is reshaped . . . For only acting changes the future, and to act, one must have hope."[10] This is echoed by Paul Hoggett, who claims that "hope is essential to human agency."[11] Both views can move someone like Anderson Jeremiah to conclude (wrongly in my view) that "Without hope, a person can be considered empty."[12] Given this perspective, children's lack of feelings of hope gave rise to a disposition wherein the future is closed, which, in turn, explains why they did not act in the sense of crying out. While I will address some problems with this formulation later, for now we need only indicate that hope comprises feeling, disposition, and action.

Things get more complicated when we consider that, for many Christians, hope is not simply a feeling or experience or disposition; it is also a cherished, if not essential, virtue.[13] The idea of virtue moves us to consider that hope entails particular practices aimed at a good, at least ideally, and this entails an evaluative capacity.[14] Put differently, we could say "that hope entails an expectation of the good."[15] Individuals exercise the virtue of hope through various skills they develop and these skills are directed toward a desired good.[16] The view that hope is a virtue is contested, especially if we consider Greek philosophers, many of whom had a negative view of hope and did not consider it a virtue.[17] In one Greek myth, Zeus places hope in the bottom of Pandora's box, "beneath greed, vanity, slander, envy, and other dark realms of human experience."[18] Indeed, Aristotle, who had a more balanced view, considered hope to be integral to the virtue of courage,

10. Farley, *Deep Symbols*, 97.

11. Hoggett, "Climate Change in a Perverse Culture," 83.

12. Jeremiah, "Farming Grief and Hope," 84.

13. See Bochanski, *The Virtue of Hope*; Pieper, *Faith, Hope, and Love*; Wilson, *Gospel Virtues*.

14. Nussbaum, *The Monarchy of Fear*, 203.

15. Henriksen, "Hope," 128.

16. If one argues that hope is a basis for action in relation to the future, then it appears to be a contradiction that hope is also a practice associated with virtues. Does hope precede action? And if so, it appears that one needs to have hope to practice the virtue of hope. This may be why Aristotle argued that hope was a part of the virtue of courage and not a virtue in and of itself.

17. See Bloeser and Stahl, "Hope."

18. Mitchell, *Hope and Dread in Psychoanalysis*, 228.

though he did not see hope as a virtue.[19] For the Greek Stoics, it was best to live in the now and not pin your hopes on some future good.[20] Roman philosophers also had a negative view of hope. Seneca, a Stoic Roman philosopher, claimed that "You will cease to fear, if you cease to hope. Both belong to a soul that is hanging in suspense, to a soul made anxious by concern with the future."[21] While relying on Greek and Roman philosophers, it has been Christian theologians and philosophers who altered this perspective, opting for hope to be one of the cardinal virtues.

Hope, as a virtue, does not stand alone from other Christian virtues. Henriksen points out that some theologians understand "Christian hope as an activity-shaped and faith-based hope that expresses itself in love for all humankind."[22] The source of the interconnected virtues of hope and love is God, which makes "a difference in faith and action, prayer and work."[23] This virtue, Henriksen claims, "allows us to see and engage with the social world in a new way.[24]

Of course, if we believe that hope is a virtue, then it follows that despair is a vice or what the early Church Fathers called a deadly sin. Vices, like virtues, entail practices, though they are not directed at a good. Despair, for instance, views the future as not only bad, but determined. This said, is there a difference between the feeling/disposition of despair and an individual having no hope of rescue? The elderly couple in the movie realized the ship was rapidly sinking, leaving them no hope to be rescued. We might imagine that they believed their immediate future was determined and bad. Was their embrace an act of despair or perhaps an act of love in spite of hopelessness?[25] The men and women who played music on the deck of the sinking Titanic likely knew they would not be rescued. They played music despite the hopelessness of the situation. My aim here is not to delve into the complexities of despair as a vice, but rather to briefly note the challenges of viewing hope in terms of virtue and its opposite as a vice.

19. Gravlee, "Aristotle on Hope," 471–77.

20. Sorabji, *Emotion and Peace of Mind*, 235.

21. Seneca, quoted in Nussbaum, *The Monarchy of Fear*, 204.

22. Henriksen, "Hope," 127.

23. Henriksen, "Hope," 130.

24. Henriksen, "Hope," 130.

25. The reader may recall in the Introduction my mentioning the novel *The Coming*, where a man and woman secretly expressed their love for each other on a slave ship. If there was ever a situation of despair or hopelessness, this was it. Yet, they acted to affirm their love in spite of the realities of their situation. Was their love an expression of hope? I would say it was not. It was an affirmation of the good of each other—a good more powerful than the despairing realities of slavery. Black, *The Coming*.

When we consider that hope is the expectation of a good and, for many, a virtue, then it follows that there must be some means of achieving the good, some practice or method that both represents and reaches for the good. If I hope to win the lottery, I have to at least do the work to purchase a ticket. If Robert hopes to be a nurse, then he will need to go to nursing school. When we hear someone say they hope to serve the country by being elected to Congress and, in the process, engages in nefarious practices to obtain the seat, then we could hardly say the individual's hope reflects a virtue. To use corrupt or evil methods to realize a "good" is a distortion of hope. Let me shift to an example from the Anthropocene Age, which will tease out another factor of hope and means of fulfilling hopeful expectations. In a previous chapter, I mentioned that some economists believe that, with some revisions, the Market, they hope, can be used to reduce the effects of global warming. These economists overlook capitalism's role in global warming, as well as the fact that capitalism itself lacks an ethos for the common good (for human beings and other species). All forms of capitalism, as Marx and numerous others recognized, are based on the fundamental premise of exploitative relations. Only strong protections can keep capitalist exploitation at bay, but these protections cannot eradicate the core feature of capitalist relations—between human beings, other species, and the earth. To use capitalism as a method for attaining one's hope of changing the trajectory of global warming would, in my view, reflect a distortion of hope, precisely because the means of attaining hope is corrupt.

A related feature of hope evident above is its relation to time and memory. Our hopes are founded in the past and expressed in the present toward an uncertain or unclear, yet possible future.[26] Hope, John Caputo writes, "is the affirmation of the future,"[27] though it is a future that cannot be determined. As Edward Farley notes, "hope has the character of both waiting and acting."[28] The Israelites cried out to God about their present suffering at the hands of the Pharaoh in the hope of God's present consolation and future liberation. They would not have cried out if they had not had a past relation and memories of Yahweh. While the past was clearer, the future was not. They did not know what awaited them once liberated, which gave rise to anxiety and the occasional grumble. After the diaspora, the idea of next year in Jerusalem expressed a collective hope, rooted in collective memory, the possibility of a return to living in the land of their ancestors.

26. See Whitehead, *Redeeming Fear*, 96.
27. Caputo, *Hoping Against Hope*, 141.
28. Farley, *Deep Symbols*, 100.

For some Christian theologians, like Wolfart Pannenberg,[29] hope entails a present reality of God's future kingdom. The presence of God among us, while partially realized, is connected to the future kingdom where we will experience the fullness of communion with God. The future reality reaches back into the present albeit partial in its fullness. For Henriksen, Christian "Hope opens up the future in—and of—the present world."[30] There are also innumerable quotidian examples of hope and time in everyday life. As mentioned above, children's hopes are based on past experiences/memories of parental care. Sally has hope that David, her boyfriend, will agree to marry, because of her past experiences with him. Even when David says yes, the future remains open and not fixed. In terms of the Anthropocene Age, some scientists may hope that scientific solutions will forestall climate disasters.[31] Others may hope to be an interplanetary species and escape the realities of climate change. Both groups have memories of science having altered present and future realities. For instance, we would expect that engineers and scientists who have hope work in the present to devise machines that will solve or mitigate the various problems associated with climate change or, like Elon Musk, build rockets, robots, inhabitable environments, etc., as they prepare to colonize Mars or some other orb. Someone might point out that the Anthropocene Age is unique, which suggests that we do not have a past to rely on with regard to our hopes for the future. For scientists, engineers, and others, this may be unique, but human beings have faced existential threats in the past and science has responded. The recent pandemic would be one example. Past examples may be the basis for hope, at least for some.

The issue of time and memory with regard to hope also helps us discern when action is based on hope or something else. If a scientist or engineer (who had the knowledge and skills) had hope that climate change could be reversed yet did nothing, then this would fall into the realm of wishful thinking. Also, if a person is taking the past and trying to determine the future, then this would not be hope. Another example is someone who ignores the present and likely future realties of global warming, saying they are simply going to live their lives. This person's hope is narrowed to their life and relationships, which in my view would be a distortion precisely because of a willed refusal to acknowledge future realities based on present-day behaviors.

Connected to time and memory is another feature of hope. Hope depends on the community's or society's symbol systems and rituals, giving

29. Pannenberg, *Theology and the Kingdom of God.*
30. Henriksen, "Hope," 130.
31. See Speth, *The Bridge at the Edge of the World,* 234.

hope its particularity. These symbol systems are part of a society's apparatuses, which maintain memory, provide knowledge, facilitate dwelling together in the present, and point residents toward a possible future. Israelites
hoped for liberation based on the tradition of God's promises to them as a
chosen people. Christians may hope to be with God in eternity based on
the Gospel stories. Americans may hope for the American dream of being
financially successful, having a nice home, cars, etc. At a micro level, a child
hopes that she will receive presents for Christmas, because of the stories
she has been told about Santa Claus. A less fanciful example is the hope
of Ta-Nehisi Coates when he was a young man wanting to attend Howard
University, because he believed it was an educational sanctuary for young
African Americans.

Hope as a feeling, disposition and its relation to faith, agency, virtue,
time, memory, and symbol systems suggests that it is intimately part of
the polis. When Giorgio Agamben points out that politics is humankind's
"most proper dimension,"[32] he is also, in my view, saying that hope (and
hopelessness) emerges within the context of the political. Similarly, Edward
Farley writes that hope "is something at work in a community and it arises
in individuals as they partake of it."[33] This view does not mean that all of
our hopes are political, but that the very ability to hope, as well as all of our
particular hopes, rest on spaces of speaking and acting together and the
symbol systems and apparatuses that support and maintain these spaces of
appearances and their particular expressions of hope. A negative example
will illustrate this claim. Jonathan Lear writes about the Crow people and
their leader Plenty Coups.[34] When he was a young boy, Plenty Coups had
a dream. When someone had a powerful dream, the practice was to share
the dream with the elders, who would help interpret it, relying on the Crow
symbol system. In the dream, Plenty Coups observes countless buffalo and
then the plains are empty of buffalo. In another scene, the plains are filled
with spotted buffalo (cattle), which were completely strange to him and disturbing because of the lack of the familiar buffalos upon whom the Crow
depended. There is yet another scene in the dream sequence. A huge storm
arises "in which the Four Winds begin a war against the forest. All the trees
are knocked down but one."[35] In the dream, Plenty Coups hears a voice:

> Listen Plenty Coups. In that tree is the lodge of the Chickadee.
> He is least in strength but strongest of mind among his kind.

32. Agamben, *The Kingdom and the Glory*, xiii.
33. Farley, *Deep Symbols*, 98.
34. Lear, *Radical Hope*.
35. Lear, *Radical Hope*, 70.

He is willing to work for wisdom. The Chickadee-person is a good listener. Nothing escapes his ears, which he has sharpened by constant use . . . He never intrudes, never speaks in strange company, and yet never misses a chance to learn from others. He gains successes and avoids failures by learning how others succeeded or failed . . . The lodges of countless Bird-people were in the forest when the Four Winds charged it. Only one person is left unharmed, the lodge of the Chickadee-person.[36]

The dream presents a future of devastation and loss. The Crow people, like all other native peoples, were forced to move from their ancestral lands and give up their culture. As Lear points out, the Crow people could no longer live out their ego-ideals because the symbol system that supported these ideals was inoperative, which raised the question of what the future as Crows people would mean or look like. In other words, the devastating loss of culture gave rise to the question of hope—hope as a people. Can a people hope if their cultural symbol system no longer informs people of a possible future as a distinct people? Lear argues that Plenty Coups' story is an instance of radical hope. Radical hope, Lear writes, "is directed toward a future goodness that transcends the current ability to understand what it is . . . This hope is radical in that it is aiming for a subjectivity that is at once Crow and does not yet exist."[37] The dream, then, represents a new ego-ideal—the Chickadee-person (as Crow identity). There were no more warriors counting coups. Instead, the physically weak Chickadee, who has the wisdom to observe, learn, and survive in the midst of the devastation, became the ego-ideal that helped them imagine a future of a Crow polis.

The point here is that before Euro-Americans arrived, the Crow people's hopes emerged from speaking and acting together, and this space of appearances depended on the shared symbol system that shaped their identity, memory, agency, and visions of the good. The question that arose in the midst of cultural devastation was not simply how they would live together as Crow people, but also what it might mean to hope as a Crow people—collectively and individually. The seed of hope is evident in the dream, wherein in the midst of the devastation was the Chickadee-person who survives by her wits. Instead of sinking into despair and violence,[38] Plenty Coups

36. Lear, *Radical Hope*, 70.

37. Lear, *Radical Hope*, 103–4.

38. Lear points out that Sitting Bull had a messianic, violent vision and response, which led to an overwhelmingly violent response of U.S. soldiers. Sitting Bull faced the same challenges as Plenty Coups, but chose to retain the warrior ego-ideal instead of acknowledging loss and constructing new symbols and practices. Lear, *Radical Hope*, 148–50.

and his people mourned the loss of the buffalo (read also symbol system), choosing to adapt and move into the future with a vision of survival.[39] The story of the Crow people illustrates the relation between hope and the polis.

Before moving on, I want to connect this to the challenges of the Anthropocene Age. I think Lear's depiction of radical hope in the midst of cultural devastation is, in part, an apt illustration of the link between hope and the polis, but it runs into a wall when we consider the Anthropocene Age and the very real possibility of human extinction. Obviously, the extinction of human beings means the extinction of cultures. This possibility portends that all of our particular hopes are futile, ashes in the face of the cataclysmic realities of the Anthropocene Age. If, as Farley notes, our actions are necessarily based in hope, then a future extinction of human beings would leave us paralyzed in a sea of despair. Of course, the possibility of extinction also includes the possibility that human beings will survive. Yet what does it mean to survive if the culture's dominant symbols systems (largely Western, capitalism, imperialism, nationalism—intersecting with religious symbol systems), which have given rise to climate change, remain intact? Do we hope for human survival based on these symbol systems? Do we retain memory, identity, ego-ideals, agency, faith, and visions of capitalism, imperialism, and nationalism? Or do we need to think and be otherwise like the Crow people and their ego-ideal of the Chickadee? Can we, like the Crow people, mourn, while retaining the possibility of a polis where the wise and "weak" work together in the midst of climate disasters?

## The Problems of Hope

I can imagine that many people, like my student, would be perplexed if someone were to say that there are problems with hope and, in particular, Christian hope. How could "hope" be a problem, if, as they say, millions of climate activists and scientists are devoting their lives to reduce the effects of climate change? Why problematize hope, when clearly it serves to motivate people to get involved in climate justice? Identifying some of the problems of hope does not mean that I am against hope or that I opt for embracing hopelessness/despair.[40] Acknowledging some of the problems with hope can help us from sinking into despair, violence, and apathy. But more important, understanding some of the problems of hope opens the door to

---

39. One can only imagine the struggle to hope when African men and women were ripped from the fabric of family and tribe and forced into slavery in a strange land, with a strange language and symbols.

40. De Le Torre, *Embracing Hopelessness*.

consider another, more durable and sustainable source of motivation and action. Toward this end, let me offer some thoughts about the problems of hope.

In my experience, Christians get anxious when someone questions hope or raises the possibility of hopelessness. Theologian Jason Whitehead writes that "Without hope, the possibilities of love and grace as practical acts of faith lose their flavor and meaning. Hope reveals our sense that the world can be a better place, that people can relate more meaningfully, and that God is present, active, and caring."[41] Jürgen Moltmann is, in one sense, a theologian of hope, which he understands as passion for the possible. Using Paul Tillich's view of faith as ultimate concern, Moltmann believes that "without hope for the ultimate" human beings turn violent.[42] Add to this systematic theologian Edward Farley's view that human action is contingent on hope, and we begin to see that, for many theologians, "hope" is a fundamental reality of human existence and Christianity. In terms of the Anthropocene Age, theologian Catherine Keller remarks that "To come to our end without hope, is this not the future we fear?"[43] "Does this hopelessness," she continues, "not lead many politically responsible and ecologically sensitive thinkers to abandon hope as nothing but cruel optimism?"[44] Her answer is to opt for a fibrous hope that does not entail a "heavenly happy ending,"[45] but rather faces squarely the challenges of the Anthropocene Age. Keller and others see the problems of hope in terms of wishful thinking, false optimism, or enervating despair. But Christians are not alone in gripping tightly to the importance of hope. Erik Erikson remarked that hope is "the earliest and most indispensable virtue inherent in the state of being alive."[46] If the loss of hope is equated with a decline of love and grace, an increase in violence, inability to act, and a state of deadness, one can understand why these and other writers spend so much time touting hope as integral to faith and life. For these theologians and for Erikson, then, it is inconceivable to live without hope, because, in my view, they equate the absence of hope with despair. They construct hope to be in a binary relationship with hopelessness. These strong statements, then, screen an underlying anxiety about the loss of hope, which is a problem.

41. Whitehead, *Redeeming Fear*, 37.

42. Moltmann, *The Living God and the Fullness of Life*, 180.

43. Keller, *Political Theology of the Earth*, 173.

44. Keller, *Political Theology of the Earth*, 173–74.

45. Keller, *Political Theology of the Earth*, 175.

46. Erikson, *Insight and Responsibility*, 115.

A significant problem with hope is not hope itself, but that so many people link the loss of hope with despair or hopelessness. For instance, political philosopher Martha Nussbaum claims that Kant was right that "good works need hope."[47] She goes on to cite the liberative actions of Martin Luther King Jr., Gandhi, and Nelson Mandela, arguing that they were "people of hope and vision, who saw a beautiful future and worked energetically to realize it. Despair or cynical resignation are attitudes incompatible with bold action and committed work."[48] This binary relation is also supported by collective narratives and practices. This is a fundamental problem because it reduces the complexity of human psychology and behavior into a false choice, namely hope or despair, which can heighten a person's anxiety[49] and occlude other possibilities of relating, in this case, to nature and other species. This can also be understood as a problem using the concept of differentiation.[50] Differentiation is widely used in family systems theory to refer to the capacity to be oneself while interacting with significant others. It can also refer to the ability to differentiate thoughts and feelings. In terms of hope, the anxiety associated with the loss of hope (despair) suggests that the feeling is defining who I am and how I engage the world. A more differentiated and complex stance is to say, "I have a feeling of hope (or hopelessness)," which does not define me or my behavior. So, the loss of that feeling does not shift one into despair or hopelessness. When faith, action, etc. become defined in relation to the binary of hope-despair, there is a tendency to lower one's capacity for differentiation. A more differentiated stance provides greater flexibility and freedom in our actions, even when one has a feeling of hopelessness. To return to the examples from the Titanic, the elderly couple likely felt hopeless, but this did not interfere with their love of and faith in each other. Similarly, the artists who played their instruments to provide solace in the face of anguish may have felt hopeless, yet they were able to continue their performance. Hopelessness, in other words, did not define them or their behavior. This becomes critically important in the Anthropocene Age, when intense emotional experiences will be expected given the difficulties we face. If political and religious leaders

47. Nussbaum, *The Monarchy of Fear*, 209.

48. Nussbaum, *The Monarchy of Fear*, 210.

49. Nussbaum later claims that "hope is stepping in the waters of chance, unafraid." This is highly problematic when one considers the biographies of two people she mentions, namely King and Mandela. Both men were afraid, but were able to regulate this emotion such that they could continue their work. The idea that hope is without fear only raises anxiety among people in dire situations who are afraid and then believe that they should not be or that their hopes are false or flawed. Nussbaum, 212.

50. Friedman, *Generation to Generation*, 31.

cannot retain a differentiated stance with regard to hope, if they remain caught up in the binary relationship of hope and despair, then we can anticipate more despair, violence, and apathy.

Another obvious problem of hope involves whose "hope" are we talking about. As indicated above, symbol systems of various poleis provide the particularity of collective visions and hopes. The Israelites hoped for freedom from the Pharaoh, which obviously conflicted with the vison and expectations of the Egyptian ruling class. For the Israelites to realize their hopes, many Egyptians and those who dwelled in the Promised Land had to die. For centuries, enslaved Africans hoped for liberation from literal and figurative chains. Their hopes were at odds with the visions of white supremacists and pragmatic capitalists whose desires and expectations focused on greater profits. White Europeans immigrated to the so-called New World in hopes of beginning a new life. The realization of these hopes had devastating consequences for Native peoples. I suspect it is true that many people in northern states hoped to defeat southern states in the Civil War, while southern states hoped to retain their slavocracy. If we fast forward to the present, many nations, rich and poor, have signed the Climate Accords in a collective hope to mitigate the effects of climate change. However, this hope collides with conflicts between rich and poor nations. The hope of rich nations (e.g., U.S., China, Russia) is to make changes while retaining and increasing their wealth (profligacy), as well as maintaining their political, economic, and military ascendent power. The hope of poorer nations is for rich nations to bear some of the economic burdens they face now and in the future.

Even within a polis, where people ostensibly operate within a shared symbol system, there are different hopes contesting for expression and realization. In the United States, the election year 2020 saw often-violent clashes between groups having different visions and hopes for the country. Black Lives Matter groups protested racial injustices, expressing a hope for a future of racial equality (legal, political, economic, etc.). Numerous rightwing Republicans sought to hold onto power through the dissemination of false claims of voter fraud, and when that failed, they participated in a violent insurrection. In terms of global warming, the 45th president signed an executive order in 2017 exiting the Paris Climate Accords, reflecting the hopes of many conservatives who wanted a future free of what they deemed to be economic and political constraints on their nationalistic freedoms—failing to acknowledge that extinction will make the issue and reality of freedom empty. Four years later, President Joe Biden signed an executive order rejoining the Paris Accords, enlivening those whose hopes had been dashed in 2017.

The concept of hope becomes more complicated when we consider that a polis has not one, but numerous symbol systems that often intersect in problematic ways. For instance, white evangelical Christians in the U.S. are avowedly Christian, yet many of them enthusiastically and unquestioningly embrace the prosperity gospel message. The prosperity gospel is a simplistic and uncritical amalgamation of the anthropology of neoliberal capitalism and Christian anthropology of the Gospels. For these evangelicals, cognitive dissonance has been smoothed over and the hope for resurrection and God's blessing are evident in one's portfolio. Add to this that many white evangelicals, embracing capitalism, are climate deniers, which is a response that opts for a short-term hope in the future of capitalism, while overlooking climate science.[51] Another interesting and problematic intersection of symbol systems is that many white evangelicals view themselves as patriotic Americans. For example, patriotic American Christians approved of the wars in Afghanistan and Iraq, which expressed the hope of American victory in the so-called war on terror. Patriotic Christians elide any incongruence between the hopes joined to Christian faith and patriotic faith—a faith in and of the U.S. Empire. So, it is not only whose hope that can be a problem, but also what symbols systems are the ground of our particular hopes and how these are leading to agonistic contestations in the polis.

Implicit in the discussion above is that hope, as theologian Miguel De La Torre points out, is often "responsible for maintaining oppressive structures,"[52] which includes Christian apparatuses. He goes on to claim that hope, "as a middle-class privilege, soothes the conscience of those complicit with oppressive structures, lulling them to do nothing except to look forward to salvific futures."[53] In their hoping, the middle-class numb "themselves to the pain of the oppressed."[54] Lest we think that hope is a problem associated with classism, we need only point to other oppressive contexts associated with racism, sexism, and other social-political forms of misrecognition and maldistribution. De La Torre also takes to task the problem of Christian hope. Critiquing Moltmann's theology of hope, De La Torre highlights how Christian hope is imbricated with notion of conquering[55]

51. Pew Research Center, "Two-Thirds of Americans Think Government Should Do More on Climate."

52. De La Torre, *Embracing Hopelessness*, xiv.

53. De La Torre, *Embracing Hopelessness*, 5.

54. De La Torre, *Embracing Hopelessness*, 5.

55. De La Torre, *Embracing Hopelessness*, 45. Many Christians in the U.S. have supported the numerous wars of conquest in the nineteenth, twentieth, and twenty-first centuries without apparent recognition that the central figure of Christian faith was tortured and murdered by the Roman Empire.

or what I addressed in chapter 3, namely sovereignty and political violence. If there is any question regarding the intersection of hope, privilege, power, and violence, one need only peruse Christian history and the long bloody trail of hopeful Christians realizing their visions of what they believed to be God's promises. Indeed, Henriksen's rosy portrayal of "Christian hope as an activity-shaped and faith-based hope that expresses itself in love for all humankind,"[56] is more in line with wishful thinking when considering over 2,000 years of Christian history, revealing what self-identified Christians have done and are doing to other human beings (and other species). To be sure, there have been individuals and communities that have loved strangers and enemies, but these pale against the innumerable instances of hate, oppression, and marginalization perpetrated by "good" Christians. Indeed, consider that the person who Christians seek to follow was cruelly tortured and put to death by an oppressive regime. We (Christian Americans) overlook the irony about how an avowedly Christian nation makes the Roman Empire look like a two-bit operation. The exercise of Christian-American hope has a similar bloody history.

If we turn to the Anthropocene Age, we might imagine how the problems of hope De La Torre mentions will increase as resources dwindle and nations compete instead of cooperate. Powerful nations and their elites will try to secure their futures through varied forms of political violence. The Anthropocene Age provides another angle and problem De La Torre overlooks. He focuses mainly on the oppression of other human beings vis-à-vis those human beings who have the privilege and power to hope. Christian hope, as a rule, centers around human beings (and primarily Christians, but also, at best, all human beings). Recall that Agamben contends that Western philosophy has excluded nature, which can also be said of Western political theologies. This means that when Christians talk of hope, it usually means hope for Christians or human beings in general. To add to De La Torre's perspective, it is important to note that hope—philosophical and theological visions—has supported the exploitation of other species and the earth. It is not just human beings who have suffered as a result of the hopes of the powerful and privileged. Other species and the earth itself have suffered as a result of human behaviors grounded in and supported by entitled, privileged visions of human dwelling. A corrective of this is seen in Catherine Keller's and other eco-theologians' claim that Christian hope must necessarily include all human beings, other species, and the earth.[57] While I am sympathetic to this view, Christian scriptures are deeply anthropocentric,

56. Henriksen, "Hope," 127.
57. Keller, *Political Theology of the Earth.*

largely containing and supporting, as noted in chapter 1, theologies of subjugation and subordination. As long as we depend on and operate from these theologies, hope will be a problem vis-à-vis other species and nature.

For De La Torre the problem of hope is not resolved by having a more accurate hope. "To hope," he writes passionately, "is to bury one's head in the sands of peace, making us useless to meet the inevitable struggle that is coming."[58] Instead, he wants "nothing to do with Christian hope, the protagonist of too many atrocities conducted in its name." "Do not shower me with reminders of God's future promises," he continues, "show me God's present grace through your loving mercy. Do not tempt me with riches of some afterlife; convince me of your sacrificial agape in the here and now. In the midst of unfathomable sufferings, the earth's marginalized no longer need pious pontifications about rewards of the hereafter. Nor do they need their oppressors providing the answers for their salvation."[59] It is justice in the present, not hope, that motivates De Le Torre, and we could extend this to the notion of eco-justice for other species and the earth.

A related problem, given De La Torre's critique, is the use of hope to distract people from political-economic systems that have contributed to climate change and continue to serve as obstacles for climate action. While Christian scriptures and practices facilitate our burying our heads in the sand and overlooking or ignoring injustices, political-economic apparatuses do as well. Consider the global capitalist system and its promises of wealth.[60] Of course, as Marx noted, capitalism creates a great deal of wealth, but the question is for whom and at what cost to human beings, other species, and the earth. Capitalism has become how we organize societies and many people have an almost religious devotion to it.[61] The daily focus on the stock markets, employment, future earnings, etc. all serve as distractions from capitalist apparatuses that establish instrumental, objectifying, exploitive relations vis-à-vis other-than-human beings and the earth. Other opiates are the various state and national lotteries, with their promise or hope (wish) for riches and freedom from economic and employment anxieties. And then there are economists, like Gernot Wagner and Martin Weitzman, who naively place their hopes in using market forces to save humanity from the harsh realities of global warming.[62] Their perspective not only distracts

58. De La Torre, *Embracing Hopelessness*, 96.

59. De La Torre, *Embracing Hopelessness*, 96.

60. See Dufour, *The Art of Shrinking Heads*; Novak, *The Spirit of Democratic Capitalism*.

61. Cox, *The Market as God*; Frank, *One Market under God*.

62. Wagner and Weitzman, *Climate Shock*. I say naively because it is clear that they are advocating an economic system without paying attention to the history of

us, but maintains the profligacy that is at the core of capitalism and which has been a key source of climate change.

Two other problems of hope are worth mentioning. I mentioned above De La Torre's critical comment about Christianity as conquering the Roman world. I want to extend this to the issue and problems of human sovereignty and the attending relations of subordination and subjugation. While Judeo-Christian scriptures advocate for human dominion over nature, Western philosophies and sciences do as well. All of these can be said to be anthropocentric apparatuses that privilege human beings in a vision of the future. This is a fatal problem of hope, because by subordinating and subjugating nature we exploit it for our own purposes, to include the purpose of bolstering our self-esteem, while ignoring our shared vulnerability and dependency. Recall Jonathan Schell's comment: "If we conquer nature, we will find ourselves among the defeated."[63] In my view, he recognizes that the hope of maintaining our sovereignty and anthropocentricity is futile, hopeless. If there is to be any realistic hope, we must let go of anthropocentric visions—religious or otherwise—that establish relations of subordination and subjugation.

This issue leads to another related problem. Many authors recognize that hope is a problem when it becomes entirely dependent on the realization of a specific vision (ideologies) of the future. This is not always conscious. In other words, we often do not know that in the present we are acting out of and completely dependent on a "certain" vision of the future—a closed future. We might become aware of it when the future arrives and it does not conform to our actions or visions. Human beings are interesting creatures, because we can act on our beliefs and create reality, which, in turn, confirms our hopes. For example, many U.S. citizens believe the country is exceptional—the most powerful nation in history. Even in the nineteenth-century Tocqueville noted this common belief among patriotic Americans. He observed,

> If I say to an American that the country he lives in is a fine one, aye he replies and there is none its equal in the world. If I applaud the freedom its inhabitants enjoy, he answers "freedom is a fine thing but few nations are worthy of it." If I remark on the

capitalism(s) and the rise of inequalities and the concomitant vast damage done to the lives of billions of humans, not to mention other species and the earth. To think that an altered view of capitalism will be a remedy also overlooks the fact that capitalism, for Jason Moore and others, is the central cause of climate change.

63. Schell, "The Human Shadow," 19. Alan Watts also points to Western preoccupations with conquering nature, as if nature is an object meant to serve the needs of humanity. Watts, *The Way of Zen*, 174–75.

purity of morals that distinguishes the United States he declares "I can imagine that a stranger who has witnessed the corruption which prevails in other nations would be astonished at the difference." At length I leave him to a contemplation of himself. But he returns to the charge and does not desist until he has got me to repeat all I have been saying. It is impossible to conceive of a more troublesome and garrulous patriotism.[64]

This belief is intertwined with U.S. imperialism of the nineteenth, twentieth, and twenty-first centuries. My point here is that beliefs fuel actions, which are connected to visions and which together create a reality. A problem occurs comes when reality disconfirm hopes. So, for instance, when the U.S. Empire is no more, it will be difficult to retain any realistic hope for its return, which points to the slogan "Make America Great Again." To shift to the realities of the Anthropocene Age, Western human beings have for millennia acted on the beliefs in human dominion over nature. This is a present belief connected to a vision that fuels behavior. The West's hope is, in other words, infected with anthropocentric beliefs. What is going to happen if human beings begin the process of becoming extinct because the planet is not habitable? When a belief and vision are not realized because they confront reality that disconfirms them, individuals *may* experience despair and turn to violence or apathy.

## A Radical Political Theology: Courageous Caring in the Now[65]

In Albert Camus' novel *The Plague*, the city of Oran is besieged by a plague. The indomitable Dr. Rieux, in the face of ineluctable devastation, tells his friend that "one must fight, in one way or another, and not go down on one's knees."[66] Later, he remarks "how hard it must be to live only with what one knows and what one remembers, and deprived of what one hopes."[67] Dr. Rieux is struggling with what to do in the absence of hope. Is he to embrace

---

64. Niebuhr, *The Irony of American History*, 28.

65. I do not have the space to be able to link "now" with Agamben's and Benjamin's intriguing discussion of messianic time. Both philosophers viewed messianic time not in terms of waiting for the Messiah in some future, "but instead a manner of experiencing and acting on what is already here in the present." This now-time, as I will explain, is not linked to hope because hope is always hope for something in the future. De La Durantaye, *Giorgio Agamben*, 378.

66. Camus, *The Plague*, 102.

67. Camus, *The Plague*, 225.

hopelessness, as De La Torre suggests? He chooses to fight the plague, but is his fighting based on a manic despair? Does he think that since he is going down, he is going to die fighting? Or is it that Dr. Rieux embraces his physician's oath that motivates him to care for patients even when a cure is hopeless. Camus' novel is apt for the struggles we face in the Anthropocene Age.

In this section, I discuss what a radical political theology might look like if we are to sideline hope as necessary for action. But before proceeding, it is necessary to address two related points, which are foundational to this section. First, recall Martha Nussbaum's claim that Kant was right: "good works need hope."[68] She goes on to cite the liberative actions of Martin Luther King Jr., Gandhi, and Nelson Mandela—"all people of hope and vision, who saw a beautiful future and worked energetically to realize it. Despair or cynical resignation, are attitudes incompatible with bold action and committed work." Also remember Paul Hoggett's and Edward Farley's view that hope is essential for agency. Indeed, Hoggett criticizes environmental activists who "face climate change without hope." He views these activists' view as "Concealing a bitter disenchantment with humankind."[69] While I understand these authors' perspectives, I think they are a tad myopic when it comes to the issues of hope, agency, and climate change. Biographies of King or Mandela, for instance, reveal that these men struggled with resignation and despair, yet continued to fight for justice. Their despair did not mean they were idle, apathetic, bitter, or incapacitated vis-à-vis their agency. I can think of plenty of good works that are not motivated by hope or cynicism or despair. There are thousands of daily examples of people caring for others in the face of hopelessness. Decades ago, as a hospital chaplain on the oncology floor, I saw nurses, doctors, and family members care for patients who had no hope of surviving cancer. I also observed many of these patients caring for others even as they faced death. Yes, hope can motivate people to act, but good works do not necessarily need or depend on hope, though it is impossible to imagine good works in the absence of care. Moreover, the problems of hope identified above recede when care is in the foreground.

Second and relatedly, while I resonate with most of De La Torre's critiques of hope, I do not think one needs to go as far as embracing hopelessness. In other words, as mentioned above, it is not a binary choice we face, either embrace hope or hopelessness, as De La Torre, Nussbaum, and Hoggett seem to suggest. This is a false choice, because it rests on a modernist view of the psyche as unitary or comprising a unified self. Instead, as

---

68. Nussbaum, *The Monarchy of Fear*, 209.

69. Hoggett, "Climate Change in a Perverse Culture," 83.

many postmodern philosophers and psychologists have noted,[70] the psyche is deeply complex. While each of us possesses a fictive unitary self, we are in fact much more complicated, containing numerous selves connected to varied relationships and contexts. In one context, a self-state may be dominant, while other self-states remain in the background. In addition, persons who obtain a level of differentiation can differentiate between selves (thoughts, feelings, etc.), retaining flexibility and freedom such that one particular self-state does not determine who a person is or how they relate to the world. I have seen this numerous times in therapy, where a client in the moment is captive to thoughts and a feeling, say despair, and within minutes shifts to a hopeful, realistic self. We might consider that Dr. Rieux possesses a hopeless self and caring (non-despairing) self at the same time. He has the courage to care despite his feeling of hopelessness. Indeed, I contend that De La Torre's view of embracing hopelessness (not despair) and fighting for justice reflects a complex, differentiated self, which belies the binary choice of either hope or hopelessness. If people, in embracing hopelessness, allowed hopelessness to define themselves and their way of being in the world, this would represent a struggle of differentiation and a loss of a complex self. Another illustration of this is the comment attributed to Martin Luther: "Even if I knew that tomorrow the world would go to pieces, I would still plant my apple tree." Care is necessary for the good work of planting a tree, while in the background there may be feelings of anxiety, dread, and hopelessness.

To make my case for care that sidelines hope in the Anthropocene Age, I first address care from an existential perspective. In particular, I consider acts of care aimed at goods in the present, even when there is a sense of hopelessness with regard to realizing some future good. It is important to begin this existential perspective with a discussion about parent-child relations because hope is part of this relation and the child's psychosocial development. It is during these early periods of development when the binary aspect of hope and hopelessness can exist. In other words, the lack of differentiation in childhood can mean children can be overwhelmed by hopelessness, while this is not necessarily the case in adulthood. If all goes well enough, children develop into adults who have more complex, differentiated selves, able to emotionally regulate while caring for others in the present. Of course, it is crucial to recognize that the polis' apparatuses can interfere or undermine the development of complex selves and their capacity to care without depending on hope for motivation. From here, I move to a theological discussion, focusing on the incarnation not as a symbol of hope, but one of care in the midst of oppression. In addition, I argue that

70. See Stern, *Unformulated Experience*, 156–58.

Jesus' forgiveness of his tormentors represents a moment when care was in the foreground, while hopelessness (imminent death) was sidelined or in the background.

I am pretty confident in asserting that not all parental caring actions involve, in the moment, hope, which motivates their agency. This is not to say that in the background good-enough parents do not possess various hopes for their children. It is also true that, in caring for children, parents often have to adjust their hopes or get rid of them altogether. Religious parents may hope their children take on their religious views, but have to adapt if their children choose another good. And for some parents whose children are terminally ill or have a lifelong chronic condition, moments of care may lack any hope of physical improvement, which does not mean parents are hopeless. Hope may not be relevant in parents' motivation to care for their sick child. Indeed, it is clear that "caring for the dying is not a despairing act but a courageous one."[71] There is often, in other words, a nowness to parental care, to attuning to and speaking and acting together with children in what Agamben calls now-time. An obvious illustration of this is not only when parents care for dying children, but also in playing with their children.

Things are different for infants and young children when it comes to hope. I mentioned above about orphaned infants in World War II who grew quiet after a couple of weeks. When infants cry, there is an expectation, a pre-representational hope that the world/parents will hear their cries and meet their needs. I think it is safe to say that the ongoing failure of the environment to respond will give rise to a pre-representational sense of hopelessness, which explains the extinguishing of agency associated with crying out. From this, we can see that a child's pre-representational experiences of hope are linked to parents' responsive attunements or care. I mentioned above Erik Erikson's stages of development. The first task is negotiating trust-mistrust, which is contingent on good-enough parental care. The strength that develops from this is, for Erikson, hope.[72] Because there is a very low capacity for differentiation in early childhood, we can expect that a binary perspective is present—hope-care or hopelessness-carelessness. From this, we can see that action is linked to hope, for the infant, because of a lack of the capacity for differentiation. Put differently, for an infant, hopelessness is linked to annihilation or engulfment anxieties, which are global psychic states that determine behavior. As an aside, this makes me wonder if adult fear of hopelessness is linked to this early period of development. I suspect so given the strong claims that hope is necessary for agency or the irritable

71. Malcolm, "Introduction," xxxv.
72. Erikson, *The Life Cycle Completed*, 31–32.

critiques (not understanding or compassion) directed at environmental activists who are said to have no hope.

The challenge in human development is: 1) to learn to manage or regulate one's emotions; and 2) to become more differentiated. The latter task includes learning to handle the complexity of one's subjectivity and the complexity of others and the world. As children, we depend on the care (includes repair) of adults to assist in regulating emotions and in learning that we comprise multiple self-states—complex selves. These are interpersonal or intersubjective achievements. Of course, as children or adults, we can choose to simplify ourselves, others, and the world, which reduces our anxiety about complexity and not-knowing. Good-enough parental care facilitates children being able to handle, if not enjoy, the complexity of themselves, others, and the world. In other words, good-enough parental care enables children to handle ambiguity and ignorance or develop negative capability, which "is when a [person] is capable of being in uncertainty, mysteries, doubts, without irritable reaching after fact and reason."[73] In terms of hope and hopelessness, sufficient internalization of parental care makes it possible for children (and later adults) not to become overwhelmed if they are feeling hopeless, because they possess the capacities for emotional regulation and differentiation. This means, then, that agency is not dependent on any one feeling or self-state. A differentiated adult recognizes that a feeling and thought do not necessarily have to define oneself or one's relation to the world. Just like a parent can care without hope, a child can learn to care without hope. If there was a real Dr. Rieux, we would hypothesize that he had obtained enough care in his early life to be able to regulate his sense of hopelessness so that he was able to act courageously in caring for patients afflicted by the plague.

A real-life figure, like Martin Luther King, as noted above, struggled with despair—understandably given his experiences of racism and receiving repeated death threats. One evening, alone in the kitchen, King laid his head on the table and confessed his weakness, lack of courage, and fear to God. In response to his pleas, King heard a quiet, assuring voice say: "Martin Luther, stand up for righteousness. Stand up for justice. Stand up for truth. And lo, I will be with you. Even until the end of the world."[74] I would interpret this to mean that God was not sending a message of hope that things would work out, that justice would prevail. It was rather words affirming that God was with King and encouraging him to persevere in his caring enough to

73. Letter John Keats wrote to George Keats, in Bion, *Attention and Interpretation*, 125

74. King, *The Autobiography of Martin Luther King Jr.*, 77–78.

stand up for justice for all human beings. I contend that the parental care King received in childhood was connected to King's ability to care for his enemies, while sidelining hope. I do not believe King embraced hopelessness, but I do believe he operated out of a complex self, caring for African Americans, poor people, and even white racists, all of which represented his capacities for differentiation and negative capability.

There are all kinds of instances in daily life where hope is not in the foreground, but care is. Medical personnel who care for terminally ill persons, caring for pets, helping an older person up the stairs, shoveling the sidewalk for a neighbor who is ill, etc. are routine examples of care in the foreground. In these and other examples, persons' actions are not motivated by hope, but by the imperative to care. It becomes more difficult when we encounter situations where a good outcome is in doubt. Then many of us may turn to hope as motivation to act toward realization of that good. Yet, because many adults possess the capacities for emotional self-regulation and differentiation, we can choose to set aside feelings of hope or hopelessness and choose to care. When Martin Luther said he would plant a tree today if he knew the world would end tomorrow, he was demonstrating this ability to care in spite of hopelessness. His care was not contingent on realizing a desired change or the attainment of a good. Personally, when it comes to the Anthropocene Age, I care not because I hope human beings and other species will survive or that our collective actions will change the trajectory of global warming, but because caring for others, other species, and the earth is the right thing to do now, in this moment. This does not mean I am embracing hopelessness or that I do not at times feel hopeless. Rather, I am choosing to sideline hope in order to embrace the categorical imperative to care now. Care, then, is not contingent upon hope. In terms of climate change, care is not dependent upon the hope of human survival.

I mentioned above that political, economic, and social apparatuses can interfere with individual and collective emotional-regulation and differentiation, which, in turn, interferes with our ability and effectiveness to care for Othered human beings, other species, and the earth. In the previous chapter, I highlighted obstacles to change, like global capitalism, imperialism, and nationalism. These apparatuses, which often include religion, shape our motivations, visions of the good, and hopes. They can, along with leaders, heighten our fears and anxieties, thus undermining our capacity for differentiation. As difficult as it is, we can identify and critique these forces and systems, while retaining our own capacities for emotional-regulation and differentiation. But we cannot do this if we are not aware of the apparatuses that are obstacles to change and that undermine hope and heighten fear, despair, and political violence. Naturally, we are aided in this endeavor to be aware and to emotionally regulate ourselves by engaging with individuals and groups who are responsive and thoughtful/reflective, instead of reactive and polarizing—groups that appreciate complexity and eschew the psychosocial defenses of simplification, denial, and splitting. In light of the Anthropocene Age, the international group XR (Extinction Rebellion), for example, pursues nonviolent civil disobedience with the aims of challenging local, state, and national governments and citizens to act to reduce the impacts of global warming.[75] There are also religious and secular communities who are engaged in caring for the environment. In my view, individuals and groups who are emotionally and thoughtfully responsive (versus reactive) in caring for other human beings, other species, and the earth are acting in the now. I suspect that many of them have hope for change, but it is also likely that many people are acting not out of hope per se, but because caring in the moment is the right thing for us to do together.

As a segue from this existential perspective to a theological view, I consider briefly Agamben's notion of now-time. Agamben stated that he is "not in the slightest interested in apocalyptic prophecies, but rather in ways we might respond at the present time to the catastrophe in which we live."[76] I think another way of saying this is that he is not interested in hope in the sense of possessing an end or a vision of the end. This now-time "is conceived of in the most literal possible sense as a conception of time focused on the radical opportunity that every moment brings with it."[77] This radical opportunity is often evident in good-enough parents' acts of care, as well as our acts of care in the now for each other, other species, and the earth itself.

I now want to shift from this existential perspective on the relation between hope and care to a theological view. Christianity is certainly a religion of hope, but I want to argue that hope is secondary and, to take this further, not necessary for Christianity. In previous chapters, I discussed the incarnation from a variety of angles, but each perspective is based on the foundational premise of God's indeterminate and infinite care for human beings and, indeed, all creation. I want to suggest that the event of the incarnation is a moment of care wherein hope is inoperative. It is an event that is not aimed at changing humanity or giving people hope that humanity can change, for there is scant evidence that human beings have changed as a result of the incarnation. Indeed, a cursory reading of the history of Christianity will provide mountains of evidence that Christians are no more and no less likely to be loving and virtuous than people from other faiths.

75. Website: https://xramerica.org/.

76. De La Durantaye, *Giorgio Agamben*, 103.

77. De La Durantaye, *Giorgio Agamben*, 102.

Someone may counter, stating that the incarnation event was aimed at providing assurance of God's presence and human salvation for those who believe in Jesus Christ. Fair enough, but there are the frequent scriptural admonitions for change—metanoia, conversion—that are often linked to salvation. Change is inextricably tied to hope. What if we were to consider the incarnation event to be God's communication to the world that God is with us in the moment, in the now-time, regardless of whether we change, regardless of the future? Put differently, the incarnation event is God's communication of care for us as we are—in our suchness in the present. This is analogous to parents who care for their children unconditionally, which means caring for their suchness in the present regardless of the future. This does not mean that parents are devoid of hope, but in the moment of unconditional care, hope is inoperative.

Would this view not lead people to avoid change or doing the right thing? Would this theological depiction lead to quietism or passivity? Perhaps, but there is a quite a bit of passivity among Christians throughout history—passive about the injustices they see or cause. Also, the idea of being saved because of one's beliefs and actions assumes that hope for salvation (or fear of punishment) is the motivation for change and for some people this may be the case. But this strikes me as a contractual faith dependent on the conditional love of God. Moreover, being motivated by a future reward for good behavior represents a less differentiated psychological and spiritual stance. It is better for a Christian to seek change, to be virtuous simply because it is the right thing to do now; whether one achieves eternity with God is secondary—not the motivation to change. A more differentiated person of faith, then, cares because it is the right thing to do. Punishment or reward is not the source of motivation. To return to the analogy of parents' unconditional love, yes, they hope their children change for the good, but with regard to their adult children, they recognize that it is their decision and their love for their children is not contingent on whether they change or not.

For most Christians, longing for the Messiah is realized in the incarnation of Jesus Christ the Savior. The incarnation, then, is tied to the hope of personal salvation, which is decidedly anthropocentric and deeply problematic. The most obvious example of this are Christians who ignore (or do not care about) the fact that human beings are responsible for the extinction of other species and the degradation of the earth, basically because they believe they will be saved. This indifference, if not outright hostility, is, theologically, a sin and psychologically profound narcissism. I am not suggesting that we get rid of the link between incarnation and salvation. I am arguing that the link, given the realities of the Anthropocene Age, be made inoperative—Bartleby's "I would prefer not." I would prefer a more radical

Christianity that considers the event of the incarnation to be an event of care for all human beings, all species, and the earth. This event is fully a moment of care—a realization of the ontological imperative to care in the present and in each subsequent present. The incarnation makes inoperative the empires preoccupation of realizing a determined future of power and authority for themselves. Put differently, whether human beings are saved (on earth or afterlife), or what salvation looks like or means, is inoperative. What is operative is God's grace to care. This is radical, not in the sense of revolutionary, but rather as the foundation of creation and creative acts of care that lead to survival and flourishing. As Christians, we are called and commanded to care for all human beings, other species, and the earth because of the event of the incarnation and not because we hope for salvation for ourselves or others and not because we hope to survive as a species.

Consider the example of King above. Facing constant threats, King teetered on the edge of despair. And then he heard God's voice. This was not a voice to assure King that everything would be fine or that King was going to be with God in heaven. It was an assurance that God was with him even in the moments of despair, which was followed by a command to stand up for justice. Again, no reward offered. It was an imperative to act for justice in spite of despair. King's actions, then, were not based on gaining a reward. Yes, I am sure King hoped that the arc of the universe would bend toward justice, and I think that was part of his motivation. It may also be that he hoped for personal salvation. But King possessed enough self-differentiation, emotional regulation, and faith to care about justice for all God's creatures in now-time.

Let me add two other thoughts about the incarnation. The notion that God incarnates Godself as a communication for human beings may reinforce believers' views that human beings and especially Christians, are special, privileged, etc. This can serve to strengthen beliefs in human sovereignty/dominion, as well as hierarchical valuations (e.g., other species have less value). If we locate the incarnation within the context of the Anthropocene Age, a different picture emerges. The incarnation is not a demonstration of humanity's specialness, but rather of our limited capacity for freedom—the freedom to care (or not to care), which does not make human beings special or of greater value. The incarnation, then, is an invitation not only to accept God's unconditional care for creation, but also to use our freedom and our agency to care for one another (including other species and the earth). When we consider that human beings, especially in the West, are implicated in climate change, then the idea of human beings having a limited capacity for freedom becomes clearer vis-à-vis the incarnation. Indeed, the Anthropocene Age is a testament to human capacities for agency, and the incarnation is an invitation to use that agency to care for climate refugees, other species, and the earth. That many of us, for various reasons, choose not to care for other species and the earth, the incarnation serves as a judgment. I am not saying a judgment by God, but an existential judgment that comes from failing to care enough to act. It is like the judgment that comes from having been cared for by our parents, but then choosing not to care for others. Our parents do not indict us; it is ourselves who are indicted when we recognize we have failed.

If we fail to care sufficiently to effect change the direction of global warming, and it is certainly very possible we will, I do not think the incarnation as judgment means eternal damnation for human beings. The incarnation reveals God's indeterminate, infinite, and unconditional care, which is inimical to eternal punishment. But God's unconditional care will not save us or other species from the consequences of our failures to care. The deep tragedy is that many human beings and other species will bear the costs of our failures in the present and future.

A second thought regarding the incarnation event concerns God taking on the form of a slave. As mentioned in previous chapters, I argued that an enslaved person is the excluded-included other—forced by political apparatuses to take on a demeaned identity. A slave relationship is one of instrumentality, wherein the slave exists to serve the needs and desires of the master. The slave's existence, in other words, has meaning to the extent that the slave fulfills this purpose. If we extend the slave metaphor to nature, we might view the incarnation as making inoperative relations and apparatuses of objectification and instrumentality, whether it is directed toward other human beings or other species or the earth itself. What an incarnate God invites are relations wherein human beings, other species, and the earth are recognized and treated in terms of their singularity. By definition, these are relations marked by agentic care with the aims of survival and flourishing of all creation.

Taking on the form of an enslaved person may suggest hope for liberation. That is, if the incarnation is an event of God's indeterminate, infinite care embodied in Jesus, is this not also the seed of liberation in breaking the chains of instrumental, exploitative relationships? I can see liberation theologies taking up this view, but I do not think future liberation is THE hope. God taking on the form of a slave means that relations in the present that are defined by relations of instrumentality, objectification, and exploitation are made inoperative. Yes, Jesus suffered as a result of Roman apparatuses of oppression, but his care for people was not diminished as a result. These apparatuses were inoperative when it came for him to care freely for others. In other words, Jesus' care was not determined by the apparatuses of empire.

I believe this care is liberating because it is thoroughly tied to the present and not some future expectation of being free. This does not mean leaving people in places of oppression or caring for them and not being concerned about freedom. Genuine care is concerned about justice, as is evident in the ministry of Jesus. But care in the present is not solely determined by the hope for future liberation. I think De La Torre's embrace of hopelessness points in this direction in that people who are faced with overwhelming oppression place care in the foreground of their relations.

Of course, it is important to point out that decisions to incarnate care can lead people to the cross. In my view, Jesus' numerous decisions to love and offer compassion for those on the lower rungs of society put him at odds with religious and political authorities who benefited from structural inequalities (and the hope of future benefits for themselves). Love and compassion are always a threat to established power brokers and the political, economic apparatuses that serve their needs by exploiting other human beings and other species. Put another way, the threat of care stems from offering a relation of singularity or suchness in contradiction to relations of hierarchy, instrumentality, and objectification. The cross is a symbol of Roman terrorism, as well as all other forms of terrorism that seek to keep persons in subjugated and subordinate relations.[78] The cross is not inevitable, but it is likely for those who, in their decisions to care for other human beings and other species, transgress the anthropological machines of capitalism, imperialism, and nationalism. I add that the cross can take many forms, public-political ridicule, ostracism, loss of jobs, imprisonment, etc.

The idea that incarnating care can lead to the cross leads me to revisit Jesus' forgiveness of the soldiers who tortured him. Above, I discussed the importance of differentiation and emotional regulation with regard to caring in anxious times, placing our individual and collective hopes to the side. Facing torture and imminent death on the cross had to evoke in Jesus a great deal of anxiety and other intense feelings, including fear, anger, and hopelessness. To be able to care for and forgive those who were torturing him and who would nail him to the cross required an incredible amount of self-differentiation, emotional regulation, and courage. Perhaps De La Torre would say that Jesus embraced his hopelessness and decided that the just thing to do was to forgive these imperial soldiers. A slightly different idea is that Jesus possessed sufficient emotional regulation and differentiation not to be defined by feelings of hopelessness, fear, anger, etc. This is different than embracing hopelessness. Instead, it reveals a more complex self able to

---

78. A modern example of terroristic practices is portrayed in James Cone's book, *The Cross and the Lynching Tree*.

experience a variety of intense emotions, while being able to care enough to forgive the soldiers.

Let me add another interpretation. The cross represents the profound injustices of Roman oppressors. I am confident that this would have been known by the Jews and Jesus, in particular. Jesus' care/forgiveness was not aimed at some future justice for himself and other Jews, which does not mean this was not a concern. Rather, justice in the moment meant forgiving these soldiers, because care/forgiveness represented the present (though, in this case, unrealized) possibility of relations free of instrumentality, objectification, and subjugation. A future hope for justice was inoperative in that moment of care, which, again, does not mean it was absent.

This perspective regarding Jesus' forgiveness, when confronted by the realities of the Anthropocene Age, encounters a twist. Most of the privileges obtained by Western nations have been (and continue to be) achieved through the exploitation of other peoples,[79] other species, and the earth itself. Perhaps one of the first steps, after acknowledging this, is having the courage to embrace our guilt and to seek forgiveness from those we have harmed. Naturally, other species cannot grant forgiveness, but human beings can atone for the exploitation and destruction of other species. Genuine atonement represents an act of care, yet it must also be accompanied by acts of care in the present toward othered human beings, species, and the earth. I add that genuine atonement/care must be free of any anthropocentric, narcissistic hope for our survival, our salvation from guilt or from the consequences of our own actions. The aim of forgiveness or atonement is to care in the now for the needs of othered human beings, other species, and the earth.

In brief, a radical political theology is not a theology that embraces hopelessness. Instead, it embraces the complexity of being human, recognizing that we can care and pursue justice in spite of feelings of hopelessness. Complexity rejects the false binary of either having hope or despair that so often frames our understanding of Christian hope. My motivation to care makes inoperative feelings that would undermine my caring acts. My use of the incarnation and Jesus' forgiveness is aimed at framing the possibility of caring for all human beings, other species, and the earth without focusing on hope or some possible future. To care in the present does not mean we will not have feelings and thoughts about the future, but my care is not dependent on these. Care is also not contingent on whether my acts lead to some future change. Indeed, even if a situation becomes hopeless, like the Titanic, hopelessness will not impede our caring. This radical view of care

---

79. See Piketty, *Capitalism and Ideology*.

sets aside the problems of hope. Put differently, a radical Christian political theology focuses on care and compassion for creation in the present (now-time), making inoperative anthropocentric and narcissistic expectations of our salvation.

## Conclusion

Martin Luther King Jr. remarked that "We are confronted with the fierce urgency of now."[80] He was not speaking about the Anthropocene Age, but the sentiment rings truer today. As mentioned above, King, in the fierce urgency of his time, struggled with despair, but it did not get in the way of his caring for people in the present—in the now-time. This ability to care without depending on hope is also seen in a literary example. In Virginia Woolf's novel, *Mrs. Dalloway*, one of her characters remarks to herself, "we are a doomed race, chained to a sinking ship, as the whole thing is a bad joke, let us, at any rate, do our part; mitigate the suffering of our fellow-prisoners; decorate the dungeon with flowers and air-cushions; be as decent as we possibly can."[81] A sinking ship is reminiscent of the Titanic and, as noted in the beginning, people cared for others even though the ship was doomed. These are examples of the human capacity to care despite the specter of hopelessness. In the Anthropocene Age, we face a frightening future—a future that may not include human beings. In the face of this future, each day brings with it the invitation for courageous care—acts of care that do not depend on hope, but rather on the existential imperative to care for all of creation. Whether our caring actions are sufficient to achieve changes needed for survival and flourishing of human beings and other species is what we may hope for, but not our reason for caring. Like many human beings, we courageously care in the now-time even as we face a dark future. To end, "This is our defiance—to practice love even in hopelessness."[82]

80. Martin Luther King, Riverside Speech, "Beyond Vietnam."
81. Woolf, *Mrs. Dalloway*, 117–18.
82. Kaur, *See No Stranger*, 241.

# Bibliography

Agamben, Giorgio. "Capitalism as Religion." In *Agamben and Radical Politics*, edited by Daniel McLoughlin, 15–26. Critical Connections. Edinburgh: Edinburgh University Press, 2016.

———. *The Coming Community*. Translated by Michael Hardt. Theory Out of Bounds 1. Minneapolis: University of Minnesota Press, 2013.

———. *The Highest Poverty: Monastic Rules and Forms-of-Life*. Translated by Adam Kotsko. Homo Sacer IV,1. Meridian: Crossing Aesthetics. Stanford: Stanford University Press, 2013.

———. *Infancy and History: The Destruction of Experience*. Translated by Liz Heron. London: Verso, 1993.

———. *The Kingdom and the Glory: For a Theological Genealogy of Economy and Government*. Translated by Lorenzo Chiesa with Matteo Mandarini. Homo Sacer II,2. Meridian: Crossing Aesthetics. Stanford: Stanford University Press, 2011.

———. *Means without Ends: Notes on Politics*. Translated by Vincenzo Binetti and Cesare Casarino. Minneapolis: University of Minnesota Press, 2000.

———. "On the Limits of Violence." In *Towards the Critique of Violence*, edited by Brendan Moran and Carlo Salzani, 231–38. London: Bloomsbury, 2017.

———. *The Open: Man, and Animal*. Translated by Kevin Attell. Meridian: Crossing Aesthetics. Stanford: Stanford University Press, 2004.

———. *Opus Dei: An Archeology of Duty*. Translated by Adam Kotsko. Homo Sacer II,5. Meridian: Crossing Aesthetics. Stanford: Stanford University Press, 2013.

———. *Potentialities: Collected Essays in Philosophy*. Translated by Daniel Heller-Roazen. Meridian: Crossing Aesthetics. Stanford: Stanford University Press, 1999.

———. *Sovereign Power and Bare Life*. Translated by Daniel Heller-Roazen. Homo Sacer I. Meridian: Crossing Aesthetics. Stanford: Stanford University Press, 1998.

———. *State of Exception*. Translated by Kevin Attell. Homo Sacer II,1. Meridian: Crossing Aesthetics. Stanford: Stanford University Press, 2005.

———. *What Is an Apparatus? And Other Essays*. Translated by David Kishik and Stefan Pedatella. Meridian: Crossing Aesthetics. Stanford: Stanford University Press, 2009.

Akeel, Randall. "Voting and Income." *Econofact*, February 7, 2019.

Alexander, Michelle. *The New Jim Crow*. New York: New Press, 2010.

Anderson, Carol. *White Rage*. New York: Bloomsbury, 2016.

Appelbaum, Anne. *Twilight of Democracy: The Seductive Lure of Authoritarianism*. New York: Doubleday, 2020.

Appiah, Kwame. *Cosmopolitanism: Ethics in a World of Strangers*. New York: Norton, 2006.

Applegate, Jeffery. "The Transitional Object Reconsidered: Some Sociocultural Variations and Their Implications." *Child and Adolescent Social Work* 6 (1989) 38–51.

Arendt, Hannah. *The Human Condition*. Chicago: University of Chicago Press, 1958.

———. *On Violence*. New York: Harvest, 1970.

———. *The Origins of Totalitarianism*. New York: Harvest, 1968.

———. *The Promise of Politics*. New York: Schocken, 2005.

———. "We Refugees." Authors for Peace. https://www.authorsforpeace.com/we-refugees-by-hannah-arendt.html.

Augustine. *The Confessions of St. Augustine*. New York: Mentor, 1963.

Badiou, Alain. *I Know There Are So Many of You*. Translated by Susan Spitzer. Medford, MA: Polity Press, 2019.

Baldwin, James. *The Fire Next Time*. New York: Dial, 1990.

———. *Notes of a Native Son*. Boston: Beacon, 1984.

Balibar, Étienne. *Violence and Civility: On the Limits of Political Philosophy*. Translated by G. M. Goshgarian. New York: Columbia University Press, 2015.

Banerjee, Neela. "U.S. Intelligence Officials Warn Climate Change Is a Worldwide Threat." *Inside Climate News*, January 30, 2019. https://insideclimatenews.org/news/30012019/worldwide-threat-assessment-climate-change-intelligence-agencies-national-security/.

Baptist, Edward. *The Half Has Never Been Told: Slavery and the Making of American Capitalism*. New York: Basic Books, 2014.

Baracchi, Claudio. *Of Myth, Life, and War in Plato's Republic*. Studies in Continental Thought. Bloomington: Indiana University Press, 2002.

Barker, Ernest. *The Politics of Aristotle*. Oxford: Oxford University Press, 1971.

Barry, John. *Roger Williams and the Creation of the American Soul*. New York: Viking, 2012.

Bateson, Gregory. *Steps to an Ecology of Mind*. Chicago: University of Chicago Press, 1972.

Baumgartner, Christoph. "Transformations of Stewardship in the Anthropocene." In *Religion in the Anthropocene*, edited by Celia Deane-Drummond, Sigurd Bergmann, and Markus Vogt, 53–66. Eugene, OR: Cascade Books, 2017.

BBC News. "Europe and Right-Wing Nationalism: A Country-by-Country Guide." https://www.bbc.com/news/world-europe-36130006.

———. "Saudi Arabia Widens Crackdown on Women's Rights Activists." https://www.bbc.com/news/world-middle-east-44223285.

Bechtel, Trevor, Matt Eaton, and Tim Harvie, eds. *Encountering Earth: Thinking Theologically with a More-Than-Human-World*. Eugene, OR: Cascade Books, 2018.

Beebe, Beatrice, and Frank Lachmann. *Infant Research and Adult Treatment*. Hillsdale, NJ: Analytic Press, 2002.

———. "Representation and Internalization in Infancy: Three Principles of Salience." *Psychoanalytic Psychology* 11 (1994) 127–65.

Bekoff, Marc, and Jessica Pierce. *The Animals' Agenda: Freedom, Compassion, and Coexistence in the Human Age*. Boston: Beacon, 2017.

Bell, Daniel. "State and Civil Society." In *The Blackwell Companion to Political Theology*, edited by Peter Scott and William Cavanaugh, 423–38. London: Blackwell, 2007.

Bellinger, Charles. *The Unrepentant Crowd: Søren Kierkegaard and Ernest Becker on the Roots of Political Violence*. Fort Worth: Churchyard, 2016.

Benhabib, Seyla. "The Generalized Other and the Concrete Other: The Kohlberg-Gilligan Controversy and Feminist Theory." In *Feminism as Critique: Essays on Politics and Gender*, edited by Seyla Benhabib and Drucilla Cornell, 158–72. Cambridge, MA: Polity Press, 1987.

———. *Situating the Self*. New York: Routledge, 1992.

Benjamin, Jessica. "Sameness and Difference: Toward an 'Over-inclusive' Model of Gender Development." *Psychoanalytic Inquiry* 15 (1995) 125–42.

Berlin, Isaiah. *Four Essays on Liberty*. Oxford: Oxford University Press, 1969.

———. "Two Concepts of Freedom." In *Liberty*, 166–217. Oxford: Oxford University Press, 2002.

Bialik, Kristen, and Kristi Walker. "Organic Farming Is on the Rise in the U.S." Pew Research Center. https://www.pewresearch.org/fact-tank/2019/01/10/organic-farming-is-on-the-rise-in-the-u-s/.

Bignall, Simone. "On Property and the Philosophy of Poverty: Agamben and Anarchism." In *Agamben and Radical Politics*, edited by Daniel McLoughlin, 49–70. Critical Connections. Edinburgh: Edinburgh University Press, 2017.

Bilgrami, Akeel, ed. *Nature and Value*. New York: Columbia University Press, 2020.

Bingaman, Kirk. *Pastoral and Spiritual Care in a Digital Age: The Future Is Now*. Lanham, MD: Lexington 2018.

Bion, Wilfred. *Attention and Interpretation*. London: Tavistock, 1970.

Birch, Kean. *A Research Agenda for Neoliberalism*. Cheltenham: Elgar, 2017.

Black, Daniel. *The Coming*. New York: St. Martin's, 2015.

Bloeser, Claudia and Titus Stahl, "Hope." In *The Stanford Encyclopedia of Philosophy*, edited by Edward N. Zalta. Spring 2017 ed.

Bochanski, Phillip. *The Virtue of Hope: How Confidence in God Can Lead You to Heaven*. Charlotte: TAN Book, 2019.

Bodin, Jean. *On Sovereignty: Four Chapters from "The Six Books on the Commonwealth."* n.c.: Seven Treasures, 2009.

Boesak, Alan. "Coming in Out of the Wilderness." In *The Emergent Gospel: Theology from the Underside of History: Papers from the Ecumenical Dialogue of Third World Theologians, Dar es Salaam, August 5–12, 1976*, edited by Sergio Torres and Virginia Fabella, 76–95. Maryknoll, NY: Orbis, 1976.

Boer, Roland. *Criticism of Heaven: On Marxism and Theology*. Chicago: Haymarket Books, 2009.

———. *In the Vale of Tears: On Marxism and Theology*. Chicago: Haymarket, 2014.

———. *Political Myth: On the Use and Abuse of Biblical Themes*. Durham: Duke University Press, 2009.

Boggs, Carl. *Crimes of Empire*. New York: Pluto, 2010.

Bollas, Christopher. *The Shadow of the Object*. New York: Columbia University Press, 1987.

Bowlby, John. *A Secure Base: Parent–Child Attachment and Healthy Human Development*. New York: Basic Books, 1988.

Bracke, Sarah. "Bouncing Back: Vulnerability and Resistance in Times of Resilience." In *Vulnerability in Resistance*, edited by Judith Butler, Zeynap Gambetti, and Leticia Sabsay, 52–75. Durham: Duke University Press, 2016.

Brody, Sylvia. "Transitional Objects: Idealization of a Phenomenon." *Psychoanalytic Quarterly* 49 (1980) 561–605.

Bromwich, David. "Natural Piety and Human Responsibility." In *Nature and Value*, edited by Akeel Bilgrami, 261–76. New York: Columbia University Press, 2020.

Brown, Wendy. *Politics Out of History*. Princeton: Princeton University Press, 2001.

———. *Regulating Aversion: Tolerance in the Age of Identity and Empire*. Princeton: Princeton University Press, 2006.

———. *States of Injury: Power and Freedom in Late Modernity*. Princeton: Princeton University Press, 1995.

———. *Undoing the Demos*. New York: Zone, 2015.

———. *Walled States, Waning Sovereignty*. New York: Zone Books, 2014.

Brown-Crawford, Elaine. *Hope in the Holler: A Womanist Theology*. Louisville: Westminster John Knox Press, 2002.

Bubeck, Diemut. *Care, Gender, and Justice*. Oxford: Clarendon, 1995.

Buber, Martin. *I and Thou*. Translated by Ronald Gregor Smith. 2nd ed. New York: Scribner, 1958.

Bunge, Marcia. *The Child in Christian Thought*. Religion, Marriage, and Family Series. Grand Rapids: Eerdmans, 2001.

Buthelezi, Manas. "Toward Indigenous Theology in South Africa." In *The Emergent Gospel: Theology from the Underside of History: Papers from the Ecumenical Dialogue of Third World Theologians, Dar es Salaam, August 5–12, 1976*, edited by Sergio Torres and Virginia Fabella, 56–75. Maryknoll, NY: Orbis, 1976.

Butler, Judith. *The Force of Nonviolence*. London: Verso, 2020.

———. *Precarious Life: The Powers of Mourning and Violence*. New York: Verso, 2004.

Campbell, Constantine. *Paul and the Hope of Glory*. Grand Rapids: Zondervan, 2020.

Camus, Albert. *The Plague*. 1947. Reprint, New York: Penguin, 2002.

Caputo, John. *The Weakness of God: A Theology of the Event*. Bloomington: Indiana University Press, 2006.

———. *Hoping Against Hope: Confessions of a Postmodern Pilgrim*. Minneapolis: Fortress, 2015.

Cavanaugh, William. *The Myth of Religious Violence*. Oxford: Oxford University Press, 2009.

Chakrabarty, Dipesh. "The Climate of History: Four Theses." *Critical Inquiry*, 35 (2009) 197–222.

Climate Science Special Report, 2017. https://science2017.globalchange.gov/.

Coates, Ta-Nehisi. *Between the World and Me*. New York: Spiegel & Grau, 2015.

Colebrook, Claire, and Jason Maxwell. *Agamben*. New York: Polity Press, 2016.

Cone, James. *A Black Theology of Liberation*. 1970. Reprint, Maryknoll, NY: Orbis, 2010.

———. *The Cross and the Lynching Tree*. Maryknoll, NY: Orbis, 2011.

Connolly, William. "The Complexities of Sovereignty." In *Agamben: Sovereignty & Life*, edited by Mathew Calarco and Steven DeCaroli, 23–42. Stanford: Stanford University Press, 2007.

Conroy-Krutz, Emily. *American Imperialism: Converting the World in the Early American Republic*. Ithaca: Cornell University Press, 2015.

Cox, Harvey. *The Market as God*. Cambridge: Harvard University Press, 2016.

Crawford, Neta. "Pentagon Fuel Use, Climate Change, and the Costs of War." Watkins Institute, Brown University, 2019. https://watson.brown.edu/costsofwar/files/cow/imce/papers/2019/Pentagon%20Fuel%20Use,%20Climate%20Change%20and%20the%20Costs%20of%20War%20Final.pdf.

Croatto, J. Severino. *Exodus: A Hermeneutic of Freedom*. Maryknoll, NY: Orbis, 1981.

Crockett, Clayton. *Radical Political Theology: Religion and Politics after Liberalism*. Insurrections. New York: Columbia University Press, 2012.

Crossan, John Dominic. *Jesus: A Revolutionary Biography*. New York: HarperOne, 1995.

————. *God and Empire*. San Francisco: HarperSanFrancisco, 2007.

Cvetkovich, Ann. *Depression: A Public Feeling*. Durham: Duke University Press, 2012.

Daly, Mary. *Beyond God the Father*. Boston: Beacon, 1973.

Danner, Mark. *Stripping the Body Bare: Politics, Violence, War*. New York: Nation Books, 2009.

Danticat, Edwidge. *Everything Inside*. New York: Vintage, 2019.

Davenport, Coral. "Pentagon Signals Security Risks of Climate Change." *New York Times*, October 13, 2014. http://www.nytimes.com/2014/10/14/us/pentagon-says-global-warming-presents-immediate-security-threat.html?_r=1.

Davis, Duane. "Umwelt and Nature in Merleau-Ponty's Ontology." In *Merleau-Ponty and Environmental Philosophy: Dwelling on the Landscapes of Thought*, edited by Suzanne Cataldi and William Hamrick, 117–32. SUNY Series on the Philosophy of the Social Sciences. Albany: State University Press of New York, 2007.

DeCasper, Anthony, and William Fifer. "Of Human Bonding: Newborns Prefer Their Mothers' Voices." *Science* 208 (1980) 1174–76.

DeCasper, Anthony, and Melanie Spence. "Prenatal Maternal Speech Influences Newborns' Perception of Speech Sounds." *Infant Behavior and Development* 4 (1986) 19–36.

DeCaroli, Steven. "Boundary Stones: Giorgio Agamben and the Field of Sovereignty." In *Agamben: Sovereignty & Life*, edited by Mathew Calarco and Steven DeCaroli, 43–69. Stanford: Stanford University Press, 2007.

————. "Giorgi Agamben and the Practice of Poverty." In *Agamben and Radical Politics*, edited by Daniel McLoughlin, 207–33. Critical Connections. Edinburgh: Edinburgh University Press, 2016.

De Dijn, Annelien. *Freedom: An Unruly History*. Cambridge: Harvard University Press, 2020.

De La Durantaye, Leland. *Giorgio Agamben: A Critical Introduction*. Stanford: Stanford University Press, 2009.

De La Torre Miguel A. *Embracing Hopelessness*. Minneapolis: Fortress, 2017.

Deleuze, Gilles, and Félix Guattari. *A Thousand Plateaus: Capitalism and Schizophrenia*. Translated and foreword by Brian Massumi. Minneapolis: University of Minnesota Press, 1987.

————. *What Is Philosophy?* Translated by Hugh Tomlinson and Graham Burchell. European Perspectives. New York: Columbia University Press, 1991.

————. *Anti-Oedipus: Capitalism and Schizophrenia*. Translated by Robert Hurley, Mark Seem, and Helen R. Lane. Minneapolis: University of Minnesota Press, 2003.

D'Entreves, Maurizio. *The Political Philosophy of Hannah Arendt*. London: Routledge, 1994.

Desmond, Matthew. *Evicted: Poverty and Profit in the American City*. New York: Crown, 2016.

de Vries, Hent. "Introduction: Before, Around, and Beyond the Theologico-Politico." In *Political Theologies*, edited by Hent de Vries and Lawrence Sullivan, 1–90. New York: Fordham University Press, 2006.

Dewey, John. *Freedom and Culture*. Buffalo: Prometheus, 1989.

Dickinson, Colby. *Agamben and Theology*. New York: T. & T. Clark, 2011.

Dickinson, Colby. "The Absence of Gender." In *Agamben's Coming Philosophy: Finding a New Use for Theology*, edited by Colby Dickinson and Adam Kotsko, 167–82. New York: Rowman & Littlefield, 2015.

———. *Agamben and Theology*. New York: T. & T. Clark, 2011.

———. "Cur Deus Homo Sacer." In *Agamben's Coming Philosophy: Finding a New Use for Theology*, edited by Colby Dickinson and Adam Kotsko, 201–18. New York: Rowman & Littlefield, 2015.

———. "Gestures of Text and Violence." In *Agamben's Coming Philosophy: Finding a New Use for Theology*, edited by Colby Dickinson and Adam Kotsko, 51–66. New York: Rowman & Littlefield, 2015.

———. "Immanence as Revelation." In *Agamben's Coming Philosophy: Finding a New Use for Theology*, edited by Colby Dickinson and Adam Kotsko, 87–110. New York: Rowman & Littlefield, 2015.

———. "On the 'Coming Philosophy.'" In *Agamben's Coming Philosophy: Finding a New Use for Theology*, edited by Colby Dickinson and Adam Kotsko, 21–40. New York: Rowman & Littlefield, 2015.

Dickinson, Colby and Adam Kotsko. *Agamben's Coming Philosophy: Finding a New Use for Theology*. New York: Rowman & Littlefield, 2015.

———. "Conclusion." In *Agamben's Coming Philosophy: Finding a New Use for Theology*, edited by Colby Dickinson and Adam Kotsko, 245–53. New York: Rowman & Littlefield, 2015.

Dodds, Susan. "Dependence, Care, and Vulnerability." In *Vulnerability: New Essays in Ethics and Feminist Philosophy*, edited by Catriona Mackenzie, Wendy Rogers, and Susan Dodds, 181–203. Oxford: Oxford University Press, 2014.

Doran, Chris. *Hope in the Age of Climate Change*. Eugene, OR: Cascade Books, 2017.

Dufour, Dany-Robert. *The Art of Shrinking Heads: On the New Servitude of the Liberated in the Age of Total Capitalism*. Cambridge: Polity, 2008.

Dufresne, Todd. *The Democracy of Suffering: Life on the Edge of Catastrophe, Philosophy in the Anthropocene*. Montreal: McGill-Queen's University Press, 2019.

Dugan, Lisa. *The Twilight of Equality: Neoliberalism, Cultural Politics, and the Attack on Democracy*. Boston: Beacon, 2003.

Dumouchel, Paul. *The Barren Sacrifice: An Essay on Political Violence*. East Lansing: Michigan State University Press.

Dykstra, Laurel A. *Set Them Free: The Other Side of Exodus*. Eugene, OR: Wipf & Stock, 2014.

Eagleton, Terry. *After Theory*. New York: Basic Books, 2003.

———. *Tragedy*. New Haven: Yale University Press, 2020

Easterly, William. *The Tyranny of Experts: Economics, Dictators, and the Forgotten Rights of the Poor*. New York: Basic Books, 2013.

Eaton, Mathew. "Beyond Human Exceptionalism." In *Religion in the Anthropocene*, edited by Celia Deane-Drummond, Sigurd Bergmann, and Markus Vogt, 202–17. Eugene, OR: Cascade Books, 2017.

Edkins, Jenny. "Whatever Politics." In *Agamben: Sovereignty & Life*, edited by Mathew Calarco and Steven DeCaroli, 70–91. Stanford: Stanford University Press, 2007.

Eggemeier, Matthew. *Against Empire: Ekklesial Resistance and the Politics of Radical Democracy*. Eugene, OR: Cascade Books, 2020.

Ehrenreich, Barbara. *Bright-sided: How Positive Thinking Is Undermining America*. New York: Picador, 2009.

Engster, Daniel. *The Heart of Justice: Care Ethics and Political Theory*. Oxford: Oxford University Press, 2007.

Erikson, Erik. *Childhood and Society*. New York: Norton, 1952.

———. *Insight and Responsibility*. New York: Norton, 1964.

———. *The Life Cycle Completed*. New York: Norton, 1982.

Fanon, Frantz. *Black Skin, White Masks*. Translated by Charles Lam Markmann. 1952. Reprint, New York: Grove, 2008.

Farley, Edward. *Good and Evil: Interpreting a Human Condition*. Minneapolis: Fortress, 1990.

———. *Deep Symbols: Their Postmodern Effacement and Reclamation*. Valley Forge: Trinity, 1996.

Ferguson, Kennan, and Patrice Petro. *After Capitalism*. New Brunswick: Rutgers University Press, 2016.

Flew, Anthony. "Transitional Objects and Phenomena: Interpretations and Comments." In *Between Reality and Fantasy*, edited by Simon Grolnick and Leonard Barkin, 483–502. Northvale: Aronson, 1978.

Floyd, Richard. *Down to Earth: Christian Hope and Climate Change*. Eugene, OR: Cascade Books, 2015.

Foucault, Michel. *Power/Knowledge: Selected Interviews and Other Writings, 1972–1977*. Edited by Colin Gordon. Translated by Colin Gordon et al. New York: Pantheon, 1972.

———. *The Birth of Biopolitics: Lectures at the Collége de France, 1978–1979*. Edited by Michel Senellart. Translated by Graham Burchell. New York: Picador, 2004.

Francis, Pope. *Laudato Si*. http://www.vatican.va/content/francesco/en/encyclicals/ documents/ papa-francesco_20150524_enciclica-laudato-si.html.

Frank, Thomas. *One Market under God: Extreme Capitalism, Market Populism, and the End of Economic Democracy*. New York: Anchor, 2000.

Fraser, Nancy, and Axel Honneth. *Redistribution or Recognition? A Political-Philosophical Exchange*. New York: Verso, 2003.

Freud, Sigmund. "Totem and Taboo." In *Standard Edition*, 12, vii–162. London: Hogarth, 1913.

———. "The Future of an Illusion." In *Standard Edition*, 21, 5–58. London: Hogarth, 1927.

Friedman, Edwin. *Generation to Generation: Family Process in Church and Synagogue*. London: Guilford, 1985.

Frye, Northrop. *The Great Code: The Bible and Literature*. New York: Harcourt Brace, 1982.

Fussell, Paul. *Class*. New York: Ballantine, 1983.

Galtung, Johann. "Structural Violence and Direct Violence: A Note on Operationalization." In *Essays in Peace Research*, vol.1: *Peace: Research, Education, Action*, edited by Johann Galtung, 135–39. Copenhagen: Ejlers, 1975.

Gander, Kashmira, "What Do Evangelical Christians Really Think About Climate Change?" *Mother Jones*, September 22, 2019. https://www.motherjones.com/politics/2019/09/what-do-evangelical-christians-really-think-about-climate-change/.

Gasparino, Charles. *Bought and Paid For: The Hidden Relationship between Wall Street and Washington.* New York: Penguin, 2012.

Gaudium et Spes. *Vatican Council II: The Conciliar and Post Conciliar Documents,* edited by Austin Flannery, 903–1001. Collegeville, MN: Liturgical, 1975.

Gauthier, David. *Martin Heidegger, Emmanuel Levinas, and the Politics of Dwelling.* Lanham, MD: Lexington, 2011.

Genel, Katia, and Jean-Philippe Deranty. *Recognition or Disagreement: A Critical Encounter on the Politics of Freedom, Equality, and Identity: Axel Honneth, Jacques Rancière.* New Directions in Critical Theory. New York: Columbia University Press, 2016.

Gentry, Caron. "Feminist Christian Realism: Vulnerability, Obligation, and Power Politics." *International Feminist Journal of Politics* 18 (2015) 449–67.

Gilens, Martin, and Benjamin Page. "Testing Theories of American Politics: Elites, Interest Groups and Average Citizens." *American Political Science Association,* September, 12 (2014) 564–81.

George, Andrew. *The Epic of Gilgamesh.* London: Penguin Classics, 2003.

Gibson, Danjuma. *Frederick Douglass, A Psychobiography: Rethinking Subjectivity in the Western Experiment of Democracy.* Cham, Switzerland: Palgrave Macmillan, 2018.

Girard, Rene. *Violence and the Sacred.* Baltimore: Johns Hopkins University Press, 1972.

Giroux, Henry. *Disposable Youth: Racialized Memories and the Culture of Cruelty.* London: Routledge, 2012.

Go, Julian. *Patterns of Empire: The British and American Empires, 1688 to the Present.* Cambridge: Cambridge University Press, 2011.

Goldberg, David Theo. *The Threat of Race: Reflections on Racial Neoliberalism.* Malden, MA: Wiley-Blackwell 2009.

Gottlieb, Roger. *Radical Philosophy: Tradition, Counter-Tradition, Politics.* Philadelphia: Temple University Press, 1993.

Grady, John. "Panel: Rise of Authoritarian Governments Pose the Biggest Threat to NATO." USNI News, June 28, 2019. https://news.usni.org/2019/06/28/panel-rise-of-authoritarian-governments-pose-biggest-threat-to-nato.

Gravlee, Scott, "Aristotle on Hope." *Journal of the History of Philosophy* 38 (2000) 461–77.

Grayling, Anthony. *The History of Philosophy.* New York: Penguin, 2019.

Greenough, Chris. *Queer Theologies: The Basics.* New York: Routledge, 2020.

Gricoski, Thomas. *Being Unfolded: Edith Stein and the Meaning of Being.* Washington, DC: Catholic University Press of America, 2020.

Gutiérrez, Gustavo. *A Theology of Liberation: History, Politics, and Salvation.* Translated and edited by Sister Caridad Inda and John Eagleson. Maryknoll, NY: Orbis, 1985.

Haley, Alex. *The Autobiography of Malcolm X.* New York: Ballantine, 1964.

Hamington, Maurice. *Embodied Care: Jane Addams, Maurice Merleau-Ponty, and Feminist Ethics.* Urbana: University of Illinois, 2004.

Hamman, Jaco. *Growing Down: Theology and Human Nature in the Virtual Age.* Waco: Baylor University Press, 2017.

Hardt, Michael and Antonio Negri. *Commonwealth.* Cambridge: Belknap, 2009.

————. *Multitude*. New York: Penguin, 2005.

Harman, Chris. *A People's History of the World*. London: Verso, 2017.

Hartwich, Wolf-Daniel, Aleida Assmann, and Jan Assmann. "Afterword." In *The Political Theology of Paul*, Jacob Taubes, 115–42. Stanford: Stanford University Press, 2004.

Harvey, David. *A Brief History of Neoliberalism*. Oxford: Oxford University Press, 2005.

Hauerwas, Stanley. *Performing the Faith: Bonhoeffer and the Practice of Nonviolence*. 2004. Reprint, Eugene, OR: Wipf & Stock, 2015.

Hauerwas, Stanley, and Romand Coles. *Christianity, Democracy, and the Radical Ordinary: Conversations between a Radical Democrat and a Christian*. Eugene, OR: Cascade Books, 2008.

Hayek, F. A. *The Road to Serfdom: Text and Documents*. Edited by Bruce Caldwell. The Collected Works of F. A. Hayek 2. Chicago: University of Chicago Press, 2007.

Hedges, Chris, and Joe Sacco. *Days of Destruction, Days of Revolt*. New York: Nation Books, 2012.

Held, Virginia. *The Ethics of Care: Personal, Political, and Global*. Oxford: Oxford University Press, 2006.

————, ed. *Justice and Care: Essential Readings in Feminist Ethics*. Boulder, CO: Westview, 1995.

Hellerstein, Erica, and Fine, Ken. "A Million Tons of Feces and an Unbearable Stench: Life Near Industrial Pig Farms." https://www.theguardian.com/us-news/2017/sep/20/north-carolina-hog-industry-pig-farms.

Helsel, Phillip. *Pastoral Power Beyond Psychology's Imagination*. New York: Palgrave, 2015.

Hendricks, Obery M. *The Politics of Jesus*. New York: Three Leaves, 2006.

————. *The Universe Bends toward Justice: Radical Reflections on the Bible, the Church and the Body Politic*. Maryknoll, NY: Orbis, 2011.

Henriksen, Jan-Olav "Hope: A Theological Exploration." *Studia Theologica—A Nordic Journal of Theology* 73/2 (2019) 117–33.

Hescox, Mitch and Paul Douglas. *Caring for Creation: The Evangelical's Guide to Climate Change and a Healthy Environment*. Bloomington: Bethany House, 2016.

Hobbes, Thomas. *Leviathan*. Cambridge: Cambridge University Press, 1991.

Hoggett, Paul. "Climate Change in a Perverse Culture." In *Engaging with Climate Change: Psychoanalytic and Interdisciplinary Perspectives*, edited by Sally Weintrobe, 56–71. New Library of Psychoanalysis. New York: Routledge, 2013.

Honneth, Axel. *Freedom's Right: The Social Foundations of Democratic Life*. Translated by Joseph Ganahl. New York: Columbia University Press, 2014.

————. *The Idea of Socialism*. New York: Polity Press, 2017.

————. *The Pathologies of Individual Freedom: Hegel's Social Theory*. Princeton: Princeton University Press, 2010.

————. "Recognition as Ideology." In *Recognition and Power*, Bert Van den Blink and David Owens, 323–47. Cambridge: Cambridge University Press, 2007.

————. *The Struggle for Recognition*. Cambridge: MIT Press, 1995.

Honneth, Axel, and Jacques Rancière. *Freedom's Right: The Social Foundations of Democratic Life*. New York: Columbia University Press, 2011.

Horsley, Richard A. *Covenant Economics: A Biblical Vision of Justice for All*. Louisville: Westminster John Knox, 2009.

————. *Jesus and Empire*. Minneapolis: Fortress, 2003.

————. *Jesus and the Power: Conflict, Covenant, and the Hope of the Poor*. Minneapolis: Fortress. 2011.

Howard, Jacqueline. "US Ranks Lower than 38 Other Countries When It Comes to Children's Wellbeing, New Report Says." CNN, February 19, 2020. https://www.cnn.com/2020/02/18/health/children-health-rankings-unicef-who-lancet-report-index.html.

Human Rights Watch Report. "Saudia Arabia: 10 Reasons Why Women Flee." https://www.hrw.org/news/2019/01/30/saudi-arabia-10-reasons-why-women-flee.

Hunter, James. *To Change the World*. Oxford: Oxford University Press, 2010.

Illouz, Eva. *Cold Intimacies: The Making of Emotional Capitalism*. Cambridge, MA: Polity Press, 2007.

IPB. "The Military's Impact on the Environment." 2017. http://www.ipb.org/wp-content/uploads/2017/03/briefing-paper.pdf.

James, William. *The Principles of Psychology*. Vol. 1. 1918. Reprint, New York: Holt, 1956.

JanMohamed, Abdul. *The Death-bound Subject: Richard Wright's Archaeology of Death*. Durham: Duke University Press, 2004.

Jeffko, Walter. "Introduction." In *Conditions of Freedom*, John Macmurray, vii–xxvii. London: Humanities Press International, 1993.

Jeremiah, Anderson. "Farming Grief and Hope." In *Words for a Dying World*, edited by Hannah Malcolm, 79–87. London: SCM, 2020.

Johnson, Cedric. *Race, Religion, and Resilience in the Neoliberal Age*. New York: Palgrave Macmillan, 2016.

Johnson, Chalmers. *Blowback*. New York: Owl, 1999.

————. *Sorrows of Empire*. New York: Owl, 2004.

Jones, Stedman. *Masters of the Universe: Hayek, Friedman, and the Birth of Neoliberal Politics*. Princeton: Princeton University Press, 2012.

Jorgenson, Kiara, and Katherine Hayhoe. *Ecotheology: A Christian Conversation*. Grand Rapids: Eerdmans, 2020.

Josefson, Jim. *Hannah Arendt's Aesthetic Politics; Freedom and the Beautiful*. New York: Palgrave Macmillan, 2019.

Kahn, Paul. *Political Theology: Four New Chapters on the Concept of Sovereignty*. New York: Columbia University Press, 2011.

Kalyvas, Andreas. "The Sovereign Weaver." In *Politics, Metaphysics, and Death: Essays on Giorgi Agamben's Homo Sacer*, edited by Andrew Norris, 107–34. Durham: Duke University Press, 2005.

Kant, Emmanuel. *Idea for a Universal History from a Cosmopolitan Point of View* (1784). Translation by Lewis White Beck. From Immanuel Kant, "On History." Indianapolis: Bobbs-Merrill, 1963. https://www.marxists.org/reference/subject/ethics/kant/universal-history.htm.

Kaplan, Amy. *The Anarchy of Empire in the Making of U.S. Culture*. Cambridge: Harvard University Press, 2002.

Kaur, Valerie. *See No Stranger: A Memoir and Manifesto of Revolutionary Love*. New York: One World, 2020.

Keller, Catherine. *Political Theology of the Earth: Our Planetary Emergency and the Struggle for a New Public*. New York: Columbia University Press, 2018.

Kendi, Ibram, and Jason Reynolds. *Stamped from the Beginning: The Definitive History of Racist Ideas in America*. New York: Bold Type, 2020.

Kertzer, David I. *Ritual, Politics, and Power*. New Haven: Yale University Press, 1988

Kestenberg, Judith, and Joan Weinstein. "Transitional Objects and Body Image Formation." In *Between Reality and Fantasy*, edited by Simon Grolnick and Leonard Barkin, 75–96. Northvale Aronson, 1978.

King, Martin Luther, Jr. *The Autobiography of Martin Luther King, Jr.* Edited by Clayborne Carson. New York: Grand Central, 1998.

———. "Beyond Vietnam: A Time to Break Silence." Riverside Speech, 1967. http://www.crmvet.org/info/mlk_viet.pdf.

Klein, Naomi. *Shock Doctrine: The Rise of Disaster Capitalism*. New York: Holt, 2007.

———. *This Changes Everything: Capitalism vs. the Climate*. New York: Simon & Schuster, 2014.

Kochenov, Dimitry. *Citizenship*. Cambridge: MIT Press, 2019.

Koivunen, Anu, Katariina Kyrölä, and Ingrid Ryberg. *The Power of Vulnerability: Mobilizing Affect in Feminist, Queer, and Anti-racist Media Cultures*. Manchester: Manchester University Press, 2019.

Kojéve, Alexandre. *Introduction to the Reading of Hegel*. New York: Basic Books, 1969.

Kolbert, Elizabeth. *The Sixth Extinction: An Unnatural History*. New York: Holt, 2014.

Kompridis, Nikolas. "Nonhuman Agency and Human Normativity." In *Nature and Value*, edited by Akeel Bilgrami, 240–60. New York: Columbia University Press, 2020.

Kotsko, Adam, and Carlo Salzani. *Agamben's Philosophical Lineage*. Edinburgh: Edinburgh University Press, 2017.

Kotsko, Adam. "Agamben's Messianic Nihilism." In *Agamben's Coming Philosophy: Finding a New Use for Theology*, edited by Colby Dickinson and Adam Kotsko, 111–24. New York: Rowman & Littlefield, 2015.

———. "Genealogy and Political Theology." In *Agamben's Coming Philosophy: Finding a New Use for Theology*, edited by Colby Dickinson and Adam Kotsko, 157–65. New York: Rowman & Littlefield, 2015.

———. "Perhaps Psychoanalysis." In *Agamben's Coming Philosophy: Finding a New Use for Theology*, edited by Colby Dickinson and Adam Kotsko, 137–56. New York: Rowman & Littlefield, 2015.

Kujawa-Holbrook, Sheryl, and Karen Montagno, eds. *Injustice and the Care of Souls: Taking Oppression Seriously in Pastoral Care*. Minneapolis: Fortress, 2009.

Kumin, Ivri. *Pre-Object Relatedness: Early Attachment and the Psychoanalytic Situation*. Guilford Psychoanalysis Series. London: Guilford, 1996.

LaMothe, Ryan. *Care of Souls, Care of Polis: Toward a Political Pastoral Theology*. Eugene, OR: Cascade Books, 2017.

———. "On Being at Home in the World: A Psychoanalytic-Political Perspective on Dwelling in the Anthropocene Era." *Psychoanalytic Review* 107 (2020) 123–51.

———. *Pastoral Reflections on Global Citizenship: Framing the Political in Terms of Care, Faith, and Community*. Emerging Perspectives in Pastoral Theology and Care. Lanham, MD: Lexington, 2018.

Lane, Melissa. *The Birth of Politics: Eight Greek and Roman Political Ideas and Why They Matter*. Princeton: Princeton University Press, 2014.

Larsen, Stephen. *The Mythic Imagination*. Rochester, VT: Inner Traditions International, 1990.

Latour, Bruno. *Down to Earth: Politics in the New Climatic Regime*. New York: Polity Press, 2018.

Leahy, Stephen. "One Million Species at Risk of Extinction, UN Report Warns." *National Geographic*, 2019.

Lear, Jonathan. *Radical Hope: Ethics in the Face of Cultural Devastation*. Cambridge: Harvard University Press, 2006.

Lechte, John, and Saul Newman. *Agamben and the Politics of Human Rights: Statelessness, Images, Violence*. Edinburgh: Edinburgh University Press, 2015.

Lemm, Vanessa. "The Embodiment of Truth and the Politics of Community." In *The Government of Life: Foucault, Biopolitics, and Neoliberalism*, edited by Vanessa Lemm and Miguel Vatter, 208–24. New York: Fordham University Press, 2015.

Lemna, Keith. *The Apocalypse of Wisdom: Louis Bouyer's Theological Recovery of the Cosmos*. Brooklyn: Angelica, 2019.

Lévi-Strauss, Claude. *Myth and Meaning: Cracking the Code of Culture*. 1978. Reprint, New York: Schocken, 1995.

———. *The Savage Mind*. The Nature of Human Society Series. Chicago: University of Chicago Press, 1966.

———. *Totemism*. Translated by Rodney Needham. New York: Beacon, 1963.

Lévinas, Emmanuel. *Totality and Infinity: An Essay on Exteriority*. Translated by Alphonse Lingis. Duquesne Studies: Philosophical Series 24. Pittsburgh: Duquesne University Press, 1969.

———. *Otherwise than Being: Or, Beyond Essence*. Translated by Alphonse Lingis. Pittsburgh: Duquesne University Press, 1998.

Lincoln, Bruce. *Theorizing Myth: Narrative Ideology, and Scholarship*. Chicago: University of Chicago Press, 2000.

Litt, Carole. "Theories of Transitional Object Attachment: An Overview." *International Journal of Behavioral Health* 9 (1986) 383–99.

Lubrano, Alfred. *Limbo: Blue-Collar Roots, White-Collar Dreams*. Hoboken, NJ: Wiley, 2004.

Lukács, Georg. *History and Class Consciousness*. Cambridge: MIT Press, 1968.

Lundestad, Geir. *The American "Empire."* Oxford: Oxford University Press 1990.

Macmurray, John. *Reason and Emotion*. New York: Humanity Books, 1935.

———. *Persons in Relation*. London: Humanities Press, 1991.

———. *Conditions of Freedom*. London: Humanities Press International, 1993.

———. "The Conception of Society." In *John Macmurray: Selected Philosophical Writings*, edited by Esther McIntosh, 98–111. Exeter, UK: Imprint Academic, 2004.

Malcolm, Hannah. "Introduction." In *Words for a Dying World*, edited by Hannah Malcolm, xxix–xxxv. London: SCM, 2020.

Mander, Jerry. *The Capitalism Papers: Fatal Flaws in an Obsolete System*. Berkeley: Counterpoint, 2012.

Mann. Geoff. *Disassembly Required: A Field Guide to Actually Existing Capitalism*. Edinburgh: AK Press, 2013.

Mantena, Karuna. "Showdown for Nonviolence: The Theory and Practice of Nonviolent Politics." In *To Shape a New World: Essays on the Political Philosophy of Martin Luther King, Jr.*, edited by Tommie Shelby and Brandon Terry, 78–104. Cambridge: Belknap, 2018.

Marable, Manning. *Malcolm X: A Life of Reinvention*. New York: Viking, 2011.

Marcuse, Herbert. *One-dimensional Man*. New York: Beacon, 1964.

Margalit, Avishai. *The Decent Society*. Cambridge: Harvard University Press, 1996.

————. *On Betrayal*. Cambridge: Harvard University Press, 2017.

Martel, James. "The Anarchist Life We Are Already Living: Benjamin and Agamben on Bare Life and the Resistance to Sovereignty." In *Towards the Critique of Violence: Walter Benjamin and Giorgio Agamben*, edited by Brendan Moran and Carlo Salzani, 187–200. New York: Bloomsbury, 2017.

Marx, Karl. "Theses on Feuerbach." In *On Religion*. 1964. Reprint, Classics in Religious Studies 3. Chico, CA: Scholars, 1982.

Mauelshagen, Franz. "Bridging the Great Divide." In *Religion in the Anthropocene*, edited by Celia Deane-Drummond, Sigurd Bergmann, and Markus Vogt, 87–102. Eugene, OR: Cascade Books, 2017.

Mbembe, Achille. *Necropolitics*. Translated by Steven Corcoran. Durham: Duke University Press, 2019.

McGuire, Danielle. *At the Dark End of the Street: Black Women, Rape, and Resistance*. New York: Random House, 2011.

McLoughlin, Daniel. "Agamben on the Post-Fordist Spectacle." In *Agamben and Radical Politics*, edited by Daniel McLoughlin, 91–114. Critical Connections. Edinburgh: Edinburgh University Press, 2016.

Meijer, Eva. *Animal Languages*. Translated by Laura Watkinson. Cambridge: MIT Press, 2020.

————. *When Animals Speak: Toward an Interspecies Democracy*. Animals in Context. New York: New York University Press, 2019.

Merleau-Ponty, Maurice. *Phenomenology of Perception*. Translated by Colin Smith. Routledge Classics. London: Routledge, 2002.

Military's Impact on the Environment. *International Peace Bureau*. Geneva, 2002. http://www.ipb.org/wp-content/uploads/2017/03/briefing-paper.pdf.

Mill, John Stuart. "On Liberty." In *On Liberty, Utilitarianism and Other Essays*, edited by Mark Philp and Frederick Rosen, 5–113. Oxford: Oxford University Press, 2015.

————. *On Liberty and the Subjection of Women*. New York: Penguin, 2006.

Miller, Alice. *For Your Own Good: Hidden Cruelty in Child-rearing and the Roots of Violence*. New York: Farrar, Straus & Giroux, 2002.

Miller, Richard W., ed. *God, Creation, and Climate Change: A Catholic Responses to the Environmental Crisis*. Maryknoll, NY: Orbis, 2010.

Miller, Zoe. "The Most Environmentally Friendly Cities in the U.S." *Insider*. https://www.insider.com/greenest-us-cities-2018-5.

Mills, Catherine. *The Philosophy of Agamben*. Montreal: McGill-Queen's University Press, 2008.

Minakov, Mykhailo. "The Authoritarian Belt in Europe's East." *Wilson Center*, May 15, 2018. https://www.wilsoncenter.org/blog-post/the-authoritarian-belt-europes-east.

Mitchell, Stephen A. *Hope and Dread in Psychoanalysis*. New York: Basic Books, 1993.

Mogenson, Greg. *A Most Accursed Religion: When a Trauma Becomes God*. Putnam, CT: Spring.

Moltmann, Jürgen. *The Crucified God: The Cross of Christ as the Foundation and Criticism of Christian Theology*. Translated by R. A. Wilson and John Bowden. Minneapolis: Fortress, 2015.

————. *The Gospel of Liberation*. Translated by H. Wayne Pipkin. Waco: Word Books, 1973.

————. *The Living God and the Fullness of Life*. Translated by Margaret Kohl. Louisville: Westminster John Knox, 2015.

———. *The Spirit of Hope: Theology for a World in Peril.* Translated by Margaret Kohl and Brian McNeil. Louisville: Westminster John Knox, 2019.

———. *Theology of Hope: On the Ground and Implications of a Christian Eschatology.* Translated by James W. Leitch. 1967. Reprint, Twentieth Century Religious Thought. Minneapolis: Fortress, 1993.

Moody-Adams, Michele. "The Path of Conscientious Citizenship." In *To Shape a New World: Essays on the Political Philosophy of Martin Luther King, Jr.*, edited by Tommie Shelby and Brandon Terry, 269–89. Cambridge: Belknap, 2018.

Moon, Dawne. *God, Sex, and Politics: Homosexuality and Everyday Theologies.* Chicago: University of Chicago Press, 2004.

Moore, Jason. "Name the System! Anthropocene & the Capitalocene Alternative." https://jasonwmoore.wordpress.com/tag/capitalocene/, 2016.

Morris, Brian. *Bakunin: The Philosophy of Freedom.* New York: Black Rose, 1993.

Murdoch, Iris. *The Sovereignty of the Good.* 1970. Reprint, Routledge Classics. New York: Routledge, 2001.

Myre, Greg and Kaplow, Larry. "Seven Things to Know about Israeli Settlements." *NPR*, Dec. 29, 2016. https://www.npr.org/sections/parallels/2016/12/29/507377617/seven-things-to-know-about-israeli-settlements.

Nancy, Jean-Luc. *Being Singular Plural.* Translated by Robert D. Richardson and Anne E. O'Byrne. Meridian: Crossing Aesthetics. Stanford: Stanford University Press, 2000.

Newkirk, Vann. "Trump's EPA Concludes Environmental Racism Is Real." *The Atlantic*, February 28, 2018. https://www.theatlantic.com/politics/archive/2018/02/the-trump-administration-finds-that-environmental-racism-is-real/554315/.

Nichols, Kyle and Bina Gogineni. "The Anthropocene Dating Problem." In *Nature and Value*, edited by Akeel Bilgrami, 46–62. Columbia: Columbia University Press, 2020.

Niebuhr, H. Richard. *Faith on Earth.* New Haven: Yale University Press, 1989.

Niebuhr, Reinhold. *The Irony of American History.* Chicago: University of Chicago Press, 1952.

Nield, David. "Scientists Say It Could Already Be 'Game Over' for Climate Change." *Science Alert*, 11 November 2016. https://www.sciencealert.com/scientists-say-it-could-already-be-game-over-for-climate-change.

Noddings, Nel. *Caring: A Feminine Approach to Ethics and Moral Education.* Berkeley: University of California Press, 1984.

Noël, Reginald. "Race, Economics, and Social Status." Bureau of Labor and Statistics, May 2018.

Norris, Andrew, "Introduction." In *Politics, Metaphysics, and Death: Essays on Giorgi Agamben's Homo Sacer,* edited by Andrew Norris, 1–30. Durham: Duke University Press, 2005.

Norris, Pippa, and Ronald Inglehart. *Cultural Backlash: Trump, Brexit, and Authoritarian Populism.* Cambridge: Cambridge University Press, 2019.

Northcott, Michael. "On Going Gently into the Anthropocene." In *Religion in the Anthropocene*, edited by Celia Deane-Drummond, Sigurd Bergmann, and Markus Vogt, 19–34. Eugene, OR: Cascade Books, 2017.

———. *A Political Theology of Climate Change.* London: SPCK, 2014.

Novak, Michael. *The Spirit of Democratic Capitalism.* New York: Simon & Schuster, 1982.

―――. *Toward a Theology of the Corporation*. Washington, DC: AEI Press, 1987.

Nussbaum, Martha. "From Anger to Love: Self-Purification and Political Resistance." In *To Shape a New World: Essays on the Political Philosophy of Martin Luther King, Jr.*, edited by Tommie Shelby and Brandon Terry, 105–25. Cambridge: Belknap, 2018.

―――. *The Monarchy of Fear*. New York: Simon & Schuster, 2018.

―――. *Political Emotions: Why Love Matters for Justice*. Cambridge: Belknap, 2013.

Oksala, Johanna. *Foucault, Politics, and Violence*. Evanston: Northwestern University Press, 2012.

Oliner, Pearl, and Samuel Oliner. *Toward a Caring Society*. Westport: Praeger, 1995.

Orwell, George. *Politics and the English Language*. E-Canada Books, 1946/2018.

Our World in Data. "Extreme Poverty." https://ourworldindata.org/extreme-poverty.

Ozacky-Lazar, Sarah. "Tackling Israeli Prejudice." *Palestine-Israel Journal*, 12/2–3 (2005). http://www.pij.org/details.php?id=360.

Pannenberg, Wolfhart. *Theology and the Kingdom of God*. Edited by Richard John Neuhaus. Philadelphia: Westminster, 1969.

Parenti, Christian. *Tropic of Chaos: Climate Change and the New Geography of Violence*. New York: Nation Books, 2011.

Patterson, Orlando. *Freedom in the Making of Western Culture*. New York: Basic Books, 1991.

―――. *Slavery and Social Death*. Cambridge: Harvard University Press, 1982.

Pérez-Huber, Lindsay, and Daniel Solózano. *Racial Microaggressions: Using Critical Race Theory to Respond of Everyday Racism*. New York: Teachers College Press, 2020.

Pew Research Center. "Two-thirds of Americans Think Government Should Do More on Climate." https://pewresearch.org/science/2020/06/23/two-thirds-of-americans-think-government-should-do-more-on-climate.

Phillips, Elizabeth. *Political Theology: A Guide for the Perplexed*. Guides for the Perplexed. New York: T. & T. Clark, 2012.

Piketty, Thomas. *Capital and Ideology*. Cambridge: Harvard University Press, 2020.

―――. *Capital in the Twenty-First Century*. Cambridge: Belknap, 2014.

Pieper, Josef. *Faith, Hope, and Love*. New York: Random House, 1991.

Pieris, Aloyssius. "Political Theologies in Asia." In *The Blackwell Companion to Political Theology*, edited by Peter Scott and William Cavanaugh, 256–69. Blackwell Companions to Religion. London: Blackwell, 2007.

Pistor, Katharina. *The Code of Capital: How the Law Creates Wealth and Inequality*. Princeton: Princeton University Press, 2019.

Plato. *The Great Dialogues of Plato*. Translated by W. H. D. Rouse. New York: Mentor, 1956.

Plessner, Helmut. *Political Anthropology*. Translated by Nils F. Schott. Edited and with an introduction by Heike Delitz and Robert Seyfert. Epilogue by Joachim Fischer. Evanston: Northwestern University Press, 2018.

Polanyi, Michael. *Personal Knowledge: Towards a Post-critical Philosophy*. Chicago: Chicago University Press, 1962.

Polkinghorne, Donald E. *Narrative Knowing and the Human Sciences*. SUNY Series in Philosophy of the Social Sciences. Albany: SUNY Press, 1988.

Poole, Kristen. *Christianity in a Time of Climate Change: To Give a Future Hope*. Eugene, OR: Wipf & Stock, 2020.

Popper, Karl. *The Open Society and Its Enemies*. London: Routledge & Kegan Paul, 2002.

Porter, Eduardo. *American Poison: How Radical Hostility Destroyed Our Promise*. New York: Knopf, 2020.

Primera, German. *The Political Ontology of Giorgio Agamben: Signatures of Life and Power*. Bloomsbury Studies in Continental Philosophy. New York: Bloomsbury Academic, 2019.

Prozorov, Sergei. *Agamben and Politics: A Critical Introduction*. Thinking Politics. Edinburgh: Edinburgh University Press, 2014.

———. "Agamben, Badiou and Affirmative Biopolitics." In *Agamben and Radical Politics*, edited by Daniel McLoughlin, 165–88. Critical Connections. Edinburgh: Edinburgh University Press, 2016.

Pruyser, Paul W. *The Play of the Imagination: Toward a Psychoanalysis of Culture*. New York: International Universities Press, 1983.

Rank, Otto. *The Trauma of Birth*. 1929. Reprint, New York: Routledge, 2014.

Ramsay, Nancy. "Compassionate Resistance: An Ethic for Pastoral Care and Counseling." *Journal of Pastoral Care* 52 (1999) 217–26.

Redfield-Jamison, Kay. *Exuberance: The Passion for Life*. New York: Vintage, 2005.

Reuther, Rosemary Radford. *Sexism and God-Talk: Towards a Feminist Theology*. Boston: Beacon, 1983.

Rieger, Joerg. *Christ & Empire: From Paul to Postcolonial Times*. Minneapolis: Fortress, 2007.

———. "Christian Theology and Empires." In *Empire and the Christian Tradition: New Readings of Classical Theologians*, edited by Kwok Pui-lan, Dan Compier, and Joerg Rieger, 1–14. Minneapolis: Fortress, 2007.

Remnick, David. "One-State Reality." *The New Yorker*, November, 17, 2014. https://www.newyorker.com/magazine/2014/11/17/one-state-reality.

Ricard, Matthieu. *Altruism: The Power of Compassion to Change Yourself and the World*. New York: Little, Brown, 2015.

Riceour, Paul. "Original Sin: A Study in Meaning." Translated by Paul McCormick. In *The Conflict of Interpretations*, edited by Paul McCormick, 269–86. Evanston, IL: Northwestern University Press, 1974.

Richardson, Joanna. *Place and Identity: The Performance of Home*. Abingdon, UK: Routledge, 2019.

"R. J. Rushdoony." *Wikipedia*. https://en.wikipedia.org/wiki/R._J. Rushdoony.

Robbins, Jeffery. *Radical Democracy and Political Theology*. New York: Columbia University Press, 2014.

Robinson, Fiona. *Globalizing Care: Ethics, Feminist Theory, and International Relations*. Boulder, CO: Westview, 1999.

———. *The Ethics of Care: A Feminist Approach to Human Security*. Philadelphia: Temple University Press, 2011.

Rogers-Vaughn, Bruce. "Blessed Are Those Who Mourn: Depression as Political Resistance." *Pastoral Psychology* 63 (2014) 489–502.

———. *Caring for Souls in a Neoliberal Age*. New Approaches to Religion and Power. New York: Palgrave, 2016.

Rorty, Richard. *Truth and Progress*. Philosophical Papers 3. Cambridge: Cambridge University Press, 1998.

Rousseau, Bryant. "In New Zealand Lands and Rivers Can Be People Too (Legally Speaking)." *The New York Times*, July 13, 2016.

Rousseau, Jean-Jacques. *On the Social Contract*. Translated by Doanld A. Cress. Introduction and new annotation by David Wootton. 2nd ed. Indianapolis: Hackett, 2019.

Ruggiero, Vincenzo. *Visions of Political Violence*. London: Routledge, 2020.

Rumscheidt, Barbara. *No Room for Grace: Pastoral Theology and Dehumanization in the Global Economy*. 1998. Reprint, Eugene, OR: Wipf & Stock, 2012.

Ryan, Alan. *On Politics: A History of Political Thought*. New York: Liveright, 2012.

Safron, Jeremy, and Christopher Muran. "The Resolution of Ruptures in the Therapeutic Alliance." *Journal of Consulting and Clinical Psychology* 64 (1996) 447–58.

Saïd, Edward. *Orientalism*. New York: Vintage, 1979.

———. *Culture and Imperialism*. New York: Vintage, 1994.

Saiving, Valerie. "The Human Situation: A Feminine View." In *WomenSpirit Rising*, edited by Carol Christ and Judith Plaskow, 25–42, San Francisco: Harper & Row, 1979.

Samuels, Andrew. *The Political Psyche*. London: Routledge, 1993.

Santiago Ali, Mustaffa. "Environmental Racism Is Killing People of Color: Climate Change Will Make It Worse." *The Guardian*, July 28, 2020. https://www.theguardian.com/commentisfree/2020/jul/28/climate-change-enviromental-racism-america.

Sassen, Sakia. *Expulsions: Brutality and Complexity in the Global Economy*. Cambridge, MA: Belknap, 2014.

Sawyer, Michael. *Black Minded: The Political Philosophy of Malcolm X*. London: Pluto, 2019.

Sayer, Andrew. *The Moral Significance of Class*. Cambridge: Cambridge University Press, 2005.

Schell, Jonathan. "The Human Shadow." In *Nature and Value*, edited by Akeel Bilgrami, 13–24. New York: Columbia University Press, 2020.

———. "Nature and Value." In *Nature and Value*, edited by Akeel Bilgrami, 1–12. New York: Columbia University Press, 2020.

Schmitt, Carl. *The Concept of the Political*. Translated by George Schwab. Chicago: Chicago University Press, 1996.

———. *Political Theology: Four Chapters on the Concept of Sovereignty*. Translated by George Schwab. Chicago: University of Chicago Press, 2005.

Schore, Alan. *Affect Regulation and the Repair of the Self*. New York: Norton, 2003.

Schüssler Fiorenza, Elisabeth. *Discipleship of Equals: A Critical Ekklesia-ology of Liberation*. New York: Crossroads, 1998.

Segundo, Jon. *The Liberation of Theology*. Translated by John Drury. 1976. Reprint, Eugene, OR: Wipf & Stock, 2002.

Sevenhuijsen, Selma. *Citizenship and the Ethics of Care: Feminist Considerations on Justice, Morality and Politics*. Translated by Liz Savage. London: Routledge, 1998.

Silva, Jennifer. *Coming up Short: Working Class Adulthood in the Age of Uncertainty*. Oxford: Oxford University Press, 2013.

Smiley, Tavis, with David Ritz. *Death of a King: The Real Story of Dr. Martin Luther King Jr.'s Final Year*. New York: Little, Brown, 2014.

Smith, Mick. *Against Ecological Sovereignty: Ethics, Biopolitics, and Saving the Natural World*. Minneapolis: University of Minneapolis Press, 2011.

Sobrino, Jon. *The True Church and the Poor*. Translated by Matthew J. O'Connell. Maryknoll, NY: Orbis, 1984.

Sorabji, Richard. *Emotion and Peace of Mind.* Oxford: Oxford University Press, 2000.

Sorel, Georges. *Reflections on Violence.* New York: Dover, 2004.

Soss, Joe, Richard Fording, and Sanford Schram. *Disciplining the Poor: Neoliberal Paternalism and the Persistent Power of Race.* Chicago: University of Chicago Press, 2011.

Spanierman, Lisa, and Sue Derald Wing. *Microaggressions in Everyday Life.* Hoboken, NJ: Wiley, 2020.

Speth, James. *The Bridge at the Edge of the World: Capitalism, the Environment, and Crossing from Crisis to Sustainability.* New Haven: Yale University Press, 2008.

Steiner, Rudolf. *The Philosophy of Freedom.* Translated by Michael Wilson. London: Steiner.

Stern, Daniel. *The Interpersonal World of the Infant.* New York: Basic Books, 1985.

Stern, Donnel. *Unformulated Experience: From Dissociation to Imagination in Psychoanalysis.* Relational Perspectives Book Series 8. Hillsdale, NJ: Analytic Press, 1997.

Stiglitz, Joseph. *The Great Divide: Unequal Societies and What We Can Do About Them.* New York: Norton, 2015.

———. *The Price of Inequality.* New York: Norton, 2012.

Strauss, Leo. "What Is Political Philosophy?" https://www.goodreads.com/work/quotes/270047-what-is-political-philosophy-and-other-studies.

Strauss, Leo, and Joseph Cropsey. "Introduction." In *History of Political Philosophy,* 1–6, edited by Leo Strauss and Joseph Cropsey. 3rd ed. Chicago: University of Chicago Press, 1987.

———. *What Is Political Philosophy? And Other Studies.* 1959. Reprint, Chicago: Chicago University Press, 1988.

Tanner, Michael. "How Did Bill Clinton's Welfare Reform Turnout." *The Cato Institute.* http.

Taylor, Mark. *The Executed God: The Way of the Cross in Lockdown America.* Minneapolis: Fortress, 2015.

Taubes, Jacob. *The Political Theology of Paul.* Translated by Dan Hollander. Stanford: Stanford University Press, 2004.

Thalos, Miriam. *A Social Theory of Freedom.* New York: Routledge, 2016.

Threadcraft, Shatema, and Brandon Terry. "Gender Trouble: Manhood, Inclusion, and Justice." In *To Shape a New World: Essays on the Political Philosophy of Martin Luther King, Jr.,* edited by Tommie Shelby and Brandon Terry, 205–35. Cambridge: Belknap, 2018.

Tillich, Paul. *Courage to Be.* New Haven: Yale University Press, 1952.

Tocqueville, Alexis de. *Democracy in America.* Translated by Arthur Goldhammer. New York: Bantam, 2004.

Trepagnier, Barbara. *Silent Racism.* Boulder, CO: Paradigm, 2010.

Tronto, Joan. *Caring Democracy: Markets, Equality, and Justice.* New York: New York University Press, 2013.

———. *Moral Boundaries: A Political Argument for an Ethic of Care.* New York: Routledge, 1993.

Tully, James. "Life Sustains Life." In *Nature and Value,* edited by Akeel Bilgrami, 163–80. Columbia: Columbia University Press, 2020.

Tuttle, Brad. "The Cost of Being Black." *Money,* June 19, 2020. https://money.com/wealth-gap-race-economic-justice/.

Ugilt, Rasmus. *Giorgio Agamben: Political Philosophy.* Humanities-E-books, 2014.

United States Council of Catholic Bishops. "The Challenge of Peace: God's Promise and Our Response." May 3, 1983. https://www.usccb.org/upload/challenge-peace-gods-promise-our-response-1983.pdf.

US Department of Defense. "Climate Change Report, 2019." Jan 29, 2019. https://media.defense.gov/2019/Jan/29/2002084200/-1/-1/1/CLIMATE-CHANGE-REPORT-2019.PDF.

Valencia, Sayak. *Gore Capitalism*. Translated by John Plueker. Semiotext(e) Intervention Series 24. South Pasadena: Semiotext(e), 2018.

Valverde, Miriam. "Have Deportations Increased under Donald Trump? Here's What the Data Shows." *Politifact*, December 19, 2017.

Van Den Noortgaete, Francis. "Reconsidering the Anthropocene Milieu." In *Religion in the Anthropocene*, edited by Celia Deane-Drummond, Sigurd Bergmann, and Markus Vogt, 155–70. Eugene, OR: Cascade Books, 2017.

Vogt, Markus. "Human Ecology as a Key Discipline of Environmental Ethics." In *Religion in the Anthropocene*, edited by Celia Deane-Drummond, Sigurd Bergmann, and Markus Vogt, 235–52. Eugene, OR: Cascade Books, 2017.

Von Mises, Ludwig. *Theory and History: An Interpretation of Social and Economic Evolution*. 1957. Reprint, New York: Garland, 1985.

Wacquant, Loic. *Punishing the Poor: The Neoliberal Government of Social Insecurity*. Durham: Duke University Press, 2009.

Waggoner, Matt. *Unhoused: Adorno and the Problem of Dwelling*. New York: Columbia Books, 2018.

Wagner, Gernot, and Martin Weitzman. *Climate Shock: The Economic Consequences of a Hotter Planet*. Princeton: Princeton University Press, 2015.

Walsh, Niall Patrick. "The Facts about Architecture and Climate Change." *ArchDaily*, 3 January 2020. https://www.archdaily.com/931240/the-facts-about-architecture-and-climate-change.

Walzer, Michael. *In God's Shadow: Politics and the Hebrew Bible*. New Haven: Yale University Press, 2012.

Warburton, Nigel. *Freedom: An Introduction with Readings*. London: Routledge, 2001.

Watts, Alan. *The Way of Zen*. New York: Vintage, 1957.

Webb, Whitney. "The U.S. Military Is the World's Biggest Polluter." *EcoWatch*, May 15, 2017. https://www.mintpressnews.com/on-earth-day-remembering-the-us-militarys-toxic-legacy/227776/.

Weil, Simone. *The Need for Roots: Prelude to a Declaration of Duties toward Mankind*. Translated by Arthur Wills. New York: Routledge & Kegan Paul, 1952.

West, Cornel. *Democracy Matters: Winning the Fight against Imperialism*. New York: Penguin, 2004.

Whitehead, Jason. *Redeeming Fear: A Constructive Theology for Living into Hope*. Minneapolis: Fortress, 2013.

Whyte, Jessica. *Catastrophe and Redemption: The Political Thought of Giorgio Agamben*. SUNY Series in Contemporary Continental Philosophy. New York: SUNY Press, 2013.

———. "Praxis and Production in Agamben and Marx." In *Agamben and Radical Politics*, edited by Daniel McLoughlin, 71–90. Critical Connections. Edinburgh: Edinburgh University Press, 2016.

Wilkerson, Isabel. *Caste: The Origins of Our Discontents*. New York: Random House, 2020.

Williams, Raymond. *The Long Revolution*. 1961. Reprint, Cardigan: Parthian, 2011.

Wilson, Edward O. *The Future of Life*. New York: Knopf, 2002.

Wilson, Jonathan. *Gospel Virtues: Practicing Faith, Hope, and Love in Uncertain Times*. 1998. Reprint, Eugene, OR: Wipf & Stock, 2004.

Winnicott, Donald. *The Maturational Environment and the Facilitating Environment: Studies in the Theory of Emotional Development*. International Psychoanalytic Library 64. 1965. Reprint, London: Routledge, 1990.

———. *Playing and Reality*. 1971. Reprint, Routledge Classics. New York: Routledge, 2005.

———. *Through Paediatrics to Psychoanalysis: Collected Papers*. International Psychoanalytic Library 100. 1975. Reprinted, London: Routledge, 2014.

Wolin, Sheldon S. *Democracy Incorporated: Managed Democracy and the Specter of Inverted Totalitarianism*. Princeton: Princeton University Press, 2008.

———. *Fugitive Democracy and Other Essays*. Princeton: Princeton University Press, 2016.

———. *Politics and Vision: Continuity and Innovation in Western Political Thought*. Exp. ed. Princeton: Princeton University Press, 2016.

———. "What Revolutionary Action Means Today." In *Dimensions of Radical Democracy*, edited by Chantal Mouffe, 240–53. London: Verso, 1992.

Wonhee, Anne Joh. *The Heart of the Cross: A Postcolonial Christology*. Louisville: Westminster John Knox, 2006.

Wood, David. *Reoccupy the Earth: Notes Toward Another Beginning*. New York: Fordham University Press, 2019.

Wood, Ellen. *Origin of Capitalism*. New York: Verso, 2017.

Woolf, Virginia. *Mrs. Dalloway*. London: Penguin, 1992.

World Inequality Database. "China." https://wid.world/country.china/.

Yoder, John Howard. *A Pacifist Way of Knowing: John Howard Yoder's Nonviolent Epistemology*. Edited by Christian Early and Ted Grimsrud. Eugene, OR: Cascade Books, 2010.

———. *The Politics of Jesus*. 2nd ed. Grand Rapids: Eerdmans, 1994.

Zerbe, Gordon, "On the Exigency of a Messianic Ecclesia: An Engagement with Philosophical Readers of Paul." In *Paul, Philosophy, and the Theopolitical Vision*, edited by Douglas Harink, 254–81. Eugene, OR: Cascade Books, 2010.

Zaretsky, Eli. *Capitalism, the Family, and Personal Life*. New York: Perennial Library, 1986.

Zinn, Howard. *A People's History of the United States*. New York: HarperPerrenial, 2003.

Zizioulas, John. *Being as Communion*. Crestwood, NY: St. Vladimir's Seminary Press, 1985.

———. *Communion and Otherness*. New York: T. & T. Clark, 2006.

# Index

accountability, 204, 207–8, 264, 270

Acts

communities of faith in, 14n60, 26, 82, 108, 140, 182, 260

political violence in, 249

actualization

and caring for nature, 257

and parental care, 252

and potentiality, 22, 151–52, 156–57, 166, 179, 201–2, 252–53

and the space of appearances, 24

Adorno, Theodor, 69, 115, 118

African Americans. *See also* King, Martin Luther Jr.; the Other; slavery, slaves; systemic racism;

Black Lives Matter movement, 152, 201, 217, 256, 277

childhood traumas, 216–17

and disembodiment, 70–71, 70n121–22

and disidentification, 63

homelessness of, 118–19n130

as the included-excluded Other, 70, 144–45, 153–54, 253

Ibram Kendi, 229

intra-community care, 255

Malcolm X, 68n98, 174–75, 174n159, 199n63, 202–3, 202nn76–77, 253, 255, 255n124

and the myth of Black inferiority, 66, 84, 199–200, 205–6n85, 239–40

and political agency, 63, 84, 161–62

Ta-Nehisi Coates, 68n98, 70n106, 121, –23, 253, 272

violence towards, 144–45

Agamben, Giorgio. *See also specific categories and constructs detailed in the subheadings below*

and the anthropological machine, 104, 106–7, 124

apparatus, concept of, 9n33, 179

bare life, concept of, 130n166, 145–46n56, 163

categorical pairs, 154n88

coming community, 29

on deactivating tradition, 9

on democracy as totalitarianism, 145–46

on the dissociation of humans from nature, 6n22, 16, 55n56, 71, 98, 103n59, 104–5n66, 246

on *ekklesia* as economic, 14n60

and the excluded Other, 107, 193

and *homo oeconomicus*, 172, 179

*homo sacer*, 144

on human co-belonging, 19

on the importance of identity to the state, 78, 220n118

on infancy, 60n75

misrecognition/marginalization,
17–18, 24n106, 25, 98n47, 106,
106n76, 239, 242, 278
Moltmann, Jürgen, 81, 275, 278
monasticism, non-sovereign, 140,
150n71, 181n177
Moore, Jason, 2n12, 111, 280–81n62
mosquitoes, killing of, 243n81
Mouffe, Chantal, 232
Murdoch, Iris, 159
Musk, Elon, 36, 271
myth
Greek, 40, 40–41n22
mythic violence, 234n38m 248b95
and origin stories, 155
and philosophy, 39n8
and political theology, 39–42
reinterpreting, 42n24, 43
and science, 37n6, 43n30
of specialness/chosenness, 51
as specific to time and place, 40
and underlying existential truths,
37n6, 40–41, 40n17, 249–50

Nancy, Jean-Luc, 28n125, 193
narcissism. *See* anthropocentrism,
narcissism
nationalism, xenophobic, 25, 25n109,
113–14, 210
nature. *See also* the earth; human
beings; "state of nature;"
stewardship;
acting into, 105
caring for, 257–58
dependence of the polis on, 17,
55, 71
diversity of, 224
as the foundation of the polis and
politics, 26
and freedom, 206
human devaluing/exploitation of,
36n15, 55, 65, 205, 243
human history vs., 224
impacts of political violence on,
231–32
as included-excluded Other, 15n63,
55n56, 125, 132, 154, 205–8, 235,
246, 259–60, 279

including in the political, 72, 182,
208
native understanding of, 104–5n66
as "non-human," implications,
99n50, 104n63, 167–68
objectification of, 134n2
patterns of, vs. "laws of," 177,
177n167
plurality of, 126, 131–32, 178, 182,
195, 206
recognizing suchness/potential-
ity of, 61–62, 61n81, 157n106,
202n75
research subjects, 61n82, 137
and Toto in the *Wizard of Oz*,
155n95
unfathomableness of, 58n66, 61,
61n82, 132
negative freedom. *See* positive and
negative freedom
neoliberal capitalism. *See also*
sovereignty; capitalism, global;
totalitarianism, inverted
emphasis on the individual, 193n29
and *homo oeconomicus*, 172, 179
inequalities associated with,
110, 199n62, 204–5, 209–10,
210n101, 236
and plutocratic/oligarchic democracy, 164–65
and the prosperity gospel, 212,
212n106, 215, 278
and sovereignty, 165
and structural violence, 233,
238–39, 251
New Zealand, 208
*Nicomachean Ethics* (Aristotle), 89
Niebuhr, H. Richard, 18n76, 99n52
nihilism, 3. *See also* despair; hope
non-human beings. *See* nature
non-sovereign relations. *See also* slave,
Jesus' incarnation as
and belonging, 31, 97
civic care, 80n132, 171m148,
171–72, 175, 261
communities of faith, 140, 150n71,
160, 181, 181n177, 183–84
and democratic anarchy, 42

nonviolent, challenges to imagining, 250–51
and power, 244
and radical democracy, 260n137
resource distribution, 18
and shared public-political narratives, languages, and rituals, 14–15
and the space of appearances, 71, 245
and the struggle between exclusion and inclusion, 15–16
as a term, origins and meaning to Greeks, 12
Titanic analogy, 264
the world as, 132
the political. *See also* the polis; politics
as all-embracing, 26
characteristics, 8, 20–24, 20n85
and dwelling, 89
and freedom, 217–19
and hope, 265, 271–73
as humankind's "most proper dimension," 13, 22, 257, 272
nature as the root of, 55
and power, 23–24
political agency (citizenship). *See also* civic care; identity; the Other; subjugation/subordination; the Other
and civic care, 19, 21, 255
awarding or denial of, 2, 25, 27, 63, 153, 215
and eco-agency, 2, 4–6, 216
and political power, 4, 22–24
and self-confidence/esteem, 17–18, 55, 60n76, 184, 239, 242, 244, 253, 255–56
political theology. *See also* theologies of subjugation/subordination; theologies of vulnerability
concepts and practices, 6–9, 26–27, 27n122, 29
and democratic sovereignty, 168–69
and dwelling together, 14, 31
focus on identifying problems, 8, 8n30

foundational myths, 39–42
independence from ideas of future good, 29
and justifications for subjugation and subservience, 138n18, 211–12, 212n106
liberation theologies, 27, 41, 47–48, 179n174, 212, 4741
and modern concerns and questions, , 9–10, 41
Paul's, as anti-sovereignty, 183–84
questions raised by, 7, 27–28, 30
politics. *See also* the polis; the political; space of appearances
characteristics, 20–21, 20n85, 23
interdependent nature as the foundation of, 26, 132
as relationship, 13, 22–23, 26
acting together for the common good, 13–15, 21, 23, 26, 28, 113–14, 132, 165
and the ungovernable, 175
Western, categories for, 154n88
Wolin's view, 20, 20n85
Popper, Karl, 8n29, 94n30
Porter, Eduardo, 256
positive and negative freedom, 189–90, 193, 193nn36–37, 204, 214
potentiality. *See also* subjugation/subordination
actualizing, 22, 151–52, 166, 179
endless nature of, 61–62, 61n81, 76–78, 151, 157n106, 202n75, 252–53, 256
factors that undermine, 156, 158, 165–66, 252–53, 257
and freedom, 32, 156–58, 157n106, 201–2, 219
in non-human beings, 202n75, 205–26
and vulnerability, 56n59
power. *See also* sovereignty
and freedom, 192–93
and political violence, 246
and politics and the political, 4, 22–24, 142, 145, 233–34n37, 243–44
violence vs., 233–34n37, 243–44

pre-political space of appearances.
    *See also* infant-parent relations;
    parental care, good-enough
    *Calvin and Hobbes* example,
        120–21
    embodied relational dwelling, 118
    and good-enough parenting, 31,
        59–60, 71
    as root of radical political theology,
        55–56
    and trusting the larger world, 68,
        68n97, 267
profanation, 9n34
"the promised land" concept, 46, 107,
    125–26, 135, 189, 211, 248
property ownership, 94–95,
    94–95n34, 159n112, 161–62,
    188, 188n15. *See also* slavery;
    sovereignty
prosperity gospel, 212, 212n106, 215,
    278
Proudhon, Pierre-Joseph, 175n165
Prozorov, Sergei
    on excess of living, 58n67, 77–78
    on inoperativity, 14n59, 80, 80n129
    on inseparability of living beings,
        105, 168n138
    on sovereignty, 151–52
Pruyser, Paul, 119n139

radical democracy, 7, 7n27, 169,
    260n137
radical political theology. *See also*
    care; non-sovereign relations;
    parental care, good-enough;
    theology of vulnerability
    characteristics, 8, 38
    and courageous care, 4–5, 9, 28–29,
        34, 265, 266, 294
    existential/foundational roots,
        86–88, 91
    and freedom, 9, 32, 38
    and inclusion, 30, 85, 132, 176, 180,
        180n176
    and interactive universalism, 29
    meaning of "radical," 55
    and the non-sovereign, vulnerable
        God, 7–8, 7n27, 28, 38, 80n132,

    83–84, 138–40, 169, 176–77,
        181, 248n95, 259–60
    now-time, 282n65, 286, 289–90,
        295
    political and ecological agency, 5,
        9, 21, 131
    and reinterpreting religious myths,
        42n24, 43
Rank, Otto, 116
reason-emotion, differentiated,
    191–92, 192n31
refugees, migrants. *See also* dwelling
    climate refugees, 31, 91, 97n46,
        109, 129–30, 291
    fear and rejection of, 162, 208–9
    and homelessness, 91, 91n24
    nomadic people, 93
    in the Old Testament, 89
    recognizing and accepting as per-
        sons, 109, 129–32, 201
    retaining sense of self, 115
    stateless persons and war, 96,
        114–15, 130n168
relations, personal and political. *See
    also* bare life; the Other; parental
    care, good-enough
    and alienation, 33, 91, 100, 103,
        104n66, 105, 145–146n56,
        198–99, 226, 244
    and the experience of being, 118
    and freedom, 193n38
    and friendship, 221
    infant-parent relations, 57n62,
        60–63, 95–96, 116
    and interdependence, 4–5, 26, 30,
        116
    interpersonal recognition/mis-
        recognition, 13, 17, 19, 98n47,
        194
    and quality of life, 96, 197
    reciprocal, role of vulnerability,
        72n110
    and repair, 67, 67n96, 252, 255
    and unequal power and status, 52,
        112
    relative (relational) freedom, 193–94
    repair. *See* forgiveness

use of glory and spectacle, 155–56
space exploration/colonization. *See*
colonization, interplanetary;
science and technology
space of appearances
Arendt's concept, 14–15, 14n61
and cooperative and diverse personhood, 24–25
determinant and indeterminant
knowing, 65–66
and embodied dwelling with an
Other, 69
and exclusion, 15
and expressions of restraint-
unrestraint, 67
extending to all beings and other-
than-beings, 16
fostering through radical political
theology, 85
and the identification-disidentification dialect, 62–63
impact of trauma/collapse on, 70
and interactions among adults in
the polis, 63
King's non-violent resistance movement, 83
possibility of suchness in, 79
potential collapse during Anthropocene Era, 85
pre-political, and good-enough
parental care, 71, 215
as term for political space, 59,
59n73
species extinction. *See* Anthropocene
Era
Speth, James, 111n102
state of exception
Agamben view of as dominant in
Western societies, 142
Jesus' assumption of role of slave,
76, 76n119
and paradoxes of democracy, 148
police exercise of, 144
and the sovereign's monopoly on
decision-making, 142
and the threat and actuality of
violence, 151–52

and white supremacy, 144–45
"state of nature." *See also* nature
Agamben's views, 55n57
Freud's views, 137, 137n15
Hobbes' and Rousseau's views, 55,
115, 136–37, 175n165
and non-sovereign relations, 31
and parent-child relations, 71
recognizing human connections
to, 115
Stein, Edith, 65, 72n110
Steiner, Rudolf, 191n29
stewardship, 73, 131, 131n170, 168,
176, 258
Stiglitz, Joseph, 164–65
Stowe, Harriet Beecher, 46
Strauss, Leo, 8n30, 12, 42
strong theology, 74
subjugation/subordination. *See
also* slave, Jesus' incarnation
as; slavery, slaves; sovereignty;
systemic racism; theologies of
subjugation/subordination; white
supremacy
characteristics, 50, 54, 158
and hope, 281
and humiliation, 98n47
and the loss of potentiality, 156,
158, 165–66
meaning of, 43–44
and misrecognition, 152, 242
and threat of violence, 151–52, 163,
166–67, 171, 171n148, 242
suchness/singularity
and denial of plurality, 199–201
denying of, 182
and dwelling together, 94, 108
experiencing, as hierarchy-free, 65
implication of plurality/excess, 58,
58n66
identification-disidentification of
children, 62–63
Jesus's retention of, 128
and parental care, 59
and personal knowing/recognition,
61
and personhood, 24n106, 58